D1707659

Hybrid Histories

Studies in Social Ecology and Environmental History

General Editors: MADHAV GADGIL and RAMACHANDRA GUHA

Other Books in this Series

DAVID ARNOLD AND RAMACHANDRA GUHA (EDS)
Nature, Culture, Imperialism: Essays on the Environmental History of South Asia
(Oxford India Paperbacks)

AMITA BAVISKAR
In the Belly of the River: Tribal Conflicts over Development in the Narmada Valley
(Oxford India Paperbacks)

BARBARA BROWER
Sherpa of Khumbu: People, Livestock and Landscape

MADHAV GADGIL AND RAMACHANDRA GUHA
This Fissured Land: An Ecological History of India
(Oxford India Paperbacks)

KRISHNA GHIMIRE
Forest or Farm?: The Politics of Poverty and Land Hunger in Nepal

RICHARD GROVE, VINITA DAMODARAN AND SATPAL SANGWAN (EDS)
Nature and the Orient: The Environmental History of South and Southeast Asia

MAHESH RANGARAJAN
Fencing the Forest: Conservation and Ecological Change in India's Central Provinces, 1860–1914

CHETAN SINGH
Natural Premises: Ecology and Peasant Life in the Western Himalaya

VASANT SABERWAL
Pastoral Politics: Shepherds, Bureaucrats, and Conservation in the Western Himalaya

Studies in Social Ecology and Environmental History

Hybrid Histories
Forests, Frontiers and Wildness in Western India

Ajay Skaria

DELHI

OXFORD UNIVERSITY PRESS

CALCUTTA   CHENNAI   MUMBAI

1999

Oxford University Press, Great Clarendon Street, Oxford OX2 6DP

Oxford   New York
Athens   Auckland   Bangkok   Calcutta
Cape Town   Chennai   Dar es Salaam   Delhi
Florence   Hong Kong   Istanbul   Karachi
Kuala Lumpur   Madrid   Melbourne
Mexico City   Mumbai   Nairobi   Paris
Singapore   Taipei   Tokyo   Toronto
and associates in
Berlin   Ibadan

© *Oxford University Press 1999*

ISBN 0 19 564310 0

Typeset by Rastrixi, New Delhi 110070
Printed in India at Pauls Press, New Delhi 110020
and published by Manzar Khan, Oxford University Press
YMCA Library Building, Jai Singh Road, New Delhi 110001

Preface

In the early nineteenth century, some Bhils raided Maratha villages in the Khandesh region of western India and carried away several cattle. A Peshwa official reported: 'respectable people were sent to the Bhils to tell them that it would be well if they ceased opposing the peasants and were loyal to the state'. The Bhils retorted 'we are kings of the forest, our ways are different, do you not worry your head with them'.[1] Such replies were common: often, Bhils caught for raiding or robberies described themselves as Mahadev's thieves, thus claiming divine sanction.

Such remarks may be more than just symptoms of defiance or resistance. Perhaps we need to take seriously what the Bhils said — 'our ways are different'. Bhils in eighteenth- and nineteenth-century India participated in a distinctive discourse of wildness that has been largely glossed over. Dangs, the region in western India that this book focuses most on, was a densely forested place. The Dangis were largely Bhils, Koknis, Varlis and Chaudaris — all communities currently classed amongst the Scheduled Tribes of India, and formerly described by the British as 'wild tribes'. Even before the British came up with this phrase, these communities were often referred to by surrounding communities, and sometimes described themselves, as jangli or wild. Sometimes, they were also called, and described themselves as janglijati, — the 'wild castes' or 'forest castes'.

But what do wildness, and ascriptions of and claims to wildness mean? Conventionally, in much mainstream western thought, wildness has been understood in terms of an opposition to civilization. It usually signifies what comes before or lies outside civilization; it is the prediscursive element that is refigured by civilization. Civilization is of course valorized, and ascriptions of wildness have justified

[1] G.S. Sardesai, *Selections from the Peshwa Daftar*, Bombay, Government Central Press, 1930–4, vol. 41, p. 40; quoted in Sumit Guha, 'Forest polities and agrarian empires: The Khandesh Bhils, c. 1700–1850', *Indian Economic and Social History Review*, vol. 33, no. 2, 1996.

much violence and oppression. Consider the two most common ways in which wildness is talked about — wild spaces and wild people. The designation of spaces as wilderness has often played a crucial role in justifying agricultural expansion or even forestry. In much western thought, cultivation and forestry represented the expansion of civilization and the taming of wilderness, its conversion into economic resources to be used efficiently.

Of course, since at least the eighteenth century, there has also been the celebration of wild spaces and calls for their recuperation by civilization rather than their obliteration. But such celebrations also place wilderness before or outside civilization. They have usually served as launching pads for critiques of civilization; they have stressed communion with wilderness as being necessary to bring out the best in civilization. This celebration of wilderness has been a crucial tenet of much environmentalist thought, and environmentalism itself has often been about the need to preserve wilderness, to make modern civilizations value it.[2]

In similar ways, the characterization of people as wild has in most western thought been about placing them before or outside civilization. Wild peoples were everywhere. They were the women, lower classes, and crowds in western societies. They were the repressed or suppressed selves within every civilized person. And most of all, in our context here, they were the savages, primitives, barbarians or natural men of non-western societies.[3] Much western

---

[2] For discussions of wilderness in western contexts, see Max Oelschlaeger, *The idea of wilderness: From prehistory to the age of ecology*, New Haven, 1991; Max Oelschlaeger (ed.), *The wilderness condition: Essays on environment and civilisation*, Washington, 1991; Robert Pogue Harrison, *Forests: The shadow of civilisation*, Chicago, 1992; Hans Peter Duerr, *Dreamtime: Concerning the boundary between wilderness and civilisation*, trans. Felicitas Goodman, New York, 1987; Roderick Nash, *Wilderness and the American mind*, New Haven, 1967; Clarence Glacken, *Traces on the Rhodian Shore: Nature and culture in western thought from ancient times to the end of the eighteenth century*, Berkeley, 1967; Jane Bennet and William Chaloupka (eds), *In the nature of things: Language, politics and the environment*, Minneapolis, 1993.

[3] The connotations of being primitive, barbaric, savage or wild, though related, are different in significant ways. I explore these differences in my 'Shades of wildness: Tribe, caste and gender in western India', *Journal of Asian Studies*, vol. 56, no. 3, August 1997. Literature on the image of the wild man is considerable. See, amongst others, Richard Bernheimer, *Wild men in the middle ages*, Cambridge, Mass., 1952; E. Dudley and M. Novak (eds), *The wild man within: An image in western thought from the Renaissance to Romanticism*, Pittsburgh, 1972; Henrietta Kuklick, *The savage within: The social history of British anthropology, 1885–1945*, Cambridge, 1991; Adam Kuper, *The invention*

thought has emphasized the need to extirpate this wildness, and this has legitimized European genocides in the colonies and, no less violently, European civilizing missions.

True, as with 'wild spaces, there was also a celebration of wild peoples (more precisely, of wild men: western societies have found it much more problematic to celebrate wild women).[4] In the form of primitivism, this celebration has been enormously influential. Those who have dwelt on and developed primitivist ideas include Rousseau, Montaigne, Defoe, de Tocqueville, Marsh, and Freud, to name but a few. Primitivists have celebrated wildness to criticize western society, or to call for a recuperation by civilized man of the wild man within. But again, there is the opposition of wildness and civilization.[5]

These celebrations of wildness may seem innocent, but they are not. They are part of 'an ethnocentrism thinking itself an anti-ethnocentrism'.[6] They are about a nostalgia for wholeness, about going back to a 'natural' state of affairs. They associate wildness with the prehistory of civilization, with the moment of its origins, with authenticity, and they yearn for unity with this moment. In many ways, they are part of a modernist fable of liberation and loss, where civilization is cast as a process of liberation from wildness, a liberation in which something was also lost.[7]

Radical scholars, having now learnt to be suspicious of nostalgia

---

of primitive society: Transformations of an illusion, London, 1988; Hayden White, 'The noble savage theme as fetish', in his *Tropics of discourse: Essays in cultural criticism*, Baltimore, 1978; Harry Liebersohn, 'Discovering indigenous nobility: Tocqueville, Chamisso, and Romantic travel writing', *American Historical Review*, vol. 99, no. 3, June 1994; Roger Bartra, *Wild men in the looking glass: The mythic origins of European otherness*, trans., Carl T. Berrisford, Ann Arbor, 1994.

4 For problems with the notion of wild woman, see Sharon Tiffany and Kathleen Adams, *The wild woman: An inquiry into the anthropology of an idea*, Cambridge, Mass., 1985.

5 On the use of wildness to criticize civilization, and the development of primitivism, see Nash, *Wilderness and the American mind*, chs 3–6; Oelschlaeger, *The idea of wilderness*, ch. 4; Hayden White, 'The forms of wildness'; Liebersohn, 'Discovering indigenous nobility'; and Marianna Torgovnick, *Gone primitive: Savage intellects, modern lives*, Chicago, 1990.

6 Jacques Derrida, *Of grammatology*, trans. Gayatri Chakravorty Spivak, Baltimore, 1974, pp. 3, 120–1. Derrida makes this remark in the context of the celebration of orality.

7 For some remarks on this trope in anthropological contexts, see Stephen Tyler, 'On being out of words', in George Marcus (ed.), *Rereading cultural anthropology*, Durham, 1992.

for origins or authenticity, are suspicious of ascriptions of wildness or claims to them. It is feared that taking discourses of wildness seriously might be a collusion with the celebration of origins and authenticity. With a few exceptions, the focus has principally been on dismantling claims to wildness.[8] My doctoral dissertation, of which this book is a radically different version, shared that focus and attempted to peel away any insinuations of wildness about the actions of Dangis.

It now seems to me, however, that as much was lost as was gained in the process. What I missed out on, most of all, were Dangi constructions of wildness, and the ways in which these constructions avoided, in the nineteenth century, the western opposition between civilization and wildness. By saying this, I do not intend to subscribe to that increasingly popular strand of environmentalist thought which valorizes and celebrates the environmental ethic of non-western societies on the grounds that these do not resort to an opposition between wildness and civilization.[9] An assertion such as that still often construes the non-western Other as possessing a harmonious relationship with wildness which has not yet been ruptured by modernity; in this sense, it is part of the very oppositions that it tries to undermine.

In contrast, for Dangis, I claim no harmonious relationship or original unity between wildness and civilization. Rather, this book focuses on constructions of wildness which were so inextricably linked to notions of civilization as to make any opposition between the two pointless and misleading. I wish to get away from wildness as the inevitable term of opposition or anteriority to civilization. A brief foray into the changing meanings of *jangal* and jangli will illustrate for now what I mean. In classical Indian texts, Francis Zimmerman has pointed out, jangal referred to a particular kind of wildness — that of dry lands which were particularly suited for agriculture: 'Salubrious, fertile and peopled by Aryans, the jungle is the soil of brahminity.' Indeed, 'in ancient India, all the values of civilization lay on the side of the jungle. The *jangala* incorporated land that was cultivated, healthy, and open to Aryan colonization.'[10]

[8] One exception is Michael Taussig's *Shamanism, colonialism, and the wild man: A study in terror and healing*, Chicago, 1986.

[9] Some of the problems with such an opposition emerge in J. Baird Callicot and Roger T. Ames (eds), *Nature in Asian traditions of thought: Essays in environmental philosophy*, Albany, 1989.

[10] Francis Zimmerman, *The jungle and the aroma of meats: An ecological*

By the eighteenth and early nineteenth century, when Dangs was jangal and Dangis jangli, these meanings had changed somewhat. In western India, the jangal and the jangli were in an agonistic, even occasionally antagonistic, relationship with dominant values in surrounding plains societies. This agonistic relationship can be and is sometimes interpreted as signifying an opposition between wildness and civilization. But that is to miss the point: here, being jangli was not about some chronologically prior state of nature, some prediscursive base which civilization transcended and overcame. Rather, values associated with the jangal and being jangli were crucial to the construction of power, authority and identity in both Dangs and surrounding plains societies; it was in this sense that a discourse of wildness was influential.

Thinking about the centrality of wildness may have implications for understanding eighteenth- and early-nineteenth-century India. Formerly, the period was seen as a time of chaos and decline, an uninteresting hiatus between the Mughal and British empires. Now, a revisionist historiography has revolutionized our understanding of the period, showing us how it was a time of immense ferment and change, when a variety of post-Mughal state forms consolidated themselves and existing identities were transformed in significant ways. This historiography stresses the centrality of apparent chaos in the growth and sustenance of settled agriculture. It argues that practices formerly regarded as disruptive, such as raids, were often part of the construction of large centralized states; that regions regarded as peripheral, such as the forested tracts, were tied into complex networks that strengthened trade and settled agriculture; that marauding bands were not simply disruptive but also formed part of the armies of Mughal successor states, and so on.[11]

This approach has provided us with considerable insights, and is a useful corrective to the older disregard of 'marginal' areas. It has initiated the process of problematizing decline and has foregrounded the complex and plural processes glossed over in earlier

---

theme in Hindu medicine, Berkeley, 1987, pp. viii, 18. Michael Dove has criticized Zimmerman's reading in '"Jungle" in nature and culture', in Ramachandra Guha (ed.), *Social ecology,* Delhi, 1994.

11 This revisionist perspective has been articulated most forcefully in C.A. Bayly's *Indian society and the making of the British empire,* Cambridge, 1988 and his *Rulers, townsmen and bazaars: North Indian society in the age of British expansion, 1770–1870,* Cambridge, 1983.

narratives of 'decline'. Still, it shares with older historiography the criteria by which to gauge societies. For both, the privileged criteria are those of growth, loosely understood as a dynamism in trade, agriculture, industry or state formation, that leads in the direction of modernity. The transformations in our understanding have principally been because, instead of focusing on empires or even states, it has correlated a complex range of factors — including trade, urbanization, commercialization, degrees and forms of cultural activity, and the changing power relationships amongst various social groups — to discern dynamism in many areas and periods of 'decline' or chaos. Here, raids, pastoralism, forest communities, and unsettled powers are significant most of all for the ways in which they fit or feed into narratives about settled agriculture, greater commercialization, indigenous capitalism, and more effectively centralized states, into narratives about the growth of modern civilization.[12]

It will be pointless to deny that ideas such as these carry some truth. Nevertheless, a very different perspective may be possible if we understand laments of decline or chaos in terms of wildness. In western India, as I shall argue, these laments in the late-eighteenth and early-nineteenth century were often because of the consolidation of the power of polities organized around wildness, around being jangli. The activities of these polities do not fit into narratives of state formation, growth, urbanization or trade; nor are they necessarily opposed to it. For example, Dangi raids on surrounding settled agricultural areas were not only attempts to get resources for state-making. Rather, there was a distinctive culture around them, and they were often celebrated for enacting a particular kind of masculine wildness.

Nor was it only in forest polities like Dangs that such a celebration of raids and similar activities occurred. Raids were important also to more evidently mainstream polities such as those of the Marathas, so much so that plunder could even be described as a form of tax collection. Here too, 'decline' and 'chaos' were about the enactment of a particular kind of political power, one that put wildness at its centre. And this wildness was not necessarily seen as some kind of unsatisfactory substitute for, or precursor of, a

---

[12] Steven Feierman has pointed out how pervasive such narratives are in even some of the finest pieces of contemporary history-writing. See his 'Africa in history: The end of universal narratives', in Gyan Prakash (ed.), *After colonialism: Imperial histories and postcolonial displacements*, Princeton, New Jersey, 1995.

more centralized state dependent on settled agriculture. Rather, wildness was at least as important a dimension of political and social power in eighteenth- and early-nineteenth-century western India as any long-term shift towards centralized states. A recognition of the centrality of wildness also suggests ways to revise the controversial emphasis of the revisionist historiography on continuities with colonial rule. The consolidation of colonial power represented such a radical departure partially because it involved the extinction of wildness. The colonial distinction between castes and tribes articulated a new understanding. 'Wild tribes' as a description of forest communities was something of a redundancy, for tribes were in colonial understanding by definition wild. In many of their administrative practices, British officials sought to extinguish wildness and to replace it with civilization: by halting raids, forcibly extinguishing mobility, imposing settled agriculture, and refashioning kingship to make it more civilized. Colonial forestry, too, was often cast as a project of taming wilderness and civilizing it. This emphasis on taming existed, paradoxically enough, along with a celebration of wilderness. There was the Kiplingesque Anglo-Indian jungle, a space of the exotic opposed to the baseness of Indian civilization; there was the nobility of the wild tribes, quite like the British nobility.

By the mid-nineteenth century, settled agriculture, centralized state power, and trade came to be emphasized and construed in ways that systematically excluded and marginalized wildness. Indian communities also took over this colonial opposition between wildness and civilization, so deceptively similar and yet so fundamentally different from the former combination of affinity and agonism involved in enactments of wildness. Now there came increasingly to be a rejection of wildness. In the process, both in plains and forest communities, identities and gender relations were remade in profound ways. Wildness came to be associated with marginality, social and ritual inferiority, and political powerlessness; often, amongst forest communities, it was now invoked as part of an oppositional subaltern discourse.

Wildness was to remain crucial in the twentieth century. As nationalist thought developed, there emerged a primitivism which celebrated tribes as natural beings: spontaneous, free, and uninhibitedly masculine, possessing some of the qualities needed for a struggle against the British. But that primitivism was also underwritten by a profound marginalization of the 'tribals'. As natural beings, they could at best rebel without knowing why. The knowing mind belonged to the nationalist elite. Indeed, no future was envisaged for the tribal in postcolonial India. The wildness of the tribal epitomized Indian backwardness; this backwardness had to be overcome for the nation to become modern, or simply for the nation to become. In all of this, there was a profound irony. The jangal and jangli, once central to kingship and authority, had become the negativities through which the civilizing processes of colonialism and nationalism defined themselves in the age of modernity. The wildness of jangal and the jangli had come to be contained within Kiplingesque exoticism or caste–tribe sociologism.[13]

I started thinking about wildness and forest communities in the 1980s, when, as an undergraduate, I doubled as a journalist with the *Indian Express* and began reporting on the 'tribal' regions of Gujarat. It would scarcely be possible to acknowledge all the institutions, friends and colleagues whose support has been crucial to the ways in which my ideas have evolved since then. But some special thanks must be recorded. To those Dangi friends and acquaintances from whom I have learned stories, I cannot be grateful enough. I am especially grateful to Jiva Kharsu, Raisinh Gondusar, and Lasiya Patil for the warmth of their friendship, and for the many ways in which they converted my fieldwork into something ineffably, distinctly different.

Much of this book is a critical engagement with the three teachers and friends from whom I have learnt the most: Chris Bayly, Dipesh Chakrabarty, David Hardiman. I could not have asked for a more wonderful supervisor than Chris. He waded patiently through innumerable inchoate drafts, discussed them repeatedly and helped me develop many of the arguments of the book. This book has developed in engagement with his inspiring work and arguments — he will recognize here in mangled form many of his own ideas. Dipesh's questions have repeatedly made me revise my assumptions, and the warmth of his friendship has been an inextricable part of the stimulating discussions we have had for the last three years. It was at David's suggestion that, as an MA student in Baroda, I took to exploring the histories of forest communities. During subsequent years, it is not only his own work on them that has

---

13 I owe these points to a discussion with Ranajit Guha.

been a source of much inspiration to me but the ethics he has brought to' that work, ethics that foreground political commitment and look at research as a collaborative effort in the truest sense of the word. I do not know how to even begin to thank him for his incredible generosity both with ideas and with the very notes that he had made from archives.

I am also thankful to: Shahid Amin, for comments which clarified several points; Rosalind O'Hanlon, whose comments helped clarify the issues I was trying to engage with; Dilip Menon, for New Orleans stories, scepticism, and extensive comments without which the book would have been much poorer; Akhileshwar Pathak, for arguments over the years about our respective projects; Samita Sen, for long discussions which have left their indirect impress on this book; David Washbrook, discussions with whom, over generous doses of coffee and whisky, were crucial in formulating many of my arguments.

My colleagues in the Subaltern Studies editorial group — Shahid Amin, Gautam Bhadra, Partha Chatterjee, David Hardiman, Shail Mayaram, Gyan Pandey, Gyan Prakash, and Gayatri Spivak — have in the course of one memorable morning at Jaipur criticized some of the arguments I had made in the early parts of the book, leading to quite extensive modifications. Discussions with colleagues at the University of Virginia — Richard Barnett, Alon Confino, Tamara Giles-Vernick, Walter Hauser, Allan Megill, Bradly Reed, Brian Owensby, Elizabeth Thompson — have helped enormously in redefining my arguments.

For discussions, and support in myriad ways, I also thank: Ifthikhar Ahmed, Seema Alavi, G. Arunima, Crispin Bates, Susan Bayly, Raj Chandavarkar, Paul Connerton, Satyakam Desai, Nicholas Dirks, Richard Drayton, Saurabh Dube, David Forgacs, Jean-Claude Galey, Richard Grove, Ramachandra Guha, Sumit Guha, Rajkumar Hans, Trina Haque, Eva-Maria Lassen, Thomas Pantham, Sanjay Reddy, Ghanshyam Shah, Bill Sherman, Bina Srinivasan, and Nandini Sundar.

My friends in the Inquilabi Communist Sangaathan, the Indian section of the Fourth International, were for long remarkably patient and understanding about my obsession with the Dangs. I am grateful for all that I have learnt from them.

I thank the Cambridge Commonwealth Trust, Nehru Trust for Cambridge University, Smuts Memorial Fund, Charles Wallace Memorial Trust and the Edward Boyle Memorial Trust for financial support for my research. Much of my research for the book was done at Trinity College, and Gonville and Caius College, Cambridge. At Caius, I am especially grateful to Neil McKendrick, Ian McPherson, and Robin Porteous for their support.

I thank for their invaluable assistance the librarians and staff of the following institutions: the Maharashtra State Archives, Bombay and Pune; Gujarat State Archives, Baroda; Dangs Forest Department Records Room, Ahwa; Dangs Collectorate Records Room, Ahwa; National Archives, New Delhi; India Office Library, London; University of Edinburgh Library, Edinburgh; and University Library, Cambridge.

Finally, there are those impossible thanks. To my parents, M.A. Skaria and Daisy Skaria, for support in so many ways that I cannot even begin to list them. And to Shiney Varghese, for everything, beginning maybe, if everything has to begin somewhere, from SD Hall.

Before his death in 1991, my younger brother, Manosh, read a very early draft of what ended up as this book, and had deep reservations. I have tried to keep his concerns in mind, and I sometimes like to think that he would not have been as critical of this version. Still, I am not he, and his work, had it ever been done — he was toying with the idea of writing about the construction of insurgent communities amongst the *adivasis* of Gujarat, Maharashtra and Madhya Pradesh in the course of their struggle against the Narmada Project — would have explored the concerns of this book much better than I have. To his dreams and his passions, to his memory, I dedicate this book.

University of Virginia, Charlottesville   AJAY SKARIA

Contents

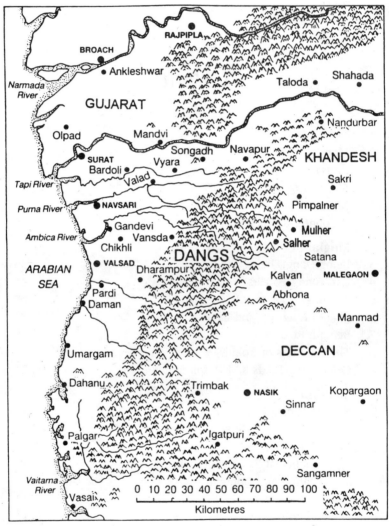

Map 1. The Hilly Regions of Western India

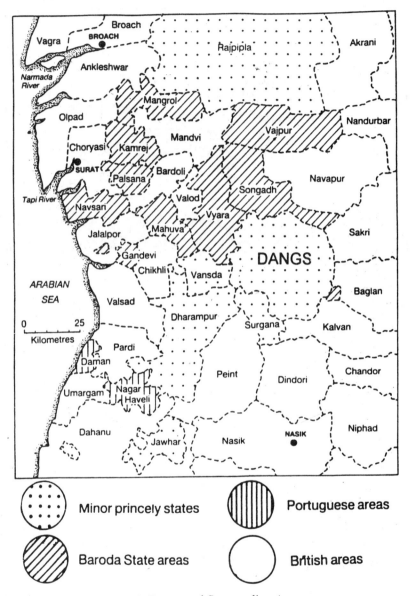

Map 2. Dangs and Surrounding Areas

Map 3. Dangs: Major Powers and Villages

Glossary

adivasi	a word often used by forest communities to describe themselves; lit. 'original inhabitants'
amir umrao	lieutenants of chiefs
Angrez	British
asan	*Bridelia retusan*
banbhag	reserved forests
beo	*Pterocarpus marsupium*
bhagat	priest
bhai pagdi	brothers by exchange of turbans
bhakar	unleavened bread
bhauband	brotherhood of chiefs
bhaus	brother
bhet	gift, often part of dues
Bhil raj	Bhil rule
bidi	cigarette made by rolling tobacco in a leaf
bigar	forced labour
chakardar	person who does service for a chief
champa	a measure of volume
chhut	freedom to
chillum	pipe
daftar	records
dahi	a form of shifting cultivation
dakan	female witch
dakanio	male witch
dang	hills
desh	plains regions to the southeast of Dangs
dev-van	forest of the gods
devdevina goth	stories of gods and goddesses
dhad	raid

dhotur	lower garment for men
dhum	disturbance
dosh	sin or fault
dukh	sorrow, often caused by witchcraft
dungar	hill
durbhin	telescope
gadi	seat of power
gairan	reserved forests
gaon	village
gavli raj	an early epoch
ghat	hills
giras	a due collected from villages
Girasia	holder of giras rights
gora	white person; the British
gora raj	white (British) rule
goth	stories or narratives
gothiya	storyteller
hak	right
halpatti	agricultural tax levied on ploughs
havildar	police official
ijaradar	revenue farmer
ikki khavana	beg or demand, and eat; a form of taxation
jagalia	watchman
jagir	grant of land or village
jagirdar	holder of jagir
jangal	forests or wilderness
jangli	wild
janglijati	wild castes
jati	caste
jod	confluence
jogani	a malevolent female spirit
juni goth	old stories
junigavthad	old village sites
kacheri	office
kadak	stern, strict
kakad	*Garuga pinata*

kalal	liquor merchant
kaliparaj	dark people; term used to describe forest communities
karbhari	person who looks after a chief's affairs
karkun	clerk
kartuk	protected forests
kath	astringent eaten with betel leaves
kayda	levy
khair	*Acacia salechu*
khari	true
khandad	a form of shifting cultivation
khuti	due paid in acknowledgement of sovereignty
khutibandhi	assigned a khuti
killedar	fort commandant
komda	chicken
kuplin bahadurin raj	an early epoch
kuver	chief
lashkar	army
mahal	palace
mahua	liquor made from mahua, *Bassia latifolia*, flowers
mal	flat area
mamlatdar	revenue official
manus	persons
markhub raj	violent rule
Mewas	hill chiefs
modal	*Lannea grabdis*
nagara	drums
nagli	a millet; *Eluisine coricaine*
naik	chief
naiki	chieftancy
naka	toll point
nau kayda	the nine levies or taxes
nishan	flag
pada	village or settlement
pagdi	turban
paiha	money

paltan	platoon
panlot	undulating lands
patil	village headman
raj	rule; chieftancy
raja	chief
raj-karbhari	regents
ram ram	a salutation
saatcoat	a kind of armour
sag	teak, *Tectona grandis*
saheb	suffix or form of address for powerful men
sahi-angutha	thumb mark used as signature
sal	*Shorea robusta*
sapati	flat lands
sarkar	state or government
saukar	moneylender
seekhel-bhanel lok	educated or literate persons
shela	shawl
shikhar	hunting
sida pani	provisions
sikka daftar	seals and records
sipai	sepoy
sirpav	mark of honour, often a dress or turban
sisu	*Dalbergia sisu*
tamasha	a genre of dramatic performance
thaali	a genre of recitation
thambla	pole
tiwas	*Ougenia dalbergioides*
tod	breaking
ujliparaj	fair people; term used for upper castes
ujyad	deserted
vadil	elder or ancestor
vadilcha goth	ancestral stories
vanarkilla	fortress of the monkeys; barren or rocky lands
wasti	populated
yad	communication

Abbreviations

Ag.	Acting
Asst.	Assistant
APA	Assistant Political Agent
BA	Bombay Archives (Maharashtra State Archives, Bombay)
BRO	Baroda Records Office (Gujarat State Archives, Baroda)
CF	Conservator of Forests
Coll.	Collector
Comm.	Commissioner
Comp	Compilation
C.D.	Central Division
C.F.	Conservator of Forests
DAAR	Dangs Annual Administration Report
DBD	The Dangs Boundary Dispute
DCR	Dangs Collectorate Records
DDG	Dangs District Gazetteer
DDR	Dangs District Records
DFAR	Dangs Forest Administration Report
DFO	Divisional Forest Officer
DFR	Dangs Forest (Department) Records
DN	Daftar Number
DWP	Dangs Working Plan
Dy	Deputy
ED	Education Department
FD	Foreign Department
FDO	Forest Demarcation Officer
FN	File Number
FRBP	Forest Reports of the Bombay Presidency
GoB	Government of Bombay

GoI	Government of India
GR	Government Resolution
HPO	Huzur Political Office, Baroda
IESHR	Indian Economic and Social History Review
IOL	India Office Library
JD	Judicial Department
KDG	Khandesh District Gazetteer
Kh.	Khandesh
KPAAR	Khandesh Political Agent's Annual Administration Report
N.C.	Northern Circle
N.D.	Northern Division
NAI	National Archives of India
NDG	Nasik District Gazetteer
NDWP	North Dangs Working Plan
No.	Number
Pol.	Political
P.A.	Political Agent
PA.DCR	Deccan Commissioner's Records, Maharashtra State Archives, Poona
PD	Political Department
PDD	Political Department Diaries
R.C.	Revenue Commissioner
RD	Revenue Department
RR	Residency Records (Baroda)
SDWP	South Dangs Working Plan
Secy.	Secretary
SN	Serial Number
SPD	Secret and Political Department
SRBG	Selections from the Records of the Bombay Government

1

Notes for a Politics of Hope

Dangis have a rich fund of *vadilcha goth* or stories about the past, stories sometimes reaching back into the seventeenth and eighteenth centuries. Storytelling is a major aspect of Dangi life, and the past provides a means to reflect on and socialize the present. Social features and identities often have their genealogies traced back to the past, and narratives dwell on the novelty or antiquity of stories. This book is titled *Hybrid Histories* because it tries to explore the distinctive sense of pasts involved in these *goth*, to recognize *goth* as a legitimate way of understanding pasts, to formulate the questions of the professional historian by taking cues from *goth*, and to attempt hybrid, contrapuntal narratives that bring together, necessarily inconstantly and incompletely, the concerns of Dangi narrators and professional historians.

THE DENIAL OF DIFFERENCE

These narrative strategies came out of a sense of dissatisfaction with many aspects of existing approaches. The older academic tradition of studying oral narratives such as Dangi stories minimizes or denies difference between oral traditions and the professional discipline of history. Such scholars as Jan Vansina (who in many senses put the study of oral traditions on a disciplinary footing) and his students have converted oral traditions into the equivalent of archival sources, and written histories that adhere to the norms of western professional history writing. They constantly invoke these norms to legitimize the study of oral traditions. Their thrust is on making oral traditions like written records, the primary sources that historians customarily depend on. Indeed, Vansina's principal achievement lies in the extensive and detailed methods for evaluations of oral sources which extract historical grain from mythical chaff.[1]

[1] Jan Vansina, *Oral tradition as history*, London, 1985, 2nd revised edition. Many works have built on and developed through internal critiques of Vansina's

2 *Hybrid Histories*

The reasons for this strategy seem clear. The study of oral traditions as a source for history developed in an Africa that was in the throes of decolonization. Denials of difference were part of a radical politics, of a manoeuvre resorted to not only by students of oral traditions but more broadly by many scholars of colonial and postcolonial societies. In imperial ideology, colonial rule was often justified by representing the colonized in terms of a lack — the insinuation that the colonized were backward, or not modern enough.[2] The insistence that the colonized lacked history was a part of this. In this context, the reclaiming of a history was almost everywhere a crucial component of the struggle of colonized peoples for liberation. To claim history is to claim speech and authority and to assert the right to independence, subjecthood, and agency.[3] Denial of difference, whether in oral traditions or histories of capitalism, nationalism, trade or development in colonized societies, is thus part of attempts to claim a specific historical identity within the narratives of modernity.

This strategy of denying difference has yielded considerable dividends. Through the use of oral traditions, agency has been ascribed to marginal actors, and histories have been produced of regions and subjects that written records would not have permitted. Politically too, the new postcolonial identities would have been more difficult without the denial of difference and the consequent use (and subversion) of the categories of the colonizers. The rendering of oral traditions in the styles of western historiography has thus often been a politically radical and empowering gesture.

Much of what follows draws heavily on this tradition of doing oral history. Yet there is a need to be aware of the particular

crucial achievements. See Joseph Miller (ed.), *The African past speaks: Essays in oral tradition and history*, Fokestone, 1980, for one classic collection. For a more recent collection of exciting work in this tradition, see Robert Harms et al. (eds), *Paths toward the past: African historical essays in honor of Jan Vansina*, Atlanta, 1994. For an important external critique of history in this tradition, see Renato Rosaldo, 'Doing oral history', *Social Analysis*, no. 4, September 1980.

2 See George Stocking, *Victorian anthropology*, New York, 1987; and Ronald Inden, *Imagining India*, London, 1991; Johannes Fabian, *Time and the other: How anthropology makes its object*, New York, 1983.

3 For a useful though not particularly insightful book on the subject, see David C. Gordon, *Self-determination and history in the third world*, New Jersey, 1971. See also Talal Asad's suggestive essay 'Afterword: From the history of colonial anthropology to the anthropology of western hegemony', in George Stocking (ed.), *Colonial situations: Essays on the contextualization of ethnographic knowledge*, Madison, 1991.

semantic load that it can carry: denial of difference is itself a form of participation in the discourse of lack. The constant appeal to the tribunal of literate historical standards is after all primarily an evaluation of these traditions by their suitability for conversion into sources for the professional discipline of history. In this sense, there is a profound dependence on the very criteria that created lack, and the legitimacy of oral sources (which is to say, their equivalence to archival ones) has to be wrested on a case-by-case basis.

Even radical historians amongst those denying difference depend on the 'hyperreal Europe', that is, a reified figure of the imagination which hypostatizes an idealized European experience generalized into a universal set of criteria. As a result, almost all major aspects of colonized societies suffered from a constitutive lack: the Indian working class was insufficiently class-like, Indian bourgeoisie insufficiently bourgeois, Indian capitalism insufficiently capitalist, and Indian revolutionary movements inadequately revolutionary. In a brilliant essay, Chakrabarty remarks that the social imaginary 'Europe' remains the sovereign theoretical subject of all those histories we call 'Indian', 'Chinese', 'Kenyan', and so on.[4] This is because all these histories tend to be written within a 'transition narrative . . . of which the overriding (if often implicit) themes are those of development, modernization, capitalism. Thus the subject of Indian history usually speaks from within a metanarrative that celebrates the nation state; of this metanarrative the theoretical subject can only be a hyperreal "Europe", a "Europe" constructed by the tales that both imperialism and nationalism have told the colonized.' The project of Indian history thus remains a mimicry of the hyperreal Europe, and is marked by lack and failure.

THE AFFIRMATION OF DIFFERENCE

It is precisely as part of the effort to refigure this kind of lack that the affirmation of difference occurs. Practitioners of the strategy assert that oral traditions are different in principle from the discipline of history. The nativist filiation of the strategy which has privileged oral traditions because they are more authentic need not detain us — it is too boring and problematic an approach to need dismantling. One of the more interesting early forms that this kind of affirmation took was the emphasis on the dichotomy between

4 Dipesh Chakrabarty, 'Postcoloniality and the artifice of history: Who speaks for the "Indian" pasts', *Representations*, 37, Winter, 1992, p. 1.

history and myth — there were the 'hot' societies that experienced change and possessed a sense of history, and there were the 'cold' societies that were relatively changeless and possessed a sense of myth. Though we have not yet been able to entirely shake off the legacy of that distinction,[5] it is no longer seriously sustained.

But the affirmation of difference continues in diverse ways, sometimes positing a difference between history and memory, sometimes calling for mytho-history, and sometimes simply describing oral traditions as forms of historical imagination quite distinct from the forms of the professional historian. The finest works within this tradition have not stopped using oral traditions as sources for a professional history, but what has been most distinctive about them is the way in which they elicit indigenous conceptions of the past, and explore different forms of historical imagination.[6]

As with the denial of difference, the affirmation of difference is a manoeuvre resorted to not only by students of oral tradition, but by students of colonial and postcolonial societies more broadly; indeed, it may be described without exaggeration as the dominant approach now. It is in this broader sense that the manoeuvre is

[5] For an unsuccessful attempt to rehabilitate the distinction, see Jonathan Hill, 'Introduction: Myth and history', in Jonathan Hill (ed.), *Rethinking history and myth: Indigenous South American perspectives on the past*, Chicago, 1988, pp. 6, 9.

[6] Amongst the most important works that have paid attention to oral traditions in this manner, by affirming difference, are: Shelly Errington, 'Some comments on style in the meaning of the past', *Journal of Asian Studies*, vol. 28, no. 2, 1979; Renato Rosaldo, *Ilongot headhunting, 1883–1974: A study in society and history*, Stanford, 1980; Marshall Sahlins, *Historical metaphors and mythical realities: Structure in the early history of the Sandwich Islands kingdom*, Association for Social Anthropology in Oceania Special Publication no. 1, Ann Arbor, 1981; Richard Price, *First-time: The historical vision of an Afro-American people*, Baltimore, 1983; J.D.Y. Peel, 'Making history: The past in the Ijesha present', *Man*, n.s., vol. 19, no. 1, 1984; Howard Morphy and Frances Morphy, 'The "myths" of Ngalakan history: Ideology and images of the past in northern Australia, *Man*, n.s., vol. 19, no. 3, 1984; Marshall Sahlins, *Islands of history*, Chicago, 1985; Robert Borofsky, *Making history: Pukapukan and anthropological constructions of knowledge*, Cambridge, 1987; Joanne Rappaport, *The politics of memory: Native historical interpretation in the Colombian Andes*, Cambridge, 1990; Alessandro Portelli, *The death of Luigi Trastulli and other stories: Form and meaning in oral history*, Albany, 1991; David William Cohen, *The combing of history*, Chicago, 1994; Lisa H. Malkki, *Purity and exile: Violence, memory and national cosmology among Hutu refugees in Tanzania*, Chicago, 1995. For India, see especially Gyan Prakash, *Bonded histories: Genealogies of labour servitude in colonial India*, Cambridge, 1990; Nicholas B. Dirks, *The hollow crown: Ethnohistory of an Indian kingdom*, Cambridge, 1987; Shahid Amin, *Event, metaphor, memory*, Delhi, 1995.

best discussed. In early formulations, the affirmation of difference often took the form of nativist histories, and the claim of a distinctive space from which the colonized subaltern spoke. But with the problematizing and decentering of the subject who speaks, the pitfalls of such straightforward affirmations of difference have come to be well-recognized. Dipesh Chakrabarty's essay represents a suggestive exploration of what it could mean to affirm difference. Where older narratives read lack, he argues, it is possible to read 'plenitude' and 'creativity'. Thus, there were persistent ambivalences in Indian appropriations of key colonial categories. They were marked by 'contestation, alliance and miscegenation . . . with other narratives of the self and community that do not look to the [western liberal] state-citizen bind as the ultimate construction of sociality'. Yet, it is not enough to stop with an acknowledgement of this, for, though they may be documented, they are so antihistorical that they will never enjoy the privilege of providing our metanarratives or teleologies; rather, they are more likely to be appropriated by history. That is to say, while the affirmation of difference from history is needed, it is not possible.

Because of this conviction about the inescapability and ubiquity of history, Chakrabarty has a distinctive vision of how to 'provincialize Europe' or limit the reach of theoretical and explanatory models drawn from the experience of European modernity.

the project of provincializing Europe must realize within itself its own impossibility. It therefore looks to a history which embodies this politics of despair. . . . I ask for a history that deliberately makes visible . . . its own repressive strategies and practices. . . . This is a history that will attempt the impossible: to look towards its own death by tracing that which resists and escapes the best human effort at translation across cultural and other semiotic systems, so that the world may once again be imagined as radically heterogeneous. . . . To attempt to provincialize this 'Europe' is to see the modern as inevitably contested, to write over the given and privileged narratives of citizenship other narratives of human connections that draw sustenance from dreamed up pasts and futures where collectivities are defined neither by the rituals of citizenship nor by the nightmare of 'tradition' that 'modernity' creates. There are of course no (infra)structural sites where such dreams could lodge themselves. Yet they will recur so long as the themes of citizenship and the nation state dominate our narratives of historical transition, for these dreams are what the modern represses in order to be.[7]

---

7 'Postcoloniality and the artifice of history', pp. 22f; see also pp. 8, 18 for

Caught between the apparent impossibilities of affirming memory and escaping history, caught in situations where the only history possible seems that of a hyperreal Europe, a radical politics of despair seems to be all that remains.

HISTORY AS A MYTH OF MODERNITY

There is of course a need to provincialize Europe, to write over privileged narratives of citizenship and modernity that make 'history' their home. But for reasons that will become clear below, I am sceptical about a politics of despair. I am fascinated rather by politics of a different kind — a politics of hope. Hope is a word that we have come to regard with kneejerk suspicion and associate with emancipatory metanarratives. If the politics of hope is to be anything more than a glib phrase, then it is necessary to indicate how we may talk of it. The most persuasive ways to do so would be to focus on the hybrid histories made possible by the recognition that history is a myth of modernity.

I use myth not in the Levi-Straussian sense which ascribed it to cold (read premodern) societies, but in the Barthesian sense, which avoids the western:non-western, traditional:modern, or cold:hot dichotomies. In Barthes' understanding, myths can be seen as the naturalization of meaning, or the moment when meanings take on givenness and fixity, and when the processes that have created meanings, as well as the contingency that always characterizes meanings, become invisible.[8]

In saying that history is a myth of modernity I refer to the naturalization of an association between history and western modernity. The empirical work of professional historians often acknowledges that premodern Europe, China or India had historical imaginations, and that several characteristics which we associate with modern and western histories can be found in modern and premodern European and non-European societies. Still, the positing of a special

---

earlier quotes. See also Nicholas Dirks, 'History as a sign of the modern', *Public Culture*, 2, no. 2, Spring, 1990.

8 See Roland Barthes, *Mythologies*, trans. Annete Lavers, New York, 1972, and 'Change in the object: Mythology today', in his *Image music text*, trans. Stephen Heath, London, 1977. Barthes vacillates between this reading and a more structuralist interpretation of myth, which depends in less interesting ways on a distinction between prior meaning and distorted meaning, seeing myth as the latter. See also on this point Sturrock, *Structuralism and since: From Levi-Strauss to Derrida*, Oxford, 1979, pp. 57, 60, 62.

relationship between history and modernity is pervasive, asserted often by those very historians whose empirical work undermines the association. For example, there is the frequent assertion that medieval writers did not recognize 'the pastness of the past',[9] and that it is with modernity that the past becomes a foreign country, thus making history possible.[10] A diverse range of thinkers over the last few centuries have in various ways emphasized how there is something modern about history, or how it is the historical sensibility which makes western civilization (often understood to include the ancient Greek world) so unique. Even the argument of several philosophers of history that the western professional discipline of history is the product of modern historical imaginations which favoured realist vehicles of representation can feed into this position.[11] And certainly, those resorting to the strategy of affirming difference draw implicitly or explicitly on such an association.

It is precisely this association that is problematic, and can lead on to a politics of despair. I would like to argue instead that the association is part of the modernist understanding of modernity or of the hyperreal Europe, and that this association leads to a curious position for non-western modern (or premodern western and non-western) styles of the past. Repressed and rendered invisible, they form the Other of history, the constitutive outside which defines history and yet cannot be acknowledged. This Other is often conceived of as memory, a category thought to hold everything — including epic, chronicle and myth — which is premodern or non-western. It is to this Other, memory, that we need to turn.

At least since Halbwachs, the distinction between history and memory has been drawn repeatedly by historians and social scientists.[12] A recent survey, though it remarked that Halbwachs'

9 Mary Carruthers, *The book of memory: A study of memory in medieval culture*, Cambridge, 1990, p. 193.

10 David Lowenthal, *The past is a foreign country*, Cambridge, 1985.

11 Amongst the works which point in this direction, especially relevant are White, *Metahistory*, and his *Tropics of discourse*; Antony Kemp, *The estrangement of the past: A study in the origins of modern historical consciousness*, Oxford, 1991; Stephen Bann, *Romanticism and the rise of history*, New York, 1995; Bann, *The inventions of history: Essays on the representations of the past*, Manchester, 1990; Frank Ankersmit and Hans Kellner (eds), *A new philosophy of history*, Chicago, 1995. For a useful survey of the relationship between history and modernity, see also Elizabeth Deeds Ermarth, *Sequel to history: Postmodernism and the crisis of representational time*, New Jersey, 1992.

12 Maurice Halbwachs, *The collective memory*, trans. F.J. Ditter, Jr. and V.Y. Ditter, New York, 1980 (1950), pp. 80ff.

'circumscribed definition of history may be one that few historians would today accept', concluded in terms not very different:

In traditional societies, the past was continually being updated in living memory, and imagination and memory were perceived to be interchangeable. One lived continually in the presence of the past. . . . The move into modern historical understanding opened up a divide between past and present.[13]

The distinction between memory and history both resembles and is tied to the more famous one between speech and writing. Memory is usually thought to be characteristic of primarily oral societies, and to be displaced by history in societies with widespread literacy and a print culture.[14] Even the emergence of history in the west is often seen as deeply intertwined with the story of writing, especially in its print form. As Frances Yates suggested, the arts of memory, such as mnemonics, were very well developed in the manuscript culture of medieval Europe, but declined with the easier availability of printed books.[15]

Derrida has explored a series of contrasts between speech and writing in western culture, where speech stands for liberty, natural goodness, and spontaneity, and writing stands for servitude, articulation and death. He describes this as logocentrism, or the privileging of speech and its treatment as authentic. At the same time, he suggests, logocentrism ascribes a civilizational role to writing. One could take his point further, as de Certeau has done, and say that a deep connection is often postulated between writing and modernity. Writing epitomizes learning, civilization, and all that distinguishes the West from the Rest:

The 'oral is that which does not contribute to progress; reciprocally, the 'scriptural' is that which separates itself out from the magical world of voices and traditions. A frontier (and a front) of Western culture is established by that separation. Thus one can read above the portals of modernity such inscriptions as 'Here, to work is to write', or 'Here, only what is written is understood'. Such is the internal law of that which has constituted itself as 'Western'.[16]

13 Patrick Hutton, *History as an art of memory*, Hanover, 1993, pp. 77, 156.
14 Jacques Le Goff, *History and memory*, trans. Steven Rendall and Elizabeth Claman, New York, 1992 (1977), p. xi. This is the subtext of Le Goff's arguments: pp. 54–62, 129–34.
15 Frances Yates, *The arts of memory*, London, 1991 (1966); see also M.T. Clanchy, *From memory to written record: England, 1066–1307*, Oxford, 1993, 2nd edition.
16 Michel de Certeau, *The practice of everyday life*, Berkeley, 1984, p. 134.

Elsewhere, I have implied that the association of writing and modernity is itself one of the myths of modernity. Both Derrida and de Certeau in some senses accept this myth, for while showing the association of writing and modernity to be a construct, they also fetishize that construct rather than challenge it.[17] Further extending that point, it seems possible to argue that the association of history with modernity is an even more central western myth of modernity. Just as writing is often portrayed as supplementary to speech, so is history seen as supplementary to memory. In this sense, both writing and history are unoriginal; only speech and memory are original. But the similarities end here. Writing is usually seen as simply the inscription of speech, not necessarily involving its trans-formation. If it is after and above speech, it is seen as so primarily in the sense that it develops after speech, and provides other ways of carrying on speech, ways that are very much more effective than speech. In this sense, writing is principally viewed as a technology, and as such capable of being exported or imported to societies. Its modernity or civilized nature springs essentially from this — it is viewed as a technological prerequisite of modernity.

Contrast this to what Le Goff says, speaking from within the common sense of the hyperreal Europe: 'Memory is the raw material of history. Whether mental, oral or written, it is the living source from which historians draw. . . . The historian must be there . . . to transform them [memories] into something that can be conceived, to make them knowable.'[18] That is to say, history is seen not as the inscription of memory but as the evolution of memory; it transforms memory.

Because of this, history in the mainstream western tradition is not simply a prerequisite of modernity or western civilization: it *is* modernity or western civilization. It is perceived not so much as a technology as a sensibility peculiar to, created by and creating, modernity or western civilization. As such, it cannot be exported or imported. And to uncover, discover or recover history requires, in this discourse, a historical sensibility, a sensibility that the tech-nology of writing amongst others enables but does not create. History is the supplement that eventually displaces its moment of origin, memory; and memory is the constitutive outside that history

---

17 These arguments are made in more detail in my 'Writing orality and power in western India', in Shahid Amin and Dipesh Chakrabarty (eds), *Sub-altern studies*, vol. IX, Delhi, 1996.
18 Le Goff, *History and memory*, pp. xif.

has to deny affinities with. Since the time of the Greeks, *mythos* or the word as a decisive final pronouncement or authoritarian thinking has been contrasted to *logos*, the word whose validity or truth can be demonstrated or enlightened thinking.[19]

Maybe this difference in the representations of writing and history explains why there is no equivalent of logocentrism in the representation of memory. Logocentrism is often part of a radical, though flawed, critique of western society. By privileging speech and oral cultures, it attempts, as in the case of Levi-Strauss's *Tristes Tropiques*, a critique of the subordination of 'primitive' peoples by 'civilized' ones, in which writing has played a major role.

What is striking is that while such radical logocentrism is a pervasive theme in western thought, the use of memory to critique history — what one might call a mythocentrism — is a very muted trope. It does occur occasionally, as in Eliade's withering remarks about the inability of modern social science to comprehend the meanings and richness of myth, or in the fascination shared by many scholars for the richness and fluidity of Homeric or other epics. But these arguments are really logocentric rather than mythocentric: they do not valorize myths and epics for epitomizing memory but for epitomizing what they take to be the fluidity of speech and orality. Consider the way Levi-Strauss views memory. In *The Savage Mind*, he suggests that the centrality Sartre accords to history is a form of ethnocentrism: just as myths of so-called primitive people invariably designate their own tribes as uniquely human and all others as inhuman, the centrality accorded to history allows Sartre to place western civilization above others. As this indicates, Levi-Strauss has been one of the few thinkers to view history itself as a myth. Yet in his distinction between hot and cold societies Levi-Strauss also affirmed the history–myth dichotomy, and claimed that there were societies 'without history'.[20] He tried to avoid the ethnocentrism of such a strategy not by deconstructing the dichotomy but by decentering it. He suggested that history,

---

[19] Peter Heehs, 'Myth, history and theory', *History and Theory*, vol. 33, no. 1, 1994, p. 3; Jurgen Habermas, *The philosophical discourse of modernity*, Cambridge, 1987, p. 107.

[20] Claude Levi-Strauss, *The savage mind*, Chicago, 1966, especially chs 8 and 9.

though not bound to disappear, would no longer dominate the social sciences. He envisioned it being replaced by anthropology, and felt that historical culture would occupy just one place amongst others in a system of differences and similarities between societies. This vision contrasts with his attempt to avoid ethnocentrism in situating societies 'without writing' and 'without history' (two themes in his work which he considered closely related). There he was logocentric and passionately affirmed the primacy of speech; here instead of being mythocentric and affirming memory he displaces the whole dichotomy.

Memory, quite evidently, is far more difficult to affirm than speech. This is why, in other writers too, even when myths or epics as memory are acknowledged as a crucial source for history, the acknowledgement is hedged in by cautions. Le Goff warns us: 'to privilege memory excessively is to sink into the unconquerable flow of time'.[21] And radical historians usually affirm history rather than memory. So it is that Jameson opens his *Political Unconscious* with the injunction 'always historicize!'. He describes this 'slogan' as 'the one absolute and we may even say "transhistorical" imperative'.[22] Similarly, the history-from-below movement was basically about recovering the history of subordinated groups; feminist scholars have tried to recover the history of women; and early volumes of *Subaltern Studies* had similar, though differently inflected, aims of recovering the history of subaltern groups.[23] Even Chakrabarty and others who are hostile to the discourse of history conclude that there is no alternative to it. In sum, history (seen as necessarily western and modern) is a central arena in which claims to legitimacy have to be made.[24]

21 Le Goff, *History and memory*, pp. xif.

22 Frederic Jameson, *The Political unconscious: narrative as a socially symbolic act*, London, 1989, p. 9; for some criticisms of this, see Geoff Bennington, 'Demanding history', Derek Attridge, Geoff Bennington and Robert Young (eds), *Post-structuralism and the question of history*, Cambridge, 1987, p. 20.

23 For the ways in which the Subaltern Studies project has developed, see Gyan Prakash, 'Subaltern studies as postcolonial criticism', *American Historical Review*, vol. 99, December 1994; Gayatri Chakravorty Spivak, 'Subaltern studies: Deconstructing historiography', *Subaltern studies IV: Writings on South Asian history and society*, New Delhi, 1985; Rosalind O'Hanlon, 'Recovering the subject: Subaltern studies and histories of resistance in colonial South Asia', *Modern Asian Studies*, vol. 22, no. 1, 1988.

24 Of course, there is also a long tradition of attacks on the inescapability of this history, a tradition which can be traced back to Nietzsche's moving 'On the uses and disadvantages of history for life', in his *Untimely meditations*, trans. R.J. Hollingdale, Cambridge, 1983.

Why should the discourse of history seem so inescapable? It seems to me that the logocentric critique of western society rests, paradoxically, on a more fundamental affirmation of that culture. Though speech is depicted as natural and original in relation to writing, it is already seen as an act of enunciation by the thinking subject. Thus there can be broad acknowledgement that oral cultures produce great western civilizations — witness the canonical position long accorded to the Homeric epics. Since writing is not seen as a qualitative transformation of speech but only its inscription, speech is not inappropriate for modernity — even if writing is more appropriate. So to reject writing is not to reject modernity or civilization as a whole but only particular aspects of these.

In contrast, since history not only inscribes but transforms memory, it is seen not merely as a technology but the very sensibility of modernity and western civilization. Because of its transformative work, it leaves memory with no legitimate existence save as the prehistory of history. If memory is represented as natural, this is so in a different way from speech: unlike speech, memory is portrayed as prior to even enunciation by the thinking subject. Put another way, one might say that speech is the articulate natural of western civilization while memory is its inarticulate and primal natural, it is the unimaginable space of wildness. An affirmative discourse centred around memory is thus a far more profound rejection of modernity and western civilization than logocentrism; and it is because history is an even more central myth of modernity than writing that mythocentrism is impossible.

HYBRID HISTORIES

Memory then is not about lack (or about permanently marginalized plenitude and creativity as Chakrabarty implies). Rather, as a site for those narratives which potentially challenge the hyperreal Europe, it is the moment of the naming of this challenge as lack. In hoping for hybrid histories, I refer to the reconstitution of this lack as surplus, to the telling of narratives which provincialize that most pervasive hyperreal of Europe — history.

But how is such provincializing to proceed? Quite clearly, it is not simply a matter of insisting that historical narratives exist in non-western or premodern societies — a manoeuvre that has been resorted to by a number of scholars over the last decade. While that manoeuvre by itself might be adequate for precolonial or premodern societies, it is not enough for contemporary non-western or agonistic western styles of the past. The problems with it are best indicated by a parallel. Derrida suggests that Levi-Strauss perceives some societies as being 'without writing' because he privileges phonetic writing, and that if one were to think of writing more broadly so as to include any form of inscription, it would be more difficult to talk of societies without writing. But in discussing inscription so broadly, Derrida also glosses over, at least in this context, the relations of power in which phonetic writing has been imbricated, and on the role that it has played in the subordination of many societies without it. It is this which has made phonetic writing seem so much more powerful than inscription that societies without the former appear to be and become societies without writing.[25]

Similarly, the association of history and modernity, part of the hyperreal Europe, is not less powerful because it is a myth; to the contrary, its power is derived from just that fact. Because it has been closely associated, since at least the seventeenth century, with western domination, because it now defines the very way in which societies can imagine themselves, it has become as much more powerful relative to other contemporary narratives about the past as phonetic writing has become relative to other forms of inscription.[26]

Given all this, hybrid histories are best understood as simultaneously produced by a constant engagement with the hyperreal Europe and by proceeding beyond its limits. I do not mean to imply that hybrid histories occupy, commence from, or end up in a sort of unsullied space untouched by the hyperreal Europe. Rather, what is being suggested is that they are created through active escape from the hyperreal Europe; they are the consequence of traversing the hyperreal to reside in sites beyond it but marked by it. It is this act of traversal which makes hybrid histories the moment when powerlessness betokens power, when blindness betokens insight, and lack betokens surplus.

Subaltern oral traditions represent a particularly fascinating kind

---

25 For this point in relation to writing, see my 'Writing, orality and power'.

26 For a superb analysis of the relationship between history and forms of western domination, see Robert Young, *White mythologies: Writing history and the West*, London, 1990. For an analysis of how the production of history has been inseparable from domination over women, see Christina Crosby, *The ends of history: Victorians and the 'woman question'*, London, 1991.

of hybridity, for they are one of the prime sites ascribed to that other of history — memory. In this sense, they are often far less collusive with the hyperreal Europe than even subalternist histories rendered from within the professional discipline. The latter, by virtue of the very fact that their challenges are situated on professional historians' terrain, are usually far more complicitous with the hyperreal Europe. In some ways we have for long recognized the peculiar hybridity of subaltern oral traditions — it is surely not accidental that radical historians, even if they ended up denying difference with history, should have turned to oral traditions so regularly in trying to tell different stories of women, forest communities, working classes, the colonized, or other groups marginal to the hyperreal Europe.

As should be clear from all this, there is nothing necessarily new about hybrid histories. To the extent that the hyperreal Europe is never hegemonic, hybrid histories are coeval with it. The very enactment of subalternity — whether female, working class, colonized or other — involves some creation of hybrid histories. Also, while they may be radical in terms of their challenges to the hyperreal Europe, there is nothing necessarily radical about them in terms of their commitment to a related politics of subaltern empowerment. In some cases, the surplus of hybrid histories springs from their fetishization of the hyperreal Europe, as for example in Hindu fundamentalist constructions of the Babri Masjid–Ram Janmabhoomi dispute.[27] It is important to recognize this, for else we slip into claiming an (infra)structural site for hybrid histories and for a politics of hope — we assume that postliberal politics broadly speaking (and challenges to the hyperreal Europe more specifically) are by themselves always empowering for subaltern groups.

The point then is not that hybrid histories are entirely new, or are always about an empowering politics, but that struggles against relations of domination will be about accentuating the hybridity of such histories, and about foregrounding ways in which they challenge the hyperreal Europe. Further, many subaltern hybrid histories — such as those involved in Dangi oral traditions — are relentlessly radical in their envisioning of the past and in the challenges they articulate to relations of domination and the hyperreal

---

[27] For analyses of Hindu fundamentalist constructions, see Gyanendra Pandey, 'Modes of history writing: New Hindu history of Ayodhya', *Economic and Political Weekly*, vol. 29, no. 25, 15 June 1994; Heehs, 'Myth, history and theory', *History and Theory*, vol. 33, no. 1, 1994.

Europe. It is precisely moments of this sort that we (both scholars and activists) need to seize on, for these are the moments for dreaming of a politics of hope.

Dangi Historical Epochs

Dangi concerns frame the broad issues that the book is concerned with. The sequential order of the book is not that of professional historians. Rather, it proceeds in accordance with the two major epochs within which most Dangis frame their past, *moglai* and *mandini*. Roughly speaking (the rest of the book will qualify these meanings) moglai is the time of freedom — freedom to move in the forests, to raid, to collect a due called *giras* from the plains, and to have a distinctive pattern of political authority. Moglai informs radical politics in the Dangs today. Mandini is both an epoch, and an event that marks the end of moglai. With mandini, often associated with British dominance, Dangi political authority was undermined and they could no longer move about as formerly, or raid surrounding plains.

These Dangi epochs are subtly different from epochs or periods in the sense that professional historians use these terms. For the latter, an epoch or a period is marked by chronological continuity: despite some overlap, it could be broadly said that one epoch succeeds another. Sometimes, Dangi narrators too talk similarly: thus, moglai is often identified with the precolonial and early colonial period, and mandini is associated with *gora raj* or British rule. Quite as often, however, Dangi epochs traverse diverse chronological times, almost running parallel to each other. It is not unusual for events that occurred as recently as twenty years back to be part of moglai, and those that occurred two hundred years back to be part of mandini. Indeed, in some very suggestive ways, moglai is about what is extra-colonial. By extra-colonial, I obviously do not only mean precolonial — it is precisely that kind of chronological separation that I am trying to avoid. What I mean is something that often includes the precolonial (and this should not be forgotten), but is in more important ways defined in opposition to the colonial, and in opposition to the relations of domination over Dangs that surrounding plains areas have established. This is not to say, again, that moglai is about some unsullied Dangi space — rather, it is about spaces and times created by traversing and exceeding colonialism and the relations of domination that it is associated with. Similarly, mandini is often about that which is extra-Dangi in origin or intent, and mandini in this sense ranges across the precolonial, colonial, and postcolonial.

INTIMATIONS OF WILDNESS

A second way in which I try to sustain hybrid and contrapuntal narratives is by searching for narratives from within the professional discipline of history which correspond to these Dangi narratives. It is this search which led me to the theme of wildness. Moglai is often about particular kinds of wildness, ways of being *jangli* that are in an agonistic relationship to surrounding plains societies; and mandini is about the transformations of these forms of wildness.

Because most work on South Asian history has been on settled agricultural or urban communities and their economies, politics and culture, it has often been overlooked that such agriculture was not practised in those widespread tracts, covering nearly a third of the subcontinent, where the bulk of those who came to be called tribals lived.

When, inspired by goth, I looked carefully at records, I felt I could read here stories about forms of wildness, and their transformations. In telling professional historians' stories of wildness, I have tried to create an overlapping epoch to moglai by attempting, like Dangi narrators, an extra-colonial history. This includes both the precolonial period and those spaces and times which might in conventional chronologies be part of the colonial period, but that could also be thought of as escaping (or, more precisely, exceeding) the colonial. In this sense, moglai cannot be understood save in the context of mandini. Similarly with professional historians' overlapping epochs to mandini: what I attempt is a history that roughly corresponds to the period of colonial domination, but is not exclusively defined by such domination.

APORIAS

One more remark. This book may be read as at least two books. The first can be read in the normal sequential fashion. It explores the various meanings of moglai for Dangis and historians' equivalents to these; it then goes on to mandini and historians' parallels to it. In this way, mandini at least can be approached with an understanding of the myriad meanings of moglai. Such a reading has its strengths, but we do need to recognize that this is just one style of reading. If it is the one preferred by professional historians and social scientists, this is most of all because of its will to comprehensiveness: it purports to be exhaustive, to begin at the beginning and tell all there is to know, to make few presumptions about what the reader might know. As the next chapter suggests, Dangis share in some ways this will to comprehensiveness. So the sequential narrative presented below is not entirely outside Dangi understandings.

Still, more is lost in the sequential narrative here than would be lost in Dangi accounts. When most Dangis discuss an aspect of moglai, they simultaneously always already know something of how it is inflected by the mandini, and vice versa. This does not only mean that they can make multiple connections between narratives, that there is a deep cross referentiality made possible by simultaneous knowledge of many goth, or that the transition from moglai to mandini consists of several narratives tacking back and forth rather than being one single overarching narrative. These are true but by now predictable points. Most of all, their simultaneous knowledge of goth makes narrators sensitive to the excess of moglai. In contrast, a sequential narrative such as the one attempted here runs the risk of missing out on this excess, on the sense in which moglai is extra-colonial rather than only pre-colonial. After all, in the narrative that I present here, we learn of moglai before we learn of mandini; there is therefore a real danger of seeing moglai as prior in some chronological or ontological sense, of forgetting that moglai and mandini are produced simultaneously, that moglai is not so much prior to mandini as about that which exceeds mandini.

In order to try and produce a similar excess, I suggest that the book be read also in some supplementary ways. These supplementary narratives, which would explore the meanings of mandini and moglai in more simultaneous ways, and maybe define and displace the sequential narrative, can be attempted through reading the book in the following manner: 3–10–11–9–16–6–17–7–12–4–13–14–15–5–18–8–19–20. (Possible subsequent chapters in this supplementary narrative are indicated in brackets at the end of each chapter.) Read this way, there are four overlapping narratives. Chapters 3, 10, 11, and 9 look at the meanings of moglai and mandini for relations with the plains, and at the meanings of the completion of the inner frontier; chapters 16, 6, 17 and 7 explore aspects of what it meant to be a raja in moglai and mandini, and of the transformation of forest polities; chapters 12, 4, 13, 14, 15 and 5 look at moglai and mandini in terms of the transformation of Dangi relations with the forests, and of Dangi identities as a forest community; chapters 18, 8, 19 and 20 look at how the meanings of being Dangi and of being wild have changed. Of course, these supplementary narratives are much more patchy and partial than the sequential narrative, but maybe this patchiness is itself reason for hope.

So the two hybrid histories, those from oral narratives and those from archival sources, remain in tension. Even when Dangi and professional historians' narratives focus on the same issues, there remain irreducible differences between them. Sometimes, there are no shared issues that can bring together in the same vision these two very different narratives. And even where the two narratives are around shared issues, an accretional approach alone ignores the distinctive trajectories of each: the two have to be simultaneously kept distinct, not within the same framework. As all this suggests, the book is intended to be read in at least two ways — as professional histories of Dangs, and as Dangi histories.

2

A Counter-aesthetics
of Modernity

By going to Dangs to learn oral traditions, I thought I was undertaking a consciously political act. In conversing with Dangis, I attempted to make my motivations and intentions clear: the accounts I had collected from the archives were partial, I was attempting a subaltern history, and by understanding and representing the past as Dangis saw it, I hoped to break away from the tyranny of the colonial categories that dominate the archives. In this, my political alliances were with the Dangis, and against the *sarkar* which has often been quite oppressive. But the solidarities that I claimed were rarely taken at face value: stories of Dangi ancestral pasts, or vadilcha goth as they are called, were far too deeply political and complex for that.

Goth can be broadly translated as story, narrative or account, and is ubiquitous in everyday life, being deployed to describe a range of narratives. People tell their goth to visiting officials, which is to say that they make a representation. They tell the goth of what they did during the day. They tell goth of divine figures, of hunting, of ancestors, of former times. So goth can be the story or account of virtually anything.

Nevertheless, there are broad genres of goth. Stories of Dangi pasts are often referred to interchangeably as *juni goth, mohorni goth* or *puduncha goth* — all phrases meaning 'stories of former times' or 'old stories'.[1] Within these juni goth there are at least two broadly distinct genres — the *devdevina goth*, or stories of gods and goddesses, and the vadilcha goth, or stories of ancestors. The bulk of the devdevina goth, literally 'stories of the gods and goddesses' tell of dealings between deities and spirits such as Vadudev, Bhutdev,

---

1 Stories of the present are called *atani goth*, or stories from now. Sometimes that word, atani, is used even to describe goth from the nineteenth or twentieth century, especially when they are being contrasted to much older stories.

Simariodev, Vaghdev, Sitalamata, Kanasarimata or the many malevolent female spirits known as *joganis*. There are also goth of the
two major popular epics of the subcontinent, the *Ramayana* and the
Mahabharata. These epics are not only radically different from the
textual versions of the plains, but are situated within Dangs. There
is the village of Pandva, where the Pandav brothers visited; the
village of Subir, where Shabiri Bhilin stayed when she met Rama;
and several other such places.[2] Devdevina goth are set in a very
distinct time — that before the time of the humans. The goth are
often about the making of the physical and geographical features of
Dangs by gods, goddesses and spirits.

In contrast, vadilcha goth is often used as a shorthand to refer
to all stories involving humans. The word *vadil* can mean both
lineage ancestor and, more broadly, elders, whether living or dead.
The time of humans does often involve divine beings, and such
stories are both vadilcha goth and devdevina goth. Some of these
tell of ancestors' encounters or dealings with spirits, gods or goddesses; they are about how Dangs and other regions were made
suitable for humans. They tell, for example, of how humans were
given corn to cultivate with, how *mahua*, the Dangi liquor, was
discovered first by Vadudev and then passed on to humans, how
kingship was given to some Dangi chiefs, and so on.

However, most vadilcha goth have an entirely human cast. Some
are about the loss of forests to the Forest Department, or the coming
of the British. Others are about the everyday lives of ancestors: of
their migrations from village to village, their harassment by the
British and the Forest Department, their modes of livelihood, their
alarm at the first motorized vehicles, the prices they paid for goods,
and of the disputes amongst Bhil chiefs.

A Counter-aesthetics of Modernity

It was for long conventional for scholars to assume that oral traditions survive most vigorously in non-literate and 'traditional'

---

[2] For an account of the Dangi understanding of the *Ramayana* and *Maha-
bharata*, as well as a list of villages with names associated with the two epics, see
D.P. Khanapurkar, 'The aborigines of south Gujarat', unpublished PhD disserta-
tion, University of Bombay, 1944, vol. II. See also K.S. Singh (ed.), *The Maha-
bharata in the tribal and folk traditions of India*, Indian Institute of Advanced
Study, Simla, and Anthropological Survey of India, New Delhi, 1993; and K.S.
Singh, *Rama-katha in tribal and folk traditions of India: Proceedings of a seminar*,
Calcutta, 1993, for accounts of other such traditions.

societies. With the emergence of a literate culture, oral traditions about the past are expected to be slowly forgotten, to be replaced by a literate historical culture. But one should not make the mistake of thinking of vadilcha goth as primarily local, as oral traditions preserved because of some presumed Dangi isolation from the larger world, as an indicator that Dangis are not 'modern', or as a case of Dangis 'still' having a mode of thinking about the past which is distinct from history.[3] Quite the contrary. It is because of the centrality of colonialism in defining their current world in crucial ways that goth stretch so far back into the past. Colonialism involved the imposition from outside and above of a particular kind of modernity on Dangs, a modernity characterized most of all by Dangi subordination. As 'development', the postcolonial state has extended this modernity further. And vadilcha goth involve a counter-aesthetics of this modernity. By this, I do not mean an aesthetic that is anti-modern. Rather, I refer to an aesthetic that engages with western modernity, but not on its terms.[4]

What I mean by this can be illustrated by contrasting it with the acknowledgement of coevalness, the preferred strategy in the classic, *Time and the Other*. Here Fabian argued that imperialism and anthropology were both fundamentally based on the denial of coevalness, that anthropologists placed the societies they studied in a time different from and before their own. In opposition to this, Fabian called for the acknowledgement of coevalness, or a recognition of the shared historical time of anthropologists and the societies they studied.[5]

I do not wish to imply that Fabian was wrong in calling for such a strategy; it is certainly often required for strategic and political reasons. But let us step back from that issue for a moment, and ask: what is the vision (broadly shared by a substantial section of the most radical social theorists of the 1980s and early 1990s) from within which the denial of coevalness seems such an imperialist act, and acknowledgement of coevalness the most appropriate

---

[3] This sense of masses having preserved something before history pervades Ashis Nandy's highly suggestive piece, 'History's forgotten doubles', *History and Theory*, vol. 34, no. 2, 1995.

[4] Paul Gilroy discusses, in similar terms, a 'counterculture of modernity', or the double-consciousness involved in striving to be both European and black. See his *The Black Atlantic: Modernity and double consciousness*, Cambridge, 1993.

[5] Fabian, *Time and the other: How anthropology makes its object*, New York, 1983.

strategy against it? A deeply modernist one, in the very direct sense that modernity is about a particular kind of relationship with time. As Vattimo reminds us, 'modernity is that era in which being modern . . . becomes the fundamental value to which all other values refer'. Modernity defines itself by claiming to be at the cutting edge of time, to be always contemporary, and to always be overcoming itself (this after all is the paradoxical sense in which one way to be modern now would be to be postmodern).[6] The acknowledgement of coevalness seized on this index, time, to claim modernity for the anthropologist's subject, and to attack the old imperializing strategy of denying modernity by denying coevalness.

The manoeuvres involved in vadilcha goth are subtly different from this. True, Dangi epochs of moglai and mandini also involve a forceful acknowledgement of coevalness. The notion of mandini seizes on colonial and postcolonial state power and accords to it a revolutionary role in the shaping of contemporary Dangs. It creates a shared historical time with imperialism and colonialism, and points to the particular forms of domination involved in that time.

Furthermore, the epochs of moglai and mandini mime the distinction between the premodern and the modern. In the truisms of western thought, for example, the modern is cast as a radical departure from history, as a revolutionary epoch — this is why all that preceded it can be lumped together as premodern, and before history. So too with mandini, which is similarly a revolutionary epoch, above all constituted by the consequences of colonial intervention. Moglai, even if its etymological roots may be a reference to Mughal rule, in everyday usage often means the pre-mandini. Indeed, subsumed within moglai are several other epochs which had been formerly important. For example, there was the time of *gavali raj*, which may be a reference to the reign of the Yadav kings of Devgiri (later Daulatabad, near Aurangabad) who reigned from AD 1216–1312.[7] Similarly, there is the epoch of *Aurung-badshah*,

---

[6] For suggestive discussions of the relationship between time and modernity, see Peter Osborne, *The politics of time: Modernity and avant-garde*, London, 1995; Gianni Vattimo, *The end of modernity: Nihilism and hermeneutics in postmodern culture*, trans. Jon R. Snyder, Baltimore, 1988, p. 99. Especially useful on colonialism and time is Dipesh Chakrabarty's 'Marx after Marxism: History, subalternity and difference', in Saree Makdisi, Cesare Casarino and Rebecca E. Karl (eds), *Marxism beyond Marxism*, New York, 1996.

[7] David Hardiman, 'Small dam systems of the Sahyadris', in David Arnold and Ramachandra Guha, *Nature, culture, imperialism: Essays on the environmental history of South Asia*, Delhi, 1994, p. 196.

the term Dangis use to refer to what may be the Mughal emperor Aurangzeb. There is also the period of what is known as the *kuplin-bahadurin*, which may be a reference to the Company Bahadur, as the British East India Company was sometimes called. But now these epochs are not associated with any major events; they are invoked by narrators principally as a chant of names. And goth from the periods that these epochs refer to are subsumed under moglai.

However, goth of moglai and mandini also go beyond the acknowledgement of coevalness, for they refuse to stop with modernity's privileging of time, and go on to create normativity out of the initiatives of the sarkar. Ranajit Guha has pointed to how much history writing is statist, which is to say that it 'authorizes the dominant values of the state to determine the criteria of the historic'. Even stories of resistance to this narrative are comprehensible within its terms:

This is a level quite accessible to statist discourse: it is never happier than when its globalizing and unifying tendency is allowed to deal with the question in gross terms. It is a level of abstraction where all the many stories . . . are assimilated to the story of the Raj. The effect of such lumping is to oversimplify the contradictions of power by reducing them to an arbitrary singularity — the so-called principal contradiction, that between the colonizer and the colonized.[8]

Goth of mandini and moglai can be regarded as sustained engagements with this statist narrative. Goth of mandini speak of the interventions of the British and the postcolonial state — mandini, above all, is about the initiatives of the sarkar. But they extensively displace that statist discourse and focus instead on Dangi refigurings of it. Goth of moglai move further beyond the 'arbitrary singularity' of that discourse: they traverse mandini (rather than being always before it) and create a multiplicity of local and regional narratives that have little to do with the concerns of statist power. Through their refiguring of time by the initiatives of the sarkar, through their exceeding of statist narratives, goth underscore the domination and exteriority that have marked their colonial and postcolonial modernity; they are a counter-aesthetics of that modernity.

8 Ranajit Guha, 'The small voice of history', in Amin and Chakrabarty (eds), *Subaltern studies* IX, 1996, pp. 1, 6.

TRUTH AND PLAY

Within this broadly shared counter-aesthetics of modernity, there is
an abiding concern with establishing whether stories of the past are
khari goth, a phrase which can for the present be glossed as 'true
stories'. Maybe we can begin understanding khari goth through what
is beyond them, such as the many tall tales in Dangs. Often very
whimsical, with a sting in the tail, they are about a range of themes
— about the sexual peccadilloes of men and women and gods and
goddesses, about heroic figures who successfully undertake daunting
tasks, or about tricksters who get out of the most difficult situations.
While there is no specific word designating these stories, they are
recognized as a distinct genre. Most of all, they are considered
imaginary, in the sense of bearing no relation (or very tangential
ones at best) to figures of the past or present.

These stories could be called false, but that is not a word many
Dangis would voluntarily use to describe them. Instead, it may be
helpful to think of these goth as being about play. By calling these
goth playful, I do not simply refer to their ludic element, though
they are often very funny. Rather, because of their independence
from time and place, they are considered to be beyond the claims
to truth and falsity which khari goth involve. While khari goth are
those that successfully sustain a claim to refer to a particular time
and space, these stories do not even advance that claim, whether
successfully or unsuccessfully.

Of course, their playfulness does not mean these goth are outside
politics or power. They are widely known, and casual references
repeatedly occur in conversations to characters from them; they
form part of the cultural repertoire of most Dangis.[9] It is not unusual
for arguments to take the form of narrating these goth to one
another, with each goth valorizing the kind of behaviour the narrator supports. The values involved in the goth are also often under
challenge. As such, these goth posit, create, sustain, challenge and
contest values central to many Dangis.

Imaginary goth are often narrated at occasions known as
tamashas, usually held in the slack agricultural period before the
monsoons. Large events where alcohol flows freely, tamashas are
sometimes spread across two or three evenings, and are attended by
hundreds of men and women, many of whom walk over a day or two

---

[9] For some of these stories, see Khanapurkar, 'The aborigines of south
Gujarat', 2 vols, Bombay, 1944.

from distant villages to participate in it.[10] Enacted increasingly by semi-professional performers and troupes from the neighbouring area of Khandesh, what is especially valued in these performances is the inventiveness of the narrators and their ability to put a new spin on familiar themes. In addition to imaginary goth, other genres of stories are also enacted and narrated at tamashas. But the tamashas' emphasis on inventiveness and fun converges with the tropes of imaginary goth.

Imaginary goth are also narrated at casual or spur-of-the-moment gatherings, when men and women are relaxing in the evenings. Such occasions are overwhelmingly preponderant in relation to the tamasha: they occur almost every second or third evening in some corner of every village. On such occasions, some person, with a particularly good reputation as a *gothiya* or teller of tales may, under pressure from others, start off on a goth; slowly, others from surrounding huts may join in. And if there is mahua to lubricate the telling and the listening, the occasion gains in gusto and vigour.

The emphasis on play is also evident in the way the figure of the gothiya is constructed. In all genre of goth, the gothiya is so central as to render meaningless conventional oppositions which assign such oral traditions to a pre-authorial folk world, and contrast it to the culture of print and the emergence of the author. But the reasons for and manner in which the gothiya is accorded centrality vary. In imaginary goth, it is the narrative skill and style — the pauses, interjections, glosses, gestures, and sudden flurries of detail that narration involves — of the gothiya (usually, though not necessarily, a man) which is valued: he makes the goth anew with each telling.

The Truth of Vadilcha Goth

In contrast to imaginary goth, both vadilcha goth and devdevina goth posit an intimate connection with time and space; every narration constitutes a claim to tell what actually happened at some specific place in some specific time. They involve the claim to be khari goth.[11] Devdevina goth are established as *khari* in a relatively

---

10 Ibid., p. 929.

11 Not all Dangi uses of the word khari posit an intimate relationship with actual happenings in a specific time and place — the remark that women are more vulnerable to evil spirits, or that all Bhils are rajas, would be regarded as khari by most Dangis without reference to any actual happening.

straightforward manner — through being narrated in a particular form, known as the *thaali*. Unlike the tamasha, the thaali is a local performance, attended usually only by persons of the village. Unless accompanying a special ritual occasion, it can be organized quite informally and quickly, without much notice. A wooden stick or branch is stuck on a metallic plate or thaali (the genre derives its name from this) and one man runs his hands down it, creating a regular, plangent drone. Against this background, either he or another person recites devdevina goth in a particular singsong intonation. Since devdevina goth involve a time before the humans, knowledge of them requires special training, usually through extended association with *bhagats* or priests, who are believed to know these goth best. The highly skilled nature of the thaali performance demonstrates that the narrator has indeed undergone such special training, and thus usually attests to the khari nature of the goth.

In the case of the vadilcha goth, the genre this book is principally concerned with, establishing them as khari is a far more difficult task. This is not merely because they are highly fragmented and diverse, with virtually every locality, lineage or even individual having a different goth. It is also because of their inextricability, in the eyes of most Dangis, from practical, partisan, political, emotive, calculative or other considerations. Consider goth around the lineage of male descent. The lineage has since the early twentieth century been one of the crucial arenas within which Dangi politics is conducted. There are currently fourteen chiefs who are recognized by the Indian state as the descendants of the former rajas or kings of Dangs. Myriad others are recognized as their close kin or *bhauband*, while yet others are recognized as descendants of those who held *jagirdari* (land-grant) or *patilki* (village headship) rights under these rajas. Such recognition as descendants is not only an honour (turbans and shawls are publicly bestowed on the rajas, bhauband, *patils*, and *jagirdars* at a darbar held annually), but is often accompanied by a substantial pension.[12]

In this context, to know and tell goth of the power wielded by one's ancestors is to make an implicit claim to some sort of power. Also, people often narrate goth designed to impugn claims of other lineages, claiming for example that a person widely recognized as

[12] For a study of adivasi migrant workers in the fields and factories of Surat and Bulsar, see Jan Breman, *Of peasants, migrants and paupers: Rural labour circulation and capitalist production in west India*, Delhi, 1985.

the male descendant of some vadil is not the true descendant, or that the true raja or patil was not the specified vadil but someone else. Even lack of knowledge of goth takes on different implications depending on its relationship with claims to power. Officially or popularly recognized chiefs are not particularly disconcerted when they do not know goth: their authority is by now too secure in usual contexts for it to matter, and lack of knowledge is easily ascribed to vagaries of transmission. But those chiefs who are neither officially nor popularly recognized feel deeply worried when they do not know their vadilcha goth. Such is the case with one lineage of Vasurna. The father of the present lineage head did not listen much to stories when he was young, and as a result the latter does not know the stories. Since the lineage now claims a share of Vasurna dang, he has expended considerable effort in meeting persons of related lineages who might know goth of his ancestors, plying them with liquor and trying to prise stories about his lineage out from them — so far with little success. Had he known such goth, and were they persuasive, he might at least have secured some popular acceptance of his claims (though of course this would not have secured him official recognition). Well-told goth can actually create power. Haipat Lasu, a distant descendant of the Ghadvi chief, Silput raja, has through his inventive retelling of vadilcha goth secured popular authority as a chief far beyond what either descent, alliances or official recognition would allow him to claim.

Even where not so directly connected to personal claims to power, vadilcha goth are still deeply political. Goth of how the British took over the forests, of how ancestors rebelled against colonial power, of raids on plains by ancestors, of oppressive state practices, or even of the plenitude of modes of subsistence during moglai question the legitimacy of the state. Goth of how Koknis and Bhils behaved with each other in former times, of how Koknis brought agriculture to Dangs, of how a particular *dakan* or witch was dealt with, are involved in complex everyday politics.

Because of this inextricability of vadilcha goth from potentially contentious politics, they are rarely performed on occasions like the tamasha or thaali. As events in which almost anybody can participate, these are scarcely desirable occasions for discussing matters so deeply political. More appropriate is everyday conversation. Old men and women, reduced to immobility by age, might often tell children and others the stories of their youth, and the stories they learned from their vadils. In the evenings when friends get together and drink liquor, or during long afternoons when there are no pressing agricultural tasks, or while working with friends in the field, conversation may turn to vadilcha goth.

What makes such occasions particularly appropriate is that, unlike the tamasha or thaali, they are not open to everyone. As with other everyday conversation, they involve spaces of intimacy with highly flexible and contextual boundaries. When goth that are relatively uncontentious are being told, such as those of how the British took over the forests, these spaces of intimacy have bound-aries inclusive enough to take in virtually every Dangi (though not necessarily persons like me). But when the truth of the goth nar-rated is a more contentious matter, the spaces are quite restrictive: it is not unusual for narrators to segue out of one goth into another relatively inoffensive one when a new person joins the group. And when goth involve challenges to the authority of very powerful persons or lineages, they are narrated almost secretively — often after nightfall, when only members of the narrators' huts and those they have specifically invited are around. Such spaces of intimacy are themselves deeply political: they are not based simply on friendships or blood-ties, but are also part of the effort to build alliances and persuade listeners that the narrator's goth is the most khari or true.

THE PERSUASIONS OF TRUTH

Persuading listeners involves hewing close to widely shared notions of what makes a goth khari. There is the importance of *jod*, which can literally be translated as conjoining. The confluence of different accounts, especially accounts by narrators whose interests are be-lieved to diverge, is the most self-evident form of jod. In another indicator of how central colonial and postcolonial modernity is to the very constitution of vadilcha goth, the most persuasive kind of jod is provided by written documents of the sarkar. Because the sarkar constitutes Dangi realities in profoundly inescapable ways, it is thought of as enormously powerful, often even omniscient in its knowledge of Dangs — its records will contain a true account. Bhil lineages who consider themselves dispossessed often assert that proof of their having held the *gadi* or seat of power in former times will be found in the district records. The members of a dispossessed lineage of Ghadvi (one of the principal chieftaincies in Dangs) went further in 1988. Seeking to assert a claim to the gadi of Ghadvi, they searched British records at the district head-quarters at Ahwa to find proof of their having formerly held the gadi. Meeting with little success, they ventured as far as Sakri in the old Khandesh district to find the records, again with no success. Even today, they insist that a photograph of their ancestor, the early-nineteenth-century Ghadvi chief Silput raja, can be found at Delhi.

When the records of the sarkar contradict claims of goth, they are likely to be disregarded. So, while immensely important, the records of the sarkar can only confirm truth; they cannot guarantee it. Besides, other kinds of jod are very important too, and sustained efforts are made to secure them. For example, in 1994, a discussion was held between various descendants of a nineteenth-century Kokni, Dadaji Patil, where different versions of the 'same' goth (about how their ancestors moved from one village to another to eventually reach Dangs) were put together over two evenings to produce a khari account of their migrations.

Second, narrators are believed to be telling khari goth when they demonstrate a command of detail. Dangi notions of detail are different from those that professional social scientists convention-ally resort to. In the latter, at its naivest, detail forms a kind of factual cornucopia prior to discourse; in more sophisticated under-standings, detail is thought to be well-deployed when it provides solidity to an argument and confirms other narratives. In contrast, detail in a goth is evocative, linking it up in as many directions as possible with other goth. By alluding to details from other goth already considered khari, the khari nature of the narrator's goth is established by association. Indeed, there is almost a superfluity of detail, an extensive elaboration of details that do not really matter. By introducing abundant detail in this way, narrators demonstrate their knowledge, showing that what they tell is likely to be true. Goth thus abound in references to now-vanished villages, to trees that stood at the time and place of the goth, to the clothes the protagonists wore, or to how they looked.

Depth of recall is another element likely to make a goth seem more khari. The further back that a narrator can take the account, or the longer the number of ancestors through whom a person can trace descent, the greater the goth's legitimacy. Thus, ancestors' names are often recited backwards till the oldest one remembered, though no goth are known about most of the figures whose names are taken. Similarly, the invocation of former epochs such as gavli raj or kuplin bahadurin raj (of which there are few substantive memories) is part of the demonstration of depth of recall.

Finally, and most importantly, the identity of the narrator may make his goth seem more or less khari. What makes identities so important is their connection with the spaces of intimacy in which vadilcha goth are told. These spaces are of course recognized as profoundly arbitrary — many narrators who know goth may not, because of suspicion or plain disinterestedness, pass these on; disinterested persons may not even learn goth told within spaces of intimacy that they have considerable access to; interested persons may participate in several spaces of intimacy and learn a wide range of goth. Nevertheless, some identities are believed to facilitate participation in these spaces. Men, for example, are thought more likely to know and tell khari goth than women. Vadilcha goth are principally about the activities appropriate to and carried out by men. This bias towards men as subjects is almost inscribed in the word vadil itself, for the ancestors that it refers to are traced almost exclusively through men. Women figure very rarely in vadilcha goth, save as witches or the occasional ruling queen. Because goth are concerned so largely with activities viewed as male spheres, it is presumed that male narrators would have better knowledge of these activities, and that the goth would be the concern of men. Still, an acknowledgement of the crucial and constitutive role of women in Dangi pasts lurks at the margins of many goth, and emerges in sustained discussions. Furthermore, women do often know these goth as well as men — they participate as audience in spaces of intimacy, sometimes correct male narrators when they go wrong, and narrate vadilcha goth themselves.

Similarly, goth are more likely to be treated as khari if their protagonists and the narrators are from the same locality or male lineage. Many goth, lacking in depth of recall or detail, are still treated as khari because their narrators are thought to be descendants of the figures whom the goth are about. Indeed, depth of recall and detail are often drawn on precisely by those whose claims are tenuous in other ways — whether because of lack of popular recognition of their versions, or because of their marginality as narrators.

Still, no amount of detail, depth of recall, jod or identity can ensure that a goth is treated as khari, and privileged over competing versions. When the politics involved diverges drastically, different versions of vadilcha goth simply cannot be reconciled with each other. Usually, such disagreement leads to no bitterness. Narrators may insist that their version is khari, and may even be dismissive of rivals and their credentials, but things go no further than that. But sometimes, especially where goth are intimately connected to claims to power and authority in the present, there is a more concerted effort to establish a singular truth, to have only one goth considered khari. The claims involved in these goth may be so contentious that to tell them is itself a direct challenge to the authority of other persons or lineages, that their inopportune narration can lead to vehement quarrels and disputes. So these goth tend to be told within spaces of intimacy to which access is highly restricted and select, within which their khari nature is less likely to be challenged. That is to say, there is a multiplicity of rival goth claiming to be the singular truth of the same event, all of which are told in spaces of intimacy that are largely exclusive of each other.

Truth, Multiplicity, and Play

But there is not always this obsessive focus on establishing a single goth as khari. There is also, paradoxically enough, the converse phenomenon. Goth that are at variance with one another — usually either in the sense of being different accounts of the 'same' event, or in the sense of contradicting each other as units in a larger sequential narrative of which they are supposed to be a part — coexist with one another. Sometimes the same narrators may provide radically divergent versions on different occasions; in any case, they would never tell the same goth two times round with precisely the same details. Dangi listeners and narrators are aware of these contradictions, but often continue to consider all of them khari goth.

This multiplicity of truth is in stark contrast to the social sciences, which are marked primarily by the will to singularize truth. Here, within each narrative, differences have to be resolved and contradictions ironed out for it to make a persuasive claim to truth. Of course, the social sciences do allow for multiple truths, but they allow for multiple truths that are exclusive of each other, that are within themselves singular. Multiple truths always betoken multiple perspectives and narrations. For the same narration to simultaneously tell stories that do not merely supplement but contradict each other is not easy within the social sciences.

How then do we understand the Dangi multiplicity of truth, where the same narrators and audience simultaneously and comfortably hold to several contradictory truths? One kind of explanation could resort to an opposition between the episodic form of premodern or non-western cultures and the will to comprehensiveness of western modernity. The will to comprehensiveness requires a totalizing narrative where contradictions cannot be tolerated, while an episodic form allows for fragmentary narratives which do not have be reconciled within the same perspective or vision, making it possible to sustain multiple truths without demanding resolution.

Such an explanation, often implicitly resorted to even by radical scholars, is however steeped in the discourses of the hyperreal Europe, in modernity's representation of itself. In this representation, while there were multiple times in the past, modernity created a unified time — manifested in both a unified historical time and a uniform clock time better suited to the requirements of capital and industry. By creating such a time, it made possible comprehensive and singularizing narratives.[13] That is to say, it is part of western modernity's self-image that the will to comprehensiveness is impossible outside itself.

Yet this self-perception may make for a misleading and inadequate explanation. The Dangi telling of goth is also characterized by a will to comprehensiveness: narrators are often engaged in discussions to establish a khari version, or to deny other versions. What is fascinating is that this is a very distinctive will to comprehensiveness: it allows in some cases at least for multiple khari goth. How is this possible? How can many Dangis both share a will to comprehensiveness and simultaneously do the opposite — narrate several divergent stories, khari goth, about the same event, and allow these goth to coexist with each other?

Partially because the enactment of khari goth is often playful in ways quite opposed to its claims to truth. By this, I refer to the fact that the actual narration and performance of many vadilcha goth is far closer to imaginary goth than to Dangi constructions of how

---

[13] On the emergence of singularizing time, see David Landes, *Revolution in time: Clocks and the making of the modern world*, Cambridge, Mass., 1983; Stephen Kern, *The culture of time and place, 1880–1918*, Cambridge, Mass., 1983. On singularizing time in the colonial context, see Frederick Cooper, 'Colonizing time: Work rhythms and labour conflict in colonial Mombasa', in Nicholas Dirks (ed.), *Colonialism and culture*, Ann Arbor, 1992.

khari goth are to be told. In stories of how the British took over the forests, of various rebels against the British, of ancestral migrations, the emphasis is often on the gothiyas, how well they tell the story, and on how inventive they are. In this sense, play is not only the constitutive outside of truth. It also pervades the latter's will to comprehensiveness, suffusing it with a profound, inescapable fragmentariness.

Playful narratives are most resorted to when the practical, partisan, political, emotive, calculative or other considerations around goth are shared amongst narrators and listeners. For example, as Chapter 12 demonstrates, because of the widespread consensus that the British leasing of the forests was disastrous for Dangis, there are riotously different goth of how the British leased the forests, but there is virtually never any attempt to establish one of them as more true than the others. Similarly, because of widely shared hostility to the sarkar, goth of the 'same' rebellions against it are radically different versions, all revelling in detail, and all equally khari.

So, when a goth is widely considered khari, this leads not to the construction of a monolithic singular khari goth, but to the proliferation of khari goth that coexist. Conversely, when the khari nature of a goth is under question, there is again the proliferation of goth, this time with the difference that they do not coexist but rather form multiple exclusive perspectives, each told within its own space of intimacy. Whether because everybody agrees that a goth is khari or because everybody disagrees, there is always a proliferation of goth.

Learning Goth from Dangis

It was this very proliferation which shaped my learning of goth. As much scholarship over the last two decades has argued, the relationship between anthropologists and the societies they study is fraught with relationships of power, and the very knowledge that they acquire, as well as the ways in which they represent this knowledge, is marked by these relationships. The issues involved in sharing goth with me were overdetermined by the complex intersection of truth, playfulness, and the counter-aesthetics of modernity. As a plainsperson, I was often assumed to be part of the sarkar. Even when it was accepted that I was not, I was evidently part of the same modernity as the sarkar. Quite apart from being a plainsperson, there was my access to the official district archives — scarcely likely to be granted to most Dangis. There was the fact that I would produce written documents which would be more accessible to the sarkar than to the Dangis. In this context, though the questions I asked about kingship, village rights, old disputes, or rebellions against the British could also have been asked by a Dangi, the fact was that these were issues that the sarkar too could be deeply interested in.

As part of the sarkar's oppressive modernity, there was much reason to exclude me from spaces of intimacy, to not narrate too many goth to me. In one village, when other Dangi listeners urged a vadil to tell me more goth, he exploded: 'What do you know about matters, telling me "tell him the goth, tell him the goth". . . . This was how the *saheb* [white man] came. . . . Do you know what he will do with the goth?' Often, I was told primarily imaginary goth, devdevina goth, and the more playful vadilcha goth, and sometimes not even the last where these involved hostility to the sarkar. Many disclaimed knowledge of other goth, especially those around intra-Dangi claims to power.

I did, in the course of time, learn these other, more contentious, goth too. I would like to think that I was told these goth because like other Dangis, I established friendships which allowed me to participate in spaces of intimacy. But that hope may be a forlorn one, and it would be disingenuous for me to believe that these friendships were entirely independent of my position as a potentially powerful person from the plains of Gujarat. Certainly, my learning of contentious goth had to do in part with my very power. Dangis were scarcely unified in their reservations about sharing goth with me. Telling me goth involving their claims to power in relation to other Dangis was one way of constructing that power. Even the very fact of my coming to them to learn goth was not innocent: by recording and writing down their goth, I gave it more credibility, and in cases where goth involved claims to power or resources in the present, there was the hope that my writings might influence the sarkar much more than the narrators ever could. In all these senses my very knowledge of goth was acquired through an implicit, maybe inescapable, collusion with the very relations of domination that I professed to be rejecting in turning to Dangis to learn their goth and present an alternative understanding.

Moglai

3

Being Dangi, Being Wild

Some Dangis speculate that moglai is a reference to, and gloss on the Mughal period. Others are sceptical. Whatever its origins, in Dangi usage now it is a capacious word, involving very distinct identities, forms of livelihood, relationships with forests, and styles of kingship. Goth of moglai quite often involve an account of Janak raja, a liminal figure somewhere between dev-devina goth and vadilcha goth, sometimes described as the first raja or king of Dangs.

Janak raja stayed at Jalgovad village across the *ghat* [hills]. His parents died when he was young. He had an elder brother named Jankia, and then Jankia also died. He was left alone to fend for himself, and became a cowherd for the village. Janak and the daughter of one of the villagers would go to graze cattle. Around noon one day, a calf was killed by a tiger. Janak came upon the calf, and was curious, and cooked it. When the girl came, she asked, 'what have you got'. He said, 'deer'. So she also ate it.

When they reached home with the cattle that day, one calf was missing. Janak said 'A tiger carried it away'. The villagers thought, 'it is alright if one calf is missing from such a large flock'.

Then Janak began to kill a calf every day and cook it. By now, the girl also knew, and they would eat the calf together.

In the meantime, people in the village became suspicious.

They thought, 'How can so many cattle be lost to tigers?' But with all the meat he was eating, Janak had by then become very strong. So they were very scared of him. They conspired to kill him by stealth.

The girl heard her father talking about it, and she ran and told Janak raja. Both of them took the cattle and fled to Dangs. They came by the Rotni ghat, and they reached Chinchli. Then they came to Atala Dungar, near Anjankund. From Anjankund they came to Linga.

At Linga there was a small tree — it is still there, though it is now very old — and they kept the cattle around the tree. They made *sagdas* [burning torches from twigs and branches], and tied them to the horns of the cattle at night. They also lit a large number of *bidis* [tobacco wrapped in a leaf and smoked like a cigarette], and scattered them around. When the pursuing party of villagers came and saw the bidi stubs, and the large number of torches, they thought, 'he must have a very large army', and went back.

During their month at Linga, they continued to eat one cow a day. After a month, they went to Bilia dungar, near Bhend village. And they began to stay there. When in the morning, they would clear their throats while washing their mouths, people would wake up in Surat at the sound. And Janak raja was so strong that when he shot an arrow from the *dungar*, it would land at the gates of Surat.[1]

There are several variants of this goth about Janak raja, and it is told in a variety of contexts: to establish which is the seniormost lineage in Dangs, to speculate about how Dangs came to be populated, how Dangis lived in the past, or to tell a playful story. This multiplicity of contexts in which Janak raja is invoked may be because he is so often cast as the quintessential Dangi of moglai, because telling goth about him provides a means to reflect on what it meant and means to be a Dangi. Taking cues from these reflections, this chapter explores the agonisms that were involved in the construction of wildness in moglai, in the precolonial and extracolonial epochs.

DANG AS IMAGINED GEOGRAPHY

One of the ways in which Janak raja became a Dangi was by moving from his village in the plains of Khandesh into the hills of Dangs. In this goth, being Dangi is not about being autochthons

[1] Keshrio Kaman, 3.4.1994, Nilsakia.

of the region. Rather, it is about inhabiting a particular kind of geographical space, and about a distinctive agonistic relationship with surrounding plains areas. It is possible to find allusions to this geography for the eighteenth and nineteenth centuries. As a term, dang refers to either hilly tracts or those regions with dense bamboo growth.[2] The dang in western India (of which Dangs was part) comprised the hilly areas, and was characterized by steep, separated peaks. A broken ridge of the dang or ghat ran roughly parallel to the western Indian coastline, at a distance ranging from about fifty to a hundred kilometres from it, all the way from Dangs into eastern Nasik, and across Maharashtra.[3] Dangs itself was often 'so strong in hilly and raviney ground [that] nothing can travel there but bullocks and ponies and even these animals have great difficulty in keeping their footing'. The people who lived in the dang were often called dangi, or *pahadi*, a word meaning 'hill people'.[4]

The term dang provided the basis for the colonial and current name of the area. After colonial officials consolidated their hold over the region, they referred to it as 'the Daungs' or 'the Dhangs'. The phrase was a gloss for the local practice of referring to different tracts within it by using the word variably as a suffix or prefix, speaking for instance of 'dang Amala' or 'Ghadvi dang'. This practice occurred also in other dangi or *ghati* areas of western India.[5] Because of the vagaries of colonial classification, however, these other areas came to be called by their proper names, whereas the adjective emerged as the proper name of the whole tract which is now known officially as 'the Dangs' or Dangs District.

The dang was also situated in relation to the broader region's imagined geography. Stewart Gordon identifies the ghat (a synonym for dang), the *desh*, and the Konkan as the three major regions south of the Dangs. Desh referred to the villages on the broad plateau which lay to the east of the ghat or dang in Maharashtra. The plains of Khandesh were part of this territory, as were those

---

2 *BA.RD.1872.Vol 77.Comp 556.*

3 Government of Bombay, *Gazetteer of the Bombay Presidency, Vol. XVI, Nasik*, Bombay, 1883; Goldsmid to Vibert, 11.10.1841 in *SRBG 6*, Bombay, 1853; *SRBG 216*, pp. 59ff.

4 Morriss to Reeves, 22.5.1843, *IOL.F.4.2074*; Premanand Patel, *Navsari Prantni kaliparaj*, Baroda, 1901, pp. 1–10.

5 For examples of the practice, see Maharawal Raisingji to John Morrison, 16.6.1804, *SPD 158 (16)*; the 1828 list of giras rights of Dangs chiefs reproduced in *BA.PD.1855.Vol. 36.Comp 577*; and *BRO.DDR.DN 1.FN 2.*

of Nasik. These regions, especially beyond the rainshadow of the ghat, were moderately fertile and well populated. The Konkan was the relatively flat and highly productive western coastal strip with many important ports, about fifty kilometres wide, which ran across Maharashtra.[6]

Towards Dangs, the imagined geography was slightly different. Situated at the northwest tip of the ghat or dang, Dangs was contiguous not to the Konkan, but to Gujarat. The three locally prevalent distinctions were between the desh, the dang, and Gujarat. In the late eighteenth and early nineteenth century, the dang, the desh and Gujarat also roughly coincided with some political bound- aries. Dangs itself was ruled by several chiefs from the Bhil com- munity, which was politically dominant in much of the forested areas of western India. The principal chiefs in Dangs during this period appear to have been six — those of Amala, Ghadvi, Deher or Dherbhavti, Pimpri, Kadmal, and Vasurna. In addition, as later chapters will make clear, there were several chiefs who were almost as powerful, and authority was deeply shared amongst Bhil chiefs, also known as the bhuband. Towards the east and southeast of Dangs, in the desh, lay the Peshwa-controlled province of Khandesh; it was to become part of British territory after 1818. In the Gujarat region to the northeast, another Maratha successor-state, that of the Gaekwads, was dominant. Both powers had very close ties with Dangs, as later chapters show.

INTIMATIONS OF WILDNESS

The imagined geography which distinguished between dang, desh, and Gujarat was overlaid by another one which drew a distinction between the dang or ghat and all the other regions, whether Gujarat, Konkan or the desh. The dang was cast in opposition to the entire plains: in comparison to the dangis or people of Dangs, the people of Gujarat, Konkan or the desh seemed quite like each other.

The Bhils, Koknis and Varlis, the three major *jatis* or castes of eighteenth- and nineteenth-century Dangs were sometimes referred to as janglijati and *kaliparaj*, as were a number of large central and western Indian communities such as the Gamits, Chaudaris, Valvis, Tadvis, Dublas, Naikdas, Vasavas, and Bhilalas.[7] The Varlis were

---

[6] Stewart Gordon, *The Marathas, 1600–1818*, Cambridge, 1993, pp. 10–13.
[7] It is still common in some circles to describe jatis such as Bhils as tribes,

the least numerous of the three major jatis in Dangs. Dangs lay on the northern fringes of the regions where they were settled — they were more densely concentrated and numerically dominant in many regions to the south of Dangs, especially around Thana. In 1891, when we have our first reliable census, they numbered only around 3247 in Dangs.[8] In the rest of the book, I shall not deal much with the Varlis, focusing principally on the other two jatis.

The single largest jati in Dangs was that of the Koknis, who numbered around 15,780 in 1891.[9] Dangs was part of the core regions where they had settled. They were most densely concentrated in the British districts of Nasik and West Khandesh, the princely states of Dharampur and Vansda, and Dangs, numbering around 189,000 in 1922. As their name implied, their ancestors had been from the Konkan, far to the southwest, but their ancestors had, following a famine in the fourteenth century, commenced a slow process of northward migration. Migration both into Dangs and beyond it northwards and eastwards continued throughout the nineteenth and early twentieth centuries. Nineteenth-century migrants maintained ancestral memorial stones in their former villages outside Dangs till well after the mid-twentieth century, when the slow attenuation of ties led to the establishment of stones for ancestors within Dangs itself.

The politically dominant jati in the nineteenth century was that of the Bhils, who had a population of 12,099 in 1891.[10] Dangs was along the southern margins of areas of Bhil settlement. Spread across Khandesh, Nasik, Panchmahals, Rewakantha, and central India, the Bhils were by far the single most numerous jati or caste in the hilly and forested regions of western India as a whole, and amongst the largest of the 'wild tribes' of India. Not much Bhil migration into Dangs appears to have occurred in the last two hundred years — approximately the maximum period to which family genealogies from oral traditions can be traced. The remotest ancestors that most Bhils can recall stayed in villages either just inside or around Dangs.

---

and to distinguish them from castes. The distinction has rightly been criticized often in recent decades. I therefore translate jati as caste, and prefer to stay away from the distinction between caste and tribe. For an analysis of the discourse which made the distinction between caste and tribe, see my 'Shades of wildness'.

8 FDO to Coll., Kh., 1.9.1891, *BA.RD.1892.Vol 144.Comp 948.*
9 Ibid.
10 Ibid.

Like dangi, there were other words, amongst them janglijati and
kaliparaj, used to describe Bhils, Koknis, Varlis and communities
like them. In the nineteenth century, all three words shared one
element — intimations of wildness. One way in which they did so
was through a presumed association with forests and hills. 'Dangi'
already carried these implications. Similarly, jangli was an adjective
of jangal or wilderness; it meant of the jungle or forests. Bhils and
Varlis, like many other communities in India, were usually considered to be residents of the forests. This was very much a case
of imagined forests. Significant proportions of the Koknis, Bhils and
Varlis lived in cleared plains areas, and the bulk of some other
communities called janglijati, dangi, or kaliparaj stayed far from
any forests. But because some portion of these jatis did stay in the
forests, or were presumed to have done so in the past, they continued to be associated with forests. So one connotation of the
words used to describe communities like the Bhils, Koknis or Varlis
is 'forest communities'.

A second way in which these words intimated wildness was
through their insinuation of a very low ritual status. Many of the
communities described by these words, such as the Bhils and
Varlis, ate beef — an extremely sinful and abhorrent act by upper
caste criteria, one associated with the lowest of low castes. Because
of this and other practices, their touch was considered polluting
by many upper castes. Kaliparaj, a word which literally translates
as 'black peoples', and was contrasted to the *ujliparaj* or *ujaliyat*,
or the fair people, connoted this inferiority most explicitly. It was
so loaded with connotations of inferiority that it was often considered to be an insult to be so called, and Bhils and others often
refused to use the prefix '*ujli*' for those claiming superiority.[11] But
occasionally they must have been compelled to accept their ritual
inferiority, and even the use of words like kaliparaj for them. They
were also often politically subordinate, especially those amongst
them who lived in the desh or Gujarat, or in regions dominated
by upper castes. By the nineteenth century at least, many worked
as landless or even bonded labourers on the fields of the upper
castes.[12] And even in the case of those who lived in the dang,
traders advanced loans to them at usurious rates; timber merchants

[11] Sarat Chandra Roy, 'The black Bhils of Jaisamand lake', *Journal of Bihar
and Orissa Research Society*, vol. X, parts I and II, 1924, p. 100.
[12] Jan Breman, *Beyond patronage and exploitation: Changing agrarian relations in south Gujarat*, Delhi, 1993.

regularly underpaid them; liquor dealers from the plains settled in the dang often cheated and browbeat them.

This connotation of inferiority was far more muted in the other two words — janglijati and dangi. Dangi, as already suggested, connoted above all an imagined geography. Janglijati would literally translate as 'wild castes' or 'forest castes'. The word itself is not used much in the records and books I examined, and it does carry connotations of an insulting inferiority now. Very occasionally and with tongue-in-cheek, however, forest communities do use the word for themselves; in some senses, it is marginally less offensive to them as a description than kaliparaj. But in the eighteenth and nineteenth centuries, janglijati might have been, like dangi, a much more acceptable word.

This is so because central to these words was a third connotation of wildness: an agonistic relationship with upper caste values, an emphatic othering. In some ways, this othering persists now in goth of Janak's eating beef. The anthropological tradition of reading similar low caste accounts as doleful origin-myths explaining how such groups were placed beyond the pale of orthodox caste society would be misleading here. For the goth is not about an original unity with upper caste plainspeople which was then sundered, or about the low ritual status created by eating beef. By situating Janak amongst their ancestors, Dangi narrators displace and challenge upper caste values. In their mirthful celebration of the way he eats beef, the way he loots plains villagers, the way he fools them, and the way he is feared in the plains, the stories are about Janak raja, the dangi or the Bhil as a wild and fearsome Other.

As later chapters will make clear, this affirmation of wildness is a relatively subdued theme now, having been replaced by a very different notion of what it means to be dangi. In the eighteenth and nineteenth centuries, however, such wildness was affirmed quite often. Many of these jatis were ascribed those remarkable supernatural powers because of their wildness. The Bhils were thought to be

endowed with the faculty of assuming the shape of a tiger, but without the tail, which it seems they cannot take. They possess the powers of conjuration, and can at their will devote any human being or animal to death. By the same art, they can make a man mad. It requires but a space of 4 minutes for effecting any of these diabolical purposes.[13]

[13] Walker of Bowland papers, University of Edinburgh Library, MS 13861,

Some moneylenders, it was reported, even refused to lend money
to these communities because of a fear of their witchcraft.[14] Those
Bhils who lived in dense forests were thought to have more powerful magic than others. Dangi witchcraft and sorcery was thought
to be especially potent and dangerous.[15]

Similarly, another community called the Malivad Bhils were
much dreaded towards Panchmahals, and a common curse amongst
cartsmen was, 'May the Malivads take you'.[16] Most intriguing of all
was the case of the Bhats. The Bhats were a highly respected caste
who often travelled with traders for a fee. Their person was supposed to protect traders from robbery, since they would threaten
to kill themselves and curse robbers in case of any attacks. This
strategy, useful with most robbers, was however ineffective with
the Bhils, who paid little heed to the threats or curses of Bhats and
Charans. As a result, Charans and Bhats often refused to be surety
for travellers through Bhil areas.[17]

What is especially striking is that these communities were not
only considered wild by others: they too emphasized their powers
of witchcraft and cast themselves as a wild and potentially fearsome
Other. By doing so, they undercut and challenged their ritual
inferiority and, where it existed, political subordination. Amongst
the Kolis, Bhils and Girasias, one observer reported in the early
nineteenth century, there was even a saying: 'Guzerat-pela Lauth,
peche Baut i.e., first a kick — then words with a Man of Guzerat.'[18]
Similarly, another forest community, Kathkaris, during funerals
exhorted the departed soul not to be reborn as a Brahman, 'for he
has to write and die, nor a Kunbi [cultivator] for he ploughs till
death . . . but be thou a Kathkari for then thou shalt be Junglacha
raja [king of the forests]'.[19]

'An account of castes and professions in Guzerat'. I am extremely indebted to
Raj Kumar Hans for providing me with the reference to this volume.

[14] Government of Bombay, *Gazetteer of the Bombay Presidency: Vol. IX:
Gujarat Population: Hindus*, Bombay, 1901, part I, p. 426.

[15] Khanapurkar, 'The aborigines of south Gujarat'.

[16] Government of Bombay, *Gazetteer of the Bombay Presidency: Vol. VI: Rewa
Kantha, Narukot and the Surat States*, Bombay, 1880, p. 28.

[17] *DDR.DN2.FN4Uc.* For accounts of the Bhats, see Neil Rabitoy, 'Administrative modernisation and the Bhats of British Gujarat, 1800–1820', *Indian
Economic and Social History Review*, vol. 11, no. 1, 1974.

[18] Walker of Bowland papers, 'An account of castes and professions in
Guzerat'.

[19] Quoted in Anon., *Notes on the criminal classes in the Bombay Presidency*,
Bombay, 1908, p. 86.

It is very tempting to read all these remarks as part of an overarching opposition between wildness and civilization, with the latter being identified with plains values. But that would be misleading. Wildness was not something that only the janglijati affirmed: it was also affirmed in some ways by upper castes in the plains. Claims to wildness were often produced through an agonistic relationship with upper caste values rather than being entirely outside these. Furthermore, this was a very complex, even fragmented, discourse of wildness. The wildness of women was quite different from the wildness of men, and that of Koknis was quite different from that of Bhils. Wildness also imparted very distinctive meanings to forms of livelihood, to forests, and even to kingship and personhood. It is to these complexities of wildness, and the many sites at which it was produced, that we now need to turn.

(10)

4

Cathecting Forests

Moglai was a time of *chhut*, literally 'freedom to' or 'permission to'. The notion of chhut is imbricated in the mandini. The freedom referred to in chhut, after all, is freedom from those colonial and postcolonial restrictions which are believed to mark the beginning of mandini. In thinking of precolonial and extra-colonial times, the old argument that non-western, premodern or precolonial societies had harmonious and ecologically sustainable relationships with the environment need not detain us — critics have by now pointed often enough to its flaws.[1] More sophisticated approaches have emphasized societies' 'cultural understanding of their environment'. These approaches have shown that the opposition between culture and nature or environment is a false dichotomy that is often not relevant in many non-western societies, that in many of these societies there is a 'mutual constitution' of persons and the environment.[2]

Yet, to view the matter in these terms — whether 'cultural understanding' or 'mutual constitution' — is still to be defined by the categories of 'nature' and 'environment'. Understood this way, 'nature' and 'environment' become self-evident entities, categories that have universal relevance, categories that only need to be fleshed out with any particular cultural understanding, rather than themselves being the culminations of particular European, western and colonial trajectories of thought and practice.

[1] The political impulse that informs these depictions of precolonial or local harmony is often admirable. See Ramachandra Guha, *The unquiet woods: Ecological change and peasant resistance in the Himalaya*, New Delhi, 1989, pp. 27–34. For a critique of ecological functionalism in the Indian context, especially relevant is K. Sivaramakrishnan's 'Colonialism and forestry in India: Imagining the past in present politics', *Comparative Studies in Society and History*, vol. 37, January 1995, pp. 3–40.

[2] See Elisabeth Croll and David Parkin, 'Cultural understandings of the environment', Tim Ingold, 'Culture and the perception of the environment', both in Elisabeth Croll and David Parkin (eds), *Bush base, forest farm: Culture, environment and development*, London, 1992, p. 40.

In this context, the evocation of chhut is suggestive, for it configures in deceptively similar but fundamentally different ways the Dangi themes that would otherwise be appropriated by the universalist narratives, academic and popular, of 'nature' and 'environment'. Above all, chhut cathects several distinctively Dangi spaces during moglai, amongst them the spaces of the *pada* or village, the jangal or forests, the dang as a region, and the dang as a political entity. These spaces are intercalated, superimposed and combined in multiple ways, all the time constituting, undermining and consuming one another. Taking cues from this, I explore how nineteenth- and early-twentieth-century Dangis, rather than simply having a concept of space or 'cultural understanding of the environment' which they imposed on an external nature or environment, actually produced and cathected the distinctive spaces that they inhabited.[3]

Chhut and the Dang

One kind of space cathected in chhut is that of the dang as a region — the dang as contrasted to Gujarat or the desh. The dang is almost the paradigmatic space produced by the enactment of chhut in moglai, for the dang ended where chhut ended: what characterized the desh and Gujarat was the lack of chhut.

First, chhut is about the freedom to use trees, plants or forests of the dang. In the nineteenth century, Dangis used forests in multiple and complex ways. Dangs was part of the semi-moist deciduous teak forests that ran virtually all along the ghats of western India, and extended in several areas into the plains.[4] In Dangs, teak trees accounted for anything between thirty-five to sixty per cent of the large trees in most areas by 1913, a time when its proportion would have been diminished by nearly a century of vigorous colonial felling.[5] Dangis had myriad uses for the teak tree:

3 I am obviously influenced in this chapter by Henri Lefebvre's classic (*The production of space*, Oxford, 1991, trans. Donald Nicholson-Smith), though Lefebvre himself here often remains hostage to the evolutionist arguments that he is rejecting. I adapt the notion of cathexis from Freudian psychoanalysis; amongst other reasons, I am drawn to it because of the forceful ways in which it allows us to think of the production of space.

4 Possibly teak had once been dominant across much larger areas, but had been slowly edged out from areas where the *sal* tree, *Shorea robusta*, could also flourish. J. Forsyth, *The highlands of central India*, London, 1919, pp. 20f.

5 Government of Bombay, *North Dangs working plan*, Bombay, 1913 (henceforth *NDWP*), p. 10.

its branches were considered excellent lopping, its leaves were used as roofing material, and its poles for the construction of houses. Almost all the species of plants and trees in the dang were used in various ways by Dangis.

There was also commerce in forests and forest produce. Merchants from the plains, as Chapter 12 details, often had leases of forests by the early nineteenth century. In addition, ordinary Dangis took headloads of firewood, gum, honey, and other forest produce into the large villages in Khandesh, and exchanged or sold these for necessities. Vanjaras, with large herds of pack-bullocks, would also pass through Dangs in the summers, carrying with them goods like salt, ornaments, and garments. These were exchanged for forest produce. Some Dangis also made bamboo mats and baskets, or other items for sale. In addition, there was a small community of Kathkaris, who made their living by felling *khair* trees, and preparing from it an astringent called *kath*, which was chewed with betel leaves extensively in India.[6]

CHHUT AND MOBILITY

Second, as already implicit in the notion of using forests and trees, chhut is about the ability to move. And mobility was crucial to nineteenth-century Dangi life. All the major Dangi forms of livelihood — shifting cultivation, hunting, fishing, gathering, and the collection of mahua flowers — presumed mobility. Many Dangis stayed in two or even three places in a year. Around February or March, when the mahua trees flowered, some Dangis put up huts near the sites where they were collecting mahua flowers. If foodgrains were short, the flowers on the tree would be eaten fresh. After drying, they provided both food and liquor for two or three months at least. By around April or May, many Dangis moved again, this time to the riversides or pools. Subsequent months, the height of summer, were the period when dependence on fishing was the greatest, when the rivers began drying up, leaving behind pools of water in which it was easier to fish. It was also the period when hunting (which commenced around September or October, when the principal agricultural operations were over) was at its peak. As

---

6 This account is gleaned from *KDG*, p. 602; KPAAR, 1872–3, *BA.PD.1873. Vol 87.Comp 1551, SRBG 26*, p. 165, KPAAR, 1888–9, *BA.PD.1890. Vol 122. Comp 205* and Shuttleworth to Secy., GoB, 19.6.1888, *BA.RD.1889.Vol 164. Comp 948.*

the monsoons approached in June, families moved house again, now to the villages where their fields were. Already, by late summer, before they moved for cultivation, tubers could be dug out for consumption, and the onset of monsoons saw various edible leaves and mushrooms springing up. Gathering was most important from May till September, the period which began at the height of summer and continued through monsoon almost till the reaping of crops.

Patterns and directions of mobility depended on the activity being undertaken, the persons involved, and their interests. Consider the threefold division of lands involved in mobility for agriculture. Koknis were often more interested in a form of cultivation called *dahi*, which involved cattle-drawn ploughs. *Sapati* lands were thought best for dahi. These were the mild slopes or plateaus, and included the flat patches where deeper reddish soil was likely to be found, as well as the patches of black soil along the river valleys. Bhils were more involved in a form of cultivation called *khandad*, which involved hand-drawn ploughs. *Panlot* lands were considered best for khandad. These were usually higher up and on much steeper slopes, and often had shallow red soil.[7] Broadly speaking, Koknis were more likely to move from and to sapati land, and Bhils from and to panlot lands. What was roughly clear was that nobody in their right minds would shift to the *vanarkilla*, literally 'fortresses of the monkeys'. Spots where neither khandad nor dahi was considered desirable, these were not much use even for gathering, fishing, or hunting. They were the closest in Dangi imaginations to useless regions.[8]

Even Dangi houses were geared towards mobility. These were small round huts, with one central teak pole in the middle from which the thatch came down to the bamboo walls, usually occupied by a nuclear family, with each married son establishing his independent hut. Since material for construction was not in short supply, these huts were largely abandoned when moving to a new spot; only some of the choicest material was carried along. The handful of prosperous Koknis who did have larger, square houses were also, strikingly, those who were not as mobile. They stayed in one residence in the village, though they like others changed the spot they cultivated every two or three years, moving to a new site

7 Annual Report, 1906–7, *BA.ED.1908.Vol 63.Comp 739*. I discuss khandad and dahi in the next chapter.
8 Khandu Ravji, 6.5.1990, Vakaria.

within the village itself. They also did not depend to the same extent on fishing, gathering, hunting or mahua-collection.[9]

Nor was the mobility referred to in evocations of chhut only associated with forms of livelihood. If a person fell ill or died, the house was usually abandoned. Dangis moved residence often to be closer to their relatives, or other persons with whom they had built particularly intimate relations. They moved to escape excessive tax demands from chiefs.[10] People, in other words, could move for myriad reasons, so many reasons that it would not only be pointless to attempt an exhaustive account of them, but would actually militate against the spirit of that mobility.

But one point should be made. The response to scarcities and famines (which occurred only too regularly, usually when agricultural or mahua crops failed) was a further escalation of mobility, especially of that required for gathering and hunting. Some forest produce, like the tubers *kadukand* and *vajkand,* were consumed largely in difficult seasons, when other kinds of food were not available. Both tubers were believed to be poisonous, and were sliced and kept in running water in a brook for a few days to be made edible.[11] During serious famines, such as the 1899–1901 *Chhapinayakad* (literally, the famine of 1956 — the year is reckoned by the Samvat calendar), even these strategies were not enough, and many hundreds of Dangis died.[12] By the end of that famine, census reports indicate, the population of Dangs had been nearly halved by death and migration.[13] Chhut, it should be remembered, is not about a prelapsarian time in goth.

MAKING THE DANG

A third meaning of chhut in the dang, again not so much distinct from the other two as already implied in them, is that of the freedom to make, or remake, the dang. Dangi patterns of use and mobility engaged with and produced the mosaic complexity of the dang. By the nineteenth century, the dang had been remade to such an extent that it does not make any sense to separate for any causal analysis the 'human' and 'natural' influences.

9 Ramji Patil, 9.6.1990, Pandva.
10 KPAAR, 1888–9, *BA.PD.1890. Vol 122.Comp 205.*
11 Coll., Kh., to Secy., GoB, 7.5.1856, *BA.PD.1856.Vol 48.Comp 987.*
12 Sayaju Lasya and Janya Kalu, 11.3.1991, Godadia.
13 Government of Gujarat, *Dangs District Gazetteer,* Ahmedabad, 1971, p. 159.

Dangi practices had produced considerable regional differences in the dang. Towards the east and south, cultivation was more extensive and forests were less dense, and towards the west, and to a lesser extent the north, lay the densest forests.[14] The denser forests may have been a recent development, caused by cultivators moving away from the west, where many recent chiefs had been oppressive, to the east, where some important chiefs actively encouraged cultivation.[15]

Lopping and firing, pervasive aspects of Dangi agriculture, also remade the forests in very basic ways. In order to provide manure for seedbeds and fields, the branches of trees near fields were lopped annually. Mainly because of this, trees rarely grew to a very large height or girth — something that did not matter to Dangis since they had little use for large timber anyway. Firing the forests was very much part of Dangi life, and it was common for some areas to be burnt several times a year:

the Bheel . . . burns jungle for the sake of shooting game of all sorts. If he thinks there are panthers around he feels safer in a burnt maidan than if surrounded by grass; the sporadic cultivation is the chief offender in this respect; the woodcutter and bamboo contractor can do their work with much more comfort after a fire; mowra flowers are much easier gathered from a burnt floor.[16]

Not all Dangis may have felt the same way about fires. For those, largely Koknis, who kept cattle, fires cut into fodder supply which was scarce. In years of drought, cattle could die for want of water or grass.[17] But whether because the benefits of fires outweighed the disadvantages for them too, or because they realized that fires were too important a part of the strategies of subsistence of the politically dominant Bhils to be abandoned, or simply because they considered fires to be unavoidable, most Koknis too participated in firing the forests.

It may not have been accidental that teak, *kakad* and *modal* were the three dominant species in nineteenth-century Dangs: they could stand lopping and fires very well. Another tree which could take both lopping and fires was *khair*, but the fact that it was felled in such large numbers to make kath, combined with its relatively poor

14 *BA.RD.1872.Vol 17.Comp 556.*
15 See KPAAR, 1888–9, *BA.PD.1890. Vol 122.Comp 205*; *DCR.DN 2.FN4Uc.*
16 Shuttleworth to Chief Secy., GoB, 19.6.1888. *BA.RD.1889.Vol 164. Comp 948.* See also *FRBP, 1884–5,* p. 23.
17 Hodgson to PA, 31.3.1910, *BA.PD.1911.Vol 198.Comp 944.*

reproduction, may have resulted in its being not so common. The *beo*, despite being the 'stoutest fire-resister' in Dangs; was even less common because it did not take lopping very well.[18]

The prevalence of teak may in fact have been partly due to Dangi lifestyle. Teak seeded after the rainy season, but the seeds were covered by a hard shell and had to be decomposed by long exposure to moisture and heat before they would germinate. In Dangs moisture by itself was often not enough: germination of teak seedlings was prolific in the moist areas along the lower reaches of river valleys, but they were soon choked off by the dense undergrowth. The repeated conflagrations thus helped seeds germinate, cleared the undergrowth, and ensured sunlight for the seedlings. This was why teak did so well in those areas which were either cultivated or at least regularly fired.[19]

As far as animals like sambhar or antelope were concerned, fires were a double-edged phenomenon. They burnt the undergrowth and cut into the grass supplies that these animals could depend on to survive the most difficult season of the year. But by clearing the undergrowth, and by reducing the density of trees, the fires created in the long run and maintained in the short run an ecological environment between forests and grasslands. Here, especially after the rains, grass was plentiful. This was the ideal habitat for many herbivores, such as sambhar, antelope, or even hare, which would not have flourished as well in dense forests.[20] In turn, the presence of these herbivores attracted both birds of prey, and larger carnivores like tigers and panthers. In this sense, Dangi fires actually helped create the environment which supported and perhaps even increased the wildlife in the area.

Dangi practices may have influenced soil, gradient, and flora and fauna.[21] Dangs varied dramatically on different sides of its hills: forests were much thicker on the northern and eastern side of hills, while on the southern side tree growth was sparser and there was greater soil erosion. This may have been because of the social meanings of winds. Easterly winds prevailed only in the

---

[18] Janya Lahanu, 11.4.1994, Sukmal.

[19] Janya Lahanu, 14.4.1994, Sukmal. Some forest officials also recognized the importance of fires in propagating teak. See the correspondence in DFR.DN 3.FN 8Uc.

[20] Cumine to Comm, CD, n.d. (August 1895), DFR.DN 3.FN 8Uc.

[21] The rest of this section is gleaned from *DWP, NDWP, SDWP,* and K.R. Bomanji (ed.), *Dangs boundary dispute,* Bombay, 1903 (henceforth *DBD*).

winter, a time when Dangi practices led to fewer fires; southwestern winds, in contrast, prevailed in summer, when Dangis used fires extensively. Thus there were more extensive fires on southern slopes, and the relative openness of these slopes, in turn, also encouraged their greater use for cultivation and cattle-grazing.

Dangi practices may also have caused significant soil erosion in some places. By the early twentieth century, trees on the southern aspects of upper hills in many areas were stunted because of soil erosion in the past. The most dramatic manifestations of such erosion were the stag-headed teak trees which occurred on some steep slopes. Here, the crowns were either half-dried — giving them a stag-headed shape — or looked as though they 'had been crushed down and made to grow sideways for a period and since made various degrees of recovery'. The deformity was partly the result of growing on a steep slope, which caused a one-sided domination of each crown by the one immediately above it, causing the leading shoot to die off. But this had been aggravated by the hard, rain-washed condition of the soil, caused most of all by cultivation on high plateaus and steep slopes. Besides, the fact that many stag-headed trees were quite tall indicated that the soil had been deeper when they were young, and had been eroded as recently as the late nineteenth century. This erosion had also prevented the re-generation of young trees on some of these slopes.[22]

As all this suggests, Dangi practices were not designed to be ecologically sustainable, nor were they based on a comprehensive knowledge of the dang. Only some men were good trackers and good hunters; only some men and women knew where to find medicinal herbs or leaves; ordinary Dangis did sometimes get lost in the forest; and many of them were quite apprehensive of travers-ing dense forests. While Dangis and similar communities elsewhere in India knew a lot about their localities — forests, trees, seasons, and produce — this knowledge remained deeply fragmented and partial, and most Dangis were aware of this.

CHHUT AND POLITICAL POWER

I have so far focused on one kind of dang cathected in the evocation of chhut — the dang as opposed to the desh. But chhut involved also a cathexis of another dang — the dang as a political territory,

22 *NDWP*, p. 173.

as one amongst several dangs that were involved in complex claims
to be simultaneously independent and interdependent. In Dangs,
there was a welter of such dangs, and their boundaries and frontiers
were far from clear. Since the complex politics of these dangs will
be discussed in later chapters, I shall here limit myself to looking
at the ways in which the dangs were cathected in chhut.

The mobility of mahua collection was deeply involved in the
cathexis of the frontiers of various dangs. Members of the bhauband
usually possessed rights over the mahua trees of their dang.[23] In
villages shared between two dangs (as was often the case) one
group of bhauband might possess the mahua-collection rights while
the other held rights for collecting agricultural revenue.[24] The
collection of mahua flowers thus occurred primarily within the dang
with which a Bhil or Kokni was associated — though, since dangs
were interrelated in so many ways, persons were often associated
with several dangs. The bhauband went with their followers (which
included the bulk of the Bhils of the dang, and a significant proportion of Koknis) to collect mahua flowers.

The mobility of shifting cultivation also constructed the frontiers
of various dangs. If individuals or families moved to another dang
to cultivate, they had to pay *palanpatti*, a tax of around Rs 5 in
cash or its equivalent in kind. Migration for cultivation was also
influenced by the conditions in each dang. If the tax demands of
Bhil chiefs or bhauband of a dang became excessive, or if they
became oppressive, cultivators could protest with their feet, as they
did in dang Ghadvi in the 1890s, deserting it in large numbers.
They could also show their approval with their feet. The late-
nineteenth-century *naik* of Chinchli-Gadad in the east, who did not
allow any harassment of Koknis, had one of the most flourishing
tracts in Dangs. Similarly, the 'mild and equitable' rule of Trimbak
raja of Pimpri attracted cultivators not only from other dangs, but
from the surrounding states of Vansda, Dharampur, and Baroda in
the 1860s.[25]

Because important Bhil bhauband symbolized their dang, their
mobility was often more restricted than that of ordinary Bhils and
Koknis, for it threatened to cathect new frontiers. In 1851, Aundya
raja of Vasurna, along with several men and women, went fishing

[23] Hodgson to Coll., Surat, 22.12.1906, *BA.RD.1907.Vol 126.Comp 632.*
[24] *DBD,* II, pp. 167ff.
[25] Report of a march through Dangs, March 1867, *BRO.DDR.DN 3.FN 12*;
KPAAR, 1888–9, *BA.PD.1890.Vol 122.Comp 205.*

in the Pimpri area without informing the Pimpri chief Trimbak naik. In retaliation, Trimbak naik and his men attacked the fishing party, and carried away all their clothes and utensils. Similarly, senior members of the bhauband could not move so easily to another dang. In 1910, the Pimpri naik went to live in Bhendmal village of Vasurna. 'As a [mark of] respect and system', the Vasurna raja did not collect revenue assessment from the Pimpri chief or his men. But the naik proceeded to bring some Koknis to the village to undertake cultivation, and he collected revenue from them. Coming to know of this, the Vasurna raja took the money from the Pimpri naik and 'forced' the naik to leave the village.[26]

VAGRANT VILLAGES

Involved in the evocation of chhut in moglai is also a cathexis of the pada or *gaon* — the village. But which village? Hypothetically, there were several villages possible in moglai and in the early nineteenth century — the community of those who cultivated in the same locality, the community of those who fished jointly by the riverside, or the community of those who gathered to collect mahua. But for most Dangis, both then and now, it is the community constituted in cultivation that was the only one considered a village — the others were considered temporary abodes.

What was this village? Cultivation was usually carried out by nuclear families, and villages consisted of anything from three to fifteen families. After paying a fixed tax, which varied depending on whether a hand-plough or bullock-drawn plough was used, a cultivator could cultivate any land anywhere in the village area, though it was best to have the prior consent of the headman or patil. Appointed by the principal bhauband of a dang, the patil was the principal person in a village, collecting taxes from it for the bhauband and managing its affairs. As the person who had usually established the village, he tried to attract cultivators to the village, and received a share of the tax for each additional cultivator.

The space of the village was also marked out to some degree in the enactment of grazing. Grazing took place primarily within its borders, though graziers also took their cattle into neighbouring lands in times of drought if these held more fodder.[27] Similarly,

---

26 Annual Report, 1851, *BA.PD.1852.Vol 42.Comp 1415*. Diwan to APA, 26–7.6.1910, *DCR.DN 1.FN 58*.
27 Such grazing in other villages was usually unproblematic, but when the

people were rarely denied access to mahua flowers within their village. In view of the importance of these flowers for subsistence, that would have constituted a provocation to cultivators to migrate to another region.[28]

But the village was itself hardly permanent. The members of any village changed regularly, with individuals moving out to join relatives or friends in other villages, and new members coming in. Apart from this, villages themselves were usually abandoned after three to ten years, most often because soil productivity had dropped, and loppings were exhausted. Such village sites often remained deserted for anything from ten to thirty or more years.[29]

This pervasive mobility blurred the very location of the village. In one sense, all the lands in Dangs were within one village or the other: there were no unclaimed forests, outside all villages. Stones representing various gods, especially the boundary god Simariodev, were placed along village boundaries.[30] In another sense, however, mobility problematized geographical location. When a village became *ujyad* or deserted, for example, did it exist? Its boundary stones remained in place. Sometimes, its territories became part of an adjoining populated or *wasti* village, and at other times it became part of two or three adjoining villages. In the latter case, new boundary gods sprang up reflecting this changed situation, but so slowly that it was quite likely that one of the neighbouring wasti villages would be deserted before that process was completed.[31] So boundary stones could not be read in themselves: only locals would know which stones were relevant, and not all of them would agree. Also, if all land actually fell within the bounds of one village or the other, there could be no conceivable deserted spot, and all of Dangs was wasti. Yet in goth and in nineteenth-century accounts, new villages are always portrayed as being established in a deserted spot — either where there had been no recent village, or where there had been an ujyad village. Thus, village boundaries could be easily redrawn, and tracts that fell within a village, especially a large one, could easily become a separate village altogether.[32]

---

adjoining villages belonged to dangs that were on hostile terms, such grazing could cause fights. Navsu Nathu, 7.6.1994, Jamnisonda.

28 Navsu Nathu, 7.6.1994, Jamnisonda.

29 Manglia Rayji, 30.4.1990, Garmal.

30 Bomanji's *Dangs boundary dispute* records the different placements of village and boundary gods in great detail.

31 Several such cases are noted in *DBD*.

32 Manglia Rayji, 30.4.1990, Garmal.

Even the very names of villages partook of mobility. The fact that place names in so many mobile societies all over the world refer to dominant floral and faunal species or physical features has led to speculation that 'the purpose of such names was to turn the landscape into a map which, if studied carefully, literally gave a village's inhabitants the information they needed to sustain themselves'.[33] Such an explanation may seem tempting. Certainly, village names carried all kinds of meanings. Villages were sometimes named after ancestors: Nanapada was named after Nana patil, who had established the village in the late eighteenth or early nineteenth century. Or they could be references to pools, dominant tree species, and physical features: Bardipada had in former times several *bor* (*Zizyphus jujuba*) trees; the water or *pani* in the stream that flowed by Bhurapani was *bhura* or white; Borkhal was situated in *khal* or depression, and had several bor trees; Chinchli had several tamarind or *chich* trees; Chikalda was situated near a spot on the river which was so full of mire or *chikal* that if a buffalo fell in, it was difficult to get it out; Dabadmal was a plateau or *mal* on which some fine *dabad* (*cynosuroides*) grass grew; Dhongiamba had a mango or *amba* tree which had, unlike other trees, grown crooked or *dhongi*; Khajurnia had near it a pool which caused itching or *khaj* to persons who bathed in it; and as for Junner, the lands around it used to be so fertile that grain from the old or *june* year used to last right through till the next year's crop was ready.[34]

Still, such an explanation, with its dependence on the ideas of cataloguing, is untenable. The information contained in these names provided at best only fragmentary information about environmental resources; the names were created at too many diverse moments by too many diverse groups for them to be concerned with a social mapping — a notion that anyway carries far too many comprehensive implications to be appropriate for thinking of societies like Dangs. The process of naming seems to have been much more part of a logic of metaphor — hence, for example, all the names that carried no such directly 'useful' information. Besides, both in India and many other regions, names carrying information about a place were not even an exclusive characteristic

33 William Cronon, *Changes in the land: Indians, colonists, and the ecology of New England*, New York, 1983, p. 65.
34 See Khanapurkar, 'The aborigines of south Gujarat', vol. I, pp. 84ff.

of highly mobile communities: similar names can be found in long-settled agricultural communities.[35]

The striking feature of village names in forest communities was not that they gave information about an area, but that the meanings that names carried could not be forgotten because of the profound role that mobility played. In most plains areas in the late nineteenth century, a name was associated with a village on a relatively fixed site. Here, the village and the site soon came to be identical with the name. In this sense, the connotative meanings of the name were subsumed under its denotative meaning, or the meaning it carried as a proper noun associated with a village on a fixed site. The former therefore became a sort of withered appendage, often even being forgotten altogether. One might say, figuratively speaking, that the act of naming took place once and for all.

In Dangs, however, naming was shaped by the pervasive mobility of villages. If an erstwhile village remained ujyad for more than a generation, its name might be forgotten. Alternatively, it might be subsumed entirely by the name of the wasti village of which it became part.[36] Dangis might move to spots which had not previously been named by any of the communities they were in touch with, or whose names they might feel no compulsion to retain. Similarly, when members of a village moved (and especially when they moved only a short distance, or even within the larger boundaries of the village) they sometimes took the village name to the new spot. Indeed, so extensive was this process of renaming that by 1899, at least fifty per cent of the names of villages noted in a British map from 1882 were in the wrong places because people had shifted around and named places differently.[37]

Naming, then, was not an act that took place once and for all; rather, it occurred over and again. So the connotative meaning remained distinct from the denotative one, and the two did not meld into each other. That is to say, the connotative meaning was important not because of the inherent value of the information it

[35] For a fascinating discussion of naming, see Paul Carter, *The road to Botany Bay: An exploration of landscape and history*, New York, 1987, ch. 1.
[36] See, for example, *DBD*, I, p. 15. For this process of disappearance and re-emergence in the case of Kalibel, see Mr Boyce's memorandum, n.d., *IOL. F.4.2074*; *BA.RD.1892.Vol 144.Comp 948*; and Khanapurkar, 'The aborigines of south Gujarat', vol. I, pp. 84ff.
[37] FDO to Coll., Kh., 12.7.1899, *BA.RD.1901.Vol 151.Comp 949, Pt II*.

carried, but because of mobility. Mobility kept open the possibility, always, in very ordinary and everyday circumstances, of renaming a place, making a space into a place again. And names rarely survived long enough to move from being both connotative and denotative to being primarily denotative.

CATHECTING FORESTS

It was in relation to this blurred village that the jangal was cathected. We should not make the mistake of taking forests to be a self-evident category in the nineteenth century, we should not assume them to be simply any dense growth of trees, scrub or undergrowth. Dense growth within the village, for example, was not part of the jangal. The jangal was created primarily through the placing of stones for various gods. Stones for the gods associated with the forests, amongst them Rajavadu, Bhutdev, Simariodev, and Vagdev (tiger-god), were set up at the boundaries or frontiers of the village, and the rituals for them took place there. This was so because these gods threatened to constantly invade the village and disturb its peace. Their position at the frontiers was indicative of the Dangi desire to bar them from the village.

The position of boundary gods is best understood by contrasting them to the village gods, especially Gaondev and Hanmat. Stones for these gods were kept at the centre of the village. Of course, Dangi villages did not have a physical centre. Patches of cultivation were scattered across the villages, separated by the trees or even forests that were within village boundaries. And houses were located near the fields, rather than being clustered in one place. In this sense, any centre was an imagined one. But the imagining of such a centre was the basic act on which a village was founded. When a patil or a Bhil chief wished to establish a village, he declared his intention by setting up a stone for Hanmat or Gaondev, amongst others. That site became the imagined centre of the village, with the boundary gods marking the outer limits of the village. All the trees, undergrowth, and scrub within this village were not part of the jangal — they were part of the village.

In some ways, there was a strong opposition between the jangal and the village. One major reason for migration was when forest gods engulfed a village. The death of one or two persons in the village from cholera, or the sickness of cattle — these were signs that spirits associated with the forests were no longer being contained

outside the village but reached into it.[38] At such times, the frontier
between the village and the jangal had to be reasserted through
appropriate rituals. Almost always, the family of a person killed by
misfortune would build a new house, often just beside the old one;
sometimes, they would move out of the village itself, hopefully
beyond the reach of the spirits plaguing them. At worst, the entire
village itself had to be abandoned, with all houses and cultivation
being moved to a new site. Nowhere possibly is the crucial importance of the village gods more emphatically brought out than in the
practice that when a patil deserted a site, he usually left the boundary
gods where they were, but transported the Gaondev to the new
site.[39] It was thus the Gaondev rather than the forest gods who
sustained the inner space of a village; its removal let the boundary
gods in, and symbolically marked the old site as ujyad, consigning it
back to the forests.

From my argument so far, it might seem that even if one allows
for the peculiarities of the Dangi jangal, most Dangis did somewhere draw a fundamental distinction between nature and culture,
between wildness and civilization. In academic literature, the drawing of this distinction is often presumed to be basic to all human
civilization. When humans emerged as sentient beings, it is often
suggested, they sensed their difference from nature, and distanced
themselves from it. At other times, it is suggested that the distance
was a result of a neolithic revolution.[40] A recent essay wishing to
abandon the dichotomy expressed its perplexity at what it saw as
the pervasiveness of the opposition between village and forest or
bush: while 'people cope and experiment by flexibly transcending
set ideas; simultaneously they commonly resort to [these] seemingly timeless cosmological dichotomies'.[41]

But our ascription of persistence and fundamental importance
everywhere to these dichotomies and distinctions may often have
to do with the tenacity with which we have been trained to look
for them, rather than to any construction of 'forests' or 'nature'
amongst peoples such as nineteenth-century Dangis. In Dangs, for
example, it would be fundamentally misleading to treat the village

[38] Report of the Commission on Dang forests, *BA.RD.1879. Vol 90.Comp 947.*
[39] Tanu Kalu patil, 28.5.1990, Pipalghodi.
[40] For an illustration of this point of view, see Oelschlaeger, *The idea of wilderness,* New Haven, 1991, chs 1 and 2.
[41] Croll and Parkin, 'Cultural understandings of the environment', in Croll and Parkin (eds), *Bush base, forest farm,* London, 1992, p. 16.

as a primary identity, privilege the opposition between village and forest, and then elide that into a wildness–civilization opposition. Let us not forget that Dangi practices also involved productions of space that undermined the village: in the practice of chhut, the dang as a whole, including its villages, was identified with jangal. In that sense, the village was part of the jangal.

Besides, the village was only one of the complex and shifting identities involved in chhut. No one village had all the fauna that villagers might wish to hunt, all the flora they wished to gather, or the fish they wished to catch. For securing them, sometimes people from a village moved together. Mobility in these activities effectively erased the very identity of the village: it was those bound by ties of kinship, friendship, proximity, or politics who came together.[42] And in all these contexts, it was the jangal which was foregrounded as a space for the enactment of chhut. If despite all this we accord primacy to the village of cultivation, this is only because our imaginations return timidly, over and again, to the comforting metanarratives of civilization and settled agriculture.

Refiguring Forests

Communities like Dangis did not only construct the forests and the dang as wild; they also tried to align with and refigure that wildness. Maybe sacred groves, sometimes brandished as proof of 'traditional' ecological conservationism, were part of such a realignment.[43] While rare in Dangs, the groves were common in Bhil-dominated regions further to the north in Panchmahals, and ranged in size from a large grove to a single tree.[44] It may not be a simplification to treat them as symbolic representations of the jungle. One of the words for them was *dev-van*, which literally means forests of the spirits or gods. The dev-vans were located at the outskirts of villages, and boundary goddesses and gods, as well as ancestral deities, were believed to reside in them. Rituals for them were regularly performed here, and there were very strict prohibitions on felling, drinking, and sexual intercourse in dev-vans. Through these prohibitions and rituals,

42 Manglia Rayji, 30.4.1990, Garmal.
43 See, for example, Madhav Gadgil and V.D. Vartak, 'The sacred uses of nature', in Ramachandra Guha (ed.), *Social ecology*, Delhi, 1994.
44 Government of Bombay, *Gazetteer of Rewakantha, Cambay and Surat States*, Bombay, 1860, vol. VI, p. 15; Y.V.S. Nath, *Bhils of Ratanmal: An analysis of the social structure of a western Indian community*, Baroda, 1960.

groups like Bhils sought to align themselves with the wildness of these deities, and to ensure that the wildness with which these deities figured the forests would not be hostile to them.

Another kind of refiguring involved the gender of wildness. Writing about the Demoiselles in nineteenth-century France, Peter Sahlins has pointed out that local communities viewed the forests simultaneously as a disorderly space, a creative force, and a destructive force, and that this combination led to the forests being conceived of as female, or 'like a woman'.[45] Again, these oppositions draw on the wildness–civilization or nature–culture distinctions which are pervasive in western thought.[46] In the north Indian context, Shiva has suggested a similar association, even affinity, of women to forests in the Garhwal Himalayas.[47] For western India, however, it would be too simplistic to regard the jangal as always already female. Rather, the jangal was an uncertainly gendered space, simultaneously male and female, and always emphatically jangli.

Some of the most important forest deities, such as Mavalimata, literally mother of the hills, articulated a distinctly female wildness. Also, the most emphatically wild spirits such as the joganis who fed on the livers of humans, were regarded as female. And witchcraft, significantly, was about the possession of women by the malevolent female spirits of the forests such as the joganis. Female witches or dakans were often killed by Dangis, and female witchcraft was a form of wildness which most Dangis abhorred but which they thought was particularly prevalent amongst themselves. They must have viewed its pervasiveness as the troubling dimension of being wild and dangi.[48]

But there were also forest deities which articulated a masculine wildness explicitly associated with the forests, amongst them

[45] Peter Sahlins, *Forest rites: The war of the Demoiselles in nineteenth century France*, Cambridge, Mass., 1994.

[46] On the association of women with nature and men with culture in western thought, see Carolyn Merchant, *The death of nature: Women, ecology and the scientific revolution*, New York, 1983; Donna Haraway, *Primate visions: Gender, race and nature in the world of modern science*, London, 1989; Donna Haraway, *Simians, cyborgs, and women: The reinvention of nature*, New York, 1991; Helene Cixous and Catherine Clement, *The newly born woman*, trans. Betsy Wing, Minneapolis, 1988.

[47] Vandana Shiva, *Staying alive: Women, ecology and survival in India*, New Delhi, 1988.

[48] I discuss witchcraft in my paper, 'Women, witchcraft, and gratuitous violence in western India', *Past and Present*, no. 155, May 1997.

Dungariodev, Vagdev or Nagdev. Some of these deities could also be very malevolent. The *dakanio* or male witch, who was supposed to be more in touch with malevolent male spirits of the forests, was a figure regarded with ambivalence and even hostility. It was not unusual for him to be expelled from a village; in at least one case, a person claimed to be persecuted because he was a dakanio.[49] However, dakanios were very rarely killed, and there existed no elaborate procedures to locate or exorcize them.

Maybe the greater tolerance for dakanios rather than dakans is suggestive of the ways in which dominant Bhils sought to refigure the forests. Quite possibly, it was because dakanios enacted a masculine wildness, however malevolent, that they were tolerated; and it may have been the female wildness of dakans that made them particularly intolerable. Infusing the forests with a male wildness was very important to dominant Bhils. Above all, they invoked ancestral deities, who often resided in the dev-vans, for this purpose. Many rituals were directed at long-dead male ancestors (usually lineage heads, kings, or great hunters), trying to secure their support for a range of activities. These figures were represented sometimes by inch-high stones, kept at home and, more rarely, by two or three feet high stones placed in the village. These commemoration stones also provided potential sites of residence for the ancestors. The ancestors were believed to be equally at home roaming the forests and villages, quite often taking the form of tigers or panthers. These ancestors were close to and quite like the male and female forest deities; they were able to align with these deities and subtly inflect the forests with their own masculine wildness, one that potentially would not threaten Dangis as much.[50]

Such refiguring of the forests is quite a different matter from 'mastery' — Dangis were not trying to master the forests. After all, deities associated with a distinctive female wildness, such as Mavalimata, remained crucial, and were a major presence in dev-vans where these existed. Besides, the support of ancestral deities was not considered adequate or effective — forest gods and goddesses, as well as malevolent spirits, were often too powerful for ancestors. Nor was it as though protection from ancestral deities, despite their ties to Dangis, could be taken for granted: the regular rituals every year were part of the attempt to ensure

49 *BA.PD.1886.Vol 79.Comp 1703*; see also Nath, *Bhils of Ratanmal*, p. 196.
50 Narsinh bhagat, 6.6.1994, Amthawa.

that they stayed in the village and were allied with their descendants.[51] Not only could the wildness of the male ancestors turn
against Dangis; even if dominant Dangis affirmed a male wildness
that would protect them, it was feared that there were too many
others around — amongst them the dakans and dakanios — who
affirmed and celebrated female wildness, or aberrant male wildness. In this sense, though Dangis affirmed and celebrated their
wildness, they also remained deeply apprehensive and anxious
about its many forms.

(13)

51 Ibid.

5

Anxious Pleasures of Livelihood

Moglai was the time of shifting cultivation, hunting, fishing, gathering, and mahua-collection. The many cessations of that time lie scattered across the twentieth century. Largely as a result of state intervention, shifting cultivation in the older sense ground to a halt by the early twentieth century; hunting, fishing and gathering more or less ceased as significant activities around thirty years back, and mahua-collection is now in rapid decline. Goth of these activities are in some senses ruminations on what it was that ceased with their cessation, what it was that changed. And in thinking about or trying to characterize them, vadils resort not to a dense description, not to a piling of detail one upon the other, but rather to an evocation of the distinctive aesthetics that runs through all these activities. That aesthetics is one of a certain kind of wildness, a wildness shot through with pleasure and anxiety.

Nineteenth-century colonial officials thought that the only aesthetics involved in Dangi forms of livelihood was laziness. They returned repeatedly to the topoi of the lazy or happy-go-lucky nature of Dangis in general, which made them avoid work. Dangis, officials remarked, 'will take ever so much trouble in digging for a rat [hunting], but will not cultivate or do any other work'.[1] The lazy native, as we know only too well, was a persistent colonial trope.[2] That trope sometimes persists, now restated as an opposition between the hardworking castes of the plains and the more fun-loving tribals.

This evidently misleading understanding has been attacked in various ways. One tack has been to defend or celebrate this idleness, associating it with 'the original affluent society' or to argue that

---

1 Note by Mr Muller, 27.4.1868, *BRO.DDR.DN 3.FN 12.*

2 The classic study of this trope remains Syed Hussain Alatas, *The myth of the lazy native: A study of the image of the Malays, Filipinos and Javanese from the 16th to the 20th century and its function in the ideology of colonial capitalism,* London, 1977.

'primitive societies . . . are characterized by the rejection of work'.[3]
Yet this is not a very satisfactory approach, for it is often part of a
deeply questionable 'search for authenticity',[4] and ascribes to communities like Dangis a proximity with nature: they were 'lazy'
because they were more 'natural'. Another tack could be to deny
laziness altogether. It could be plausibly argued that though such
groups were less involved in settled agriculture, they were involved
heavily in other forms of producing food, and there was a considerable amount of hard work involved in these forms, as much as
in agriculture. Besides, to the extent that there was no natural
abundance that could be reaped, the notion of 'the tribal' making
less effort certainly cannot be sustained. And if Bhils, Varlis and
poorer Koknis were less involved in settled cultivation, this might
have been because it required cattle and large cattle-driven ploughs,
neither of which they had easy access to.[5] Furthermore, there were
the cultural factors. The Bhil imagining of themselves was primarily
as rajas or kings. Cultivation did not sit very well with this identity,
and so they were relatively unenthusiastic about doing settled
agriculture themselves.[6]

While all such explanations are partially true, there is something
dissatisfying about them. Their subtext is often a privileging of both
hard work, that lodestone of the bourgeois ethic, and of settled
agriculture. The paradigm remains the same as that of colonial
officials; only, now extenuating circumstances have been found for
the behaviour of groups like Dangis. Maybe we need to take a more
radical stance, and consider the possibility that in their own uncomprehending way, the British were right in seeing Dangis as
opposed to the norms they were committed to. That is to say, rather
than getting lost in the question of whether Dangis were 'really'
lazy, it is much more satisfying to focus on the aesthetics of livelihood, and to view Dangi and especially Bhil activities as part of an
aesthetics that affirmed pleasure and wildness.[7] Of course, I say

---

[3] I quote from Marshall Sahlins, *Stone age economics*, Chicago, 1972; Pierre
Clastres, *Society against the state*, trans. Robert Hurley in collaboration with
Abe Stein, New York, 1989, p. 196. For a sophisticated invocation of idleness,
see J.M. Coetzee, 'Idleness in South Africa', in his *White writing: On the culture
of letters in South Africa*, New Haven, 1988.

[4] See especially Edwin Wilmsen, *Land filled with flies: A political economy
of the Kalahari*, Chicago, 1989, pp. 1–63, 195–7.

[5] David Hardiman, 'Power in the forest: The Dangs, 1820s–1940s', *Subaltern
studies III*, Delhi, 1994.

[6] Report of a march through Dangs, March 1867, BRO.DDR.DN 3.FN 12.

[7] For an interesting early effort to look at the aesthetics of livelihoods, see

this from a position very different from those involved in colonial or postcolonial invocations of the 'happy primitive', 'lazy native' or 'original affluent society'. All of these are based on the assumption of proximity with nature, on the idea that it was because these communities were more natural that they were lazy.

In contrast, I here depend on a point that Zizek has made in a very different context: that enjoyment is not natural or spontaneous but is closely connected to and impossible without repression or prohibition. He suggests, 'enjoyment itself, which we experience as "transgression", is in its innermost status something imposed, ordered — when we enjoy, we never do it "spontaneously", we always follow a certain injunction'.[8] This way of questioning the association between pleasure and the natural opens up the possibility of a more radical stance. Dangi and especially Bhil affirmations of pleasure and wildness are best understood not as natural but as constructed through an agonistic relationship to a discourse centred around the upper caste ideals of rightful work and living. This discourse organized to a considerable extent the forms of livelihood in the plains of western India. It was influential in significant ways amongst Dangis too: recall, for example, that Janak raja was cast as having come from the plains, as having chosen to reject dominant values and become Dangi.

Of course, the prohibition that Dangis violated was not only a 'no-saying power', one that only legislated, censored, and prohibited. As Foucault has pointed out, it is inadequate and misleading to understand repression and power in a restrictive way, as 'poor in resources, sparing of its methods, monotonous in the tactics it utilizes, incapable of invention, and seemingly doomed always to repeat itself '.[9] Rather, the prohibitions that Dangis violated were part of complex regimes of power which elicited and even produced wildness. Dangi violations were not only rejections of dominant values; they were also tied up with these values rather than being outside them or innocent of them.

Stephen Gudeman, *Economics as culture: Models and metaphors of livelihood*, London, 1986. In a related vein, though with a greater focus on consumption, see Emiko Ohnukhi-Tierney, in her *Rice as self: Japanese identities through time*, New Jersey, 1993.

8 Slavoj Zizek, *For they know not what they do*, London, 1994, p. 9; see also his *The sublime object of ideology*, London, 1989, pp. 49–53.

9 Michel Foucault, *The history of sexuality: An introduction*, vol. I, New York, 1978, p. 83.

THE DILEMMAS OF CULTIVATION

Agriculture was the principal source of livelihood for many Dangis. Usually, one crop was taken annually, and that was reaped in October and November. The principal crop was *nagli*, a hardy millet which did quite well on hillsides and with scanty water. Rice was also grown in the low-lying areas. The other crops in the region were the millets *kodra* and maize, as well as the lentil *urad*. The Dangi adoption of cultivation was an acknowledgement of affinity with upper caste values, a significant corpus of which valorized settled agriculture. But this was a profoundly qualified acknowledgement. In many goth, the activities and work associated with cultivation are subsumed under metaphors of drudgery, of work that had to be avoided. This fits in well, from a very different perspective, with the complaints of nineteenth-century officials that Dangis considered cultivation 'infra dig', and did not wish to be involved with it.[10] By refusing to privilege and celebrate cultivation the way surrounding plains societies did, Dangis were taking their distance from these societies, and stressing instead their wildness.

The fact that most Dangis practised shifting cultivation may also have been related to this affirmation of wildness. After two to five years (or longer) on the same spot, cultivators would shift to a new spot; sometimes, it could be as much as a generation before the same spot was cultivated again.[11] Now, it could be argued that the absence of settled agriculture had to do with Dangis being unfamiliar with it, lacking the resources for it, and with the terrain not being suitable for it; it could be argued that shifting cultivation was ecologically perfect for Dangs, since it prevented the exhaustion of thin topsoils, required less resources, and used technologies that Dangis were familiar with.[12] It would be pointless to deny that such ideas as these carry some truth. Still, we should not be too quick to read economic, ecological or technological necessity into social practices. Settled cultivation was easily possible in several tracts of Dangs. Many Koknis had spent time in plains areas, were familiar with settled agriculture, were reasonably prosperous, and did even very occasionally practise settled cultivation. Rather than being dictated by necessity, then, the adoption of shifting cultivation may

---

[10] KPAAR, 1877–8, *BA.PD.1878.Vol 116.Comp 681*, and KPAAR, 1875–6, *BA.PD.1876.Vol 108.Comp 1887*.

[11] *DBD*, I, p. 14.

[12] This is the line I take in 'A forest polity', ch. 5.

have been part of a distinctive politics. While affinity with upper caste values was acknowledged by according centrality to agriculture, distance from them, and wildness, was articulated by practising mainly shifting cultivation, by rejecting settled cultivation, and by regarding cultivation itself as drudgery.

The affirmation of wildness took many forms, as was evident in the two broad styles of cultivation, dahi (also called *adar*) and khandad.[13] In khandad, preferred by Bhils, a reasonably well-wooded area was selected, and 'bamboos and saplings are all cut. Large trees are stripped of their branches. Round each large tree plenty of bamboos and branches are piled to kill them and prevent their injuring the crop by shading it'.[14] The loppings, which were usually cut around March, were allowed to dry for a few months, and were burnt just before the monsoons, usually around June or July. After the loppings were burnt, a *pawada* or hand plough was sometimes drawn across the field, and the seeds scattered or dibbled in.[15] They were then left to grow, with occasional weedings.[16]

Khandad was often less productive than dahi, but Bhils preferred it 'because they consider that the necessary labour required is less . . . and a saving of exertion in the Dangs is considered of more importance even than the production of a superior crop'.[17] This was not an entirely accurate representation: goth indicate that khandad involved just as much work as dahi. But the work involved in khandad, narrators agree, was much less tedious and boring: dahi required far more repetitive and regular operations, and more tending of the fields, while khandad required intensive effort over short bursts of time. Also Bhils may have preferred it since khandad was considered more jangli or wild because of its radical mobility, its use of hand ploughs, and dependence on dibbling.[18]

13 We do not find adar as commonly used in colonial records. However, the word is widely used by narrators now to refer to what colonial officials called dahi, and there are some indicators that the word was known in the early twentieth century too.
14 'Proposals for the improvement . . . Dangs forests', *BA.RD.1902.Vol 107. Comp 949, Part II.*
15 KPAAR, 1875–6, *BA.PD.1875–6.Vol 108.Comp 1887.*
16 'Proposals for the improvement . . . Dangs forests', *BA.RD.1902.Vol 107. Comp 949, Part II.* For the cultivation cycle, see Khanapurkar, 'The aborigines of south Gujarat', vol. I, pp. 337ff, and *BRO.DDR.DN 7.FN 20.*
17 'Proposals for the improvement . . . Dangs forests', *BA.RD.1902.Vol 107. Comp 949, Part II.*
18 Lucas to Coll., Kh., 1.9.1891, *BA.RD.1892.Vol 144.Comp 948*; Jiva Kharsu, 20.3.1990, Ghadvi.

For dahi, preferred by Koknis, a relatively flat area or mal was usually selected. Around the same time as for khandad, the trees in the field were lopped to their stems. Just before the monsoons, the 'loppings are laid neatly in the form of a square on the ground and eventually fired. Seed, most often nagli, is sown in the ashes; the seedlings, when large enough, are transplanted close by into the open land which has been ploughed'.[19] Sometimes, instead of making one large seedbed, several small seedbeds would be prepared across the field, so as to make the task of transplantation easier. Dahi usually required cattle-driven ploughs.[20]

Maybe some Koknis were involved in dahi because they were not prosperous enough to rent cattle or ploughs. Still, that so many Koknis, including prosperous ones, practised dahi — not settled cultivation and not khandad — may also have been the articulation of a distinct politics. As I argue in Chapter 8, while most Koknis affirmed wildness, they carefully distinguished their own wildness from that of Bhils, and cast it as having closer affinities with dominant plains values. Dahi, neither quite part of plains' values nor quite Bhil, nicely staged this politics.

WILDNESS AND PLEASURE

Cattle-rearing, hunting, fishing, gathering and mahua-collection, the principal forms of livelihood for nearly two-thirds of the year, were occasions for the production and enactment of some very different kinds of wildness. Consider cattle-rearing. There were around 24,039 cattle in 1891 — more than the population of the Dangs.[21] Most Koknis kept at least enough cattle for ploughing, and some of the better-off ones had well over a hundred head, selling milk products from the herd in the plains. Some activities associated with cattle-rearing, such as grazing, were privileged sites for the articulation of a distinctive aesthetics. Grazing took place ideally in the open grasslands, a space ambiguously between the village and the forests. Cattle themselves were part of the complex of cultivation, being used as bullocks. In that sense, grazing connoted a kind of dalliance with wildness that could be affirmed from

[19] 'Proposals for the improvement . . . Dangs forests', *BA.RD.1902.Vol 107. Comp 949, Part II.*

[20] KPAAR, 1888–9, *BA.PD.1890.Vol 122.Comp 205.* 'Rules for forests of Dangs'; *BA.PD.1856.Vol 48.Comp 1104.*

[21] Lucas to Coll., Kh., 1.9.1891, *BA.RD.1892.Vol 144.Comp 948.*

within upper caste values as well. Some plains Indian traditions, such as in the romantic motifs around the god Krishna as a cowherd, saw grazing in these terms.[22] In Dangs too, these motifs surround grazing; it may be significant that Janak raja should be repeatedly cast in goth as a cowherd — wild, and still potentially associated with plains values.

Fishing was a crucial component of subsistence from around March till the end of summer, a period when stocks of foodgrains from cultivation would be running low even for the more prosperous Koknis.[23] But more seems involved here than economic or ecological needs. For example, there was the mobility that was enacted in fishing, one which emphasized its wildness as a lifestyle. Bhils and many Koknis would, once summer really set in, shift to the riverside from the hilltop huts around which they cultivated.[24] Fishing was also made into a wild activity by imbuing it with pleasure. It was reported in the 1850s that Kerulsinh raja of Ghadvi had, around the time of the *Shimga* festival in March,[25] gone as was usual every year to the Purna river to fish and 'take air', accompanied by around ten to twenty Bhils.[26] Though we do not know the original Dangi phrase which was translated in this way, it would not be surprising if the phrase connoted, as the former activity of fishing does in many goth today, a pleasant change of surroundings. Such taking of air was not, of course, limited to chiefs: ordinary Dangis, both men and women, were involved in it. The pleasure of the occasion also had to do with the fact that it often involved working in large groups, usually of relatives and friends from other villages; for married women, it was often an occasion to meet agnates.

Another major form of livelihood was mahua-collection, which started in March, just before the period when people shifted to the riverbanks for fishing, and continued for well over a month or two. The mahua crop, coming at a time when grain was running low or scarce, was of vital importance throughout the forest tracts: 'when

22 Haberman, *Journey through the twelve forests: An encounter with Krishna*, New York, 1994, esp. p. 49.

23 Jiva Kharsu, 20.3.1990, Ghadvi.

24 Khanapurkar, 'The aborigines of south Gujarat', vol. I, p. 141.

25 *Shimga*, the Dangi equivalent of the plains festival *Holi*, was amongst the most important festivals of the region. Khanapurkar, 'The aborigines of south Gujarat', vol. I, pp. 337ff.

26 Daulat to Morriss, 24.4.1852, *BRO.DDR.DN 2.FN 6*.

mahuda flowers are scarce . . . the Bhils are in a very bad plight, finding the greatest difficulty in keeping body and soul together.'[27] A couple and three children, by one estimate, could be supported for a month on two maunds.[28] And a mahua tree yielded around 6–8 maunds of flowers, and in exceptional cases as much as thirty maunds. The flowers were used not only as food but for distilling liquor, and mahua seeds provided an oil for cooking, *doliu*.

While Bhils kept most flowers for consumption, Koknis sold the bulk of the dried flowers to merchants, or bartered it for other goods.[29] This may have been because Koknis were marginally better off than the Bhils, and did not have to use the flowers as extensively for consumption.[30] But it may also have been because mahua flowers could be used for producing liquor, and this gave a particular inflection to flower-collection. Of course, most families required so much of the mahua for food that there was only a little left over for distillation into alcohol. But let us not equate meaning with quantity: that little was what constituted the aesthetics of mahua-collection. The mahua season was (and to some extent still is) treated as a period for an exceptionally pleasant state of drunkenness. Dangi fondness for mahua liquor in particular, and drinking in general, was part of colonial lore: 'as long as [they] . . . have any property or money — they live in a state of perpetual intoxication — and when these are exhausted they are reduced to starvation.'[31]

The consumption of liquor, and especially the celebration of excessive consumption evoked in the whole spirit of the mahua season, was also at odds with dominant strands in upper caste thought. To participate enthusiastically in mahua-collection and consumption was to affirm a particular conjuncture of wildness and pleasure; to distance themselves from it, as at least some Koknis did, was to articulate an ambivalence towards the predominantly Bhil conjuncture of pleasure and wildness.

---

[27] Government of Bombay, *Gazetteer of the Bombay Presidency, Vol. VI, Rewa Kantha, Narukot, Cambay and Surat States*, p. 53. See GR 1274. Famine Department 25.6.1902, *BA.RD.1902.Vol 102.Comp 1004A*. For a detailed discussion of the politics of liquor in the region, see David Hardiman, *The coming of the Devi: Adivasi assertion in western India*, Delhi, 1987, ch. 7.

[28] Anon., 'Rab in Thana', *Indian Forester*, vol. 12, 1886, pp. 186ff.

[29] Gibb to Loch, 8.7.1890, *BA.RD.1890.Vol 93.Comp 948*.

[30] Ramji patil, 9.6.1990, Pandva.

[31] Coll., Kh., to Secy., GoB, 7.5.1856, *BA.PD.1856.Vol 48.Comp 987*.

Hunting and Masculine Wildness

Hunting, another major source of livelihood, constituted a very distinctive aesthetics of pleasure where both affinity and distance from plains values was clear. When there was no other work, or when enough people had been collected, individuals or large groups ventured out for a hunt. There was nothing fixed about the period which might be spent in hunting. A hunter might occasionally not go hunting for weeks, and might at other times go hunting on several consecutive days. It was this very ascription of impetuosity to the hunt that constituted its aesthetics of pleasure.[32]

The hunt was also bound up with the enactment of a masculine wildness. This was not because hunting was an activity carried out by men. Women were involved in beating the forests and flushing animals out; occasionally they were also part of the group that killed the animals. One well-known Mughal miniature depicts a night-hunt by a Bhil woman and man, with the woman using a bell to attract animals, and holding a torch so that they could be shot by the man.[33] We should not, then, take the masculine wildness of hunting to be some simple reflection of or correspondence with a sexual division of labour. Rather, it was a particular way of imagining or figuring the activity, one that excised the involvement of women and foregrounded men instead.

Ebba Koch has argued that for the Mughal nobility, hunting was associated with daring, strenuousness and adventure; the mastery of wildness demonstrated the fitness of the hunter for kingship. The association of hunting with kingship was articulated in the understanding amongst the Mughal and Rajput nobility that the killing of tigers and lions was a largely royal prerogative.[34] Other South Asian plains' traditions of kingship, it is likely, made a similar association between kingship and the wildness of hunting. There are evident affinities between Dangi understandings and this plains celebration of the association between hunting, kingship, and wildness. Certainly, they emphasized the daring, strenuousness, and

---

[32] Soma Gangaji, 20.3.1991, Ghogli.

[33] Ebba Koch, 'Hunt and landscape in imperial Mughal paintings', Paper presented at the McIntire Department of Art, University of Virginia, 18 April 1996.

[34] Ibid. See also Mahesh Rangarajan's important book, *Fencing the forest: Conservation and ecological change in India's Central Provinces, 1860–1914*, Delhi, 1996, especially ch. 1.

adventure involved in it; excellence in it secured the admiration of other men; there is an endless fund of goth centred around ancestors who are remembered as particularly good hunters; and great kings are almost always cast as good hunters too. It may have been because of these affinities that both the Mughals and the Rajputs, and the former especially, were fascinated with Bhil hunting — the Bhil hunter was to be a staple of miniatures.[35]

But in contrast to the Mughal practice of reserving tigers and panthers as royal game, there was virtually a prohibition amongst Dangis on killing tigers and panthers. The spirits of dead ancestors were believed to take the form of these animals and roam the forests; also, tigers and panthers were treated as forms of Vagdev, a tiger-god.[36] In refusing to kill tigers and panthers, maybe, Dangi men underscored their distance from plains communities. While for the latter, the affirmation of masculine kingly wildness involved mastery over tigers, panthers and lions, for the former the affirmation of masculine kingly wildness occurred through alignment with the power of these animals. After all, even the martial prowess of groups like Bhils was thought to derive from their knowledge of esoteric spells that allowed them to invoke the forest spirits, deities and animals.[37] Again, then, the affirmation of the wildness and pleasure of hunting was, as transgression, in an agonistic relationship to upper caste plains values rather than simply convergent or antagonistic.

The Problems of Female Wildness

Nowhere possibly are the affinities with upper caste values more clearly evinced than in the ambivalence towards women's enactments of wildness. Women's participation in wildness was unproblematic only in activities where affinities with dominant plains values were most marked, such as shifting cultivation, grazing and fishing. Elsewhere, there was much more ambivalence. While women were involved in collecting mahua flowers, and even in distilling liquor, their consumption of it was regarded with hostility,

---

35 I thank Ebba Koch for this point.
36 Report of a march through Dangs, March 1867, *BRO.DDR.DN 3.FN 12*. See also E.M. Shull, 'Worship of the tiger-god and religious rituals associated with tigers among the Dangi hill tribes of the Dangs district, Gujarat state, western India', *Eastern Anthropologist*, vol. 21, no. 2, May–August 1968.
37 Soma Gangaji, 20.3.1991, Ghogli.

though in the nineteenth century they did still occasionally drink
mahua with the immediate nuclear family or even publicly (there
are some colonial reports of drunken women at darbars and
bazars). Similarly with hunting — women were not only excluded
in the imagining of *shikhar* and goth about it, but they were also
less likely to eat meat than men, for this could on occasion lead to
charges of witchcraft.[38]

This ambivalence towards female wildness was most marked in
gathering, the principal source of livelihood in the two to four
months after the monsoons started — a period when grain and
mahua stocks would have run out, and hunting and fishing were
no longer easy, and agricultural operations for the next season had
just started.[39] While men often accompanied women on gathering
expeditions, and several men knew as much as women about where
to find particular kinds of leaves, tubers, fruits or herbs, the activity
was constructed as female, and associated with female wildness.

The ambivalence towards gathering may have been because it
was construed as potentially refiguring the forests with a female
wildness, and potentially also refiguring women with the female
wildness of some of the forest spirits. For example, dakans were
often thought to be especially good at gathering. Maybe because
of this ambivalence, it was not associated with pleasure. Like
cultivation, rather, it tended to be subsumed under metaphors of
drudgery. But in the case of cultivation, the ascription of drudgery
had been part of an agonistic relationship with upper caste values.
With gathering, it was an acknowledgement of the affinities with
upper caste values. That is to say, in their opposition to these values,
most Dangis affirmed either a masculine wildness or a wildness
that was not sharply gendered; the claim to wildness itself was
intended to be enacted primarily by men, and women were intended to be the site for the acknowledgement of affinity with upper
caste norms.

Still, this was not a consistent rejection of female wildness.
After all, there is the fact that gathering persisted as a form of
livelihood and men participated in it, and this when greater effort
in other modes of subsistence such as hunting, agriculture or
mahua-collection could have substantially reduced dependence on

38 Govt. of Bombay, *Gazetteer of Bombay Presidency: Gujarat Population: Hindus*, vol. IX, part I, Bombay, 1901, p. 426; *DCR.DN 2.FN 4Uc.*
39 FDO to Coll., Kh., 1.9.1891, *BA.RD.1892.Vol 144.Comp 94; SRBG 26*, p. 185.

it, maybe even eliminated it altogether at least in good seasons. Besides, as pointed out in Chapter 6, many women affirmed a female wildness that was profoundly disruptive and destabilizing of both upper caste and dominant Dangi norms.

(18)

6

Shared Kingship and Lack

At the very beginning of moglai, according to many goth, there was one raja and one naik. In other accounts, there was only one raja. He is sometimes identified as Paharsinh Dongarsinh (both words that, without the suffix 'sinh', mean hills), sometimes as Chitangan, and sometimes as Janak raja. Each of these figures is associated with different stories. But quite as often, narrators do not know who the first raja was, and this is not regarded as especially worrying. What is clear is that whoever the first raja was, he gave raj to the Bhils. Moglai was a time of Bhil raj, literally, the reign of Bhils. Though Bhil raj continues even after the mandini in many goth, it is certainly most strongly associated with moglai. Bhil raj was a time when Bhil chiefs ruled in the region, and when values espoused by dominant Bhil groups were very influential.

One parallel to Bhil raj could be the point that in eighteenth- and nineteenth-century Dangs, as well as in large tracts of Rajputana, Bharuch, Surat, and central India, power was wielded principally by chiefs from forest communities such as Bhils, Kolis, Girasias, Vasavas, Naikdas and Bhilalas, and that furthermore such chiefs were very powerful in plains areas. But it is not enough to stop with this, for forest chiefs not only wielded power but did so often through a distinctive discourse of wildness.

This discourse poses some knotty problems for the way we usually understand kingship, and to some extent even caste. It is now recognized that caste had to do not so much with purity and pollution 'but rather with royal authority and honour, and associated notions of dominance and order'. Indeed, the king was 'a central ordering feature in the social organization of caste'.[1] This point is well taken, but we should be careful not to presume that the centrality of the king rests on classical textual constructions

1 Nicholas Dirks, *The hollow crown*, Cambridge, 1987, p. 7; Dirks, 'The original caste: Power, history and hierarchy in South Asia', *Contributions to Indian Sociology*, vol. 23, no. 1, 1989, p. 59.

which associate kingship with Kshatriya values. True, such associations were widespread in western India, with the claim to be Kshatriya often being conflated with that of being a Rajput.[2] Thus, to recall a famous example, after the Maratha chief Shivaji had established his political authority, he hired priests in order to construct for himself a genealogy that denied his more humble origins and traced his descent from one of the most illustrious Rajput clans.[3] Many of the smaller kingdoms in Gujarat and central India had similar genealogies. Because such claims were often made even by Bhil chiefs and other similar forest groups, it may seem that kingship in these communities too conformed broadly to this model.[4] In Dangs too, there were often claims to Rajput descent, and the bhauband of dang Amala often now claim the suffix Suryavanshi — that is to say, descent from the legendary solar dynasty of Kshatriya rulers.

Nevertheless, the departures from Kshatriya kingship, both in Dangs and elsewhere, may be more important than the convergences. Rao, Shulman and Subrahmanyam have shown how in Nayaka-period Tamilnadu, 'the Sudra now proudly claims the summit'.[5] Similarly, it seems likely that the ideology of Maratha *svarajya* represented a significant departure from either Kshatriya or Mughal models of kingship.[6] In Dangs, while we do not know whether the word Bhil raj was used in the late eighteenth or early nineteenth century,[7] there was a distinctive Bhil style of kingship that diverged profoundly from dominant understandings.

Bhil relations with ritually powerful groups like Brahmans — whose ritual authority Kshatriya and classical kingship was supposed

[2] Rajput identities were not associated only with kingship. Rajputs seem to have been an open status group, and the identity seems to have been claimed by a range of mobile, martial groups, some of whom later adopted and passed on to their heirs a landed status. See D.H.A. Kolff, *Naukar, Rajput and sepoy: The ethnohistory of the military labour market in Hindustan, 1450–1850*, Cambridge, 1990, chs 3 and 4.

[3] Gordon, *The Marathas, 1600–1818*, Cambridge, 1993, pp. 87–9.

[4] See, for example, the entry on Bhils in R.V. Russell and Hira Lal, *The tribes and castes of the Central Provinces of India*, London, 1916, vol. II, esp. pp. 279–82.

[5] V.N. Rao, D. Shulman and S. Subrahmanyam, *Symbols of substance: Court and state in Nayaka period Tamilnadu*, Delhi, 1992.

[6] Wink, *Land and sovereignty*. Wink, of course, does not make this argument, preferring instead to foreground the continuities between Mughal rule and the Marathas. However, his work also recognizes, in subdued ways, a distinctive Maratha construction of kingship.

[7] The first reference I have found to the phrase dates from the late 1860s. See *BA.PD.1868.Vol 102* and *DDR.DN 3.FN4Uc*.

to complement and even sustain — were often tense and even hostile. And Bhil kingship involved rule by a community lower down ritual hierarchies than even Sudras. Such kingship, with its privileging of wildness and very distinctive forms of political power, often constituted a powerful alternative to Brahman- or Kshatriya-centred claims to social power. Furthermore, this style of kingship was not confined to forested areas such as Dangs: it often spilled over into the 'mainstream' plains areas, and may actually have inhibited the influence in these regions of Brahman- and Kshatriya-centred ways of claiming power. In surrounding plains too, the power of kings may have been derived to a substantial extent from their association with the wildness of forests and forest chiefs.[8] In this and the next chapter, I shall deal specifically with how Bhils enacted Bhil kingship; Chapter 8 will turn to the ways in which Koknis participated in this kingship; Chapter 9 will explore how the wildness of that kingship entailed particular kinds of relationships with plains powers.

KINGSHIP, PARTICIPATION, AND LACK

In telling goth of Bhil raj, one motif now is that of shared kingship — every Dangi man, and certainly every Bhil man, was a raja. In the nineteenth century, kingship was widely shared. Several terms carried connotations of a widespread Dangi participation. Amongst these were *girasia* and *mewasi*. The *Girasias* or Girasia Bhils were a community living in the hills around Mewar, depending on both cultivation and raids in the early nineteenth century. More broadly, girasias referred to those groups or communities who, like Dangi chiefs, claimed political allowances called giras from plains villages, and attacked these villages if the allowances were not paid. In this sense of the word, which will be discussed in greater detail later, many Bhils, Rajputs and Kolis in western India were girasias. Mewasi, it is speculated, was an appellation introduced around the twelfth century, deriving from an Arabic root which meant, 'to oppose', or 'to rebel'.[9] By the late eighteenth and early nineteenth century, it was quite routinely used to describe even submissive hill

8 For an argument that makes, from a very different perspective, a similar point in relation to the kingdom of Puddukottai, see Joanne P. Waghorne, *The Raja's magic clothes: Re-visioning kingship and divinity in England's India*, Pennsylvania, 1994, ch. 6. The centrality of wilderness in constituting the power of the king in India is also explored in Nancy Falk, 'Wilderness and kingship in ancient South Asia', *History of Religions*, vol. 13, 1973, pp. 1–15.

9 Wink, *Land and sovereignty*, Cambridge, 1986, p. 197.

or forest chiefs. Both terms were often used to describe the Dangis, the Bhils of Rajpipla, or other Kolis and Rajputs who held giras rights.

The very names of the jatis with which the most powerful forest polities were associated carried connotations of political power. This was most strikingly the case with two names, 'Koli' and 'Bhil'. The Kolis were a large and amorphous community quite like the Bhils, for the most part concentrated in central and north Gujarat, practising a little agriculture, but depending crucially in the late eighteenth and early nineteenth century on raids, and attacks on plains villages.[10]

This association of entire jatis with political power was because power was very widely shared. As nineteenth-century colonial officials came into intensive contact with Dangs, a refrain developed, one which even finally elbowed its way into the *Khandesh District Gazetteer*: all Dangi Bhils regarded themselves as rajas.[11] Part of the emphasis was surely because of the quixotic and distinctly ludicrous texture of the fact to officials ensconced in social-evolutionist categories — the primitive Bhil laying claim to the insignia of royalty! Yet they had inadvertently made a very important observation about the eighteenth- and nineteenth-century forest polity. Kingship was deeply shared in Dangs, and 'every Bhil from the humblest to the most haughty expects the term [raja] applied to him when spoken of, and every one of them is proud of the fact that he is a Bhil or raja. Let it be remembered that the two terms Bhil and raja are synonymous among all the people of the Dangs'.[12]

Hardiman has shown how ties of kinship could have been extensive enough for the bulk of Bhils to consider themselves rajas. In 1954, there were 668 persons officially listed amongst the bhauband — a word which can for the present be glossed as the principal adult male Bhils associated with the ruling chiefs. Working with the very reasonable assumption of five members to each family, he points out that around 3140 Bhils, around a quarter of all Bhils in Dangs, were of 'direct royal lineage' — and this was only the most immediate family circle! Since the bhauband intermarried a lot

10 For an early-nineteenth-century account of Kolis, see Heber, *Narrative of a journey*, vol. III, Philadelphia, 1829, pp. 25–9.

11 *KDG*, p. 601.

12 Quoted in David Hardiman, 'Power in the forests', in Arnold and Hardiman (eds), *Subaltern studies VII*, Delhi, 1994.

with ordinary Bhils, quite evidently the majority of Bhils would have been at least related to bhauband.[13]

And there certainly was explicit recognition of ordinary Bhils as rajas in the nineteenth century. No Bhils had to pay agricultural tax for the cultivation they undertook — an exemption that affirmed their status as a community which owned the land. Of the giras dues that the Ghadvi chief received from the neighbouring state of Baroda, Rs 30 was distributed amongst all the naiks of Ghadvi Dangs 'including all Bheels of Dhang Ghadi'![14] While it was surely not distributed to all Bhils, a payment so designated may be regarded as a symbolic recognition of the extent to which all Dangi Bhils were rajas.

What do we make of this extensive participation in Bhil raj? In some other Asian contexts where widespread sharing or participation in kingship has been noticed, explanations have put the principal king at the centre of their explanations. Here, the king is the ultimate source of authority, and shared kingship basically amounts to participation in the substance of this authority. Thus, in Dirks' argument about Puddukottai, participation in authority or sovereignty was basically through receiving royal gifts of lands or other markers of power, and it was proximity to the king which was the principal source of power. Simultaneously, by making gifts, virtually to the limits of his abilities, the king created his own power. In a different vein, Geertz emphasizes how the king's rituals created his authority in the Balinese state, and how that ritual was extended to include lower levels of the chiefly hierarchy.[15] Though deeply insightful, such a centripetal view may sometimes be 'overly formal, top-down' and 'largely unresponsive to "ground up" centrifugal tendencies which threatened to undermine it'.[16]

Nor however can this view simply be replaced with a perspective that emphasizes ground-up, centrifugal tendencies involved in kingship. In the context of societies like Dangs — after all conventionally described as 'tribal' — this may be a move especially fraught with

13 Ibid.

14 'List of *haks* acknowledged by the Gaekwad', 1828, in *BA.PD.1866.Vol 24.Comp 607.*

15 Nicholas Dirks, 'The original caste'; *The hollow crown: Ethnohistory of a south Indian kingdom*, Cambridge, 1987; Clifford Geertz, *Negara: The theatre state in nineteenth century Bali*, Princeton, 1980.

16 Norbert Peabody, 'Kota Mahajagat, or the great universe of Kota: Sovereignty and territory in 18th century Rajasthan', *Contributions to Indian Sociology*, vol. 25, no. 1, 1991.

danger. By emphasizing centrifugal tendencies, we run the risk of drawing implicitly on that liberal model of society before (or, more precisely, just after) the social contract — a society of fully formed, independent men, with each man his own master, conceding only some of his power to the chief. In this model, well-developed hierarchies are a sign of civilization and development. This commonsensical image has been very influential in thinking about a wide range of societies, from 'feudal' ones to those like Dangs, which are often described as 'stateless' or 'primitive' societies, or in Clastres's memorable phrase, 'society against the state'.[17]

Maybe goth can suggest an alternative way of thinking about the sharing of kingship. In accounts told by vadils, there is fierce dispute on the question of which group of bhauband (brotherhood of chiefs) is seniormost. The ruling bhauband of Ghadvi, Amala and Pimpri tell a goth which begins similarly, almost identically. According to it, the god Vishnu visited each of the five principal chiefs — those of Ghadvi, Amala, Vasurna, Pimpri and Deher — disguised as a mendicant. He asked that they give what was most precious to them. But the various goth diverge on the question of how each chief responded to the request. Narrators from each group of bhauband claim it was their ancestor who offered his life, while those of other groups baulked at this ultimate sacrifice. Each group goes on to claim that in recognition of this ultimate gift, Vishnu recognized their ancestor as the principal chief of Dangs. The giving of one's own life — the ultimate gift possible after all — is here a means of establishing hierarchies. There are innumerable goth in this vein which tell of how relatively minor bhauband rose to prominence, and how their dangs grew alongwith; or how major bhauband were marginalized.[18] That is to say, there is a profound, almost constitutive, underdetermination of political hierarchies in

[17] Pierre Clastres, *Society against the state*, trans. Robert Hurley in collaboration with Abe Stein, New York, 1989. Clastres has a much more complex perspective than that of simply producing a modern version of social contract theories — indeed, his main thrust is to show how these theories are seriously inadequate. However, his efforts remain seriously compromised, in part because of his deeply problematic Levi-Straussian allegiances. I use the word 'men' deliberately in discussing these theories. As Carole Pateman has pointed out, the 'social contract' is preceded by an unspoken sexual contract. See her *The sexual contract*, Cambridge, 1988.

[18] One such goth, focusing on the decline of the Kadmal bhauband, who had apparently been very powerful till around the early nineteenth century, is narrated in Chapter 9.

goth — hence the intense uncertainty and debate about which bhauband were seniormost.

Taking my cues from the emphasis in goth on both shared authority and contestation, I suggest that widespread participation in Bhil kingship was associated with a politics of lack — a lack, that is to say, of self-sufficient loci for kingship. Because of this lack of self-sufficient loci, kingship resided in no one place, and there were multiple hierarchies of kingly authority. In order to situate what I mean, consider the enactment of kingship in Dangs.

Of Bhauband and Multiple Hierarchies

The gadi or seat of power was held by the head of the group of bhauband who controlled a dang — he was the raja in the most restricted sense of the word. As remarked earlier, while dang symbolized the forest communities and forest polities in general in relation to the desh or Gujarat, within the dang, there were several entities called dangs.

In the early nineteenth century, the most powerful dangs were those of Ghadvi, Amala, Vasurna, Deher, Kadmal, and Pimpri. Between them, the bhauband of these six dangs possessed nominal suzerainty over most of the Dangs. The Ghadvi bhauband was the most powerful of these six. This may well have been a recent development, partially because the Ghadvi chief who held the gadi had used his resources to employ Makranis and Sidis.[19] The Makranis and Sidis had formerly been part of Maratha forces, but the disintegration of Maratha armies in the late eighteenth century resulted in many of them migrating into Bhil areas. Here, with the assistance of their more powerful horses and weapons, the chiefs who employed them quickly gained dominance over other Bhil chiefs.[20]

But the holders of the gadis of these dangs were in no sense unambiguously on top of a clear hierarchy. Almost comparable in power to them were their close bhauband. While many bhauband were related to each other, the bhauband should not be thought of as a local instantiation of that anthropological construct, the lineage of patrilineal descent.[21] Blood relationships or genealogical

[19] Statement of Nathu patil and Sivaji Balaji, *BA.PD.1829.Vol 8/332.*
[20] See Willoughby's letters about their role in Rajpipla, reproduced in *SRBG 23.*
[21] There are already so many critiques of the lineage that there is little need

ties were not necessary to being part of the bhauband. Being a member of the bhauband was rather about a metaphorical kinship and kingship, about ties created through participation in political authority — this, after all, was the sense in which all Bhils were rajas.

Most narrowly understood, the bhauband were those closely associated with ruling chiefs in the various dangs. These principal bhauband were not much better off than ordinary Bhils. In the early nineteenth century, none of them possessed a permanent house; they moved with other Bhils for fishing, hunting, or mahua-collection; and they were almost as vulnerable as ordinary Bhils during seasons of want. But they possessed considerable authority over ordinary Bhils. When Daulat raja, one of the principal members of the Ghadvi bhauband, confronted a large group of Bhils and beat up two persons, nobody retaliated because, they said, he was a raja and they were poor people.[22]

The major bhauband's participation in kingship was very extensive. The various dues and revenues received by Dangi chiefs were distributed principally amongst them, with every powerful member of the bhauband getting a share. The participation of the bhauband in the power of the principal chiefs was evident when merchants tried to secure leases of timber in Dangs forests in the 1830s and 1840s. In almost every case, the agreements were signed by several members of the bhauband together, and the principal chiefs even claimed that they did not possess the authority to sign agreements without first securing the consent of their bhauband.[23]

The bhauband were quite independent of the local chiefs. Each group of bhauband stayed in a village or group of villages separate from the chief's, and they often collected revenue directly from these villages.[24] They paid only a token share of the revenue to the principal raja as a mark of their submission.[25] So marked was this independence that many bhauband held smaller dangs within the

---

to add my mite to them. See Roy Richard Grinker, *Houses in the rainforest: Ethnicity and inequality among farmers and foragers in Central Africa*, Berkeley and Los Angeles, 1994, ch. 1; Adam Kuper, 'Lineage theory: A critical retrospect', *Annual Review of Anthropology*, vol. 11, 1982, pp. 71–95. For a discussion of the evolutionary implications of kinship models, see also Wilmsen, *Land filled with flies*, Chicago, 1989, chs 1 and 2.

[22] Deposition of Sooklya Reshmya, *BRO.DDR.DN 2.FN 6*.

[23] *IOL.F.4.2074*; *DFR.DN 1.FN 9*.

[24] KPAAR, 1888–9, *BA.PD.1890.Vol 122.Comp 205*.

[25] *DBD*, I, p. 14.

larger dang. Thus, part of dang Ghadvi were the chiefs of dang Kirli, dang Sivbara, and dang Malangdeo; part of dang Dherbhavti was dang Palasvihir, and so on.[26] More than half of the Dangs villages were part of such dangs within dangs, some consisting of just one or two villages.

As powerful actors, the bhauband could demand to share in the authority and resources of the principal chief; if he did not oblige, they could seriously undermine, or refuse to constitute, his authority. Contestation was marked both during succession disputes and in more everyday interactions. Sometimes the heads of subordinate bhauband regarded the authority of the dominant raja as illegitimately obtained, and laid claim to the gadi themselves. Similarly, challenges could also come from within the principal chief's own bhauband: from brothers, uncles, nephews or other followers who disputed his right to the gadi.

Because of this kind of power of their bhauband, the holders of the gadi had to share authority with at least some bhauband. If the principal chief did not do so by distributing resources, his authority would be quite quickly undermined. To extend or maintain his dominance, he had to enter into alliances with other bhauband, and this involved sharing his resources and authority — it was the very process of sharing authority that constituted his kingship. This sharing of resources and kingship was always represented and perceived in different ways: by the principal chief as grants from above, and by the bhauband as their rightful share which the chief could not keep away.

The power of the bhauband should not however lead to the mistake of thinking of them as self-sufficient loci of kingship; their authority too was characterized by a pervasive lack. Not only was it unclear who was a member of the bhauband (since all Bhils were rajas), but the bhauband too needed to participate in the power of the principal chiefs and other bhauband. Certainly, support from senior rajas could create bhauband. Amongst the bhauband were jagirdars and *amir umraos* (military retainers), figures who had attained their status through grants from powerful chiefs. Thus, for instance, when Nawji naik, one of the amir umraos of Vasurna, was killed in the early nineteenth century during an attack by his chief Aundya raja on Rajhans raja of Ghadvi, Nawji's wife, who was at

26 *BA.PD.1870.Vol 57.Comp 1213; BRO.DDR.DN 3.FN 12; KPAAR, 1888–9; BA.PD.1890.Vol 122.Comp 205.*

the time pregnant, was promised the jagir if she gave birth to a male child. She did, and the jagir was granted. These territories secured as jagirs were sometimes referred to as dangs.[27] The principal chiefs could also unmake members of the bhauband, as could unfortunate circumstances. Senior bhauband or holders of gadis regularly took back villages and other grants from those they considered rivals, from former grantees who had offended them, backed the wrong side in a dispute, or had simply lost the power to sustain their grant. Daulat raja took back Vahutia village from a naik; his father Rajhans took back Jhari Gharkhedi from another bhauband.[28]

As all this suggests, the rajas and the bhauband were not part of a single neat hierarchy. There were often attempts made by powerful groups to assert such a hierarchy, but they did not make much headway. Most rajas or bhauband owed allegiance and had close ties simultaneously with several chiefs. Because of this, even the boundaries of a dang were not always clear. While at one level the naik of Kakadvihir owed allegiance to Ghadvi and his village was part of Ghadvi, at other times there are references to dang Kakadvihir. Many smaller dangs like Kakadvihir both were and were not dangs. Sometimes, a smaller dang owed allegiance simultaneously to two larger dangs. Even the six principal dangs were, because of this, distinct but overlapping entities. Amala and Vasurna had originally been held by the same group of bhauband, as had been those of Ghadvi and Deher. In the mid-nineteenth century, similarly, Ankus raja of Deher divided villages with the Kadmal chiefs in order to avoid quarrels. Such fission occasionally resulted in some villages being co-shared, with each group of bhauband possessing rights in them but collecting their revenue independently.[29]

There was thus a profound lack in loci of authority: at every level, ties and alliances with other chiefs and bhauband were essential to construct or sustain claims to kingship and authority. With pressure from above and below to share kingship, the ties and alliances of shared kingship were in constant flux; they were constantly being made and negotiated. The profusion of intermeshed hierarchies is evident in the malleability of titles of the principal chiefs. For example, it was broadly accepted that only the most

---

27 *BRO.DDR.DN 6.FN 34.*
28 *DBD*, II, p. 109.
29 *BRO.DDR.DN 6.Fn 34*; *DBD*, II, pp. 111, 171; Report of a march through the Dangs, March 1867, *BRO.DDR.DN 3.FN 12.*

important chiefs, and their close bhauband had the term 'raja' regularly attached to their names; the other chiefs were to be called naiks. Another suffix was *kuver* or prince, and it was meant to be used by those bhauband who had claims of succession to the gadi. But even important figures like the chiefs of Pimpri or Vasurna were sometimes referred to as naiks; conversely, several minor naiks were often referred to as rajas. Who was a raja, who a naik, and who a kuver? — these were difficult questions in a situation where all Bhils were rajas.

Of Bridewealth and Dakans

There was also an even more pervasive lack involved in nineteenth-century Bhil kingship — a lack in the authority of Bhil men because of what was perceived as the power of Bhil women. In comparison to surrounding plains societies at least, both Kokni and Bhil women were quite powerful. Consider the complexities of bridewealth. When one of the Ghadvi bhauband, Chipat, wanted to marry a woman from the village Masli, he came to visit her father with around twenty friends, and Rs 5 worth of mahua liquor. Chipat's proposal was accepted, and the men drank the liquor — often a way of marking a friendship or alliance.[30] In Dangi marriages, it was customary for the prospective groom to visit the father of a girl and offer him mahua liquor and an amount in cash. This gift formalized the engagement or *pen*, which was followed later by marriage.

Certainly, some meanings of bridewealth enacted the subordination of women. Thus, bridewealth transformed marriage into a relationship between men — here, the prospective groom and the father of the woman — through the exchange of the woman. In Chipat's marriage, an alliance was established between him and the bride's father. That is to say, the bride was 'the object that both consolidates and differentiates kinship relations'. 'Given as gift . . . from one patrilineal clan to another', the woman is the 'conduit of a relationship rather than a partner to it'; 'the bride functions as a relational term between groups of men; she does not have an identity, and neither does she exchange one identity for another. She reflects masculine identity precisely through being the site of absence'.[31] In addition to establishing in this way a relationship

30 *BA.PD.1882.Vol 60.Comp 1452.*

31 The quotes are from Gayle Rubin, 'The traffic in women: Notes on the "political economy" of sex', in Rayna Reiter (ed.), *Towards an anthropology of*

between men, bridewealth also enacted the control of women's labour by men. Thus, in goth, the payment to the father is often described as a recognition of his loss of a valuable pair of hands for labour, and of the gain of that pair of hands by the groom. In these ways, it may seem bridewealth staged the subordination of women to men in Dangi society.[32]

However, in many ways these meanings of bridewealth were also subverted. It was quite common for Bhil women especially to elope with men, or to marry men of their choice, rather than participating in a regulated exchange. Such actions undercut the postulated absence of women in these exchanges, and made that absence into something that had to be established post-facto, usually by the man paying bridewealth to the woman's parents after the elopement. Similarly, there was the relative ease with which a woman could separate from her husband, either to go back to her affinal village or stay with another man. In the former case, her parents paid back the bridewealth to the husband in settlement of his claims, and in the latter case the new husband or man did so. Here, then, the relationships that bridewealth sought to establish — between men exclusively — were disrupted by the foregrounding of relationships between women and men, or in other words by women refusing to assent to their absence.[33]

Nor did the control of women's labour by men, whether as fathers or husbands, actually prevail. In comparison to most women from surrounding plains societies, Dangi women had a striking degree of control over their own labour and its products. True, they had little independent access to land or control over the disposal of crops produced through a significant contribution of their labour. Still, women had considerable control over resources obtained through gathering, fishing and mahua-collection. In the Rewa Kantha area, inhabited by forest communities similar to Dangis, women referred to the mahua tree as their parent, because they used the

---

women, New York, 1975. p. 174; Judith Butler, *Gender trouble: Feminism and the subversion of identity*, London, 1990, pp. 39–41, 75. Both Rubin and Butler make these remarks in the course of a critique of Claude Levi-Strauss's *The elementary structures of kinship*, Boston, 1969. Butler also provides a highly suggestive and sympathetic rereading of Rubin's essay, which by now seems to suffer from the problem of positing a prediscursive sexuality: see pp. 72–8.

[32] Chimna Navsu, 8.4.1994, Songir.

[33] Government of Bombay, *Rewa Kantha Gazetteer*, pp. 31f; Government of Bombay, *Gujarat Population: Hindus Gazetteer*, part I, pp. 308–9; DCR.DN 2.FN 4Uc.

money generated by their sale of mahua flowers to buy goods they required.[34] Other forms of livelihood over which they had some independent control over included forest produce and, for Kokni women, milk products from cattle. Through the sale or barter of these, women could secure goods quite independently of men. This ability, however limited, to disrupt the meanings of bridewealth as a relationship between men, to displace these with other meanings, was precisely what constituted the greater power of Dangi women in relation to women in surrounding plains societies.

But while Dangi women were relatively more powerful, that power was a deeply contested one, and was often considered illegitimate. Contact with them was in many ritual contexts believed to be polluting. The perceived autonomy of women in choosing partners remained on the margins of appropriateness, which may be why it was associated most of all with clandestine liaisons. Most strikingly, there was the celebration of abducting women as a way of securing a wife. When such abduction took place, the woman's parents and affinal family would give chase. If they did locate the couple, a serious clash could ensue. Usually, however, only a perfunctory search was made before the man's relatives or friends approached the woman's parents and offered a bridewealth payment — more than normal — as settlement. With this, the marriage would be regarded as formalized. Such abductions were considered quite honourable acts, and several folk-songs celebrated the daring involved in these;[35] further north in the Central Provinces, there was even an annual fair, Bhagoria, where such abductions were supposed to occur.[36] Indeed, abductions were so accepted a means of marriage that the abduction itself was often gestural: the girl would go or be taken to the boy's house with the knowledge of people in her village, and stay with him publicly. Later, her parents would visit him and fix a bridewealth; if this failed, she would return to her parents. What makes the language of abduction all the more striking in these situations is the fact that it took place most of all in those cases where women had previously indicated interest in or developed liaisons with the men who 'kidnapped'

34 Government of Bombay, *Rewa Kantha Gazetteer*, p. 28.

35 Government of Bombay, *Rewa Kantha Gazetteer*, pp. 31f; Government of Bombay, *Gujarat Population: Hindus Gazetteer*, part I, pp. 308–9; Narsinh bhagat, 6.6.1994, Amthawa.

36 Amita Baviskar, *In the belly of the river: Tribal conflicts over development in the Narmada Valley*, Delhi, 1995, p. 96.

them — where women had exercised a significant degree of autonomy in the choice of their partners. That is to say, the rhetoric of
abduction erased women's agency and transmuted it into its opposite at the very moment they exercised it most visibly.

The tension between the power of women and its illegitimacy
is most visible in the image of the dakan or witch. In principle, any
woman could become a dakan. Usually, it was the older and more
articulate women who were suspected of being dakans. There were
two or three such suspect women in some small villages.[37] Dakans
were regarded as extremely malevolent and dangerous, capable of
killing people through their spells. This malevolence and power
was thought to derive from their proximity to malevolent female
forest spirits like joganis — in this sense, dakans were the epitome
of female wildness.

Sanctions against dakans could be brutal. Quite often, when
Dangis suspected witchcraft, they consulted a bhagat to identify the
dakan. The violence of the dakan was conceived of as gratuitous, or
not socially determined. This was why consultations with the bhagat
were necessary: his enhanced sight enabled him to see the violence
that was independent of social causation. He would identify the
dakan. After this, the male members of a village would try to
mobilize social opinion for action against a suspected dakan.

If they did succeed, she was seized and her eyes usually tied
shut with a cloth containing ground chillies. This was amongst the
several 'tests' to determine whether she was actually a witch — if
she was innocent, her eyes would water. After this test, she was
suspended by her feet from a tree or a pole between uprights, and
a fire lit under her, her body just beyond the reach of its flames.
This treatment continued for three days, though most women died
long before that. If they did survive, they were freed, and permitted
to stay on, since they were thought to have been deprived of their
powers of witchcraft.

Swingings were not very common. Many relatives of a suspected
dakan, especially her agnates, were likely to stand by her, and
protect her against swingings. Attempt to override them could
lead to disputes and clashes. As a result of these fissures, dakans
often stayed on unharmed in villages for long after they had been
identified as dakans. But even if they were not very common,
swingings had an air of rightness to them as far as most Dangis

---

[37] The discussion of witchcraft is drawn from my paper, 'Women, witchcraft
and gratuitous violence in the Dangs'.

were concerned. It was the most appropriate way to take action against a dakan, and to deprive her of her power.

Yet dakans were respected in some ways, or at least regarded with ambivalence. Many Bhils 'to protect themselves from the consequences of being bewitched will not marry into a family in which there is not a reputed witch to defend them from others of her species . . . '.[38] Even a whole village could benefit from witchcraft: in the 1940s, the health of the cattle of one village was attributed to the protective presence of a witch. Besides, it could benefit entire communities: 'Konkanas [Koknis] and Warlis are afraid of Bheels. They think that Bheels are expert in magic and witchcraft.'[39] And the witches of forest communities like the Chodhras, Naikdas or Dublas in other areas of western India were so feared that many 'moneylenders will have no dealings with these early tribes'.[40] A dakan's reputation sometimes 'secured her a free supper of milk and chickens',[41] by itself quite a considerable benefit in a poor society. Often,

through fear of offending her the village people supply the witch with all articles of everyday use. As even things praised by a witch do not thrive, presents are made to her to secure her absence from marriage and other festive occasions. She is also free from a share of the articles collected for the use of travellers and moneylenders.[42]

Whatever their reasons — maybe because of the resources and respect they secured, or because this was one of the few means by which they could claim authority in Dangs — many women in fact claimed to be witches.

The power of women threatened always to draw attention to Dangi masculinity as a prosthetic reality — 'a "prefixing" of the rules of gender and sexuality; an appendix or addition, that willy-nilly, supplements and suspends a lack in being'.[43] It is striking that the belief in dakans, as well as the practice of swinging them, was so much more marked amongst the forest communities of western India than it was amongst neighbouring plains communities. As I have argued at greater length elsewhere, it was the paradox of the great power of women, and the simultaneous illegitimacy of that

38 *NAI.FD.Pol.16.2.1853.Nos 121–3.*

39 Khanapurkar, 'The aborigines of south Gujarat', pp. 63, 141.

40 *Gazetteer of the Bombay Presidency*, vol. IX, part I, p. 426.

41 Russell and Hira Lal, *The tribes and castes*, II, p. 290.

42 *Gazetteer of the Bombay Presidency*, vol. IX, part I, p. 430.

43 Homi K. Bhabha, 'Are you a man or a mouse', in Maurice Berger, Brian Wallis, and Simon Watson, *Constructing masculinity*, New York, 1995.

power that was articulated in Dangi images of the dakan. The dakan was the figure above all who threatened to reveal the prosthetic dimension of Dangi enactments of masculinity.

BHIL RAJ AND MASCULINITY

It is in the context of this considerable but illegitimate power of women that the enactment of the bhauband's authority in the nineteenth century has to be understood. In many ways, Dangi chiefs enacted Bhil raj as a denial of this prosthetic reality, as a claim instead to an accentuated masculinity. That is to say, the masculinity of Bhil raj was meant to challenge and control the presumed power of women.

For example, bhauband constructed a distinctive masculinity in their marital relationships. There was a concerted effort amongst them to control the meanings of the bridewealth they paid, and to cast women as conduit or absence. There was much more concerted effort than amongst ordinary Dangis to confine it to one exclusive meaning — that around the relationship between men which it created. Senior members of the bhauband often had as many as 'a dozen wives'.[44] This was usually depicted as a matter of status, an indicator that the bhauband was powerful enough to support that many wives, but it may also have had to do with the multiple alliances senior bhauband were likely to be involved in — each marriage allowed, after all, alliances with additional groups of bhauband. The honour and authority of the bhauband was intimately linked with transforming affinal or agnatic women into conduits for relations amongst the bhauband. Such women had a less active role in the choice of partners: their marriages were intended to construct alliances with other prominent bhauband. One of the wives of Daulat raja, a major mid-nineteenth-century Ghadvi chief, was the daughter of a prominent member of the Vasurna bhauband, Purtea raja.[45] Daulat's elder brother, Devisinh, was married to the daughter of Trimbak naik, the chief of Pimpri dang.[46]

Of course, as daughters, women within a family were persons to be given away, and an abduction, though a serious provocation,

[44] *BA.PD.1873.Vol 87.Comp 1551.*
[45] Morriss to Mansfield, 13.9.1853, *BRO.DDR.DN 2.FN 6.*
[46] Sheppard to Coll., Kh., 11.5.1861, *BRO.DDR.DN 3.FN 13*; Morriss to Mansfield, 13.9.1853, *BRO.DDR.DN 2.FN 6.*

could be transformed into an alliance between the male bhauband involved. When in the early nineteenth century, the Ghadvi raja Rajhans — elder brother to Devisinh and Daulat — carried away the daughter of the Vasurna raja, Aundya, the latter initially retaliated by attacking Rajhans, but the two later converted the abduction into a marriage alliance.[47] But the abduction of wives was a more serious matter — they had been taken into the patrilineal family, and honour was directly involved in retaining them within it. In cases where such women fled to rival bhauband, the kind of settlement with the new husband that was ordinarily possible became difficult. When Somee, the 'kept woman' of a senior Vasurna bhauband, Shendia raja, abandoned him to live with his arch-rival Bapu raja, the son of Aundya, he was so enraged that he sought her out and killed her.[48]

Nor was it only in the context of their individual relationships with women that a distinctive masculinity was claimed. The bhauband would, when any marriage took place within their dang, claim a marriage tax.[49] It may not be too far-fetched to interpret the tax as an acknowledgement of the role they were supposed to play in sustaining appropriate relations between men and women. Certainly, we know that controlling dakans was one of the major responsibilities of the bhauband and the rajas. Once a dakan had been located by a bhagat or priest, they played a major role in mobilizing crowds and swinging dakans. Villages in which dakans had been located were also expected to pay a tax to the bhauband.[50]

The bhauband were also more involved in those activities which Dangis associated with a masculine wildness. In goth by vadils, the Bhil chiefs or bhauband who are most celebrated are cast as figures who excelled in hunting, a masculine activity. It was they above all who invoked male ancestors to traverse and transform the forests. Their warfare involved secret spells that they learnt as male warriors from forest gods and spirits. And it was they, with their claims to a distinctive masculine wildness, who were most deeply involved in controlling dakans — after all the epitome of a dangerous female wildness.

[47] *BRO.DDR.DN 6.FN 34*; Raisinh Gondusar, 14.4.1990, Jamulvihir.
[48] Proceedings, *BA.PD.1854.Vol 40.Comp 915*.
[49] Raisinh Gondusar, 14.4.1990, Jamulvihir.
[50] See my 'Women, witchcraft and gratuitous violence in the Dangs'.

SOME RESERVATIONS

Two lacks, then, involved two strategies. The lack of self-sufficient loci for kingship was associated with the participation and inclusion of all Bhil men in kingship. In sharp contrast, the lack of Bhil masculinity was associated most of all with its denial, with the exclusion and subordination of women, with the enactment of Bhil kingship as distinctively masculine.

But is this neat formulation too easy a dichotomy? Did these refigurings and extinctions of the wildness of women succeed? Going by the prevalence of dakans, the ways in which women continued to exercise power, and subvert dominant meanings of bridewealth, maybe not. Though Bhil raj should have been, in dominant Dangi understandings, only the enactment of masculine kingship, that masculinity continued to be haunted by apprehensions of its prosthetic nature. The power of figures like dakans was not simply part of some illegitimate margin: recall the role they played in protecting village cattle, in restraining the power of moneylenders, or in marking out the distinctive power of the dang.

We do not know much about Kokni women, but Bhil *ranis* or queens figure in goth of moglai in more than the relatively trivial sense that many Bhil ranis effectively ruled their dangs after their husbands died. Consider for a moment goth of a dispute between the Ghadvi and Kadmal bhauband which, we know from records, occurred around 1799.

> Fatehsinh raja was the brother of Bada Udesinh [a Ghadvi chief]. He had two wives. Of them, the younger one, Chauti, she was from Vasurna, she left him and went away. She went to Virsinh raja of Kadmal, and said, 'will you keep me?' He told her, 'I will not keep you. But I will give you a bullock, and you can sell that and wear bangles.' She said, 'I do not want the bullock.' But then she took the bullock and went away. On her way, she met some Bhils. She told the Bhils, 'take this bullock'. The Bhils took it and ate it. Then they said, 'Virsinh raja will not keep you, but go to Gondu raja [another Kadmal chief] and he will keep you'. So she went, and Gondu raja kept her.
>
> [After several months] Gondu raja asked the rani, 'there is no shortage of food in my house, but you keep getting thinner. Tell me why'. She said, 'your face and Fatehsinh raja's face are the same. Maybe he will kill you, or you will kill him. I do not know, and this is why I grow thin.' Then Gondu raja told her, 'do not worry, I shall kill him'.

Fatehsinh raja had gone to cast nagli. The others who were with him went out into the jungle to hunt. Only one old man remained with him. He heated water for the raja to wash his face. Just then, the people from Kathikaldar came and killed the raja. When everybody came back from hunting, the old man said, 'you go away for hunting, and look what happens. The raja has been killed.' Dasari rani [Fatehsinh's senior wife] was called. They told her, 'the raja is calling you'. The rani came. She pulled off the sheet, and saw that he was dead. Then the body was burnt.

Then Dasari rani went to the Baduda [Baroda] sarkar. She said 'My raja has been killed. Now you put the *nishan* [flag] of the Gaekwad in my raj and help me catch them. Do not put the nishan elsewhere, but put it up in my raj. You may put it elsewhere later.' So the nishan was put up. This showed that Ghadvi was the first of the rajas. Then the Gaekwad came and helped the Ghadvi raja kill Gondu raja and others.[51]

Quite evidently, ranis are important here not simply as inter-changeable substitutes for rajas. They enact rather a very distinctive politics. The actions of Chauti rani negate any notion of women simply being the means of constructing ties between groups of bhauband; rather, Chauti not only leaves Fatehsinh but actively seeks out other bhauband who will keep her, thus constructing relationships both between herself and potential partners, and between bhauband. As for Dasari rani, it is she who is associated most of all with what is regarded in many accounts as an event of especially great importance: the establishment of close relations between Gaekwadi officials and Ghadvi. It is this relation which, in many goth, is identified as the cause of the dominance of Ghadvi bhauband over other bhauband.

The power of Bhil ranis may also have had to do with their distinctive wildness as women. Let me briefly summarize a goth which is narrated in detail in Chapter 8. During moglai, a Kokni village headman, Ghobria patil, challenged the authority of one of the most feared bhauband of Amala, Rajhans raja. The latter was initially confused as to how to retaliate. He came back with his wife, Jegi rani, who tied a rope to Ghobria's neck, got him down on his knees, and rode him around the village as she would have ridden a horse. This *dosh* of being ridden by a woman (with all its obvious sexual innuendoes) led to Ghobria patil's death, from mortification and shame, the next day. In this way, one of the most

51 Raisinh Gondusar, 1.4.1990, Jamulvihir.

powerful Kokni patils, who till then had without reprisals defied the most powerful Bhil bhauband, was finally subordinated by a Bhil rani. Maybe then, Bhil raj was not only about the masculine power of the bhauband, maybe it was also about the wildness of Bhil women.

(17)

7

Being a Raja

Early one summer morning, Kama Rupdev and I went to Khatal village to meet his uncle. Kama was a new friend, about my age, and his uncle, he believed, knew stories about Khem raja, a bhauband of the Ghadvi chief Silput raja. The uncle was not at the village. On the way back, Kama told me that though he did not know much of these goth, he knew that they were about clashes amongst Ghadvi bhauband. In the fragments he told me, there figured several important Ghadvi chiefs who I had read of in nineteenth-century records: Silput raja, Khem raja, Silput's brother Udesinh raja, Silput's sons Rajhans, Devisinh, Daulat and Rupdev, Udesinh's son Kerulsinh, and several others made fleeting appearances. That was my first introduction to a dispute between two powerful groups of Ghadvi bhauband. The dispute's consequences still reverberate in the present: quite by accident, I was initially associated with Kama and the group of bhauband who felt they had the rightful claim to the gadi of Ghadvi, and who told stories of how they had been dispossessed. Because of this accidental association, members of the other group of bhauband were often suspicious of me, and it was difficult for me to learn their goth of these purported incidents. The goth that follow, then, are all from the perspectives of only one group of bhauband.

Many of these goth revolve around how the ancestors of the narrators lost the gadi to their rivals, the bhauband associated with Nana Udesinh.[1]

> Nana Udesinh's people lived at Popirkilla. There was no grain available there one year, and so they came to Dangs, four of them, Soman Bhil, Kaman Bhil, Budea Bhil and Eria bahas [old man.] Udesinh was from Soman Bhil's family. Silput raja saw him and took him as his *chakardar* [servant/military retainer.] He moved

---

[1] I learnt these stories principally from two persons: Raisinh Gondusar, a descendant of Vanwasia, and Linga Partam, a descendant of Rahirao.

around with Silput raja, cooked food for him, and did other *chakar* [service]. His salary was also fixed, at Rs 60 a year.[2]

By casting Udesinh as hailing from Popirkilla — outside Dangs — it is his royal authority that is being denied, for most senior bhauband claim to be autochthons.[3] As a figure from Popirkilla, he would not even belong to the clan of Dharegad Pawars, from which all bhauband are. The imagery of how Udesinh's ancestors came to Dangs has been drawn, obviously, from Kokni goth of migration into the region during times of famine; the implicit parallel depicts Udesinh and his ancestors in a supplicatory position when they first came to Dangs. His position as a chakardar is also damaging, for it is traditionally a post held by junior members of the bhauband, who did anything from tending horses to being a *sipai* with the chief, and were given some perquisites in turn. The chakardar is a common figure in stories which delegitimize claims of ruling bhauband to the gadi. The Kadmal chiefs sometimes describe the Dherbhavti rajas as originally their chakardars, while a section of Amala kuvers again deride the present Amala rajas in similar terms.[4]

In recalling how their ancestors lost the gadi to this upstart Udesinh, narrators often draw on motifs of violent treachery.

Rajhans raja went from Ghadvi to Bandhpada to collect mahua, and he made his house there. Devisinh raja, Daulat raja, and Rupdev raja [his three younger brothers] went to meet him. Behind them went Nana Udesinh, with bow and arrows, in hiding. Rajhans' wife welcomed them, and Rajhans called for mahua. All four brothers drank together. His wife made food inside the house, and then Rajhans called them in to eat. While they were eating, Udesinh parted the grass walls of the house and shot Rajhans with an arrow. Rajhans shouted, 'who has shot me' and ran out. He ran and fell into the lake of Bhurapat. From there he got up and went to the Devi at Bandhpada, fell at her feet and died. Behind him ran his three brothers, Devisinh raja, Daulat raja and Rupdev raja, but by the time they reached him, he was dead. Then they tried to find Nana Udesinh, but he had run away. They came back and performed the funeral rites for Rajhans. That same night, Nana Udesinh went back to Ghadvi and started

[2] Raisinh Gondusar, 1.4.1990, Jamulvihir.

[3] An exception to this is the group of bhauband associated with Chinchli, Sivbara, and Kirli, amongst other places. But they see their place of origin as just outside Dangs district, and certainly do not see themselves as migrants into Dangs.

[4] Indarsinh Somansinh, 29.4.1990, Kadmal, and Chandu Bhausinh, 30.4.1990, Anjankund.

harassing the wives of Devisinh raja, Daulat raja and Rupdev. He also took away their *sikka daftar* [seals and records] and burnt their houses. They [the brothers] were alone and weak; he had made a *jodi* [alliance] with his relatives.[5]

One thrust here is the attempt to delegitimize the claims of Nana Udesinh and his descendants (who hold the gadi today); the other is the attempt to legitimize their own claims. Thus the emphasis on Rajhans having possessed the gadi prior to Udesinh's family. As Rajhans's brother (Rajhans had no sons, according to narrators), Devisinh had a strong claim to the gadi, and by virtue of this so do his descendants now.[6]

Many goth also tell of Devisinh's revenge for the killing of his brother: he later killed Kerulsinh, who had succeeded his father Udesinh to the gadi, cut Kerulsinh's body into pieces and threw it into the forest. But while Devisinh's descendants tell stories of how Kerulsinh was killed, they are also anxious to deflect any potential stigma on Devisinh for this. They emphasize that this was revenge for Udesinh's act in killing Rajhans by despicable means, when Rajhans was not even expecting an attack. Especially radical is the account below, which does not even allow that Kerulsinh was bound when killed (as is mentioned by many other descendants of Kerulsinh and Devisinh, and also in nineteenth-century court testimony).

Then Nana Udesinh died and his son was Kerulsinh. Devisinh told Kerulsinh, 'you have killed my brother, and so I will kill you'. Devisinh called Kerulsinh over to his village for a meeting, but Kerulsinh did not go, fearing that he would be killed. Then all three brothers went to Kotba [where Kerulsinh lived] at night. Two stayed at one door each, while the third went in and caught him. Devisinh said, 'we will not kill you, but we will take you to our village'. Then they brought him to Ghadvi. There, Kerulsinh fought with Devisinh. Devisinh thought, 'If I do not fight back, I will be killed by him, just as his father killed my brother'. So Devisinh fought back and Kerulsinh was killed.[7]

To kill in a fight where both opponents faced each other was the

5 Raisinh Gondusar, 1.4.1990, Jamulvihir. Udesinh is usually referred to in goth as 'Nana [junior] Udesinh' in order to distinguish him from the eighteenth-century Ghadvi chief Bada [senior] Udesinh.

6 I met no figures who claimed descent from the bhauband associated with Rajhans, Daulat or Rupdev — most narrators who associated with this group of bhauband claimed descent rather from Devisinh. According to goth told by them, there have been no male descendants from Rupdev for around three generations, and none from Daulat for around four.

7 Linga Partam and Mosru Jalal, 30.3.1990, Ghavria.

most honourable way of doing so, quite different from the way Udesinh killed Rajhans, shooting him in the back as he sat down to eat.

INALIENABLE MARKERS

Because of cues from goth, I slowly came to realize that many events narrated in colonial records as stray clashes fitted, for Ghadvi bhauband, into the narrative of a series of related disputes that had continued, with several confrontations, for over a century. Piecing archival sources together in the light of goth, the account that emerges is briefly this. Around 1829, the Ghadvi chief Silput raja was succeeded by his son Rajhans. In the late 1830s, Silput's brother Udesinh killed Rajhans and succeeded to the gadi. Rajhans's brothers — Silput's three other sons, Devisinh, Daulat, and Rupdev — were at the time too young to be involved. On Udesinh's death in 1844 (?), Devisinh however made a claim to the gadi. He was bypassed, and it was given to Udesinh's son Kerulsinh by the British. As a compromise, Devisinh and Daulat were made the *raj-karbharis* to Kerulsinh, or the persons who looked after the management of the state. But Kerulsinh resented their regency, and following his complaints to the British as well as an attack by Devisinh on some of his followers, Devisinh was imprisoned in 1849. Sometime later, in 1853, Daulat was also imprisoned by the British on charges of having attacked Kerulsinh's followers.

Devisinh escaped and returned to Dangs in 1860, joined forces with Daulat, and declared that the gadi should either be returned to him, or he would seize it by force. A series of clashes followed, culminating in his capture of Kerulsinh from Kotba village. During negotiations for Kerulsinh's release, he progressively raised the stakes. When some Ghadvi zamindars came to negotiate, he first demanded Rs 500 as ransom. When this was met with, he asked for Kerulsinh's seal, which too was handed over. Then he asked for Kerulsinh's wife and children, and when that demand was not met, he killed Kerulsinh. Following this, the British undertook a punitive expedition, captured Devisinh and Daulat, and restored the gadi to Kerulsinh's son.[8]

The dispute however persisted across generations, and has lasted now for well over a century and a half. One of Devisinh's sons,

<hr/>

[8] Sheppard to Ag. Coll., Kh., 11.5.1861; Trial of Devisinh, Daulat and others, *BRO.DDR.DN 3.FN 13*. Trial of Devisinh, 1862, *BRO.DDR.DN 2.FN 10*.

Rahirao, was involved in a clash with Udesinh's son Murharrao; another son, Vanwasia, successfully got Kerulsinh's descendant Umbarsinh imprisoned in 1899; Daulat's son Chipat was involved in repeated clashes with Kerulsinh's sons, and was finally imprisoned. Around the 1930s, one of Vanwasia's sons was involved in a clash with Umbarsinh's son. There were some minor confrontations in the 1970s, and to some extent the two groups of bhauband are still on hostile terms.[9]

In the nineteenth century, disputes were not uncommon: colonial officials complained repeatedly of the 'interminable feuding' amongst Bhils.[10] The pervasiveness of disputes was because of a fundamental paradox in Dangi thought about what the gadi was. On the one hand, as the previous chapter has suggested, Dangi polities had no centre. Authority was so deeply haunted by a lack that there was no clear hierarchical apex to political power in Dangs. On the other, Dangi bhauband were deeply concerned to locate an apex or centre to their polities. The Dangi idea of a gadi was about it, as were disputes over succession such as that between the bhauband associated with Devisinh and Udesinh. It is the implications of this paradox, or the question of what it meant to be a raja, that I would like to tease out in this chapter.

Because of the extent of participation in power by bhauband, conventional criteria like control of the region or domination over the bhauband would have been inadequate by themselves to determine who held the gadi — after all, Devisinh may even have controlled more villages and the allegiance of more bhauband than Udesinh. The gadi also had to be conceptualized and understood through a range of what might be called markers of kingship. These markers were crucial to the construction of power: since the gadi could not be conceptualized in itself, it was the markers that even made the gadi visible. Markers of kingship was so diverse and access to some of them so widespread (as I suggest below, seals, kinship ties, women, land grants, even small grants of money, shawls, or turbans could all become markers) that they were important not

---

[9] Quite evidently, any understanding of the dispute would, from the perspective of professional historians, be partial without taking account of the crucial role of the British. I nevertheless excise the British here because my attempt here is not to provide a comprehensive understanding of the dispute or disputes as a genre, but, as I have already argued, to attempt parallels to the theme of Bhil raj and *dhum* in moglai.

[10] Fenner to Robertson, March 1860, *BRO.DDR.DN 2.FN 9*.

only in social relationships amongst chiefs but also in those between more ordinary people. Differential access to markers of kingship was associated with myriad subtle and not so subtle distinctions: between ordinary Bhils and bhauband, between ordinary bhauband and important ones, and between important bhauband and the rajas who held gadis. The deployment of these markers was crucial for bestowing honours on allies, for insulting rivals, for laying claims to being the principal raja, and for simply maintaining one's position in kingly hierarchies. In everyday life, it was above all these markers that constituted and gave form to the authority of the chiefs, that were invoked in efforts to resolve knotty questions raised by multiple hierarchies, that were deployed to try cover the lack involved in claims to kingship.

What was distinctive about these markers of kingship was that they were constructed as inalienable possessions or relationships, as entities inseparable from the persons of the people associated with them. It was the claim that these possessions or relationships embodied (and I use that verb almost literally) the power of the person involved that made them so important. Yet, this claim to inalienability was always haunted by the spectre of alienation. Markers of kingship could be alienated from the persons whom they embodied and empowered in myriad ways — by accident, by the actions of rivals, or by the transformations of the meanings that they carried. It was at the junctures of these anxieties and contingencies that markers of kingship were constituted.[11]

Consider first the claims to inalienability involved in markers of kingship. One of the most exclusive markers of authority was the seal or sikka. The seal had reached Dangs at least by the late eighteenth century, when we find the first documents which use

[11] My understanding of inalienable possessions and relationships is quite different from that articulated by Annete Weiner in her *Inalienable possessions: The paradox of keeping while giving*, Berkeley and Los Angeles, 1992. First, Weiner suggests that the notion of inalienable objects will help us understand exchange in small-scale societies since 'all exchange is predicated on a universal paradox — how to keep while giving'. In contrast, I am not particularly interested in universalist understandings of exchange: my focus is on the construction of authority. Second, and more importantly, in Weiner's analysis, inalienable possessions are themselves an already given category or entity; her focus is on the implications of these possessions for social life. In contrast, my focus is far more on the contingencies and anxieties that haunted claims to inalienability. I thank Tamara Giles-Vernick for suggesting a focus on inalienable possessions as a way of exploring kingship.

it.[12] But documented agreements which required a seal were not very common within Dangs: when the British made an attempt to draw up a list of jagirdars of Dangs as late as the early twentieth century, it was found that most held them on oral agreements.[13] The sikka was principally associated not with transactions within Dangs but with dealings with important plains powers or figures, such as the Gaekwads, the deshmukh and the merchants. By the mid-nineteenth century, the possession of a sikka indicated that a chief was powerful enough to be dealing not only with powers within the dang, but also with powers of the desh. Because of this, only the really powerful amongst the bhauband, and usually only the holder of the gadi, usually laid claim to it.

Maybe the kind of power that the sikka epitomized is best understood in conjunction with other similar forms of authorization. Like the seal, the arrows of powerful chiefs could also embody their authority. After a meeting that Silput raja of Ghadvi had with a Havildar sent by the British,

he regretted that he could not send a suitable present to the Circar as a fire had destroyed all his cloth turbans &c. but says he, drawing an arrow from the well-filled quiver at his back 'Take this and give it to the people of my village of Kehl and demand 9 rupees'. To the companion of the Havildar he gave another arrow telling him to demand five rupees at another of his villages. They delivered the arrows as described and instantly received the money.[14]

Like the arrow, the power of the seal had little to do with the fact that it represented writing, or that writing was a powerful technology of the plains. To assume this would be an instance of what Mudimbe has described as epistemological ethnocentrism.[15] That is to say, it runs the risk of presuming that the valorization of writing in non-literate societies must necessarily be a consequence of incomprehension and wonderment in the face of an external stimulus. Rather, the seal, like the arrow, was construed as an inalienable possession, as an entity that embodied and enacted the power of those laying claim to it. Its power was derivative

12 As, for instance, the documents reproduced in *BA.RD.1850.Vol 95.Comp 1283, BA.PD.1851.Vol 24.Comp 273*. This discussion of seals and writing is drawn from my 'Writing, orality and power in the Dangs'.

13 Memo by Mr Hodgson, 22.7.1905; Diwan to APA, 30.10.1910; APA to PA, 13–15.3.1911, *BRO.DDR.DN 6.FN 34*.

14 Giberne to Newnham, 16.10.1828, *BA.PSD.1828.Vol 29/230*.

15 V.Y. Mudimbe, *The invention of Africa: Gnosis, philosophy and the order of knowledge*, Bloomington, 1988, pp. 13–22.

not from writing but from its construal as such an inalienable possession.[16]

Claims to inalienability were also involved in a slightly less exclusive marker, the *nagara*, a drum usually possessed by the head in each village or settlement, and used primarily to summon Bhil followers. When on the move, the *nagarchi* or drummer commenced playing as the chief approached a village; this was notice for the patil to prepare to meet the raja and pay respects. The playing of the nagara was an assertion of authority and sovereignty over a village; 'one small raja is not allowed to play his drums while passing through the village of another'.[17] In 1877, Devisinh's son Rahirao ordered his drums to be played as his retinue passed through the forests of Kerwan village, where Udesinh's son Murharrao resided. Infuriated, Murharrao raja and his men attacked them, killing one of their men. Here, it was precisely the inalienability of the nagara from the authority of Rahirao which led to the clash.

Maybe the most inalienable relationship was that claimed through kinship. This, after all, was the meaning of bhauband in the most narrow sense of the word — 'the kinsmen of powerful chiefs, persons who could claim a relationship by blood to authority. Certainly, kinship was very central to claims to kingship. Many claims to succession to gadis were made on the basis of primogeniture, or on the basis that the claimant was the eldest son of the chief he was succeeding. Kerulsinh, for example, succeeded his father Udesinh partially because he was the eldest son. Similarly, the brother of a deceased chief sometimes succeeded to the gadi, especially when the son of the chief was a minor.[18] Within the family constituted by kinship, women also became inalienable possessions: as the last chapter already suggested, bhauband enacted the prosthetic masculinity of Bhil raj by exercising greater control over women within their family.

Even in death, the inalienability of markers of kingship was emphasized. The difference between ordinary Bhils and bhauband was enacted in mortuary practices. Rajas were normally cremated, while ordinary Bhils were buried. This difference in practices may

---

[16] I thank Tamara Giles-Vernick for pointing this out.

[17] Nanju Raut, 8.6.1990, Payarghodi; Proceedings, *BA.PD.1877.Vol 106. Comp 500.*

[18] See, for instance, the succession of the Chinchli naik in *BA.PD.1855. Vol 36.Comp 1606*, and the succession in Sivbara reported in *BA.PD.1858. Vol 97.Comp 1317.*

have been due to varying financial means — cremation needed more resources than burial.[19] To bury a member of the bhauband instead of burning him would thus have been an acknowledgement of the lack of authority necessary to garner resources; it was to be that much less of a raja. Bhil cremations, in other words, enacted an inalienable relationship with kingly authority.

THE ANXIETIES OF INALIENABILITY

Yet, claims to inalienability, despite their rhetoric, were always contingent and unstable, under threat from rivals and circumstances. In 1862, when Devisinh and Daulat killed Kerulsinh, they bound him, took him to the forests, and hacked him to death there with a sword. They returned leaving his body out in the open.[20] To be killed thus, and then be thrown in the forest and left for the wild animals to pick clean was the most degraded kind of death possible. It was to die improperly, as less of a raja. In demanding revenge against Devisinh, members of Kerulsinh's bhauband dwelt more on how Kerulsinh had been killed than the fact of killing itself. It may have been because of the fear of improper mortuary rituals by enemies that, when an umrao of Aundya raja of Vasurna was killed in a clash with Rajhans raja of Ghadvi, Aundya raja cut off his head and took it to Vasurna. In Vasurna, presumably, the head was given a proper cremation.[21]

The presumed inalienability of arrows and seals was also under constant threat. When Aundya raja of Vasurna was engaged in a dispute with a rival Vasurna bhauband, he tried to have Shendia's seal taken from him. Aundya demanded that the British confiscate the seal, since Shendia might sign documents with it, and Aundya would be held responsible for them.[22] And when Devisinh and Daulat were appointed raj-karbharis to Kerulsinh (at the time around twelve years old) *c.* 1845, the two took immediate possession of the seal. Their possession of it was one of Kerulsinh's principal grievances, and he made several efforts to get it back. One evening in 1849,

[19] Report of a march through the Dangs, March 1867, *BRO.DDR.DN 3.FN 12.* The distinction, however, was not immutable. See *BA.PD.1882.Vol 60. Comp 1452*, and Khanapurkar, 'The aborigines of south Gujarat', vol. I, pp. 154ff.

[20] Trial of Devisinh, *BRO.DDR.DN 2. FN 10.*

[21] 'Vasurna jagir case', *BRO.DDR.DN 6.FN 34.* For similar accounts, from south India, of the importance attached to a proper death in warfare, see Rao et al., *Symbols of substance*, Delhi, 1996, pp. 305–8.

[22] Yad by Aundya, n.d., 1849, *BRO.DDR.DN 1.FN 2.*

in 1849, finally, when Kerulsinh threatened to complain to the British, Devisinh gave in and told his karbhari (key administrative official to important chiefs, usually also a member of the bhauband) Budea, to hand it over. But the seal was so valuable that Budea initially refused, saying that Devisinh would later blame him for the loss. Only after Devisinh insisted did Budea finally follow his instructions.[23] Still later, the seal was to come back into play again. When he had made Kerulsinh prisoner, Devisinh's penultimate demand was for Kerulsinh's seal. It was handed over to him.[24] Maybe this acquisition, which made him more of a raja, gave him the confidence that he could get away with killing Kerulsinh.

The inalienability of women as possessions was equally under siege. Leave aside for the moment the point already explored in the previous chapter — that Dangi masculinity was prosthetic, that women themselves challenged the inalienability, from their husbands, brothers or fathers, which was ascribed to them. In disputes, it was not so much women as rival male bhauband who challenged this inalienability, trying repeatedly to demonstrate that their rivals did not have the power to make women into their inalienable possessions, and were thus not powerful chiefs. Clashing bhauband thus often carried away women associated with rival groups. In 1852, Kerulsinh's followers carried away his rival Rupdev's wife, telling her that she was to be put into Kerulsinh's house, a phrase which is interpreted for us as meaning that she was to be made Kerulsinh's 'unlawful wife'. But they were intercepted by Rupdev's elder brother, Daulat, who 'recovered' her. Later, Kerulsinh 'seduced' Devisinh's wife while the latter was in prison, an act for which other rajas were sure that Devisinh would want revenge.[25] Eventually, when Devisinh captured Kerulsinh, he demanded, after the seal had been handed over to him, that Kerulsinh's wife and children be handed over as a precondition to the chief's release. If Kerulsinh's bhauband refused to meet this demand,[26] it was because the voluntary handing over of the women of the family or their group of bhauband was almost the ultimate acknowledgement of

23 *BA.PD.1850.Vol 38/2404.Comp 593.*

24 *BRO.DDR.DN 2.FN 10.*

25 Daulat to Morriss, 24.4.1852; Morriss to Mansfield, 29.9.1854, *BRO.DDR. DN 2.FN 6.*

26 Kerulsinh to Diwan, September 1860, *BRO.DDR.DN 3.FN 13*; Sheppard to Ag. Coll., 11.5.1862, *BRO.DDR.DN 2.FN 6*; Ashburner to Secy., GoB, 2.1.1862, *BRO.DDR.DN 2.FN 10.*

subordination, and would have seriously threatened their authority even in villages directly under them.

Even kinship ties, on the face of matters the most inalienable markers of kingship, were characterized by a profound alienability. True, primogeniture could be deployed to claim an inalienable relationship with a gadi, or with any position of power. But primogeniture itself could take on a host of meanings. Consider a dispute over succession between the bhauband of Vasurna following the death of Aundya raja of Vasurna in 1851. Claims to the gadi were made by three persons, and all were on the basis of some reading of primogeniture. Bapu kuver, the eldest 'legitimate' son, and Dalpat kuver, the eldest 'illegitimate' son, both claimed the gadi on these grounds. Then there was Shendia kuver, a long-time rival of Aundya raja within the Vasurna bhauband. Shendia kuver belonged to the elder branch of the family, which had originally possessed the gadi of Vasurna. But Aundya or his ancestors had seized it by killing Shendia's brother and two senior rajas of Shendia's branch.[27] Now Shendia made a claim to the gadi on the basis of ruptured primogeniture — he would have been raja if his ancestors had not been deposed. In other words, the idea of primogeniture itself could support a host of different claims to an inalienable relationship with the gadi, or more broadly with any position of authority.

Besides, forms of descent other than primogeniture could be important too. In one instance, a claimant demanded the gadi by insisting that he had been the favourite son of the deceased chief.[28] Devisinh similarly claimed the gadi partially on the grounds that his brother Rajhans had held the gadi formerly. Indeed, one colonial official was to remark that there was 'no peculiarity or local custom with respect to the order of succession to the different Gadees'.[29]

Furthermore, ties of kinship could also be entirely set aside or marginalized. Sometimes, as when Udesinh killed his nephew Rajhans, the rivals too were related by descent. Similarly, the three brothers Devisinh, Daulat and Rupdev did not always present a joint front against Kerulsinh. They occasionally clashed amongst themselves, and Rupdev was once wounded in such a clash.[30] Kinship relations created through marriage did not work all the

---

[27] *BA.PD.1851.Vol 24.Comp 1578*, and Annual Report, 1848, *BRO.DDR. DN 1.FN 2*.

[28] Sheppard to PA, Kh., to Comm., CD, 11.5.1861, *BRO.DDR.DN 3.FN 13*.

[29] *SRBG 26*, p. 166.

[30] Sheppard to Ag. Coll., Kh., 11.5.1861, *BRO.DDR.DN 3.FN 13*.

time either — Devisinh's father-in-law, Trimbak naik, the chief of
Pimpri, was allied with Kerulsinh, and Devisinh tried once to kill
Trimbak. Similarly, Daulat was captured in 1853 with his father-
in-law Purtea's assistance.[31] Kinship, then, though often cast as
embodying an inalienable relationship with kingship, was more
metaphorical than about any binding blood ties; it was a language
within which different claims could be cast, or even a language
that could be set aside, when inconvenient, without too many
twinges of conscience.

THE MUTABILITY OF MARKERS

Fears over the alienability of markers of kingship also had to do with
the very mutability of their meanings. Consider turbans or pagdis,
important maybe due to their ubiquitousness. While senior members
of the bhauband 'barely [have] their nakedness covered' even on
formal occasions like darbars, they made it a point to not move
around without 'good turbans'.[32] The most ordinary Dangi men,
whether Kokni or Bhil, wore turbans. Precisely because it was so
widely shared, the meanings of a pagdi were determined by a variety
of factors. In addition to its quality and cost, there was the way it had
been received. The most honourable way to possess a turban was to
be gifted one, and many members of the bhauband received turbans
annually from the villages upon which they possessed dues, or from
powerful neighbours like the Gaekwads, the Vansda raja, or the
Baglan deshmukhs. Important members of the bhauband usually
gave either their old turbans, or the surplus ones that they received,
to other junior members of the bhauband. To give or receive a pagdi
was to become *bhai-pagdi*, or brothers by the exchange of turbans.

And, of course, the deployment of turbans was one of the most
basic and widespread ways of creating alliances, as during the
claims to the gadi made at the time of the Vasurna succession in
1851, after the death of Aundya raja. Shendia had been a long-time
rival of Aundya, and had on occasion successfully demanded a
greater share of the dues that Aundya received.[33] When Aundya

31 Sheppard to Coll., Kh., 11.5.1861, *BRO.DDR.DN 3.FN 13*; Morriss to
Mansfield, 13.9.1853, *BRO.DDR.DN 2.FN 6*.
32 Quoted in David Hardiman, 'Power in the forests', in Arnold and Hardiman
(eds), *Subaltern studies VIII*, Delhi, 1994.
33 Annual Report, 1848, *BRO.DDR.DN 1.FN 2*, and Elphinston to Secy., GoB,
26.4.1852, *BA.PD.1852.Vol 42.Comp 1415*.

died, most bhauband, including Shendia raja, initially agreed to the succession of Bapu raja. But Shendia was clandestinely engaged in constructing alliances to undermine Bapu raja's claims. At the 1852 British darbar, where the succession was to be ratified, he put forth his own claim to the gadi.[34]

In support of it, he produced three turbans and one *dhotur* (lower garment), implicitly claiming three sources of support. One turban, he said, was a gift from Hasusinh raja of Amala. By claiming a gift from Hasusinh, Shendia was claiming both the support of the wider constellation of important Dangi chiefs and, more specifically, the support of major Amala bhauband, of which Vasurna was believed to be a junior branch. The second turban was, he said, from Dalpat raja, the eldest but 'illegitimate' son of Aundya raja — thus claiming support from within Bapu kuver's own bhauband. The third turban as well as the dhotur were from the zamindars or jagirdars of Vasurna — proof of support from the important Vasurna bhauband too. Shendia thus claimed the gadi on the grounds that the turbans from key figures were symbolic of their alliances with him.

The strategy did not work. Hasusinh said that he had given the turban to Shendia kuver not in support of his claim to the gadi, but during a feast that Hasusinh had held. The zamindars said that Shendia had himself come with the turbans to them and asked them to place it on his head. As this suggests, even when success-fully construed as inalienable possessions, markers of kingship were not complete semiotic systems. Whether the gift of a turban was the acknowledgement of subordination rendered to a superior figure, a conferral of honour upon an inferior, or a mark of honour to an equal depended on circumstances. Markers of kingship, in other words, were not transparent entities but had to be constantly read and re-read. Their meanings were profoundly mutable, and in this very mutability resided the possibility of their alienation.

Who was the Raja?

The alienability of markers of kingship — the ways in which these markers, though always cast as inalienable possessions, were al-ways profoundly unstable — created some of the paradoxes of Dangi kingship. Markers of authority derived their meaning not internally from themselves — they had no fixed meanings — but

[34] The account below is drawn from Elphinstone to Secy., GoB, 14.5.1852, *BA.PD.1852.Vol 42.Comp 1415.*

with reference to the gadi and social relations. They were no more anterior to power than power was anterior to them. Yet the gadi, as well as subtler gradations within hierarchies of the bhauband, were thought of principally through these markers. Indeed, the gadi is possibly best described as a particularly powerful cluster of several markers of kingship. And because the meanings of the markers were derived from changing social relations, this cluster could never precisely define the gadi, or even be singular. Put differently, there was always a slippage between the singularity which many Dangis wished to ascribe to the gadi and the multiplicity of ways in which it could be thought of. Kingship was so profoundly characterized by lack that attempts to conceive of a clearly defined gadi failed. The distribution and accumulation of these markers was an attempt to demonstrate a plenitude of power, one that would cover the lack which haunted kingship. Such efforts at demonstration were often a game of brinksmanship, where contenders claimed a power that they did not possess, and when successful, actually managed to augment their power and authority in this way. But whether they succeeded or failed, the gadi virtually never became entirely singular.

As an illustration, consider this question: Did Devisinh hold the gadi? No, one would think, quite evidently not. Udesinh's son, Devrao, recalling matters nearly three decades later also thought not. He remarked in 1886 that Devisinh 'did not reign, nor his sons', Rahirao and Vanwasia.[35] However, Devisinh would not have agreed. In a petition made in 1850, he complained that when he was ruling his dominions, one Kiro (Kerulsinh), son of Udesinh, caused him annoyance. But neither Devisinh nor his people took notice of this annoyance.[36]

Notice: Kerulsinh is the annoyance and Devisinh the holder of the gadi. But could Devisinh really have meant this? After all, did he not threaten to kill Kerulsinh unless the latter handed over the gadi (which implies that he did not think he possessed the gadi), and did he not later carry out his threat? In all likelihood, while Devisinh thought of himself as having lost the gadi, he also simultaneously thought of himself as being on the gadi. This apparently paradoxical understanding was possible because by questioning the social relations which constituted them, he could deny the meaning of Kerulsinh's markers of kingship. Also, he could put together his

[35] *DBD*, II, 167.
[36] Petition of Devisinh, *BA.PD.1850.Vol 38/2404.Comp 593.*

own cluster of markers of kingship, represent the social relations involved in them as the right ones, and claim on this basis to already possess the gadi. Nor was such a claim necessarily self-delusionary. To the extent that Dangis believed that there was only one gadi, one of the two was of course potentially a pretender. But it was never immediately clear who was the pretender, nor did it ever need to become clear. Through claims to markers, different claims to the gadi could coexist hostilely for very long, creating in effect almost different gadis.

Nor was it only claims to high positions like the gadi which coexisted hostilely, erupting occasionally into disputes. Because of the ubiquitous reach and irresolution of markers of kingship — after all, even ordinary Bhils received turbans, and a share, however nominal, of dues such as giras — disputes were pervasive amongst Bhils in general rather than only amongst senior bhauband. To the degree that every Bhil was a raja, to have not responded to provocations, especially when they came from a person not very much higher up on hierarchies, would have been to become that much less of a raja, and to accept a seriously traduced degree of honour and authority. Indeed, where the markers of kingship stopped, so did disputes. Thus Koknis, who were much less of rajas than the Bhils, were as colonial officials remarked far less given to 'interminable feuding'.[37]

THE POLITICS OF FORGETTING

The persistent emphasis on the inalienability of markers of kingship may also help us understand a curious lopsidedness of memory: while goth of dhum dwell on violent incidents, they rarely mention peaceful resolutions. And yet, these must evidently have occurred, for else Dangs would be a maelstrom of disputes. It would be inadequate to treat this lopsidedness of memory as merely one more manifestation of the truism that oral traditions come to be dominated by the more spectacular events, with the mundane dimensions erased. More to the point, involved in evocations of dhum is a distinctive politics not only of remembering, but also of forgetting.[38]

[37] Fenner to Robertson, March 1860, *BRO.DDR.DN 2.FN 9*. The British, predictably, attributed this difference between Koknis and Bhils to the former being higher up on a civilizational hierarchy.

[38] As Nietzsche recognized, forgetting plays as or more important a role as remembering in the construction of societies. See his 'On the advantages and disadvantages of history for life'. It is only recently that forgetting has come

Both remembering and forgetting were evident in nineteenth-century disputes. Dangis feared that disputes could always flare up into violent clashes, or could escalate. And sometimes they did. Devisinh did not consider all scores settled after killing Kerulsinh. Accompanied by around 200 or 300 followers, he attacked Trimbak naik, one of Kerulsinh's supporters.[39] It was because of this fear of getting into clashes that, during the standoff in Vasurna dang between Shendia and Bapu, many rajas refused to take sides — they remarked that it 'made them enemies'.[40] Even Koknis were pulled into disputes: clashing groups attacked or looted rivals' cultivators, trying to make them desert villages. A patil who helped Kerulsinh, Dadaji, was singled out for attack by Devisinh in 1849.[41]

Spurred by this fear of the escalation of violence, and by the desire to defuse challenges from rivals, bhauband regularly attempted to re-establish relations with their challengers. After having warded off Shendia's claim to the gadi of Vasurna, Bapu kuver and his bhauband offered Shendia some compensation, and persuaded him to formally support Bapu kuver's claim to the gadi.[42] We do not know what Shendia was offered. But other cases indicate that compensation usually took the form of markers of kingship. In 1851, after Daulat raja looted some of Kerulsinh's villages, Kerulsinh tried to arrive at an agreement. He promised to pay Daulat Rs 5 every month from his personal allowance if he would abstain from attacks on cultivators, not get drunk, or create other disturbances. He also offered Daulat a turban, a *shela* or shawl, a bullock and a female buffalo.[43]

These attempts to orchestrate forgetting were not necessarily successful in the short run. Both Daulat and Kerulsinh, for example, kept up low-level hostilities against each other, culminating in Kerulsinh's complaint which led to the imprisonment of Daulat in 1853, and later still in Daulat and Devisinh's killing of Kerulsinh. At best compensation could establish only an uneasy truce, one that could either crumble or solidify over the years. As for the long run, maybe that is best exemplified by looking at what nineteenth-century

---

to be explored in the social sciences as a theme. See Benedict Anderson, *Imagined communities: Reflections on the origins and spread of nationalism*, London, 1991, revised edition, ch. 11, for an extremely insightful discussion of forgetting in the construction of nations.

39 Trimbak naik to Coll., Kh., 6.11.1861, *BRO.DDR.DN 3.FN 13*.
40 Elphinstone to Secy., GoB, 14.5.1852, *BA.PD.1852.Vol 52.Comp 1415*.
41 Trial of Devisinh, *BA.PD.1850.Vol 50/5204.Comp 593*.
42 Elphinston to Secy., GoB, 14.5.1852, *BA.PD.1852.Vol 52.Comp 1415*.
43 Kerulsinh to Morriss, 13.4.1852, *BRO.DDR.DN 3.FN 6*.

disputes mean today. Narrations of many of these disputes today are rarely innocent. They are often part of an orchestration of remembering, especially important because many Dangis fear that unless such remembering is attempted, issues that they want to keep alive will be forgotten. These goth are told within very carefully constructed spaces of intimacy, for else they can trigger off an escalation of hostilities, or conversely not be adequate to the task of remembering. Of course, not all narration of disputes is this directly political. Often, especially when no group of bhauband claims direct affiliation to the figures about whom the goth are being told (and this happens often), they become part of a broad genre of stories about dhum which can be told to virtually any other Dangi.

Then there are those disputes which are remembered, but not so deliberately or publicly. These are often either early-twentieth-century incidents, or disputes that have been settled, but where normal relations between the two groups of bhauband have not yet been re-established. Memories of these disputes are thus a potent means of organizing hostility if relations between the two groups sour again. Yet tensions have become subdued enough for conscious rehearsals of these memories to be undesirable, or even disruptive.

Finally, many — in fact most — disputes are simply not remembered. Thus it is with Devisinh's hostility to Trimbak naik, or a late nineteenth-century clash between the Pimpri and the Vasurna chiefs over fishing rights.[44] Such extensive, maybe even complete, erasure is an indicator of the considerable success of the orchestration of forgetting. But forgetting, like remembering, is never complete. After all, involved in dhum were markers of kingship. In this context, there is often the fear that a rehearsal of old grievances and issues can foreground the inalienable nature of these markers, and thus re-ignite disputes. This is the main reason why vadils do not narrate any goth of dhum without considered attention to the audience — telling a goth to a wrong person could potentially heighten tensions. It was also why so many narrators responded sharply to my indiscriminate and enthusiastic narrating of stories I had learnt from the archives. Though I did not realize it in the early months, by narrating these stories I inadvertently often threatened to open up disputes that listeners had chosen to forget. For it is not only the narration of goth of dhum that is political — even the refusal to narrate or know them is a profoundly political act.

(12)

---

44 Elphinstone to Secy., GoB, 26.4.1852, *BA.PD.1852.Vol 42.Comp 1415.*

8

The Wildness of Koknis

'In moglai,' Jiva Kharsu said once, 'my vadils used to call them-selves Bhil.' Jiva Kharsu is a Kokni from one of the most powerful lineages in Dangs. Many of his vadils had been influential patils for the rajas of Ghadvi, Vasurna and Amala; some of them had been patils of the village of Ghadvi itself. Nor was Jiva Kharsu's remark unique. Many Koknis, from both comparable and much more ordinary backgrounds, were to say the same thing: their vadils had called themselves Bhil.

I do not know how widespread such renaming was in the Indian subcontinent in the eighteenth and nineteenth centuries — it has not been mentioned much by historians. Going by goth, it was very common in regions of western India where forest polities played any significant role at all. Both in Dangs and in surrounding areas, narrators repeatedly mention how, during Bhil raj, many com-munities — Koknis, Varlis, Naikras, Gamits, Valvis and Chaudaris amongst others — were called Bhils, and referred to themselves as such. Once alerted to this custom, we can find implicit parallels to it in nineteenth-century archival sources. The occasional reference in records to 'Gamit Bhils', 'Dhanka Bhils' or 'Kokni Bhils' can now be seen not as the result of ill-informed transcription by colonial officials but as the result of persons describing themselves as such.[1]

Yet there is something profoundly counter-intuitive about all of this, for it flies in the face of much that we have learnt to regard as 'natural' about caste. In simpler times, it was common to talk of Sanskritization (the adoption of Brahman values) or Rajputization (the adoption of Kshatriya values) as two related ways by which lower castes claimed higher status. Now such talk would rightly be regarded as far too simplistic, for lower castes were often ap-propriating upper caste values to challenge Brahmans and Rajputs, rather than simply adopting these values. Nevertheless, it is still taken as axiomatic that castes make claims to ritually higher status.

1 DCR.DN 1.FN 4Uc.

It is this commonsensical assumption that is challenged by claims to be Bhil. Jatis like Gamits, Chaudaris, Valvis or Koknis were ritually superior to Bhils. And in many ways, they stressed this superiority. Koknis, the largest community in Dangs, did not eat beef while Bhils did. While Bhils were willing to accept Kokni women or Kokni men into their community in case of marriages, Koknis were usually not willing to accept Bhil men married to Kokni women into their community, and only very reluctantly accepted Bhil women who had married Kokni men. Similarly, while Bhils accepted most prepared food from Koknis, Koknis refused to accept food from Bhils. When Kokni and Bhil men went hunting together, it was common for meat to be roasted over a fire so that utensils would not have to be shared.

Given all this, by calling themselves Bhil, they were accepting a lower caste position which they rejected in other contexts. Why should they have done this? This was because there was a distinctive discourse of wildness, of being jangli, a discourse that all these communities appropriated in different ways. Bhils were the single largest forest community in western India. This made the very name Bhil a ready marker of difference, covering all groups in the region which pursued those lifestyles and forms of political power of which Bhils were considered paradigmatic. In describing themselves as 'Kokni Bhils', Koknis laid claim to the wildness and political power of Bhil raj; they asserted a shared political identity with Bhils. If it were not such a clumsy and misleading neologism, one might even talk of Bhilization, and contrast this to those two other misleading names — Sanskritization and Rajputization. I say misleading because Koknis and other communities did not simply become part of the Bhil jati. Rather, they claimed to be Bhil in distinctively Kokni ways; they were simultaneously Koknis and Bhils. They infused the notion of being Bhil with novel meanings; they participated in Bhil wildness and Bhil raj in distinctive ways, even sometimes questioning Bhil enactments of these.

PARTICIPATION IN BHIL RAJ

In goth, one of the ways in which Koknis constituted Bhil raj was simply by introducing cultivation. At nights, the occasional good mimic parodies the older dialect of the Bhils to describe how they reacted to the first taste of cultivated food, as opposed to the wild food they had eaten so far.

'*Ui*, patil, what is this strange thing you have made. It tastes very good'.

'That is a *nagli bhakar*, rajasaheb'.

'Ui, patil, this tastes much better than the roots I eat. Ui, what is this you have made?

'That is rice, rajasaheb'.[2]

Here, then, Koknis are the moment of constitution of Bhil wildness; it is through their introduction of the contrastive element of cultivated food that Bhil wildness becomes visible, and comes to be seen as radically other.

The constitutive role of Koknis is stressed also in Lasu Jiva's goth of how his ancestors were brought into Dangs as the first Koknis.

> Our vadil [ancestor] was at Sindia [a village across the ghats in Khandesh]. At that time, there were no Koknis in Dangs, only naiks. The Ghadvi naik went, with a nagara [drum] and nishan [flag], to Sindia to get our vadil. The people at Sindia saw a large party and were frightened, saying that a *dhad* [raiding party] had come. There were seven brothers, and six of them ran away. Only our vadil Goru patil remained. Then the naik said, 'do not worry. I have not come to harm you. You are a *sonani chidi* [bird of gold] because you are a Kokni. I have come to take you to Dangs'. Then they came by foot-track to Dangs. At that time there were no horses here. At that time it was not Ghadvi raj, it was only a *naiki*. That night, the naiks made a roof and a hut of grass and teak leaves for the patil. The next morning all the naiks had a meeting. Goru patil went there, and said, 'Raja saheb, Ram Ram'. Before that, nobody would say ram ram in Dangs. With that, the naik became a raja. And the Koknis started cultivation in the Dangs.[3]

Central here are the juxtapositions which emphasize the Kokni role in constituting Bhil kingship. The period is marked by its ordinariness: the chiefs did not even have horses, that most elementary marker of kingship and authority. Also, there are no rajas, only naiks. But in descending the ghats from Khandesh, Goru patil transforms the situation. By addressing the naiks as 'Raja saheb, Ram Ram' (narrators accompany the salutation with a genuflection with folded palms) he effects the first transformation. He casts himself as politically subordinate, and thus initiates the conditions for the differentiated polity that is necessary for substantive authority; there can be no real chiefs amongst equals such as the bhauband, after all.

2 Soma Gangaji, 20.3.1991, Ghogli.
3 Lasu Jiva, 29.5.1990, Kotba. Bhils usually acknowledge the role of Koknis in bringing cultivation to Dangs.

It is the Kokni, both as a sonani chidi and as a subordinate, who gives Bhil raj many of its meanings.

In the nineteenth century, Koknis were central to Bhil raj most of all through their ability to create resources for a dang by cultivation. While many Koknis, maybe even the bulk of them, were doubtless almost as poor as the Bhils, it seems clear that prosperous Koknis outnumbered prosperous Bhils. The major reason for this was that the dahi which Koknis practised was more productive than Bhil khandad. Prosperous Koknis sometimes did so well that they employed Bhils during the agricultural season as labourers on their fields, paying them in grain.[4]

Because Koknis were so crucial to the prosperity of a dang, rivals often tried to drive them away from the territories of those bhauband with whom they had ongoing disputes. After his escape from the asylum, Devisinh forcibly carried off grain from several villages, causing eleven of them to be totally deserted. Several other villages were at least partially deserted because of his attacks. In one case, he carried off 12 heads of cattle from a Kokni patil, and in another case he carried off 20 heads of cattle. Similarly, in the late 1870s and early 1880s, when Daulat's sons, Chipat and Tikam, clashed with the bhauband who held the gadi, they carried away cattle from Koknis in villages controlled by their rivals.[5]

Crucial in creating prosperity for a dang was the patil, usually Kokni, who founded a village and managed it, collecting taxes from villagers for the Bhil chief, deciding who would cultivate where, how to attract more cultivators to the village or the dang, and when appropriate to abandon a village. The patils were often quite 'well-to-do men, with good cattle and fairly comfortable homesteads'.[6] Being a patil involved working closely with Bhil chiefs.

We are originally from Ladgaon, in Surgana. Navsia Chaudari stayed at Ladgaon. His wife died, and there was a lot of apda [poverty]. With only a blanket he left the place and wandered around. He reached Rauchond [a village in Amala Dangs]. Then Ratansinh raja told him 'Pipalghodi has become deserted, so go and settle there. Do the patilki at Pipalghodi. I will find a wife for you here' [in Amala]. The raja gave him Rs 10. He went with the money, found a wife in Borkhal, and married her with the money, spending Rs 5 on liquor. After this he went to Rauchond, and the

---

4 KDG, p. 601.
5 BRO.DDR.DN 2.FN 10; KPAAR, 1880–1, BA.PD.1881.Vol 73.Comp 1518.
6 KPAAR, 1888–9, BA.PD.1890.Vol 122.Comp 205.

raja gave him *sirpav* and pagdi, and then he went to Pipalghodi as the patil. He brought people from Ladgaon and Rauchond, and populated the village. Slowly, it had five houses. And now, it has thirty houses of Chaudaris.[7]

Ratansinh raja's actions were comprehensive, giving Navsia the money to marry, and a shawl and turban to incorporate him into the authority of Bhil raj. Such practices were often part of the establishment of a village. Bhil rajas would install, with appropriate rituals, a flag at the site of the village, and would appoint as patil a person who could persuade cultivators to settle on the spot.[8] From the point of view of Bhil chiefs, effective patils could not only create resources in a dang; they could also provide substantial resources from their own reserves at short notice to the chiefs. Also, as relatively recent migrants from the plains, many Kokni patils were perceived as better equipped in helping the chiefs deal with plains authorities.

Patils were often as and sometimes more powerful than even senior bhauband. In a striking parallel with Bhils, a patil did not have to pay revenue on the land he cultivated. Like the bhauband, he was often given a pagdi, and a sirpav (set of clothes) by the chiefs. The patils also adjudicated disputes and shared in the punitive powers of the rajas. In Chakdara village, out of a fine of a goat and Rs 6 imposed on a rapist by a Ghadvi chief, the goat was given to the patil. Furthermore, some especially important patils received a share of the lease amounts that were paid to the rajas. In Amala, three patils had been assigned a *khuti* or royalty. Such khuti patils were expected to help the chiefs in administering their territory and were often amongst the closest advisors of the principal Bhil chiefs, far more powerful and respected than most bhauband.[9] Records indicate that Dadaji patil, the principal advisor to the Ghadvi chief Kerulsinh, was a figure of this sort. After the death of Kerulsinh's father Udesinh, Dadaji played a crucial role in persuading British representatives to accept Kerulsinh's claims to the gadi instead of Devisinh's. Again, in 1849, when Kerulsinh had complaints to make against Devisinh, Dadaji was one of those who accompanied him to Pimpalner. At Pimpalner, Devisinh singled him

---

[7] Tanu Kalu patil, Pipalghodi, 28.5.1990.

[8] Bapu Purshottam to Coll., Kh.,14.3.1874, *BA.PD.1874.Vol 109.Comp 619*.

[9] Report on the future administration of the Dangs. *BA.RD.1902.Vol 107. Comp 949, Part II*; *DBD*, II, pp. 6, 66; Testimony of Jania Manjia, *BA.PD.1847. Vol 21/1902.Comp 162*; *FRBP*, 1856–7 to 1859–60, p. 40; Statement of Gulalsinh Kamansinh, *BRO.DDR.DN 6.FN 34*; *KDG*, pp. 604–6.

out for an attack. In compensation, Kerulsinh later granted Dadaji a jagir of Jamnia village, in addition to the village of Kakadvihir which he already held.[10]

Goth by Dadaji patil's descendants tell a slightly different version. According to them, he had gone with Kerulsinh raja to fight in a battle near Pimpalner. At night, however, Kerulsinh in a drunken fit of anger took out his sword and brought it down on Dadaji's head. The powerful blow sliced through the many folds of the large turban that Dadaji patil was wearing and inflicted a deep scalp wound. The next day, when Kerulsinh saw the wound, he was remorseful. He gave Kakadvihir and Jamnia to Dadaji patil in jagir as compensation for this.[11] Here, then, the clash with Devisinh is entirely excised, maybe because of the tensions with Devisinh's group of bhauband that it involves.

It would be seriously mistaken to consider the power of prosperous Koknis or patils as an economic power that can be contrasted with the political power of the senior bhauband. Wealth was not, in this context, an abstract carrier of power. True, wealth and prosperity always carried connotations of power, but the very generation of the wealth of Koknis was sustained and made possible by support from senior Bhil chiefs. In this very important sense, Kokni prosperity was not opposed to Bhil raj but derived from participation in Bhil raj.

Even the role of more ordinary Koknis in Bhil kingship may not have been insignificant. There was their participation in Bhil power through proximity to the patil. Many Koknis in a village were kin of the patil, having been invited by him to settle there. In addition, it is likely (though not clear) that even if Bhils were the principal raiders, at least some Koknis participated in Bhil raids on plains.[12] These forms of participation in Bhil authority must have provided one of the most important senses in which Koknis could call themselves Bhils.

10 Trial of Devisinh, *BA.PD.1850.Vol 38/2404.Comp 593*; Case III, *BRO.DDR. DN 6.FN 34.*

11 I learnt this account from the descendants of Dadaji patil in Jamnia on 3.4.1991. A slightly different version was told to me at Kakadvihir, where another line of descendants resides.

12 There is an intriguing reference to 'large numbers' of Koknis in a band of Bhil raiders in 1819. See *DCR.DN 4.FN 4Uc*. However, most other records mention only Bhils as raiders. Also, Kokni narrators are emphatic that raiding was a Bhil activity; some concede the possibility that their vadils may have participated in Bhil raids, but say that my reference is the first they have heard of it.

Subordinating Koknis

Yet if Koknis called themselves Bhils, such an appropriation of the word could be problematic for both Bhils and Koknis. For many ordinary Bhils, Bhil raj was about a kingship in which Bhils participated to the exclusion of other communities. It was this meaning, after all, which was acknowledged in their description as rajas, or in the exemption of all Bhils from taxes even while ordinary Koknis, or members of other communities, had to pay taxes.[13] And Kokni participation threatened to obliterate this meaning of Bhil raj, with prosperous Koknis exercising considerable power over ordinary Bhils.

In this context, Bhils often tried to assert other meanings of Bhil raj, ones that excluded Koknis and enacted Kokni subordination. For senior bhauband, the subordination was enacted most of all in the many *kayda* or levies which provided the means by which they cultivated. Under the *aut kayda*, each Kokni cultivator had to go with his plough to the fields of the raja or local jagirdar for a specified period and till them. There was also the *bigar kayda*: Koknis would work on the rajas' fields for a specified period during different agricultural operations, such as sowing, transplantation, weeding, and reaping. The amount of bigar or unpaid labour that was taken appears to have varied: eleven days in the Pimpri area, eight in the Ghadvi region, and six around Chinchli–Gadad. During bigar, the Koknis would be paid nothing, but would be given meals.

But for more ordinary Bhils, these levies were scarcely an enactment of their dominance over Koknis — they were almost as prone to be drafted for work under the bigar kayda as ordinary Koknis; and far more so than Kokni patils. For these Bhils, the most important enactment of their power came in the collection of levies and taxes from Koknis. There was the *halpatti* or plough tax, levied directly, in cash or kind, on cultivation: those who cultivated by hand paid Rs 2-8-0 to the local chief and those who used a plough paid five rupees.[14] Then there were the *nau kayda* or nine levies, which stipulated how much grain, flour, clarified butter, chickens or other items each cultivator should supply to the chiefs.[15]

What made these levies an enactment of Kokni subordination was the way they were collected — through *ikki khavana*, a phrase

---

[13] Report of a march through Dangs, March 1867, *BRO.DDR.DN 3.FN 12*

[14] 'Proposals for the improvement . . . Dangs forests', *BA.RD.1902.Vol 107. Comp 949, Part II.*

[15] For a detailed account of the nau kayda, see my 'A forest polity', pp. 163ff.

which in this context can be translated as 'demand/ask and eat'. In the late nineteenth century, ikki khavana came in for criticism from colonial officials: it seemed to them that Bhils were only too ready 'to importune or to demand at the arrow's point from their more industrious neighbours the Kocanas their daily meal'.[16] But what appeared like importuning to colonial officials was actually part of a complex process of tax collection. Collections were made not directly by the principal chief, but by those members of the bhauband who held rights over the specific village. The bhauband would venture out to collect kayda, accompanied by a large number of followers, mostly Bhils, but also some of the poorer Koknis. The kayda were often paid by the patil in kind as grain, and provided a source of subsistence to the naik and his Bhil followers for quite some time. A visit to a village for collecting kayda would usually last two or three days, during which period the group camped outside the village, and was fed and provided liquor by the patil. Sometimes, the group would also during this time make demands of other villagers — both Bhils and Koknis.[17]

There can be no doubt that for poor Bhils (amongst whom most of the bhauband numbered), ikki khavana was a major source of subsistence during difficult months.[18] By participating in expeditions for ikki khavana to several villages, subsistence for a significant portion of those times could be taken care of. But in our context, possibly what was important was the subordination of Kokni patils that was staged in ikki khavana. The patils, themselves exempt from taxation, were for the duration of the visit subordinate to even ordinary Bhils in the group — the very Bhils whom the patils usually exercised authority over. In this sense, one might say, ikki khavana was a moment when the Bhil enactment of Bhil raj was visibly dominant over the Kokni enactment of Bhil raj. Indeed, ikki khavana was considered part of the exercise of kingship, and Bhils believed they had a right to resort to it. Many major Bhil chiefs often encouraged or at least tolerated ikki khavana by junior

16 Fenner to Robertson, March 1860, *BRO.DDR.DN 2.FN 9.*

17 FDO to Coll., Kh.,1.9.1891, *BA.RD.1892.Vol 144.Comp 948*; KPAAR, 1888–9, *BA.PD.1890. Vol 122. Comp 205*; *BA.PD.1852.Vol 42.Comp 1415*. Other taxes also provided occasions for groups of Bhils to visit villages: there was one on marriage, another on divorce, and a third when a suspected witch was discovered in a village. See KPAAR, 1888–9, *BA.PD.1890. Vol 122.Comp 205.*

18 Annual Report, 1848, *BRO.DDR.DN 1.FN 2*; Kerulsinh to Morriss, 13.4.1852, *BRO.DDR.DN 2.FN 6*; Kerulsinh to Coll., Kh., 3.6.1861, *BRO.DDR.DN 2.FN 10*; *BA.PD.1882.Vol 60.Comp 1452* and *BA.PD.1890.Vol 90.Comp 205.*

bhauband. When some Koknis complained to the Deher chief about Bhils who had looted nagli from them, he remarked that they did it only because they were hungry.[19]

Yet ikki khavana could also be problematic and counterproductive. For example, Ghadvi and Deher were largely deserted by the late 1880s because their chiefs did not check ikki khavana.[20] Given the plenitude of land and the ease of mobility, Koknis faced with excessive exactions only too easily shifted to another dang where Bhil enactments of Bhil raj were not so clearly dominant over Kokni enactments of it, or over Kokni ways of being Bhil. Maybe because of this potential to move, ikki khavana does not seem to have been enacted too forcefully. There is the telling fact that during the later half of the nineteenth century, a large number of Koknis preferred to migrate to Dangs rather than stay in regions which had introduced British-inspired revenue settlements. Quite evidently, ikki khavana was more than compensated for by the low taxes and abundance of land and grazing area that the chiefs provided for the Kokni enactment of Bhil raj.

The Ambivalences of Wildness

While one source of ambivalence in relations between Koknis and Bhils involved the feared excessiveness of Kokni claims to be Bhil, and Kokni participation in Bhil raj, the other source, paradoxically enough, was often the precise opposite — a suspected Kokni questioning of Bhil raj.

> At Pipalghodi, there was Ghobria patil. He had populated a very large village. There were *annwada* [people with grains] and *paihawada* [people with money] in the village. He did not fear anyone. If the rajas came, he would not give them anything. He did not get on well with anybody, and would not give anything to beggars, or even on loan to people. The rajas went there several times, but were not given anything.
>
> When Rajhans raja came to Pipalghodi, Ghobria patil said, 'the *Bhilda* [derogatory form of Bhil] has come. Get *sida* [provisions] for him'. The raja came and told his rani, Jegi rani, 'he called me Bhilda. In all the other villages, they call me raja'. Then Jegi rani sat on a horse and came to Pipalghodi. She tied the horse at a mango tree — it was standing till recently — and went with a

[19] Remarks by Mr Muller, 27.4.1868, *BRO.DDR.DN 3.FN 12*; Report of a march through Dangs, March 1867, *BRO.DDR.DN 3.FN 12*.
[20] KPAAR, 1888–9, *BA.PD.1890.Vol 122.Comp 205*.

paltan [platoon] to the house of Ghobria patil. The whole paltan stopped outside the house, and the sipai said, 'the rani has come'. Then Ghobria patil said, '*Bhilin ani, Bhilin ani,* [The Bhil woman has come, the Bhil woman has come] give her sida'. Then she got the sipai to catch him, and put a bit in his mouth. She sat on him and said *chal ghoda* [come, horse], and went with him. She got off, and told the sipai to tie her horse, and the patil was tied up. She gave stones from the riverbed to the patil to eat. Then they all drank *daru* from the shop, and then took him back. Then she told the patil, 'you do not have the standing to be a patil'. Three days later, he died [from the dosh or ill-fortune of being ridden by a woman].

He had seven sons. They thought, 'if the patil was not safe, how can we carry on?' Two of them went and found a new place. Then they put their Maruti, Vagdev and other gods in a hole and buried it. Within one night, they left with all the grains and the family for some other place. Then the village became deserted.[21]

I have already shown how the manner of Ghobria's death is indicative of the power of women in Bhil raj. Here I pursue another parallel — the relationship between Koknis and Bhils that it hints at. Towards this end, consider a similar incident in the nineteenth century. In 1859, two Koknis, Hulia, a patil, and Rupji, were going with a Bhil, Chumbhar, to the village Chinchli to consult a bhagat. En route, they stopped at a village, where the patil gave Chumbhar some rice since he was one of the local raja's men. They went on, only to halt later at a Parsi's liquor shop near the village Panaganer. Chumbhar exchanged his rice for some liquor, and the three settled down to drink. Dalpat kuver, one of the Vasurna bhauband, happened to come by around that/time with about twelve or fifteen others. Hulia, Rupji and others offered salutations to Dalpat, saying 'Ram Ram'. Hulia patil then offered some liquor to Dalpat kuver, but the Parsi's wife came out and said 'you three drink what you have purchased and Dulput Rajah can have as much as he likes from me'. Dalpat was seated on a cot and given liquor. After some time, Hulia patil again offered some liquor to Dalpat raja. At this Rupji asked, 'why do you give those black-faced fellows liquor?' This led to a scuffle, in which the Bhils fell on Rupji angrily, saying, 'Rupji has made money at Rambaj and has gone to live at Pimpri, so let us give him a bellyful of liquor' (a phrase which the records translate as a beating).[22]

21 Tanu Kalu patil, 28.5.1990, Pipalghodi.
22 Case II of 1859, *BA.PD.1859.Vol 92.Comp 589.*

It may be too easy a reading to view these two incidents as the manifestation of a ritual superiority that was always at odds with Bhil raj, that had always been at least a kind of hidden transcript challenging Bhil raj but becomes visible to us only occasionally.[23] First, this takes for granted the prior, separable, and already constituted nature of ritual superiority. But this was hardly the case. As I have already suggested, in claiming to be Bhil, Koknis were not usually seeking to erase the distance between Kokni and Bhil. While they were willing to appropriate the wildness of being Bhil, they also wished to distance themselves from aspects of it — hence the abjuring of beef, the greater commitment to agriculture, and so on. Yet there was always the danger of becoming Bhil, of the distance actually being erased. Lifestyles, after all, were quite mixed up with Bhils. Like Bhils, Koknis were involved in gathering, fishing and hunting. Even dahi, though closer to settled agriculture than khandad, was still also very different from settled agriculture. This kind of blurring of jatis led to at least some Koknis not just claiming to be Bhils, but actually becoming part of the Bhil jati. And Bhils were quite willing to accept persons from other jatis.[24] Thus, the very strict Kokni dining and pollution taboos may not have been so much an expression of an already existing distance between Koknis and Bhils but part of concerted attempts to create that distance, to shore up fragile, crumbling boundaries. Even for more powerful Koknis like Hulia or Ghobria, participation in Bhil raj remained essential: their ritual and economic power was made possible by Bhil raj rather than being prior or separable from it. In this context, their actions and remarks are best understood as trying, in very tenuous and even hesitant ways, to constitute that ritual superiority as prior and separable.

Second, this reading presumes that Kokni ritual superiority, when so constituted, had meanings that were always at least implicitly opposed to Bhil raj, or to subordination to lower castes. Such an understanding, though maybe appropriate for later periods, is unhelpful in this context, when after all Koknis could call themselves

[23] The argument about hidden transcripts is of course developed most explicitly by James Scott in his *Domination and the arts of resistance: Hidden transcripts,* New Haven, 1990. For a persuasive critique of Scott, one which also has implications for the notion of hidden transcripts, see Timothy Mitchell, 'Everyday metaphors of power', *Theory and Society,* vol. 19, 1990, p. 545.

[24] R.E. Enthoven, *The tribes and castes of Bombay,* Bombay, 1975 (1920), vol. 1, p. 156; Tanu Kalu patil, 28.5.1990, Pipalghodi; Khandu Ravji, 4.5.1990, Vakaria.

Bhils. Quite evidently, two kinds of readings of ritual superiority were possible. One of these, maybe the more influential one, acknowledged Bhil raj and participated in it. Though it sometimes seemed to threaten the distance between Kokni and Bhil, this was not necessarily always the case. And with this kind of ritual superiority, the bhauband were quite comfortable. When the powerful Ghadvi chief Daulat raja raped a (Bhil) woman in the house of a Kokni, he was charged amongst other things with polluting the house and had to compensate the Kokni for the cost of the feast the latter had to give to the Kokni community to be accepted back.[25] He quite willingly accepted that charge and agreed to pay the fine.

What the bhauband were hostile to, in other words, was not ritual superiority per se but a challenge to Bhil raj that they felt was sometimes enacted by invoking ritual superiority. Such superiority was evidently invoked in the two incidents above — 'Bhilda ani, Bhilda ani' and those 'black-faced fellows'. When such suspicions existed, even normally innocuous acts could become loaded. Kokni patils often had nagaras, and these were played at marriages or other collective gatherings with no problems. But in at least one case where relations were already tense with the Kokni patil of Lavariya village in Vasurna, bhauband reacted sharply.

> There was a big nagara at Lavariya, so big that you could hear it over the hills. It was with some Koknis, I don't know who. Once, when they played it, it was heard in Vasurna. The bhauband heard it, and they said, 'who is this that plays the nagara so loudly?' They came to Lavariya and they tore off the hide of the nagara, and used its body to cook a cow in.[26]

Here obviously, the transgression lay in having a nagara big enough to be heard till the village of Vasurna, where the rajas stayed. The reaction was an assertion of Bhil raj that made the nagara unusable not only by tearing away the hide but by eating beef in it — thus striking specifically at the ritual superiority of the Koknis which the bhauband suspected lay behind the possession and playing of such a nagara.

(20)

25 Trial of Daulat, *BRO.DDR.DN 2.FN 6.*
26 Madho Bhivsan, 25.4.1990, Nadagkhadi.

9

Celebrating Raids and Desolation

Bhil raj and moglai were times when Bhils used to raid the desh, and when they used to collect from plains powers a due called giras. The plains powers named depend on the region where narrators are from. Those from northern, eastern, and southern Dangs mention their neighbours — the Gaekwads of Baroda, and the deshmukh of Baglan, who was the representative in the region of the Peshwa-controlled district of Khandesh. Those from western Dangs are more likely to mention their neighbours, the Gaekwads and Maharaja of Vansda; they often do not even know of the deshmukh.

In travellers' and archival accounts of the eighteenth or early nineteenth century too, raids or dhad by forest polities like Dangis loom large, almost overwhelmingly so since these polities were usually written about only when they raided. Bhils, Bhilalas, Gamits, and other forest communities regularly attacked plains villages, or looted travelling merchants. Complaints about this echoed throughout western and central India — in Udaipur, Gujarat, Khandesh, and the Nizam's territories.

In older writings, relationships between forest polities and surrounding societies were often seen as fundamentally antagonistic, with raids just the most dramatic expression of this antagonism. Now such simplistic understandings are no longer adequate. Recent writings have stressed the highly complex relationships of interdependence between forest polities and Maratha powers in eighteenth-century western India. They have emphasized how these states were also involved in raiding, and in plunder as a form of tax collection.[1]

---

[1] Amongst the works which stress this complex relationship are Stewart Gordon, *Marathas, marauders and state formation in the eighteenth century*, Delhi, 1994; Sumit Guha, 'Lords of the land versus kings of the forest: Conflict and collaboration in peninsular India, c. 1500–1981', unpublished paper, 1995; and his 'Forest polities and agrarian empires: The Khandesh Bhils, c. 1700–1850', *Indian Economic and Social History Review*, vol. 33, no. 2, 1996; Andre

It is precisely the point about interdependence that I would like to take further. Interdependence by itself does not imply any particular sort of discourse. But there is often the tendency, maybe through force of habit, to ascribe meanings to this interdependence which privilege growth and state-making. Now, this is not wrong, but it is certainly partial. Articulated in this interdependence was also an aesthetics and politics of wildness, one in which eighteenth- and early-nineteenth-century plains powers participated to a significant degree. And this aesthetics and politics problematizes narratives around growth or state-making, for it suggests that the deep involvement of plains powers in raids and other similar activities seem so clearly directed towards the building of centralized states only because of our post-facto teleologies. During the period itself, these activities may have been also about an enactment of wildness not very different from that which Dangi chiefs were involved in.

Many goth dwell on the plains powers with whom Dangi chiefs had relations.

> The deshmukh was a *Bahman* [Brahman]. He was the raja of Dangs. He came to Dangs to collect his haks. The rajas did not know anything and the Rao would look after their affairs. He kept all the sikka-daftar [seals and records] of the rajas.[2]

The deshmukh did actually handle at least some of the writing that was done in non-literate Dangi society. The late-eighteenth-century copperplate inscription recording the grant of the village of Vakaria, for example, was prepared under his instructions. In other stories he is mentioned as keeping all the maps of Dangs. That he should be remembered thus suggests that a considerable proportion of his power has been attributed in retrospect to his familiarity with the powerful technology of writing. Maybe the persistence of this association also has to do with his having been a Brahman, a caste associated in much Dangi thought with power derived through their knowledge of writing.

Memories of the Gaekwads of Baroda are far more common.

Wink, *Land and sovereignty*, Cambridge, 1986; Chris Bayly, *Indian society and the making of the British empire*, Cambridge, 1988; Chetan Singh, 'Conformity and conflict: Tribes and the agrarian system of Mughal India', *Indian Economic and Social History Review*, vol. 25, no. 3, 1988, pp. 319–40; and his 'Forests, pastoralists and agrarian society in Mughal India' in David Arnold and Rama-chandra Guha (eds), *Nature, culture, imperialism: Essays on the environmental history of South Asia*, Delhi, 1994.

2 Khandu Ravji, 2.5.1990, Vakaria.

Often, these memories have to do with the role they played in Dangi clashes, such as that between the Kadmal and Ghadvi bhauband. One goth of this clash was narrated in Chapter 6. It told of how the Ghadvi queen Dasari rani secured Gaekwadi assistance against Gondu raja of the Kadmal bhauband after the latter killed her husband. In return for this assistance, she agreed to fly the Gaekwadi flag at Ghadvi.[3] For descendants of the Ghadvi lineage today, the flying of the flag is a problematic event. The close ties with the Gaekwads that it implies are valued — bhauband often describe their ancestors as bhai-pagdi to the Gaekwads, or brothers related through the exchange of turbans. Still, such accretions were double-edged. Already by the late nineteenth century, many Bhils felt hostile about the flag. Now, in some goth, Silput raja and the Gaekwads had a battle because of the flag.

> Then the flag began to be hoisted. First, it was hoisted near Sajupada, and then at the hill near Nilsakia [both villages in the former Ghadvi dang]. There were two teak trees there. One flag was put on one tree, and the other [the Ghadvi flag] on the other. With that, Ghadvi raj began to be pulled into Gaekwadi raj.
>
> Silput raja said, 'the Gaekwad has taken our raj. What do we do?' He told Suklia naik [his karbhari both in goth and in colonial records] 'Get ready with me for a fight'. Neither bullets nor arrows could hurt Silput raja or Suklia naik. Silput was on his horse, whose name I do not remember, and Suklia on his horse. They both went to the banks of the Narmada. There the Baduda sarkar also came, and a battle took place. Earlier, the raja had broken the flag. The battle went on for two hours. On one side of the river was the Gaekwadi paltan and on the other side were Silput and Suklia. Every day they would fight for two hours. This went on for ten days, or maybe a month.
>
> Then Suklia naik said to Silput raja, 'We have been fighting for very long. Now I want to go home'. Silput said, 'Do not go. Do not go home'. But Suklia naik did not listen, and went home.
>
> His wife said, 'Stay tonight, and go tomorrow'. The next morning, he washed and left.
>
> Silput raja told him, 'now do not come to the battlefield. You have slept with your wife, and are impure. Do not come to the battlefield, for you will not succeed'.
>
> But Suklia naik did not listen. He went for the battle. A bullet

---

[3] Descendants of the family of Gondu raja sometimes tell a very different version of this goth, stressing how Gaekwadi officials wiped out their ancestors. It is from this catastrophe that they trace the decline of their power, and the fact that they are not today on the official list of fourteen rajas and naiks (about which more in Chapter 16). Gajesinh Monsu, 26.4.1990, Kadmal.

hit him. Silput raja tied Suklia to his horse and sent the horse to Ghadvi. Then the raja stood alone against the Gaekwad. In the fighting, the Gaekwad defeated Silput. Silput was made prisoner and taken to Baduda.

There the Gaekwad gave him a poisoned bidi. But Silput had been warned, and he did not smoke or eat. Later, he escaped from Baduda, got a horse, and rode back to Ghadvi. And so Ghadvi raj stopped being pulled into Gaekwad raj.[4]

Giras is also often treated as an indicator of the political power of the chiefs. This power is emphasized in accounts by the Pimpri bhauband about the giras their ancestors collected from the raja of Vansda to their west:

> We helped Partapsinh raja of Vansda in a war, and he gave Trimbak raja an elephant in return. In addition, he was also given a giras of Rs 250 from Vansda. Our vadils went to Vansda for collecting giras around Dusshera. They would stay in Vansda for eight to ten days, and all their needs would be taken care of by the Vansda Maharaja during that time.[5]

Though records do not mention how he came by it, Trimbak raja did possess an elephant in the late nineteenth century, a very grand means of transport for Dangs.[6] Anyhow, to represent it as a gift along with giras, is to claim an especially strong alliance with Vansda. (And the alliance was important to the Vansda rajas too: after independence, they paid till the 1970s out of their personal allowance a token giras payment to the Pimpri bhauband.)

The foregrounding of giras and dhad also has to do with their association with wildness. The wildness of raids is explicitly acknowledged: they are often attributed to vadils or ancestors having been jangli. In a similar vein, goth tell of how, till the 1940s, and maybe even the 1960s,

> Every year, there would be sent to Songadh and Baroda five pots of water from Bokarvihir, five baskets of the *umbar* fruit from Donumbria, five baskets of the *tembrun* fruit from Divantembrun and five baskets of the *payar* fruit from Kahapayar. In acknowledgement of this, the Ghadvi raja was given his giras every year by the Gaekwadi sarkar.[7]

4 Linga Partam, 30.3.1990, Ghavria.
5 Indarsinh Dhanorsinh, 14.4.1990, Pimpri.
6 *BA.RD.1892.Vol 144.Comp 948.*
7 Raisinh Gondusar, 7.4.1990, Jamulvihir. As noted earlier in Chapter 4, villages are here named after the trees or other physical features dominant around them. There are not too many umbar trees around Donumbria now,

It is surely suggestive that so many items sent were wild, and associated with forests: after all, it would have been quite possible to send the shawls, sets of clothes or turbans that were more conventional gifts amongst both the chiefs and Gaekwadi officials. By deliberately choosing products that carried connotations of being jangli, perhaps the chiefs were representing themselves as wild.

This wildness made for the distinctive power of the dang.

> Our vadil [ancestors] would go from here to Khandesh, leaving their wives and children at home. The naik would lead the band, and they would go and raid a village, and come back with cattle, grain, and utensils. At that time, it was Bhil raj in Dangs, and so nobody could follow them here.[8]

The details of how each giras right had been acquired, or which villages were raided and why — these are no longer narrated, though they were as late as the early twentieth century. These have long ceased to have relevance for Dangis: as Chapter 11 argues, raids were brought to an end by the British by the 1830s, and the nature of giras was fundamentally transformed. Because raids were extinguished with the coming of mandini, they are now amongst the most compressed and evocative markers of all that was involved in moglai and Bhil raj.

BHILS AND MARATHA POWER

Bhil relationships with Maratha powers changed in dramatic ways over the centuries. In the seventeenth century, the Maratha founder-chief Shivaji's armies had thousands of Bhils and other forest communities, and these communities played a major role in the consolidation of Maratha power. In the eighteenth century, however, as the Marathas ceased to levy tribute and instead attempted a settled government, and as 'Brahmanical attitudes' became 'increasingly rigid', relationships with forest dwellers were renegotiated in the three major Maratha centralized states of the region — those of the Peshwa, the Gaekwads, and the Holkars. In the territories of central India held by the Holkars, for example, Ahilyabai Holkar successfully adopted a series of measures which

---

nor any tembrun near Divantembrun. When there were, these and the other fruits were prized across Dangs for their flavour, as was the water from Bokarvihir for its sweetness. See also Khanapurkar, 'The aborigines of south Gujarat', vol. I, p. 106.

[8] Boodal Ulsya, 5.4.1990, Sajpuada.

curbed raids and extended settled cultivation. There were efforts to follow a similar policy in the Peshwa-controlled regions of Khandesh. Here, Maratha officials sought to control raids, primarily through agreements with the chiefs that granted them rights to collect dues from passes they controlled, and recognized their rights in Maratha villages. In 1789–90, after the fort of Kanhera had been captured back from some Khandesh Bhil chiefs, an agreement was arrived at by which these Bhils agreed to leave their forest and hill residences and settle down in plains villages and perform the duties of *jagalias* or watchmen. While doing such duty, they were to use only arrows, and not carry swords or guns. They would also wear around their necks a packet bearing the seal of the sarkar, and those not wearing such a packet would be punished. In return, all existing Bhil haks or rights would be protected.[9]

The agreements were combined with the use of force. One mode of control involved setting up a chain of armed outposts along the foothills at times when Bhil raids were particularly high, as for example between Ajanta and Kasarbari in Khandesh between 1776 and 1777. These outposts as well as additional soldiers were financed by a *Bhil-patti* or Bhil-tax, levied on the inhabitants of the area in addition to other land revenue. Measures could be tougher too. Bhils in general were prohibited from living in the plains around Ajanta in the late eighteenth century after they were suspected of helping hill Bhils in raids. Those Bhils suspected of being involved in raids were severely punished.

Even at their most effective, these measures did not entirely stop raids. Bhil chiefs occasionally raided Maratha areas, they were often drawn on for support by rival Maratha factions, and their employment of Makranis or professional soldiers continued to be a source of tension to the new centralized Maratha states. And sometimes these raids became very extensive, as during the time between 1750 and 1753, when internal rebellions, drought and war combined to weaken the Peshwa's authority over Khandesh. During this period, raids by Bhil chiefs from the hills increased, and large cultivated areas were abandoned. But the Peshwa's control was later re-established through forces sent in to crush the rebellion and put down the raiding Bhil chiefs.[10]

9 This paragraph and the next are based on B.A. Saletore, 'The Bhils of western India', and Sumit Guha, 'Forest polities and agrarian empires', *Indian Economic and Social History Review*, vol. 33, no. 2, 1996.
10 Gordon, *The Marathas*, Cambridge, 1993, pp. 108ff.

A more profound challenge to the authority of the centralized Peshwai state in Khandesh came in the late eighteenth and early nineteenth centuries. This was in part a fall-out of disputes amongst Maratha chiefs, the Ahmadnagar Nizam and, indirectly, colonial involvement with the Maratha states.[11] The conflicts eventually led to the virtual extinction of the Peshwa's authority by the British in 1803, and its formal extinction in 1818. In Khandesh, raids by Pindaris, or irregular unpaid troops maintained by various Maratha chiefs, increased dramatically in the 1790s, as did Bhil raids. In 1802, Khandesh was ravaged by the army of the Maratha chief, Yesh-wantrao Holkar, and this was followed by the famine of 1803–4, which resulted in many cultivators migrating to Gujarat. With the authority of the Peshwas at Poona under siege because of other conflicts, they could not spare resources to bring it back under control as had been done in the 1750s. So raids by Bhils and Pindaris on village continued with snowballing effect. When Khandesh came under the British in 1818, only around 1836 of the 3492 former villages were populated, and the sites of 97 villages could not even be remembered.[12]

RAIDS AND THE INNER FRONTIER

How should we understand the Bhil raids? One kind of narrative, indeed the one that pervades most writings, has centred around the growth of state power. It has seen times of settled agriculture as indicative of a growing Maratha power, and raids as indicative of a Bhil power that disrupted settled agriculture on occasion. With the consolidation of nineteenth-century colonial rule, tendencies towards the emergence of centralized state power, already inherent in eighteenth-century polities such as those of the Marathas, were brought to fruition.

In this kind of narrative, understandings of areas such as those where Bhils were dominant are framed by the metaphor, implicit or explicit, of the inner frontier. Here, the inner frontier denotes areas beyond the effective political governance of large centralized states.

---

[11] See *KDG*, pp. 250ff for a brief background to developments in late-eighteenth-century Khandesh.

[12] For accounts, see A.M. Deshpande, *John Briggs in Maharashtra: A study of district administration under early British rule*, New Delhi, 1987, p. 124; Government of Bombay, *Gazetteer of the Bombay Presidency, Vol. 16, Nasik* (henceforth *NDG*), Bombay, 1883, pp. 193ff.

In the Indian context, the inner frontier has been depicted as part of a ragged and oscillating edge just beyond the control of the centralized states.[13] Further, because of an understanding of the inner frontier as simply an area within the ambit but beyond the effective governance of large centralized states, colonial intervention can be seen as taming the inner frontier, as bringing it under control, as finally completing the growth of large centralized states, and completing the task of subordinating communities like Bhils.[14]

The explanatory power of this kind of narrative seems undeniable. Bhil chiefs were often less committed to settled agriculture than eighteenth-century Peshwa officials or local Maratha chiefs. There was considerable hostility to Bhils amongst many Peshwa officials — if nothing else, the widespread Bhil contempt and antipathy for Brahmans would have been difficult to take for a Brahman-dominated state. And even in many smaller Rajput states, there were signs of a distancing from Bhils in the late eighteenth century, with some Rajput chiefs trying to exclude Bhils from the coronation ceremonies with which they had been formerly associated.[15]

Nevertheless, it may be too hasty to assimilate all this into narratives about the emergence of centralized Maratha states or about the growing marginality of Bhils. The aesthetics and politics of wildness was so intertwined with these developments that an interpretation which focuses only on the emergence of a centralized state runs the risk of being whiggish, of privileging in its readings of the past those differences which were to become important after the consolidation of colonial rule. Bhil chiefs, I suggest, were often as powerful in times of 'peace' as in those of 'disturbance'. The Maratha 'peace' that extended settled agriculture was not only about the suppression of Bhil power but also about its recognition in a particular way — through the payment of dues or haks, and acknowledgement of Bhil sovereignty. Similarly, an increase in raids did not signify a blanket decline of Maratha power. In the

13 J.C. Heesterman, *The inner conflict of tradition,* Chicago, 1985, p. 170; Andre Wink, *Land and sovereignty,* p. 197; C.A. Bayly, *Indian society and the making of the British empire,* Cambridge, pp. 30–2.

14 Heesterman, for instance, describes the 1857 rebellion as 'a chaotic resurgence of the inner frontier', ibid., p. 175. See also his discussion on p. 174. This metaphor, and the privileging of settled agrarian regions, pervades much of the literature cited in footnote 1 above, including my own 'A forest polity'.

15 Malcolm, 'Essay on Bhills', *Transactions of the Royal Asiatic Society of Great Britain and Ireland,* vol. I, 1827.

late eighteenth and early nineteenth century, for example, though the power of the centralized Peshwa state declined, the power of the local Peshwa representative, the Mulher deshmukh, increased enormously. Raids and settled agriculture did represent two very different strategies, but it was not unusual for the same chief to resort to both in different regions, or even in the same region at the same time.

RAIDS, KINGSHIP AND SHARED SOVEREIGNTY

These points may be elaborated by considering the different meanings of dhads or raids. Dhads were more common in bad years, when the monsoon was poor. They were often conducted around May or June,[16] the time of the year when foodstocks were lowest. Budrea raja, the naik of Zorum Kikwari, raided Umerpant in Khandesh in 1823 because, according to him, his haks in the district had been witheld and his family and dependents were 'greatly distressed for food'.[17] The large spoils that could be secured during a raid underscore its importance for subsistence. When Jararsinh attacked Kuswao in 1809, his men conducted an unexceptionally thorough sacking. They took away 77 bullocks, 106 cows, 55 calves, 11 female buffaloes, 54 brass and copper pots, 50 pieces of clothing, nine blankets, 19 iron ploughs, 65 axes, several ornaments, a good deal of grain, and other things, worth altogether around Rs 1500.[18] Since Bhils did not have any taboos on eating beef, looted cattle were often killed and consumed at celebratory feasts after a raid.[19]

The spoils were distributed so widely as to make a difference to the subsistence of a significant proportion of the population. The group under the Ghadvi chief Jararsinh which attacked Kuswao in 1809 had over 200 Bhils, and it was not exceptionally large.[20] The first rough population survey in 1859 (when the population may have been higher than in 1809) placed the Dangi population at 10344 persons with 3040 adult males. Of this, 1178

[16] See *BRO.DDR.DN 1.FN 1*, and *BRO.DDR.DN 1.FN 2*.

[17] Rigby to Robertson, 14.8.1823, *BRO.DDR.DN 1.FN 1*. Graham to Blanc, 25.3.1839, *BRO.DDR.DN 1.FN 3*.

[18] List of things taken from Kuswao, *BA.PDD.351(11)*. See Rigby to Briggs, 20.5.1821, *BRO.DDR.DN 1.FN 1*. Briggs to Chaplin, 13.6.1822, ibid. Statement of Nathu Patil and Sivaji Balaji , n.d., *BA.PD.1829.Vol 8/332*.

[19] Statement of Nathu Patil and Sivaji Balaji, n.d., *BA.PD.1829.Vol 8/332*.

[20] Morrison to Keith, n.d., *BA.PDD.351(11)*; Briggs to Chaplin, 13.6.1822, *BRO.DDR.DN 1.FN 1*. See also *BA.PD.1829.Vol 8/332*.

were reported to be Bhils while around 1714 were reported to be Koknis.[21] Even if the entire male population could be potentially drawn on (and not, as is more reasonable to assume, largely Bhils) for an attack, the raiders would have represented over six per cent of the total male population of the 1850s!

But an answer that explains raids only with reference to peculiarities of subsistence for forest-based communities is at best partial. After all, most Koknis and Varlis did not resort to raids despite bad seasons. Also, raids often took place despite good monsoons, and sometimes despite more than adequate resources for cultivation: an early British official despatched to retaliate against some raiders remarked with some surprise that their area was 'well-inhabited, and the population for Bheels are rich'.[22]

Rather than subsistence alone, dhad are best understood as particular claims to power by Bhil chiefs. Sometimes, a dhad could be a political act meant to repudiate or challenge other chiefs. In 1828, when Silput attacked Garkhedi village along the frontiers of Dangs, he did so because he had a dispute with the Mulher deshmukh, who held the village in jagir. Besides, the patil of the village had killed two of his Bhils.[23] Similarly, another attack in 1822 on some Khandesh villages was directed against the British who, Silput felt, had challenged his authority.[24] So raids could be about demonstrating a raja's authority, or responding appropriately to challenges to that authority.

At other times, a raid could be a demand by raiders for their haks, especially for giras haks. Literally, giras meant a mouthful or share, and symbolized the right to an amount as a due from a village. In eighteenth- and early-nineteenth-century western India, giras was a pervasive and central feature of forest polities, and its payment was to continue in an ossified form well into the twentieth century.[25] The Bhumia forest naiks of Malwa and central India, the Vasava and other *mewas* or hill chiefs of Rajpipla and Baroda, the Bhil chiefs around Khandesh and the Nizam of Hyderabad's territories — all of them claimed giras amongst their other haks.[26]

21 Population tables, *BRO.DDR.DN 2.FN 9.*

22 Rigby to Briggs, 18.6.1822, *BRO.DDR.DN 1.FN 1.*

23 Coll., Kh., to Chief Secy., 19.9.1828, *BRO.DDR.DN 1.FN 2.*

24 Silput and Khem to Rigby, n.d., *BA.PSD.1822.Vol 7/69.*

25 So widespread was the payment of giras in the nineteenth century that the Gaekwads had a separate department to deal with it. See the Giras Department papers at the Gujarat State Archives, Baroda.

26 See Maya Unnithan, 'Constructing difference: Social categories and Girahya

Late-nineteenth-century British and Gaekwadi officials were often to think of giras as a 'species of blackmail' paid to Bhil chiefs to avert raids on Gaekwadi territory.[27] Yet that was not how things had appeared formerly. In the late eighteenth and early nineteenth centuries, giras was above all a claim to shared sovereignty with surrounding powers. Payments were associated with specific villages, often situated at considerable distance from Dangs. Kuswao, which the Ghadvi chief Jararsinh raided in 1809 was near Buhari, at least half a day's march from Dangs.[28] The claim to sovereignty emerges even more clearly from the haks of bhet and sirpav which accompanied its payment. Sirpav (literally, head to toes) was the dress that Gaekwadi officials or village representatives gave the Dangi chiefs along with giras. Here, the sirpav was the acknowledgement of an explicit claim to authority over the village by the Dangi rajas and naiks.[29] It was also a symbol of alliance: amongst the Marathas, the Peshwa held a sirpav ceremony after Dussera, where the army assembled at a designated place, and he distributed special dresses amongst its commanders, who in turn gave him a vow of loyalty.[30] Bhet, a word which translates literally as 'gift', was usually a small sum which accompanied giras, and again an explicit acknowledgement of authority.[31] The raja of Ghadvi received annually a bhet of Re 1 from Kejban village, and every person in the village contributed 2 pice towards this amount.[32]

In sustaining or creating claims to giras haks, and the sovereignty it implied, raids were very important. New haks could be built from scratch through raids. When Budrea raja demanded two maunds of grain and Rs 2 from Chokee village during a raid, he was asking for haks that had not formerly existed.[33] Bhil raids were never ends in themselves, or complete acts directed solely at immediate subsistence. Rather, they were about creating or sustaining claims to giras,

---

women, kinship and resources in South Rajasthan', unpublished PhD thesis, University of Cambridge, 1991, pp. 42–55, for a broad account of girasia history.

27 Boyd to Secy., GoB, 9.6.1830 *BRO.DDR.DN 1.FN 3*; and T. Madhav Rao, Diwan, Baroda, to the Agent to the Governor General, Baroda, 18.7.1881, *Selections from the Records of the Baroda Government, No. X, Vol. I, Dang Case,* Baroda, 1891, *BRO.Section 8.Daftar 4.Anukram 43.*

28 Morrisson to Keith, 11.1.1810, *BA.PDD.351(11).*

29 *BRO.DDR.DN 1.FN 2.*

30 Gordon, *The Marathas,* Cambridge, 1993, pp. 181f.

31 See *BA.PD.1855.Vol 36.Comp 577.*

32 *DBD,* II, p. 153.

33 Coll., Kh., to Rigby, 29.7.1823, *BRO.DDR.DN 1.FN 1.*

and through it political power and sovereignty. Often, they were a means of ensuring payment of giras or other haks, a sort of shot across the prow. In 1825, for example, the followers of the Ghadvi chief Silput attacked Raipur village, prevented for some time reaping or mahua-collection, but eventually went away without taking anything.[34] In these senses, it is doubtful whether the agreements that Maratha officials in Khandesh and elsewhere reached with the Bhil chiefs in the eighteenth century, by which the latter undertook not to raid, were the indices of Bhil subordination that they are sometimes presumed to be. It may be more appropriate to view the agreements as acknowledging the substantial sovereignty of Bhil chiefs in these regions, and as attempts to engineer on that basis a very contingent consensus to pursue strategies promoting settled agriculture.

THE GAEKWADS AND THE DESHMUKH

Similarly, it is by no means clear that an increase in Bhil raids signified a blanket decline in Maratha power. Consider the relations with Dangi chiefs of the deshmukh of Baglan, the Peshwa hereditary official in the region, and the Gaekwads. Deshmukhs were usually figures who had spearheaded the colonization of several villages in a compact area. Important political figures with hereditary rights within the Maratha polity, deshmukhs possessed considerable independent authority. Their responsibilities included extending cultivation, maintaining a body of troops to keep peace in the area, and making these troops available for campaigns against the kingdom's enemies.

In the nineteenth century, Murharrao deshmukh was sometimes described as the raja of Dangs, and at other times as its zamindar.[35] Murharrao's son later described Dangs as part of his hereditary deshmukhi area, which the family had enjoyed for 'hundreds' of years.[36] While that was possibly an exaggeration, there is little doubt that the ties of the deshmukhs with Dangs were already extensive by the late eighteenth century, and increased further in the early nineteenth century.

One indicator of their increasingly powerful position lay in the

[34] Rigby to Silput, 21.5.1825, *BRO.DDR.DN 1.FN 2*.
[35] Coll., Kh., to Secy., GoB, 1.7.1843, *IOL.F.4.2074*.
[36] Laxman Murharrao to Governor in Council, n.d., *BA.PD.1874.Vol 108. Comp 1983*.

Hybrid Histories

growth of their jagiri villages and timber rights in Dangs. The villages of Lavchali, Temburthawa, Jambla, Kejwan and Borpada were given to them in jagir in the eighteenth century. They acquired more villages in Dangs in the early nineteenth century: Harpada, Thorpada, and Khokarvihir were given to the deshmukh by Laxman Naik.[37] In the consolidation of the deshmukhs' authority, their alliances with plains powers were the most important factor. In addition to being the hereditary Peshwa officials for Dangs, they had close ties with Baroda. In the 1790s, when some villages were transferred to Songadh officials, the then deshmukh was present to witness the agreements. He also possessed authority over the Gaekwadi territories of Sadarvihir, Pargat, Panchmori, Amba and Antapur.[38] As all this suggests, the period of intensified Bhil raids in the early nineteenth century, whatever its implications for centralized Peshwa power, did not much affect the Baglan deshmukhs.

Accounts of Gaekwadi relations with Dangi chiefs are more extensive, and allow a richer understanding. The Gaekwads, originally lieutenants of the Peshwa, had by the mid-eighteenth century established the independent successor state of Baroda, to a significant extent with the help of Bhil chiefs. While Anglo-Maratha wars might have sapped their strength in other regions during the eighteenth and early nineteenth century, in Dangs their power may have increased during the period. The initial base of the Gaekwadi kingdom had been at Songadh, a fort-town not very far from the northern frontiers of Dangs. Eighteenth-century Gaekwadi commanders had maintained close ties with Bhil rajas and naiks in the Songadh and Dangs area.[39] As the Gaekwads consolidated their hold over large tracts of Gujarat, they moved their capital to the town of Baroda, further away to the north. But Songadh continued to be an important fort, and Gaekwadi influence in Dangs continued to increase. Since around the late eighteenth century, there had been the sharing of fees collected from timber *nakas* or toll stations located in the villages with at least two major Dangi chiefs, those of Ghadvi and Dherbavti.[40] In the 1820s, the Ghadvi chief Silput raja received around Rs 5000 annually from fees at such nakas; Gaekwadi officials received a similar amount.[41]

37 *DBD*, I, pp. 111, 114.
38 *BA.PD.1850.Vol 37/2403.Comp 1983*.
39 For an analysis of similar relations, see Andre Wink, *Land and sovereignty in India*, Cambridge, 1986, pp. 117–22, 189–99.
40 Report of a march through Dangs, March 1867, *BRO.DDR.DN 3.FN 12*.
41 Rigby to Robertson, 30.10.1825, *BRO.RR.DN 144.FN 719*.

Another indicator of Gaekwadi influence was the approximately 52 villages that were co-shared with the Dangi chiefs.[42] In these villages, revenue from agriculture was divided between Gaekwadi officials and the Dangi chiefs, each collecting their portion directly from the cultivator. In the late nineteenth century, an old Ghadvi karbhari, Budea Naik, narrated a story of how some villages came to be co-shared. Some Dangi rajas, he said, had been caught by Gaekwadi officials for raiding villages. Gahenabai, a Gaekwadi rani, had fed the rajas while they were in captivity, and helped to secure their release. As a mark of gratitude, the rajas had arranged for her to receive a small amount as a gift from each village she passed through on her way to the fort of Salher. Budea claimed that this grant had, with time, led to Gaekwadi officials treating these as co-shared villages.[43]

The key figures in extending Gaekwadi influence were two: the *killedars* or fort-commandants, and the revenue farmer or *ijaradar*. Stewart Gordon has noted the general importance of hill-forts in maintaining Maratha dominance.[44] In the context of forest polities, they and their killedars were certainly indispensable. The forts of Salher and Songadh provided bases from which Gaekwadi authority in Dangs was maintained and extended. Salher was situated to the east of Dangs, just two miles from Babulna pass, the main trade route into Dangs. Formerly under the Peshwas, it was taken over by the Gaekwads in the eighteenth century. By the turn of the century, the killedar of the fort had acquired rights in Harpada, Thorpada, and other villages within Dangs.

Songadh, above the northwestern tip of Dangs, was even more important. The killedar of this fort played a major role in the acquisition of co-shared villages along the northern tracts of Dangs. He maintained more extensive ties with the Dangi chiefs than the Salher killedar did, distributing, for instance, the giras payments. Officials based at Songadh had already, by the early nineteenth century, established a *thana* or outpost at Malangdev village in northern Dangs, and taken over several villages around it.[45]

[42] See Diwan, Huzur Kacheri to Resident, Baroda, 18.12.1903, *BRO.HPO (Political).Section 214.1A.SN 3* for a list of all the co-shared Gaekwadi villages.

[43] Evidence of Budea naik, *BRO.RR.DN 144.FN 719*, and Coli., Kh., to Secy., GoB, 13.3.1871, *BA.PD.1871.Vol 56.Comp 578*.

[44] Gordon, 'Forts and social control in the Maratha state', in his *Marathas, marauders and state formation*, Delhi, 1994.

[45] *DBD*, I, pp. 106ff.

The killedar's involvement in struggles for authority amongst the chiefs further increased his influence. An important turning point was the struggle around 1799, of which we have already encountered a version in goth. According to records, a Ghadvi chief, Udesinh, was killed by the Kadmal chief Godoo raja, with whom the former's wife was staying after leaving Udesinh. Udesinh's son, Janak raja, approached the Songadh killedar for assistance against Godoo raja. He was given a loan of Rs 900 to raise men to fight the other chief, on condition that the Gaekwadi flag would fly at Ghadvi village.[46] From around 1800, then, a Gaekwadi *sowar* or mounted force came every year to Dangs around Dussera, carrying a fresh Gaekwadi flag. The Ghadvi chief was presented with a horse, a saddle, and a shawl in recognition of his authority, and the flag was hoisted at Ghadvi.[47]

The killedar also often doubled as the ijaradar for the area, or worked closely with the person who had bought the farm. Revenue farming was a technique regularly adopted by Maratha polities for dealing with 'unsettled' areas along the frontiers of forest polities.[48] But they were introducing cultivation not so much against the will of Dangi chiefs as with their active support and encouragement. Forest chiefs were quite willing to go along with revenue farmers, and often complained against ijaradars who were not effective in extending agriculture, or who collected exorbitant taxes, causing a desertion of villages and a decline in the amount the chiefs could obtain.

The sovereignty that ijaradars or killedars exercised over these regions, in other words, remained profoundly shared. If Gaekwadi officials did not meet the demands of Bhil chiefs, the chiefs could retaliate. In the early nineteenth century, a Gaekwadi official wrote to the Ghadvi chiefs Silput and Khem complaining about the non-payment of his haks.[49] Similarly with the collection of revenue from

---

[46] Coll., Kh., to Secy., GoB, 13.3.1871, *BA.PD.1871.Vol 56.Comp 578*; see also the evidence of Budea naik, *BRO.RR.DN 141.FN 710*. Records mention the name of the chief as Udesinh rather than Fatehsinh, but this is possibly a mistake, since goth are quite unanimous about Fatehsinh being the person who was killed.

[47] Coll., Kh., to Secy., GoB, 13.3.1871, *BA.PD.1871.Vol 56.Comp 578*; Ashburner to Secy., GoB, 12.4.1871, *BRO.RR.DN 141.FN 710*.

[48] Andre Wink, 'Maratha revenue farming', *Modern Asian Studies*, vol. 17, no. 4, 1983; see also his *Land and sovereignty in India*, Cambridge, 1986, pp. 339–52.

[49] Amrut Rav to Silput and Khem, n.d., no. 4, *BRO.DDR.DN 1.FN 3*.

co-shared villages. Gaekwadi ijaradars often collected exorbitant taxes, causing a decline in the amount the chiefs could obtain from the cultivators. One ijaradar collected so much in the 1820s that it led to the desertion of villages. The Ghadvi chiefs reacted strongly to this: they refused to meet the ijaradar's successor the next year, despite reassurances that he wished to collect no more than the customary settlement.[50]

RETHINKING GIRAS AND RAIDS

In such a context, to figures like the killedars, ijaradars or the deshmukhs, issues like dhad or giras were very complex matters, not to be regarded with straightforward hostility because they hindered settled cultivation. True, the killedars often pursued measures to halt raids by the Bhil chiefs on their territory. Though expeditions into Dangs were difficult because the forests were so dense, and because malaria was so rampant, counter-raids on the border villages of the Bhil chiefs were sometimes carried out and local cattle seized as retaliation.[51] They also tried to bring raiding chiefs to negotiation by restricting their access to merchants outside Dangs, or by drawing on their ties with other Bhil chiefs to put pressure on raiders. These sometimes resulted in Bhil chiefs offering either cattle or village grants in compensation.[52]

Nevertheless, they also actively encouraged raids by Bhils on rivals. Cattle raided from Peshwa and, later, British-controlled Khandesh were sometimes sold at a market near Salher in Gaekwadi territory with the full encouragement of Gaekwadi officials. Looted villagers from Khandesh would even visit Salher and pay a ransom to get the cattle back. Fifty-eight of the cattle taken from Kuswao were restored this way.[53] We do not know whether Gaekwadi officials themselves participated in Bhil raids on the former's rivals. But certainly, in the late eighteenth century, many Bhil attacks on villages in Khandesh were connected to disputes amongst

---

[50] Amrut Rav to Silput and Khem, n.d., no. 4, *BRO.DDR.DN 1.FN 3*.

[51] See, for example, *DBD*, II, p. 18.

[52] Bell to Resident, Baroda, 25.7.1845, *BRO.RR.FN 122.DN 609*; Appaji Rav to Silput, n.d., no. 5, *BRO.DDR.DN 1.FN 3*; Mansfield to Secy., GoB, 24.7.1855, *BA.PD.1855.Vol 37.Comp 123*.

[53] John Briggs to Resident, Baroda, 14.7.1821, *BA.PSD.1820.Vol 4/8*; List of things taken from Kuswao, *BA.PD.351(11)*. See also statement of Nathu patil and Sivaji Balaji, *BA.PD.1829.Vol 8/332*.

Maratha chiefs in Khandesh, with rival groups jostling for the support of Bhil chiefs for their activities.[54]

Even raids on Gaekwadi territory were not necessarily met with unconditional hostility. From the 1820s onwards, British officials complained regularly of the killedars' 'vacillating and mutable . . . policy' where all 'crime' from cattle-lifting to murder was 'alike visited with the extremes of punishment, or overlooked altogether'.[55] What the British did not realize was that Baroda officials' attitudes were an acknowledgement of the political rather than criminal nature of the dhad — its connection with giras and shared sovereignties. A dhad usually called not for retaliation but for renegotiating the sharing of sovereignty.

Giras payments were, from a Gaekwadi point of view, equally complex matters. These payments were fundamentally transformed in the course of the late eighteenth century. Formerly, towards Gujarat, giras, sirpav and bhet were paid directly by the specific villages on which they were levied. But now Baroda officials increasingly replaced village officials as the agency through which a payment was made. Consolidated into one lump sum, the giras dues from all villages were paid together by the Gaekwadi killedar at Songadh at an annual meeting, though bhet and sirpav continued to be paid directly from the village.[56] And the centralization of giras payments also transformed raids. Now raids on a village were not necessarily because of the dues from it specifically. Jararsinh, for example, raided Kuswao because he had around Rs 1000 due in giras from the district of which it was part.[57] He claimed that he had told the local official about this two years back, 'but he still continues to sleep, therefore I have given him a specimen of what I can do'.[58]

Giras payments fluctuated greatly. The Ghadvi chiefs received about Rs 1400 annually around 1799–1801, an amount which fell by half during the ensuing decade before rising again to Rs 1400 by 1814.[59] By 1828, they were getting barely half that amount

54 Saletore gives several examples of this. See his 'The Bhils of Maharashtra', *New Indian Antiquary*, vol. I, 1938–9; and also his 'Relations between the Girassias and the Marathas', *New Indian Antiquary*, extra series I, 1939.

55 Rigby to Robertson, 14.8.1823, *BRO.DDR.DN 1.FN 1*.

56 Giberne to Newham, 28.5.1828, *BRO.DDR.DN 1.FN 2*; *DCR.DN 1.FN 4Uc*.

57 Morrison to Keith, 11.1.1810, *BA.PDD.351(11)*.

58 Morrison to Keith, 11.1.1810 and Jararsinh to Trimbak Rao, Songadh, 5th Magsur, Vad, , 1866, *BA.PDD.351(11)*.

59 Graham to Coll., Kh., 8.7.1828, *BRO.DDR.DN 1.FN 2*.

again.[60] But it may be too simplistic to read these fluctuations as directly in proportion to the power of the chiefs. True, some such correlation may seem to obtain. Ghadvi was quite powerful till around 1799–1800, when the slaying of Fatehsinh raja by the Kadmal bhauband led to a period of disputes. The rise of giras payments again by around 1814 may have been due to the power of Jararsinh raja, a figure who looms large in goth as a powerful chief. And the decline after that could have been due to the consolidation of Gaekwadi power which accompanied the British takeover.

Yet such a reading may be misplaced, a case of our narratives of the growth of centralized states causing us to read too much into scanty data. Such a reading still implicitly presumes that giras payments were a form of blackmail or ransom, paid only because the chiefs would otherwise have raided the villages in question. On closer attention it is clear that a direct correlation between giras and the power of either the chiefs or Gaekwadi officials did not obtain. Gaekwadi officials were not interested in a systematic or complete repudiation of giras dues when they increased their power relative to Dangi Bhil chiefs. Rather, to reiterate a point that has already been dwelt on in the context of the creation of authority within Dangs, it was only by distributing giras and similar dues that killedars, ijaradars and deshmukhs created the authority and alliances that they needed.

Nowhere was this more sharply brought out than in disputes after 1828 over Gaekwadi giras payments. That year, British officials in Khandesh claimed that Gaekwadi irregularity in giras payments was one major cause of Dangi raids. They proposed that they take over the Gaekwadi giras, make them from the British treasury at Khandesh, and charge the amount to the Gaekwads. Gaekwadi officials fiercely opposed this measure, for such a transfer threatened the most vital means by which ijaradars and killedars made alliances and extended their authority. Nevertheless, the British ignored Baroda's protests and took over the making of giras. Then even more bizarre events unfolded — bizarre at least by British criteria. The killedar at Songadh took to paying giras clandestinely a second time — at considerable financial loss to Baroda — in order to keep up direct relations with the chiefs! Far from being a reluctantly paid blackmail amount, then, Baroda officials (like the Vansda raja till the late twentieth century)

60 Graham to Coll., Kh., 8.7.1828, *BRO.DDR.DN 1.FN 2*; Hodges to Noriss, 14.7.1829, ibid.

considered the distribution of giras as important as the chiefs did its receipt.[61]

RAIDING AND KINGSHIP

Quite apart from these implications for Bhil relations with surrounding plains powers, within Dangs itself there was also a close link between giras, raids, and the construction of kingship. A dhad needed considerable political authority to organize. For a small foray, a chief might mobilize his own men. But major raids involved alliances amongst rajas of different dangs. In 1829, Seetria naik, the karbhari of Deher, went to meet Silput raja to request that his men accompany a raiding party to collect overdue Deher haks from Khandesh. It took several days to persuade Silput, and to negotiate the division of spoils. Other alliances too were drawn on. The party that eventually raided Khandesh had 40 Ghadvi men, 51 Deher men, as well as men from the dangs of Sivbara, Kirli and Malangdev.[62]

Such large groups were necessary partially because the raided villagers often responded ferociously to raiders. If they obtained intelligence of a planned raid, they usually sent their cattle away to a neighbouring village, and prepared themselves for a confrontation. When faced with such a prepared village, the raiders sometimes refrained from attacking, and returned to Dangs. And even when attacking unprepared villages, raids were bloody and violent affairs, often with deaths and casualties on both sides.[63] Raided villagers, or Gaekwadi or Peshwai forces also often pursued the raiders. In fact, the concentration of raids around May may have been not only due to scarcity of food around that time, but also because the monsoons deluged the region around this time, making pursuit difficult. Dangs, difficult for outside forces to reach at the best of times, became virtually inaccessible in the rainy season, when malaria was rampant, the undergrowth rife and the rivers swollen.[64]

Raids and giras were also important for the maintenance of authority and power of chiefs within Dangs. Giras was widely distributed. In 1828, Silput raja, the principal chief of the powerful dang Ghadvi, and his uncle Khem raja were the chief recipients of

---

[61] See the correspondence in *BRO.DDR.DN 1.FN 2*; *BRO.DDR.DN 1.FN 3*.

[62] Statement of Malharrao Kal naik, 20.8. 1829, *BA.PD.1829.Vol 8/332*.

[63] Maharawal Raisinhji, Vansda raja, to J. Morrison, recd. 16.6.1804, *BA. SPD.158 (16)*.

[64] From Rigby, 1.5.1821, *BRO.DDR.DN 1.FN 1*.

Gaekwadi giras. But separate and independent payments were also made to at least six naiks of the Ghadvi bhauband. By receiving giras directly this way from the Gaekwads, the bhauband asserted the distinctiveness of their authority from that of the principal chief, in this case Silput. Quite apart from this, of the Rs 760 paid to Silput, he retained only Rs 300. Of the rest, Rs 40 was distributed amongst his three sons and two brothers, Rs 270 to 36 other persons connected with him, and Rs 51 to the soldiers with them.[65] By accepting money this way from Silput, they acknowledged their subordination to him. And in distributing the amount he received, Silput created hierarchical ties.

Similarly, cattle and other spoils secured during raids were an important resource, and to distribute them was to make valuable gifts. A good deal of Silput raja's authority was based on what was described as his liberality and bravery, which had made many young chiefs his followers.[66] Maybe that was why when Silput was forced in 1829 to restore cattle he and his men had carried away from a village, he preferred to send his own cattle rather than collect back what had already been distributed. To do so could have rendered him, as a similar move nearly did Khem, 'highly unpopular'.[67]

Authority could be extended considerably through the giras claims that raids sustained. Sometimes, in fact, a claim to authority and chieftaincy could be constructed virtually from scratch through raids. One of the most spectacular cases of this sort occurred in the Rajpipla region to the north of Dangs, where a minor Vasava chief, Kuver Vasava, emerged through raids as a major figure by the early nineteenth century.[68] In Khandesh during the early nineteenth century, similarly, many Bhil watchmen consolidated their authority through raids and emerged as important chiefs.[69] Though we know of no such dramatic cases in Dangs, Silput certainly increased his authority significantly through the distribution of

[65] Statement of Nathu patil and Sivaji Balaji, n.d. *BA.PD.1829.Vol 8/332.*
[66] Rigby to Briggs, 30.7.1822, *BRO.DDR.DN 1.FN 1.*
[67] Giberne to Newnham, 16.10.1828, *BA.PSD.1828.Vol 29/320.* See also Rigby to Briggs, 2.7.1822, *BRO.DDR.DN 1.FN 1.*
[68] For an account of the chiefs, see Deshpande, *John Briggs in Maharashtra,* New Delhi, 1987, pp. 97–101.
[69] See the letters from Briggs to Elphinstone, 24.9.1818, *PA.Dec.Com.Vol 172.No 212*; 19.11.1818, *PA.Dec.Com.Vol 173.No 292*; 8.1.1819, *PA.Dec.Com. Vol 174.No 367.* See also Deshpande, *John Briggs in Maharashtra,* ch. 3; A.K. Prasad, *The Bhils of Khandesh under the British East India Company*, New Delhi, 1991, ch. 2.

giras and spoils from raids.[70] Being a raja thus involved raiding in
order to create the resources to distribute amongst followers.

THE WILDNESS OF RAIDING

In the last few sections, I have tried to break away from narratives
that privilege growth by emphasizing how raids and giras were
crucial to political authority. Yet even this may not be enough. It
still runs the risk of implying that raids were simply the means to
an end, or that raids occurred only when a system of paying giras
collapsed. It may still cast raids as rational activities, and Dangis
as rational actors trying to maximize their interests. Maybe we need
to go further still, and understand raiding as inextricably part of
the enactment of wildness by Bhil men. In this sense, celebrations
of raiding were very central to Bhil imagining of themselves.

This may seem a deeply questionable statement to make, almost
subscribing to colonial stereotypes. In colonial gazetteers, it is often
claimed that Bhils considered themselves 'Mahadev's thiefs', and
described themselves as such.[71] Colonial officials picked on this
Bhil assertion, of course, because it fitted in well with their own
notions of the religiosity of vocations in India, and because many
of them disapprovingly saw Bhils as natural plunderers. Quite
rightly, these and similar descriptions have been shown to be part
of a deeply problematic colonial discourse.[72]

Leaving aside these colonial stereotypes, many Bhils celebrated
raids as enactments of masculine wildness. Both men and women
left on raids together, but the women stayed on in the foothills, or
the base village, while the men attacked the village and returned
with the spoils to join the women. Sometimes, women too wielded
slings against pursuers, and helped to herd seized cattle through
the hills.[73] The British, part of a culture that viewed such collective
violence as an even more exclusively male sphere, found this limited
involvement in activities like raids striking enough to remark on it
repeatedly. But for Bhil men, the exclusion of women from the

[70] Rigby to Briggs, 30.7.1822, *BRO.DDR.DN 1.FN 1*

[71] Malcolm, 'Essay on the Bhills', p. 89

[72] See my 'Shades of wildness'; also see Sanjay Nigam, 'Disciplining and
policing the criminals by birth' (2 parts), *Indian Economic and Social History
Review*, vol. 27, nos 2 and 3, 1990, and Nandini Sundar, 'The dreaded Danteshwari: Annals of alleged sacrifice', *Indian Economic and Social History Review*,
vol. 32, no. 3, 1995.

[73] Rigby to Briggs, 25.11.1819, no. 659 *PA.Dec.Com.Vol 178.*

actual moment of the dhad was possibly more important than their participation at prior and later moments.[74]

This association of raids with masculine wildness may be why, in goth, important rajas are also described often as active in not only shikhar, but also in raids. And just as there is even now a fund of goth around shikhar, ballads celebrating raids were known and sung in Dangs till around the early twentieth century. We now have no access to these songs; however, some similar songs recorded in the late nineteenth or early twentieth century amongst the Bhils of central India are known. The song about the Bhil chief Damor Lal is typical of the genre. It tells how Damor Lal came to Sakalia village and became the *palavi* (chief of *pal* or village) of the thieves of Sakalia. Then he sent a spy to gather intelligence of the country. The scout spied on the village Varund and saw a number of white cows in the *gundara* (relatively open place in the forest where cattle taken out for grazing are conducted at noon) and grey buffaloes enjoying themselves in the *dobanas* (pits of mire and water). He returned and informed Damor Lal. Then the Damor palavi beat a nagara to assemble his men. A large host of Bhils assembled and started the raid. They crossed the river Mahiyari and plundered Varundi. They seized the white cows from the gundaras, and they seized the buffaloes in the dobanas. After plundering and beating the villagers, they returned, crossed the Mahiyari, and came to Sakalia. They brought liquor of all sorts, and drank it in cups of gold and silver and made merry.[75]

Several of these motifs are staple ones, repeated in most songs: there are always white cows in gundaras and grey buffaloes in dobanas, the palavi always beats a drum, and at the end of it all liquor is always served in cups of gold and silver. And there is always a central figure, a Damor Lal, whose feats the song celebrates. In Dangs, some of these equivalents of Damor Lal were actual vadils: there were celebratory songs till recently about raids by Silput raja and Aundya raja. So raids were not just about an end, or just about the resources they generated for subsistence and for the construction of kingship. Rather, the very act of leading raids was crucial to imagining a raja, his bravery and his daring. To rule, in other words, was to raid.

More broadly, the songs suggest how closely raiding, with its emphasis on wildness and masculinity, was connected to being a

---

74 *DCR.DN 1.FN 4Uc.*
75 IOL, Luard MSs., Central India Songs, MSS Hindi D1 (27), Folio 31.

Bhil man. Not only do they celebrate raiding as an activity, but all those causes for raids that we have seen — poverty, authority, giras, shared sovereignty — are absent from them; the only reason to raid appears to be the enactment of the raid itself.[76] This celebratory element seems to have marked raids in the nineteenth century too: we know that raids were followed by long celebrations at which alcohol flowed freely. And when Bhil men described themselves as Mahadev's thiefs, they were possibly not claiming a religiously sanctioned vocation; rather, they were refusing to reduce their actions to instrumental causes. That refusal was also of course a particularly loaded allegory, for Mahadev was another name for the deity Siva. As Shulman has observed in his article on south Indian bandits and kings: 'Siva, the antinomian deity par excellence, is at his best not far removed from a bandit. . . . Siva remains unpredictable, delightfully mischievous, entirely unbound by conventions or properties.'[77]

THE AFFINITIES OF WILDNESS

All this is very well, but what did raids mean for regions and peoples who were raided? The answer — hardship, desertion and desolation — often seems so straightforward and so agreed upon both by historians and contemporary chroniclers that the question itself is rarely seen as even worth posing. And true enough, quite apart from the substantial and very real bloodshed and violence, the plundering of its cattle, grain and utensils could entirely impoverish a village household, and even drive it below already tenuous margins of subsistence. Many people, maybe even the bulk of cultivators, abandoned their villages and moved to more peaceful places, where they could continue with cultivation as before. This was what happened to Khandesh in the late eighteenth and early nineteenth centuries.

But from a less biased perspective it is possible to tease out several meanings that are suppressed or minimized in depictions of desertion and desolation. First, desolation did not mean that all

[76] See the songs in the IOL. Luard MSS. as well as those reproduced in T.H. Hendley, 'An account of the Maiwar Bhils', *Journal of the Asiatic Society of Bengal*, vol. IV, 1875.
[77] David Shulman, 'On south Indian bandits and kings', *Indian Economic and Social History Review*, vol. XVII, no. 3, 1980, pp. 290–1. See also J.F. Richards and V.N. Rao, 'Banditry in Mughal India: Historical and folk perceptions', *Indian Economic and Social History Review*, vol. 18, no. 1, 1980.

villages were deserted. Several villages brokered their own peace with the raiding chiefs when the political authority of figures like the Peshwa failed. In the Khandesh region, for example, some patils reached agreements of this sort with the chiefs of Amala, paying giras directly. As a result, cultivation continued in these regions across the early nineteenth century.[78] Second, in addition to this continuation of cultivation, at least a significant proportion of those from both such villages and deserted ones voted with their feet to join the raiders. Amongst them often were the plains Bhils. The plains Bhils, as colonial records designated these people, had an ambiguous relation with the plains villages in which they lived, and in which they were possibly quite numerous. In normal times, they served as jagalias in these villages. In this position, they were responsible for securing information about potential raids. Some-times, however, they instead supplied information to the raiders — they were often the spies of the sort mentioned in the song. Given their links with both sides, it is understandable that they should so often have selected to move to the hills, take up cultiva-tion or other forms of subsistence there, and join the raiders.[79]

Third, in villages that had been deserted, forests — always nearby in the late eighteenth or early nineteenth century — quickly re-established themselves. In the twenty years that they lay relatively fallow, many villages in Khandesh were overrun with forests. This sort of desolation simply meant the emergence of different modes of subsistence, of the sort we saw in Chapter 5. Sometimes Bhils moved in near the area they raided, especially if there already were a significant number of Bhils around. In 1804, for example, some Bhils from Ghadvi moved into the Gaekwadi village of Raigadh in this way, and used it as a base for further raids.[80] These villages usually remained without a permanent population, and became part of an area used for gathering, hunting, fishing, or even cultivation. The whole of Navapur taluka was virtually resettled this way in the late eighteenth and early nineteenth centuries, with its demographic profile changing so dramatically that Bhils became the principal community of the region.[81] So desolation in late-eighteenth- and early-nineteenth-century western India can be rethought as the

78 Rigby to Briggs, 28.11.1819, *DCR.DN 1.FN 4Uc*

79 Briggs to Elphinstone, 8.1.1819, *PA.Dec.Com.Vol 174.*

80 Maharawal Raisinhji, Vansda raja, to J. Morrison, recd. 16.6.1804, *BA. SPD.158 (16).*

81 David Hardiman, 'Small dam systems of the Sahyadris', in Guha and Arnold (eds), *Nature, culture, imperialism*, Delhi, 1994, pp. 205ff.

creation of areas where forest communities and forest polities were dominant. Maybe that is one way to read the insistence of goth that the dang was bigger during moglai.

Finally, and most importantly, even a sharp distinction between the dang and the desh and Gujarat may not always be helpful. There was a profound overlap between Dangi enactments of wildness and those of surrounding plains communities. The ways in which Dangis thought of themselves as jangli — in relation to forests, masculinity, femininity, modes of livelihood, raids and giras amongst other things — had significant resonances in surrounding plains communities rather than simply being opposed to the practices of these communities.

Even the floral and faunal difference between the dang and surrounding areas was not great. Till the later half of the nineteenth century, interrupted forests (small forests and wooded patches) were a significant physical feature of the cultivated plains of Gujarat or the desh.[82] Consequently, these regions too supported a wide variety of wildlife. In the early decades of the nineteenth century, a considerable number of tigers and panthers were killed in plains areas of Khandesh, Bharuch and Baroda. Later too, after most land had come under cultivation, the grasslands and croplands supported diverse wildlife, including large numbers of deer (who often devastated crops) and birds.[83] Both around Surat and Baroda in the plains of Gujarat, deer and other game were an important source of subsistence for the lower and middle castes till almost the 1930s.

Modes of livelihood were not radically different either. The collection of mahua flowers and the consumption of liquor made from toddy trees was important as a source of subsistence even

---

[82] For tracts of western India slightly to the south of Dangs, see G.D. Sontheimer, *Pastoral deities in western India*, trans. Anne Feldhaus, Delhi, 1989, p. 167. For the areas of Gujarat and Khandesh, though little scholarly research has been done, see J.F. Richards and Michelle B. McAlpin, 'Cotton cultivating and land clearing in the Bombay Deccan and Karnatak: 1818–1920', in Richard Tucker and J.F. Richards (eds), *Global deforestation and the nineteenth century world economy*, Durham, North Carolina, 1983. Such forests were characteristic of other areas of 'settled agriculture' too in eighteenth- and early-nineteenth-century India. See J.F. Richards, E.S. Haynes and R. Hagen, 'Changes in land-use in Bihar, Punjab and Haryana, 1850–1970', *Modern Asian Studies*, vol. 9, 1985, pp. 699–732.

[83] See, for example, V.K. Chavda, 'Dharavi deer preserve: A note on ecology, royal past-time, and peasant unrest, 1856–1940', *Proceedings of the forty-fifth session of the Indian History Congress, 1984*, New Delhi, 1985.

to the kaliparaj and lower castes who stayed in the plains around
Surat.[84] Little is known about dependence on gathering, though
the patches of interrupted forests could have supported it. Nor do
we know much about how these modes of livelihood were enacted
— as involving wildness, or otherwise. Certainly, pastoralism,
enacted specifically as carrying connotations of wildness, was
widespread in western India till the early nineteenth century.[85]

Settled agriculture was also not as pervasive on the plains as
is often assumed. There were considerable amounts of fallow land
in western India in the early nineteenth century, and till the
mid-nineteenth century in Khandesh.[86] Plains cultivators often
abandoned villages and shifted to new ones when the sarkar
became too oppressive. Bad seasons, a persistent feature of western
India, could also lead to migration. There was also the temptation
to move out of the more settled plains areas into regions like
Panchmahals or Dangs where more land was available. Indeed,
even residence across generations in the same village was not
necessarily indicative of settled agriculture. As in dahi and khandad, cultivators in some plains regions used loppings from trees
to manure lands. And since land was reasonably plentiful, cultivators often left fields fallow for some years in order that it
regain its fertility. They moved, in other words, from field to field
within the same village.[87] So though mobility was not as systematic
an alternative in the plains as it was in Dangs, it was important
enough to make the modern notion of settled agriculture —
cultivation in one fixed site — quite misleading.

There were affinities and similarities with the raids and giras of
forest polities too. Like giras, the famous Maratha revenue claim
chauth was about shared sovereignty and the construction of kingship; moreover, it was sustained through raids.[88] Besides, giras
itself was very important not only in the forest polities but in the

[84] Hardiman explores the relationship between alcohol and forest communities in his *The coming of the Devi*, Delhi, 1987.

[85] On pastoralism, see especially Sontheimer, *Pastoral deities in western
India*, New York, 1989.

[86] Richards and McAlpin, 'Cotton cultivating and land clearing in the Bombay Deccan and Karnatak: 1818–1920', in Richard Tucker and J.F. Richards
(eds), *Global deforestation and the nineteenth century world economy*, Durham,
1983.

[87] Richard P. Tucker, 'Forest management and imperial politics: Thana
district, Bombay, 1823–1887', *Indian Economic and Social History Review*, vol. 16,
no. 3, 1979.

[88] Gordon, *The Marathas*, Cambridge, 1993, p. 76.

plains of central and south Gujarat, especially in the Ahmedabad, Kheda, Bharuch, and Surat regions. In early-nineteenth-century Bharuch, a prosperous region of Gujarat for which we have a detailed study, the girasias claimed a fourth or a third share of the revenue, and held nearly half the land under cultivation. If their dues were not paid to them, they were likely to raid villages and collect these amounts.[89] In 1776, they held in Bharuch over 56,000 *bighas* of land, which yielded a revenue of Rs 1.2 lakh annually. Amongst the Girasias were 124 Rajputs, 81 Muslims, and 22 Kolis.[90] Around Ahmedabad, virtually the whole of Dhanduka, Ranpur and Gogha, except for the chief towns, were under their control. The Gaekwads had a separate Giras Department to look after the various claims to it made all over their territories. Similarly, raids and plundering affected not just areas close to forest polities but agricultural and urban centres. 'Near Ahmadabad, Burhanpur, Agra, Delhi, Lahore and many other cities, thieves and robbers come in force by night or day like open enemies', Pelasert wrote.[91] What Shulman suggests for south India — that the raids and other activities of bandits were celebrated, and regarded as having close affinities with kingship — may well be true of other parts of India too.[92]

The physical and cultural similarities between the dang, the desh, and Gujarat were at least partially the result of their influence on each other. For example, the role that non-agricultural modes of subsistence had in the plains was surely linked in part to the fact that the same communities, such as Koknis and even Bhils, often moved between both areas. Similarly, if power was quite deeply shared in the Maratha polities amongst the male chiefs (known like in Dangs as the bhauband), this may have been not only because Maratha hereditary chieftains and officials built up independent bases for power. It may also have been because they had to depend on alliances with Bhils or taking to the forests during disputes with the Peshwa or other Maratha chiefs. To cite only one of the most famous examples, the founder of the Baroda dynasty, Pilaji Gaekwad, rose to pre-eminence through his alliances with the Bhils and

[89] Raj Kumar Hans, 'Agrarian economy of Broach district during the first half of the nineteenth century', PhD thesis, MS University, Baroda, 1987, pp. 62ff.

[90] Raj Kumar Hans, 'The Grasia chiefs and the British power in the beginning of the nineteenth century Gujarat', *Proceedings of the Indian History Congress*, 1979, Waltair.

[91] Wink, *Land and sovereignty*, Cambridge, 1986, p. 197.

[92] David Shulman, 'On south Indian bandits and kings', *Indian Economic and Social Review*, vol. XVII, no. 3, 1980.

Kolis. His early ties were with the (Bhil?) raja of Rajpipla, who controlled the fort of Songadh near Dangs.[93] Songadh was later to be Pilaji's first capital. Even in later decades, after the Gaekwadi capital was shifted to Baroda, Songadh remained an important base, and many Gamits, at the time a janglijati, joined Gaekwadi army service, eventually settling down in distant parts of north Gujarat. Given this backdrop, it is not surprising that the Ghadvi chief Silput raja should have remarked on one occasion that 'he looked to the Guicowar as his brother'; Gaekwadi officials were to acquiesce and maybe even participate in this language.[94] Being jangli was thus not exterior or external to being Gaekwad; it was integral to the relationships that Gaekwadi officials sustained.

The role of forest polities was even greater in the small kingdoms of western and central India — those like Chhota Udepur, Baria, or Lunavada in southeast Gujarat, Boodawal and Peint towards Maharashtra, or Jura and Oghna towards Rajasthan. Most of these small kingdoms were as deeply involved in discourses of wildness as in the power of larger centralized states. Some of these had been established by Rajput adventurers between the fourteenth and the sixteenth centuries, others by Bhil chiefs who had become much more powerful than their rivals. They often had strong alliances with plains powers — those of Boodawal and Peint held grants from plains powers for their lands on condition of their controlling Bhil raids onto the plains.[95] At the same time, a considerable degree of the power of little kingdoms too was derived from their alliances with forest polities. In the Mughal period, for example, the Surgana deshmukh and the Dangi chiefs rebelled together; at one time, Dangs and the deshmukh's territories were together called bandi mulak, or rebel lands.[96] It was an indicator of the centrality of wildness in these little kingdoms that, during coronations, a Bhil chief often played a crucial role, seating the new king on the throne.[97]

Even an identity as Bhils was sometimes adopted by or ascribed to the more upper caste Rajputs in forested and hilly regions. About the rajas of Vansda, for example, there was some confusion as to

93 Wink, *Land and sovereignty*, Cambridge, 1986, p. 117.
94 *BRO.DDR.DN 1.FN 2.*
95 Briggs to Elphinstone, 24.10.1818, no. 212, *PA.Dec.Com.Vol 172.*
96 Morriss to Mansfield, 15.4.1854, *BRO.DDR.DN 2.FN 7.*
97 The practice of Bhils participating in the coronation of Rajput chiefs is noted in John Malcolm, 'Essay on Bhils', *Transactions of the Royal Asiatic Society of Great Britain and Ireland*, vol. I, 1827, pp. 68–9, and in Russell and Hira Lal, *Tribes and castes*, London, 1916, vol. 1, p. 280.

whether they were Bhil or Rajput chiefs.[98] Though often simply because of colonial ignorance, such confusion shows how thin the line between Rajput and Bhil was in many forested areas. As one official noted in the early nineteenth century, Rajput chiefs were quite willing to marry into powerful Bhil lineages.[99] Claiming and participating in the wildness of being Bhil, then, was not something that only janglijatis like Koknis did — even Rajputs were fascinated by, and claimed involvement in, enactments of wildness. In certain contexts and situations, the discourse of wildness may have been as influential as those around Brahman or Rajput values.

But all this was to change. After the British takeover of Khandesh in 1818, a new kind of centralized state was to emerge, one that was closer to historians' notions of state power. This state did not erase any inner frontier. It could not have, for no inner frontier existed. But it did create an inner frontier of sorts, in the sense that the dang was to be subordinated to surrounding areas, and that differences between the dang and these areas were to be accentuated, even as similarities were to be attenuated. Goth of mandini and gora raj speak of these transformations.

(16)

[98] *DCR.DN 1.FN 4Uc.*

[99] Central Provinces Ethnographic Survey, *Draft articles on forest tribes*, 3rd series, Pioneer Press, Allahabad, 1911, p. 46.

Mandini

10

Pax Britannica Revisited

Mandini, literally allocation or demarcation, marks the end of moglai. Mandini is almost the founding event of a particular present — that instituted from outside the dang. The mandini however is not any specific event. It straddles the nineteenth and twentieth century, and though the last mandini that goth dwell on occurred in the 1970s, it is not inconceivable that there will be more mandinis. It is an ongoing event and epoch. It is the beginning of several narratives which extend, often with portentous and minatory ramifications, into the present. The meanings of mandini overlap, most of all, with those of gora raj, and these meanings will be explored in the rest of the book.

One mandini associated with gora raj is that which extirpated dhad. In many goth, the cessation of raids is ascribed to an agreement reached between the chiefs and the British at a darbar where the former undertook not to raid in return for an annual payment. There is a frequent association between the mandini and the darbar, usually the first British darbar. From the 1840s, darbars were major annual features in Dangs; these were occasions when British officials met the chiefs, distributed turbans and shawls to them, paid their lease and giras, and supplied sida-pani for all Dangis who attended. By associating the mandini with the first darbar, narrators emphasize the profoundly political and constitutive nature of the mandini. Perhaps this emphasis is why the darbar of the mandini is often portrayed as having been held at *Bhavani cha killa* in Sattarsingi, situated to the southwest of Dangs. Not only was Sattarsingi — Suptshring to the British — often a base for colonial operations, but it also had an older ritual significance since it was an important place of pilgrimage.

Goth about the cessation of raids led, occasionally, to reflections on the power and novelty of the British sarkar:

> Hoomla sipai was sent to the jungle by the sahebs. Silput raja and his karbhari, Suklia, ran away on seeing him, thinking he was a ghost, because they had never seen a *sarkari manus* [government man] before. Then they stopped and gathered their bows and arrows to drive it away. Hoomla sipai saw this and ran away to Dhule. He reported that the Dangis had thought him to be a ghost. But the sarkar sent him back. He met Silput raja and Suklia karbhari and told them, 'let the sarkar gather timber in the forests'. . . .[1]

Hoomla is not a white man: he is frightening only because he is a sarkari manus, and dressed in the unknown uniform of a sipai. Here, the coming of the British is also the coming of the sarkar — a completely novel event.

In some goth, the Dangis resisted the British, and it is their defeat which led to the cessation of raids.

> The gora sarkar [white government] first came to Dhule and established itself there. Then the saheb came to Dangs and saw the forests. He said, 'I want to take these forests from you'. But Silput raja and Suklia karbhari said, 'we will not give you the forests'. Then the saheb came with a *lashkar* [army] and there was a battle. Silput and Suklia fought, but they were defeated. They were then taken to Delhi and kept there. Their photograph is still there in Delhi.[2]

THE TAKEOVER OF GIRAS

Perhaps we can think of these goth as allusions from below to Pax Britannica. That Victorian phrase, Pax Britannica, was a succinct, self-congratulatory description of a world over which Britain dominated and maintained order. It was a peculiar kind of order, for

---

[1] Somalia Gondusar and others, 26.3.1990, Ghadvi.
[2] Raisinh Gondusar, 7.4.1990, Jamulvihir.

central to it was a very distinctive understanding of wildness. The British constructed wildness and civilization as completely opposed and antagonistic categories rather than agonistic ones, and they privileged civilization almost exclusively. Practices like those of the Dangis — shifting cultivation, mobility, raids on plains, fluctuating giras, no clear system of succession to kingship, indeed no clear kings — were almost a litany of the kind of wildness that colonial officials saw themselves as opposed to. Pax Britannica was about the subordination of wildness by civilization, or the peace of the colonial concepts of civilization. The meanings of this civilized peace are explored here.

When the British took over Khandesh in 1818, it was certainly not civilized by their standards. A large proportion of villages were deserted, and had even been run over by forests. The main task that colonial officials set themselves was the repopulation of these villages, ensuring that they remained on one fixed site, and extending settled cultivation in them — in a word, the civilizing mission. Yet, establishing Pax Britannica in the plains involved them, almost necessarily, in confrontations with groups in the regions around Khandesh. If the practice of wildness was influential in regions like Khandesh, this had much to do with the influence of neighbouring forest chiefs like those of Dangs and their raids and giras. Pax Britannica in Khandesh was impossible without reducing the influence, in the region, of forest communities and chiefs, and of the discourses of wildness that they were associated with.

In order to better establish Pax Britannica in Khandesh, colonial officials tried to halt raids by neighbouring forest chiefs. They secured undertakings from the Dangi Bhil chiefs (as they did from other chiefs in and around Khandesh) that they would not raid the plains.[3] But these did not succeed either in Dangs or elsewhere. Raids were reported in 1821 from Dangs, and again in 1822 and 1823. In 1825, it was reported that the 'rapine' of the Dangi Bhils had increased.[4]

By that time, Khandesh officials thought they had identified the principal cause of Dangi raids: the irregularity and lack of fixity in the payment of giras by Gaekwadi officials.[5] It was proposed that these be taken over by the British, and made through the Khandesh treasury. Such a settlement would leave the Dangi Bhils with 'no

3 Briggs to Resident, Baroda, 14.7.1821, *BA.PSD.1820–21.Vol 4/8.*
4 Rigby to Robertson, 30.10.1825, *BA.PD.1826.Vol 5/228.*
5 Coll., Kh., to Comm. in Deccan, 30.7.1825, *BRO.DDR.DN 1.FN 2.*

possible pretence for any aggressions'.[6] Though Gaekwadi officials were hostile to the idea, the British decided to go ahead. Efforts to reach a settlement began in 1826, with the Baglan deshmukh playing a key role as a British intermediary. In 1829, after long negotiations, Khem raja of Ghadvi, Hasusinh raja of Amala, Ankus raja of Deher, and several others signed agreements accepting the giras transfer. Many others, including the most powerful Ghadvi chief, Silput raja, and his allies, like the raja of Pimpri, refused to accede to the transfer. But the agreements effectively ensured that their giras too would be paid by the British.[7]

The transfer held out one advantage to all the chiefs. The amounts that the British finally decided to pay after adjudicating between Gaekwadi and Dangi claims were often twice as much as what Songadh officials were paying at the time.[8] Yet that did not swing matters. Many, like Silput, remained hostile. He refused to take notice of his uncle, Khem, and also fought bitterly with one of the chiefs who along with Ankus, Khem and Hasusinh 'had gone unaccompanied by the Silput Raja to the Sarkar [in July 1829] and got the Hucks'.[9]

Some of Silput's reasons for hostility to the giras transfer may have been shared widely. He feared that the transfer was a pretext to stop payment of giras altogether in the long run. When the time came to collect payments, he would 'eventually be referred to Bombay, Delhi, Calcutta or elsewhere'.[10] Because of this fear, he insisted that he would agree to the transfer only after receiving a Gaekwadi yad (communication) authorizing it.[11]

Most of all, he was worried because of the different way in which the British perceived giras. After his uncle Khem raja had despite his opposition accepted the British transfer in 1829, he told Khem: 'you get your money from the English Sarkar, one day or other we shall be ruined. The English Government will give us Hucks as long as we

6 Rigby to Bax, 27.3.1826, *BRO.DDR.DN 1.FN 2*.

7 See the correspondence in *BRO.DDR.DN 1.FN2*.

8 Graham to Giberne, 8.7.1828, *BRO.DDR.DN 1.FN 2*; Hodges to Noriss, 16.7.1829, *BA.PSD.1829.Vol 8/332*. This was because Gaekwadi payments had declined over the previous two decades, as was noted in the last chapter.

9 Hodges to Noriss, 30.6.1829, *BA.PSD.1829.Vol 8/332*; Statement of Malharea Kal naik, n.d., 1829, *BA.PSD.1829.Vol 8/332*. Giberne to Newnham, 19.9.1828, *BRO.DDR.DN 1.FN 2*.

10 Coll., Kh., to Secy., GoB, 16.10.1828, *BA.PD.1828.Vol 29/320*.

11 Coll., Kh., to Secy., GoB, nd., *BRO.DDR.DN 1.FN 2*. Coll., Kh., to Resident, Baroda, 16.10.1828, ibid.

can do any mischief and no longer, why not take money from the Guicowar?'[12] By this, he possibly alluded to the point that while the British paid giras only to stop the raids, the Gaekwads also considered it a means of affirming and extending their own authority in the region; therefore the latter were less likely to stop payments.

Whatever the reasons of different chiefs for accepting or rejecting the transfer, the faith that officials reposed in it as a means of extirpating raids turned out to be misplaced. Not only Silput but Ankus and other Dangi chiefs who had accepted the giras transfer raided the plains villages of Chorawar and Nagjor in 1829.[13] And that led to the British expedition which finally halted the raids. Nine full years were to elapse before the next raid. And on that occasion, when the raids were conducted to protest against Gaekwadi non-payment of giras, the chiefs surrendered as soon as an expedition against them reached the outskirts of Dangs.[14] Through the rest of the century, there were to be virtually no major raids on the plains of Khandesh or Gujarat. The raid as an activity had been decisively extinguished.

THE EXTIRPATION OF RAIDS

The remarkable success in halting raids had to do with a range of factors, all related to the ways in which colonial officials worked with an opposition between the wild and the civilized. Most importantly, the British, unlike previous plains powers, consistently wished to halt raids. Raids were treated by British officials not as occasions for negotiations but rather as acts of aggression on territory over which they had exclusive sovereignty. This was manifest, first, in the colonial emphasis on firmness of conduct. In 1823, for instance, when Budrea raja of Zorum Kikwari raided a village in Khandesh, and demanded that his overdue haks be paid, this was not conceded. It was necessary, one official said, to be firm when faced with such demands, else it would 'hold out a premium to other Bheel chiefs for the commission of like irregularities'.[15] In other words, the negotiations that had been the consequence of raids formerly no longer took place to the same degree.

Then there was the British emphasis on securing reparations.

---

12 Statement of Malharea Kal naik, *BA.PSD.1829.Vol 8/332.*
13 Stevens to Hodges, 15.9.1829, *BA.PD.1829.Vol 8/332.*
14 See *IOL.F.4.1929* for accounts of the raid.
15 Rigby to Robertson, 14.8.1823, *BA.PSD.1823.Vol. 10/105.*

While these had often been demanded by the Gaekwads or the Vansda raja for raids, they had not been taken with any consistency because of the implicit recognition that a raid was also a claim to authority, giras, or other haks; it could become an occasion for the acknowledgement or granting of rights. In contrast to this was the attitude of Khandesh officials, who regarded raids as criminal acts, invariably demanded back the cattle that had been carried away, and undertook punitive expeditions, as in 1822 and 1830, if this were not done.[16]

Third, there was a consistent emphasis on retaliation against those involved in such attacks. This was the point Khem raja was making to his bhauband in 1822 when they contemplated an attack on British forces which were camped at Chikhli. He warned them that

though not a calf had been slain nor a Hut burnt at Chicklee, yet if an arrow was once let fly, our destruction was inevitable. We had not to contend with that description of men whom we had hitherto engaged with success, who had contented themselves with burning villages, who sought to avoid the remotest danger, but that now we should be hunted like the deer of our Forests, that even admitting the possibility of success, an overwhelming Force would instantly be disposed and effect our total annihilation.[17]

Involved here is the distinction between the colonial army and those which had preceded it. The latter would have burnt villages like Chikhli on attack, which to Khem does not seem excessive. It still left open the possibility of negotiations. Such demonstrations of power could lead, for instance, to the Dangi chiefs offering a village in compensation.[18] In contrast, the colonial army had already, in the process of 'settling' Bhils along the Khandesh ghats, demonstrated its commitment to the single-minded pursuit of 'offenders' and 'criminals'.[19] From a Dangi framework which saw raids as primarily part of a process of negotiating authority, and not only as ends in themselves, the British obsession with capture and punishment represented a refusal to negotiate, more destructive and dangerous than anything that had preceded it.

---

[16] See the correspondence in *BRO.DDR.DN 1.FN 2* and *BRO.DDR.DN 1.FN 3*.
[17] Rigby to Briggs, 30.7.1822, *BRO.DDR.DN 1.FN 1*.
[18] Mansfield to Secy., GoB, 24.7.1855, *BA.PD.1855.Vol 37.Comp 123*.
[19] For an account, see Deshpande, *John Briggs in Maharashtra*, New Delhi, 1987, ch. 3; Prasad, *The Bhils of Khandesh*, New Delhi, 1991, ch. 2; and Graham, 'A historical sketch . . . ' in *SRBG 26*.

Finally, there was the tremendous British military power relative to the Bhil chiefs, and the ways in which that power was enacted through the British concerns with firm conduct, reparation, or retaliation. There had long been an emphasis amongst British officials on the need to instill an awe of colonial military power. In 1809, when Jararsinh raja raided Surat territory, he was warned that 'whoever acts in this Manner with the Company must in the end suffer'.[20] After the British takeover of Khandesh, colonial power was made evident to the Bhil chiefs in the course of two military expeditions into Dangs. The first was launched in 1822, following raids by Silput raja and his uncle Khem raja on Umerpat and Pimpalner villages. The commanding officer, Captain Rigby, marched to the village of Chikhli on the eastern outskirts of Dangs, and from there sent a letter to Silput and Khem, offering a pardon if the plundered cattle were restored. Shortly afterwards, Khem visited Rigby's camp, and asked for a pardon for Silput and himself, promising to restore the cattle. Rigby, feeling that his rapid and easy progress till Chikhli had already demonstrated colonial military power, accepted this offer and withdrew.[21]

The chiefs' notion of their own power had formerly been shaped by the belief that Dangs was almost inaccessible to outside troops. This attitude informed the Ghadvi chief Jararsinh's response in 1809 when a Valod official threatened retaliation if some goods that had been carried away during a raid on a village were not restored. Jararsinh replied: 'If your Company Bahadur wish to fight with me I will advance a few paces to meet you. There is no fear. I am prepared in case any person should attack me.'[22] By the time of Rigby's expedition, there was enough and more fear to go around. The success of the British in subduing the plains of Khandesh had already made the chiefs rather more wary of tangling with them. That time, Silput raja entered into a confrontation with Rigby apprehensively, almost unwillingly.[23] Again, in 1830, while Silput remained defiant, most other chiefs were apprehensive of the consequences of a confrontation with the sarkar. A naik warned that 'unless you pay attention to the Sarkar, the Country will be ruined'.[24]

20 Komavisdar, Valod and Buhari to Jararsinh, *BA.PDD.351(11)*.
21 Rigby to Briggs, 30.7.1822, *BRO.DDR.DN 1.FN 1*.
22 Jararsinh to Komavisdar, Valod and Buhari, 5th Magsur, Vad, 1866 *BA. PDD.351(11)*.
23 Rigby to Briggs, 30.7.1822, *BRO.DDR.DN 1.FN 2*.
24 Deposition of Babul Naik, 6.5.1830, *BRO.DDR.DN 1.FN 3*. See also Statement by Nathu patil and Sivaji Balaji, *BA.PD.1829.Vol 8/332*.

By 1830 a new organizational technology had developed which increased British military domination, the Khandesh Bhil Corps. Former expeditions, such as even Rigby's, had been handicapped by relatively slow-moving conventional troops, outsiders to the region and the terrain, and were not too effective in dealing with the quick forays of the Bhils, or in making much headway in the dense forests where the raiders took refuge. But in the early 1820s, James Outram, then a junior officer posted to Khandesh, set up the Khandesh Bhil Corps. It was similar in principle to the late-eighteenth-century corps set up by Cleveland in Bhagalpur to deal with Paharia hill chiefs,[25] a precedent which Outram was in all likelihood aware of. Its principal innovation was that it consisted of Khandesh Bhils who had been put through a rigorous training. The Corps undertook campaigns against recalcitrant chiefs who conducted raids or defied Khandesh officials. Proceeding in small formations and led by persons familiar with the local terrain, the corps was remarkably effective in retaliating against chiefs.[26]

And it was the Khandesh Bhil Corps under Outram which ventured into Dangs in April 1830. Its very success in penetrating quickly into Dangs produced results. Ankus raja of Dherbhavti and Partabsinh raja of Amala met Outram, sought pardon, and promised to help against Silput raja. Later, following a night march, the toughest terrain in Dangs was occupied. After this, other chiefs too, including Khem, came in and promised assistance.[27] It took longer to actually capture Silput. But from this point on, he was constantly on the run. Within three months of the expedition setting out, Outram was back in Khandesh, with Silput and other captured chiefs in tow. Here, the names of all the chiefs were noted down, and they were warned that they were known and could be easily captured if they resorted to further attacks on the plains. As for Khem (who had later been discovered to have been less than wholehearted in supporting the British, and to have secretly colluded with Silput and helped him escape) and Silput, British officials imprisoned both of them. Silput was also removed from the gadi of Ghadvi, and replaced by his son Rajhans.

[25] Briggs to Chaplin, 16.4.1825, *BA.PD.1825.Vol 2/192*; Briggs to Elphinstone, 8.1.1819, *PA.DCR.Vol 174.No 36*. See Seema Alavi, *The sepoys and the Company: Tradition and transition in northern India*, Delhi, 1996, ch. 2, for an account of Cleveland's policy.

[26] A.H.A. Simcox, *A memoir of the Khandesh Bhil Corps, 1825–1891*, Bombay, 1912.

[27] For an account of the campaign, see *BRO.DDR.DN 1.FN 3*.

For the British, the cost of the 1830 expedition was heavy, even with the Bhil corps. Though only one man from the force died in action, later, of the five British officers, one died of malaria and three left India on sick certificate; and of the 300 Bhil regulars, only 120 marched back to their base in Khandesh, with even most of them having found Dangs too malarial.[28] Even so, it was clear to Dangis that a determined colonial force could not be kept out. The Corps' success and the attitudinal shift represented by the British approach to raids led to the emergence of a new cultural trope amongst the Dangis: a profound fear of British military power. In goth even now, the enormous power of the colonial lashkar or army is a repeated motif. This new trope became evident even in the course of the 1830 expedition. As Outram reported immediately after his night-march,

the charm which upheld the Silput's power and the spirits of his followers immediately dissolved — the latter dispersed and have not yet reassembled though strongly urged to do so by the Silput's [messengers?] bearing his own arrow, which symbol was heretofore reverenced and promptly obeyed.[29]

He reported that the chiefs were 'by now so thoroughly convinced of our power to punish, and have suffered so much by our inroad, that I am satisfied that they will endeavour to avert such an eventuality as the more angry visitation which I threatened'.[30]

The success in Dangs presaged similar developments throughout the rest of colonial western India. British stakes in the regions honeycombed by forest polities increased dramatically after 1818, when Khandesh, Ahmadnagar, Nasik, Pune were ceded to them from amongst the Peshwa's territories. In central India and Rajputana too, from the 1830s the British had to deal with regions where forest polities were influential. Using elements of the same strategies in these regions, including the creation of Bhil Corps, most of these forest polities had been subordinated by the 1850s.[31]

Within Dangs, the subordination led to the transformation of giras. After Silput raja had been deposed, the transfer of giras was

[28] F.J. Goldsmid, *James Outram: A biography*, London, 1880, vol. I, pp. 87–9; Graham, 'A historical sketch of the Bheel tribes inhabiting the Province of Khandesh', *SRBG 26*, p. 211, note.

[29] Outram to Boyd, 11.4.1830, *BRO.DDR.DN 1.FN 3*.

[30] *BRO.DDR.DN 1.FN 3*.

[31] No survey of this process of subordination exists, though records about it are plentiful at the National Archives of India, New Delhi. See especially *NAI.FD.20.12.1841.FC7–9*, and *NAI.FD.30.11.1840, FC 33–39*.

carried through with no opposition, and beginning the next year
Gaekwadi giras was paid from the treasury at Khandesh. The British
thought that they were doing this only to ensure more regular
payment of giras, and maybe to decrease Gaekwadi influence in the
region. But the transfer had more far-reaching implications. Formerly, giras had been a marker of shared sovereignty over specific
villages, and its receipt from the Gaekwads had been part of the
formation of shifting alliances with Baroda. Its irregularity and
variability was constitutive of giras, and indexed the shifts in alliances and power. Now, as a fixed annual sum paid regularly from the
Khandesh treasury, the right to it did not have to be demonstrated
any longer through the regular wielding of power. Also, new giras
dues could no longer be created through raids, nor could old ones be
modified. Furthermore, the association between giras and shared
sovereignty over specific villages in the plains was weakened. An
annual lump payment associated with no particular village, giras was
not so much a right claimed from plains villages as a conferral from
above. Its association with the active wielding of power, and with a
role in plains polities, was attenuated and made superfluous. A
mandini of giras, one might say, had taken place.

THE UNFOLDING OF PAX BRITANNICA

But enough for now about the dang. After all, the extirpation of
raids and the transformation of giras was undertaken not so much
to manage the dang as to manage the plains of Khandesh, and it
is to their transformation that I now turn. As part of Pax Britannica,
the extirpation of raids and the reduction of the influence of the
dang transformed the older enactments of wildness. It had been
principally because of the forest polities' power — their ability to
raid the plains and escape reprisals, their ability to provide sanc-
tuary to rebels against powerful rulers in settled agrarian areas —
that discourses of wildness were so influential in plains areas. But
now they were left with far fewer means of exercising authority in
the plains.

Even figures associated with plains armed forces who had been
active in forest polities had been systematically reduced. After
deposing Silput raja, the British compelled the 'Arabs', Sidis and
Makranis in his force to leave. This was because they were believed
to instigate the chiefs to 'mischief'. Such a systematic elimination
of these soldiers had earlier been undertaken in British Khandesh,

where they had put up a ferocious resistance to colonial forces. There, deporting 'Arabs' out of Khandesh and even India was one of the major tasks which British officials undertook after consolidating their power.[32]

The reduction of the influence of forest polities was one of the major factors that made possible the dramatic extension of settled cultivation in western India, and more broadly throughout India, in the nineteenth century. In Khandesh, where forest polities had been particularly influential in the preceding period, the cultivated area increased from 705,960 acres in 1818–23 to 1,053,849 acres by 1847–52, and to about 3,631,000 by 1916–20. To a significant degree, such growth was made possible by the marginalization in these regions of the politics and lifestyles associated with the dang.[33]

The exclusive emphasis on settled cultivation also meant that modes of subsistence in plains and forest areas began to diverge dramatically. Unlike earlier, mobility and seasonal migration were now systematically discouraged. Shifting cultivation was considered inappropriate for the plains, and appropriate only for primitive tribes in the forests.[34] In Thana district in western India, where many communities used loppings to manure their fields as in Dangs, the British made concerted efforts to halt the practice.[35] Permanent villages were established on fixed sites, and even the area available for fallows decreased gradually. This was in contrast to the forested areas, where maximizing land revenue and extending cultivation was not a priority, and shifting agriculture often persisted till the early twentieth century.

Even plains ecology was transformed with the subordination of forest polities. Formerly, we saw, plains areas had been characterized by interrupted forests; in this sense, the contrast between these regions and the extensive forests like Dangs was not very sharp. But agricultural colonization virtually wiped out these forests. Sometimes, as in Awadh and Bihar in northern India, the British had a

32 Deshpande, *John Briggs in Maharashtra*, New Delhi, 1987, p. 71.

33 See Richards and McAlpin, 'Cotton cultivating and land clearing'.

34 For colonial ideology towards shifting cultivation, and their privileging of settled agriculture, see Jacques Pouchpedass, 'British attitudes towards shifting cultivation in colonial south India: a case study of South Canara district, 1800–1920', and Neeladri Bhattacharya, 'Pastoralists in a colonial world', both in Arnold and Guha (eds), *Nature, culture, imperialism*.

35 Tucker discusses the effort to halt lopping in Thana in his 'Forest management and imperial politics: Thana district, Bombay, 1823–1887', *Indian Economic and Social History Review*, vol. 16, no. 3, 1979.

further incentive for wiping out interrupted forests: these forests served as bases for resistance by rebellious chiefs, most spectacularly during the 1857 uprising. Similar considerations may also have influenced the clearing of forests in the plains regions of Khandesh. For a range of reasons, then, by the late nineteenth century, there was a sharp contrast between the forest-less regions of settled agriculture largely in the plains, and the densely forested regions such as Dangs. There was now a physical and faunal dichotomization of western India, and maybe the subcontinent more broadly.[36]

Further research is needed to explore the implications of the subordination of forest polities for plains communities. But it is likely that fewer people in the plains now embraced a Bhil identity. The increasing influence in the nineteenth century of Kshatriya and, especially, Brahman-centred values may have been related to the decline of the Bhil-centred discourse of wildness. This development, combined with the decline of warfare and the warrior culture that had formerly been influential, may also have influenced the forms taken by nationalist masculinities in late-nineteenth-century western India.

The very escalation of difference between the dang and surrounding plains regions created an inner frontier. Formerly, there had been intimate ties between them, and both had influenced each other profoundly. Now the dang was contained. It did not influence the desh or Gujarat, it was influenced by them. And even this influence did not tend towards the creation of similarities. Rather, the dang came to be seen and treated as a subordinate Other of surrounding areas; it became the space of the wild tribes as opposed to civilized castes; it became the space of forestry as opposed to settled agriculture, it became the space where the civilized dalliance with primitivism took place. It is to these developments, and to the many ways in which the dang was transformed, that I now turn.

(11)

---

[36] For the ecological transformation of Khandesh, see Richards and McAlpin, 'Cotton cultivating and land clearing'. For northern India, see J.F. Richards, E.S. Haynes and R. Hagen, 'Changes in land-use in Bihar, Punjab, and Haryana, 1850–1970', *Modern Asian Studies*, vol. 9, 1985, pp. 699–732.

11

Towards Exclusive Sovereignties

Another mandini associated with gora raj is the exclusion of the Gaekwads and the deshmukh from Dangs:

The Rao Bahadur was the karbhari of the entire Dangs. The sikka-daftar of the rajas were with him, and he kept them at home. There was a quarrel between the *Angrez Bahadur* [a phrase often used for the English] and him at the darbar of the mandini. The Rao told the Angrez, 'leave Dangs'. The Angrez told him, 'go and light a candle on each hillock' [leave this place.] They fought then at the darbar. The rajas saw it. The Rao tied a big red turban. He was a *seekhel-bhanel manus* [educated man.] He took out his daftar and the Angrez took out his daftar. They began reading to each other. They kept on reading. Finally, the Rao threw away the daftar of the Angrez. The Angrez said, 'Bade [big] Rao, you threw away my daftar. I shall throw you out'. The Angrez snatched away the Rao's daftar, read it, and threw it away. The Rao said, 'I shall throw you out'. But it was the Angrez who got rid of him. The Rao ran away, and he had a pyre made, and had it burnt. He also had his wife cut off all her hair. Then he made it known that the Rao was dead, and he slipped away at night to some other place. After this, the Rao's wife went away to Malegaon.[1]

It is appropriate that the deshmukh's struggle with the British should be through the written word, and that the figure with superior records should win: the power of both the deshmukh and the British is often associated with writing.[2]

There are several goth about the exclusion of the Gaekwads too:

The gora sarkar held the mandini at Bhavani cha killa. The Gaekwad Maharaj, Sivaji [Sayajirao Gaekwad], also came. His turban had jewels in it, and he was on a black horse. He climbed off the horse. The golden turban he was wearing fell down while

---

1 Gajesinh Monsu, 26.4.1990, Kadmal.
2 I return to the theme of writing in later chapters. See also my 'Writing, orality and power'.

he was doing this. So he lost face. He took out his sword and broke the Angrez turban. He said, 'if my raj is over, then your raj is also over'. Then Sivaji Maharaj and the gora saheb went away and they had a fight. The gora saheb came back victorious. He came to Dangs and the mandini was held. Shelas [shawls], sirpav [turbans], and sida [provisions] were given to the rajas. The sida included one *man* [a measure] grain, one *man masur dal* [a lentil], goats, and twelve packets of tobacco.[3]

Unlike the deshmukh or the British, the power of the Gaekwads is not associated only with writing, but also with the insignia of royalty. Significantly, it is the loss of these — the falling of the turban and the consequent loss of face — which is seized on to explain his exclusion.

THE EXCLUSION OF THE GAEKWADS

The exclusion of the Gaekwads and the deshmukh in the nineteenth century was another aspect of the subordination of forest polities and the consolidation of an inner frontier. It did away with the shared sovereignty over loosely defined frontiers — a sovereignty that I suggested earlier had been constructed through giras, raids, and co-shared villages — where two or more chiefs could hold rights over the same villages. Instead, the British understood sovereignty as exclusive, which is to say, they felt that political authority was unified, and that there could be only one sovereign over a particular region. Associated with exclusive sovereignty was the notion of singular allegiances. Formerly, we saw, a Bhil chief maintained alliances with several plains powers simultaneously, shifting between them. Now, the British insisted on making each Bhil chief owe allegiance only to one plains power — themselves in the case of the Dangi chiefs.

Initially, the British takeover of Khandesh in 1818 increased Baroda's authority in Dangs, because it was the only power capable of providing the chiefs with support against the British. In 1829, the Songadh killedar and other Gaekwadi officials provided intelligence to Silput of Outram's plans to invade Dangs, and of his moves.[4] When Outram's expedition overran Dangs, Baroda officials helped Silput raja flee from it. Colonial corps had to march through

3 Gajesinh Monsu, 26.4.1990, Kadmal.
4 Appaji Rav to Silput, No. 1, n.d., *BRO.DDR.DN 1.FN 3*; Appaji Rav to Coll., Kh., n.d., *BRO.DDR.DN 1.FN 3*.

Gaekwadi territory in pursuit of him; they even seized a Gaekwadi official for assisting Silput.[5]

The Gaekwads continued to strengthen their ties with the chiefs even after the 1830 British expedition. Around that year, Bapu Rakshya had become the ijaradar of Songadh. Almost immediately, he strengthened an outpost at Malangdev village along north-eastern Dangs. It provided a base from which ties with the chiefs could be extended, and authority over more villages established.[6] He used the classical instruments of incorporation: the distribution of gifts which conferred authority, and possibly support to the chiefs against each other.[7]

But the British too were taking increasing interest in Dangs. Ever since their takeover of Khandesh, they had been suspicious of Baroda's involvement in Dangs. One of the reasons for carrying through the giras transfer was the desire to reduce Gaekwadi influence in the region. After the assistance given to the chiefs by Songadh officials during the 1830 expedition, they were even more convinced that Baroda was instigating the chiefs to 'mischief'. And from the 1840s, three developments led to the exclusion of Baroda from Dangs. First, British officials at Khandesh and Surat decided, in the early 1840s, to secure leases of Dangs forests from the chiefs. But Gaekwadi officials too were trying for timber leases. Some existing Gaekwadi leases to parts of Dangs were set aside, and Baroda's efforts to secure additional leases were foiled. By late 1843, the British had secured leases to most of Dangs, and by the early 1860s to all of it, overriding whatever Gaekwadi leases had survived.[8]

Second, there was the attempt to extinguish Gaekwadi rights in co-shared villages. Ever since the leases, the rights of the Gaekwads to remove timber from co-shared villages had been denied in principle, and no new alienations of villages to the Gaekwads were recognized.[9] From the 1860s, even old rights were subjected to an

[5] Outram to Boyd, 8.5.1830, *BRO.DDR.DN 1.FN 3.*

[6] Pritchard to Ashburner, 15.10. 1870, *DBD*, I, p. 9. See also *DBD*, II, pp. 18ff, 55ff.

[7] Udesinh to Blanc, 24.8.1838, *BRO.RR.DN 144.FN 719.*

[8] Boyce to Reeves, 19.2.1844, *BA.PD.1845.Vol 16/1648.Comp 444*; see the correspondence in *BA.RD.1858.Vol 77.Comp 1419*; *BA.PD.1858.Vol 96.Comp 1123*; *BA.PD.1859.Vol 92.Comp 866*; *BA.PD.1864.Vol 115.Comp 906*; *DBD*, I, pp. 11, 57.

[9] *NAI.FD.FC.181.19.4.1843*, Mansfield to Secy., GoB, 4.9.1857, *BA.PD.1858. Vol 96.Comp 1123.*

exceptionally harsh scrutiny, and curbed or extinguished wherever possible. In addition to the spectre of pilferage, a phalanx of reasons were marshalled to support this course of action: fees levied at Gaekwadi timber nakas made timber extraction financially unviable; 'primitive' Dangis were 'simple' people who needed protection against Gaekwadi 'machinations'; and Gaekwadi officials would, if allowed to retain control over co-shared villages, use these as a base for further expansion into Dangs.[10]

Eventually, in 1879, after two British committees (in 1867 and 1872) had deliberated over the issue, the British government at Bombay decided to acknowledge only Gaekwadi land revenue rights in the co-shared villages. It denied the older Gaekwadi rights to transit duties, land and *abkari* (liquor) revenues, as well as to civil and political jurisdiction over the villages. Some years later, a definitive list of co-shared villages was prepared, and an official appointed to collect the Gaekwadi share of land revenue and hand it over to Baroda.[11] Obviously, Baroda was to be allowed no dealings at all in its co-shared villages.

Third, there was the creation of a fixed boundary between Dangs and Baroda. In 1884, a Boundary Commissioner was appointed to demarcate it. This proved to be a difficult task, for villagers themselves gave contradictory information. Some claimed that a particular village belonged to the Gaekwads, others that it belonged to a Dangi chief. The Boundary Commissioner tried to weigh these claims and decide who 'really' held exclusive rights over the village. Deciding on the exact line of control was even more difficult. In principle, the boundaries of a village were indicated by the boundary gods. Yet we saw in Chapter 4 that there were several boundary gods, and the choice of which of them indicated the 'real' boundary was a vexed and arbitrary choice. Despite all these hurdles — indicative of how alien the notion of a boundary was — a clear boundary between Baroda and Dangs had been completed by the 1890s.[12]

These three developments together resulted in the almost complete exclusion of Baroda officials from Dangs. The broad band

10 See *BA.PD.1870.Vol 57.Comp 121*; Fenner to Mansfield, 13.5.1858, *BA. RD.1858.Vol 77.Comp 1419*; *BA.PD.1864.Vol 15. Comp 906* and *BA.PD.1870.Vol 57.Comp 589*; Ashburner to Secy., GoB, 31.3.1873, *DBD*. I, p. 29; Pritchard to Ashburner,15.10.1870, *DBD*, I, pp. 9ff, 53.
11 For an account of this process, see *DBD*, I, pp. 9–69, 98–105, and II, pp. 1–39. See also *BRO.RR.DN 141.FN 710*; see also V.K. Chavda, *Gaekwads and the British: A study of their problems, 1875–1920*, New Delhi, 1966, pp. 89–94.
12 The process is extensively documented in *DBD*.

of villages on which both the Gaekwads and the Dangi chiefs had possessed overlapping rights were now reconstituted as part of two territories, bounded and exclusive of each other. Such exclusive sovereignty was a profound transformation of older relations. Formerly, despite what may seem like precedents in Maratha hostility towards Bhil chiefs, the ties of Maratha chiefs had involved shifting alliances, shared sovereignty, frontiers rather than boundaries, and profound affinities with the Bhil chiefs. Now, under the British, the shift from frontiers to mapped boundaries, which more than anything else epitomized the creation of exclusive sovereignty, was carried out in most areas of colonial India by the late nineteenth century.[13]

THE EXCLUSION OF THE DESHMUKHS

The exclusion of the deshmukhs took place by quite a different process. The British takeover of Khandesh already undercut their authority in Khandesh. Formerly powerful hereditary representatives of the Peshwa, they now had little role in the emerging system of administration. But in Dangs, as an intermediary indispensable to the British during the first two decades after their takeover, and as the chiefs' conduit to colonial officials, there was initially a significant increase in the power of Murharrao, the principal deshmukh between the 1820s and 1840s.

Formerly, the Bhil chiefs in the deshmukhi area of Baglan acknowledged the suzerainty of Dangi chiefs like those of Ghadvi or Deher — more, possibly, than they did that of Murharrao.[14] In this, they had been, in the heart of the deshmukh's area of control, potential allies of the Dangi chiefs. During the colonial settlement of 1818–20, however, agreements were secured from the Baglan chiefs that they would not raid the plains; their haks were commuted to an annual allowance, which the British undertook to pay. Since Baglan could be effectively controlled, these chiefs were, on the whole, to stick to their agreements in the ensuing years. Effectively, this reduced the retaliatory power of Dangs chiefs in relation to the deshmukhs, for they no longer had allies within Baglan to bank on.

The consolidation of the deshmukh's power was furthered by his role in the 1829 giras transfer. As we saw, he persuaded some chiefs,

[13] The transformation of frontiers into boundaries is noted in Ainslee Embree, *Imagining India: Essays on Indian history*, Delhi, 1989, ch. 5.
[14] Briggs to Elphinstone, 24.9.1818, *PA.DCR.Vol 172.No 212.*

such as Khem raja and Ankus raja, to assent to the transfer.[15] He played a major role at negotiations, successfully buttressing with documents and assertions the claims of Khem and other Dangi chiefs to a larger share of giras than Gaekwadi officials were willing to concede. Though he did not succeed in becoming, as he had desired, the intermediary through whom payments were made, he did emerge as an important figure in the new system of giras payments.[16]

Murharrao deshmukh also played an important role in the British expeditions in the 1820s and 1830s which helped subordinate Dangs. As a later Collector remarked, Murharrao's

influence in the Dang is unquestionable and I might say almost unlimited. Neither Captain Outram nor Captain Graham ever went into the Daung without him, and I have been informed by the latter that his connection with the Bheel chiefs is so complete, and his authority so well recognized that the fact of his being in camp was sufficient to prevent treachery on the part of the guides and ensure success.[17]

The resultant perception of the deshmukh as a close British ally possibly helped him further consolidate his authority. This is indicated by the increase in his *jagiri* villages in Dangs during the period.[18]

But precisely because it drew largely on alliances with the British, his authority was also very fragile. And in 1844, when the British made efforts to secure direct leases of Dangi forests, the deshmukh made the mistake of initially opposing them. Though he shifted his stance later, it was too late. The British had become suspicious of him, and to the Dangi chiefs his ties with the British no longer seemed so very strong. The chiefs commenced repudiating his authority, and the leases that the British drew up drastically pruned his powers. Direct British management of the region did away with his role as the representative of the British, and terminated his haks on timber extracted from Dangs.[19] The deshmukhs' authority was further undercut by later colonial administrative reforms reducing the powers of village officials.

Officials in Khandesh also made strenuous efforts in the 1850s to do away with the compensatory allowance paid to Murharrao

---

[15] Giberne to Graham, 18.6.1828, *BRO.DDR.DN 1.FN 2*.

[16] 2nd Assistant Coll., to Coll., Kh., 8.7.1828, *BRO.DDR.DN 1.FN 2*.

[17] Reeves to Secy., GoB, 1.7.1843, *IOL.F.4.2074*.

[18] *DBD*, I, pp. 11, 111, 114. See also the agreements, reproduced in *BA.PD. 1850.Vol 37/2403.Comp 1983*.

[19] Reeves to Willoughby, 1.7.1843, *IOL.F.4.2074*.

from 1844 for the loss of his haks.[20] They were unsuccessful that time, but they succeeded two decades later. After the death of Murharrao, his widow adopted the son of Krishnaji Khanderao, the Songadh killedar, as the heir to deshmukhi haks (one can only speculate whether the Dangi goth about Murharrao's flight arose from disbelief in these stories of his death). This adoption further aroused the ire of the British. Eventually, in 1874, district officials had halted the payments, claiming that Murharrao's allowances had been personal and not hereditary.[21] In ensuing decades, the deshmukhs played an insignificant role in Dangs, and their influence was confined to those villages they held in jagir.

THE SPREAD OF EXCLUSIVE SOVEREIGNTY

What was striking was that it was not only the British who imposed their notions of exclusive sovereignty: these notions were later taken up by Gaekwadi officials and even Bhil chiefs. Initially, it is true, Gaekwadi officials and the chiefs resisted the spread of exclusive sovereignty. In its first few decades, the British takeover did not succeed in excluding Baroda the way Khandesh officials had hoped it would. An early sign that things had not been going as anticipated came in 1838, when the Dangi chiefs raided Gaekwadi territory, claiming that their giras payments had been held back that year.[22] Colonial officials were initially baffled, for had not Gaekwadi giras payments been made from the Khandesh treasury since the giras transfer in 1830? In the course of investigations, it emerged, as noted in Chapter 9, that in the years following the transfer in 1830, Gaekwadi officials at Songadh had continued to distribute giras amongst the chiefs. Baroda claimed that this was the result of a misunderstanding, and that they had not known of the transfer.[23]

That story is rather thin. Songadh officials, who managed several co-shared villages in Dangs and maintained outposts there, would certainly have been aware of the British takeover of giras. The actual reasons appear to have been somewhat different. The British

20 Coll., Kh., to Secy., GoB, 24.7.1855, *BA.PD.1855.Vol 36.Comp 1290.*

21 *BA.PD.1872.Vol 74.Comp 123.* See also *BA.PD.1855.Vol 36.Comp 1290, BA.PD.1874.Vol 108.Comp 897.*

22 Dallas to Blanc, 18.3.1839, *BRO.DDR.DN 1.FN 3.* See also the correspondence in *IOL.F.4.1929.*

23 Coll., Kh., to Resident, Baroda, 28.7.1828, *BRO.DDR.DN 1.FN 2.*

takeover of haks had been partial, in that it only covered the *gaonwar giras* (dues on villages). Several other haks remained which had to be collected from Gaekwadi territory, either directly from the villages, or from Songadh.[24] Also, Gaekwadi officials at the time had a conscious interest in continuing to pay giras themselves, since it was a crucial element in the construction of alliances with the chiefs. The most striking indicator of this is the fact that the payments continued to be made even after 1838, when it had been discovered that they were being duplicated![25] This distribution of giras sustained shared sovereignty in the early decades after colonial rule was established in Khandesh.

But in later decades, Gaekwadi officials acquiesced in the spread of exclusive sovereignty, even claiming it themselves over formerly co-shared villages. From the 1850s, Gaekwadi officials sought consciously to reduce the giras payments they made in addition to the British ones. Despite repeated complaints over the decades, these had almost entirely stopped by the early twentieth century.[26] It would be inappropriate to treat this transformation of Gaekwadi attitudes as simply a continuation of older precolonial trends towards exclusive sovereignty: as this and earlier chapters have argued, it is difficult to discern any such trends. Rather, by the 1840s, the ability of the chiefs to raid the plains, assert authority and demand payments had declined. The divorce from power transformed the payments. From being both a conferral and an acknowledgement of authority by Gaekwadi officials, the payment became a unilateral conferral of authority, one that the Gaekwads had no particular reasons for maintaining. Also, not only was the influence of chiefs in the plains less important, but discourses centred around the affirmation of wildness had in general been marginalized with Pax Britannica. Everywhere in their territories, Gaekwadi officials formalized their giras payments, making it into a fixed due paid every year, with few connotations of shared sovereignty. And once shared sovereignty was denied, giras payments appeared as a 'form of blackmail' imposed by Bhils and

<hr>

[24] Udesinh to Blanc, 24.8.1838, *BRO.RR.DN 144.FN 719.* Giberne to Newnham, 8.7.1828, ibid.

[25] See Coll., Kh., to Resident, Baroda, 28.7.1838, Resident to Coll., Kh., 10.1.1829, *BRO.DDR.DN 1. FN 2*; Dulput Vagoo and Kursal Vagoo to Boyce and Arbuthnot, n.d., forwarded 16.1.1843, *DCR.DN 1.FN 9.*

[26] For some complaints, see Coll., Kh., to Resident, Baroda, 7.8.1857, *BRO.DDR.DN 1.FN 4*; Resident, Baroda to Secy., GoB, 1.9.1862, *BRO.HPO(Pol). FN 289/2.SN 2*; and the correspondence in *BA.PD.1870.Vol 57.Comp 439.*

other similar communities on villages that were actually under exclusive Gaekwadi or British control.[27]

The shift towards exclusive sovereignty may also have been the result of a new and very conscious strategy. By the 1840s, shared sovereignties created through alliances were easily set aside by the British. Gaekwadi officials became more acutely aware of this after 1850, when the first portion of the boundary between Dangs and Gaekwadi territory was drawn. Shared rights, they saw, were likely to be treated by hostile British officials as a sign of Dangi sovereignty over a village. Unsurprisingly, they now took less interest in maintaining giras and other hak payments or making them serve their old purposes. Instead, they tried to acquire exclusive rights in villages, and to deny the haks of Dangi chiefs in them. This new emphasis on exclusive authority was evident when they stopped the naiks of Kati village from exercising their traditional right of mahua-collection from the village: they told the naik that if he 'ate' (collected) free mahua then the village would be claimed later as Dangi. Similar instances appear to have occurred in other villages like Kaldar.[28] Only by emphasizing their exclusive sovereignty could Gaekwadi officials maintain their authority in a political order where the terms were set by British domination.

In Dangs, of course, they were not successful. But this was because the more powerful British backed the chiefs, and wished to set up the chiefs as independent powers. Elsewhere, and especially in those forest polities which fell within what had been deemed Gaekwadi boundaries, Baroda was more successful. In the forested areas around Vyara, Songadh or other Bhil-dominated areas further north, Baroda had by the late nineteenth century, successfully halted raids, converted giras into a fixed annual payment, contained the forest polities, and dismantled the ties of the forest chiefs with all neighbouring powers save themselves, and established an exclusive sovereignty.

There were similar developments in smaller kingdoms too. Except where small kings were located within what had become British territory (as happened to the deshmukhs), British support often had a two-pronged effect. Working with notions of sharply defined boundaries, colonial officials systematically dismantled the

27 'The Dhang case' by T. Madhav Rao, Diwan, Baroda, *DBD*, I, p. 52; see also Giras Department records of Baroda state in Gujarat State Archives, Baroda.
28 *DBD*, II, p. 14.

extensive ties of these kingdoms with forest polities beyond colonially stipulated boundaries. But within these boundaries, they helped small kings consolidate their authority. In the Central India Agency, in the Rajputana, Rewakantha and Mahikantha agencies, the British gave military assistance to several small kings so that 'depredations' by Bhils 'within' their territories could be put down. By the late nineteenth century, the Bhil chiefs had been almost completely subordinated, their political power had been marginalized, and each little king possessed a far more uncontested authority over his 'kingdom' than had been the case formerly.[29]

These developments increasingly led small kings to dissociate themselves from the now relatively powerless forest polities. Many who had formerly hovered between a Bhil status and a Rajput one, affirming each in different contexts, now rapidly distanced themselves from Bhil status and claimed a Rajput one. So the affirmation of Bhil identities, which had been a feature of many smaller kingdoms, no longer occurred. The growing marginality of the forest polities was mirrored in the increased repudiation of the role of Bhil chiefs in coronation ceremonies. By the early twentieth century, there were very few little kingdoms left that still had the ritual of a Bhil chief applying a *tika* (mark on the forehead) with his blood on the raja during coronation, or of the chief seating the raja on his gadi.

Dangi chiefs too participated in the creation of exclusive sovereignty. Again, this was partially for the very pragmatic reason that if they did not claim exclusive sovereignty over villages, they would have lost these. As the Baroda Diwan remarked, they knew that they stood to gain directly from denying Gaekwadi rights.[30] In many cases, with the help of supportive colonial officials, they persuaded the naiks of frontier villages to show false boundaries against Baroda.[31]

The consolidation of exclusive sovereignties furthered the creation of an inner frontier. Whether areas like Dangs became self-contained territories or part of some larger plains power, their subordination was clearly marked. Now they no longer possessed the power which had formerly allowed them to sustain claims to shared sovereignty; plains powers too did not need to create shared

[29] There is rich material at the National Archives of India, New Delhi documenting the transformations in these states' dealings with Bhil chiefs.
[30] 'The Dhang Case' by T. Madhav Rao, Diwan, Baroda, *DBD*, I, p. 62.
[31] *DBD*, II, p. 33.

sovereignty to sustain their authority. Now areas like the dang could no longer be influential in surrounding plains societies as they had once been.

But a caveat is in order. Both here and in Chapter 10 (and this is a point that later chapters will return to), we should not think of mandini as occurring only after moglai. It does often so occur, but quite regularly moglai coexists with mandini in the same chronological period. As Chapter 9 points out, the Vansda rajas distributed token giras payments right till the 1970s, the chiefs sent wild products from forests to the Songadh killedar till shortly after independence, and repeatedly refer now to the Gaekwads as their *bhaus* (brothers) — all this during the same chronological period as the mandini. Practices such as these were a way of traversing and exceeding the meanings imposed through mandini, of sustaining a world beyond mandini — that of moglai.

(9)

12

Becoming Ignorant

The mandini which frequently fascinates most Dangis is that of the forests. There is one goth about it that, in some form or the other, is known by almost every Dangi adult:

> The gora saheb called all the rajas and naiks to Bhavani cha killa for the mandini. They put three sacks in front of the rajas. They said, rajasaheb, choose any of these three sacks for yourselves. The rajas went around feeling each of the sacks. They felt the first one, and said, 'this is *maati* [earth]'. Then they felt the second one, and said, 'this is *dhilpa* [bark]'. Then they felt the third one, and said, 'this is *paiha* [money]'. The rajas said amongst themselves, 'We already have bark and earth in our forests, what do we need those for? Let us take the money, since we do not have money'. At that time, there was no money in Dangs. So they told the gora saheb that they would take the third sack. Then the saheb told the rajas, 'now that you have taken the money, you shall get the money and we shall take away the forests and the land. Had you taken the sack with earth, you would have kept both the earth and the forests. Had you taken the sack with the bark, you would have kept the forests. Now you have lost both, but you will get a pension instead.[1]

Goth of the forest mandini are very different from other goth. For one, they are very widely known, with most Dangi men and women able to narrate one or more goth of how the mandini of forests took place. This may be because the loss of forests is the most definitive feature distinguishing the present from the past, the one matter that any Dangi rumination on the present has to tackle. Then, in goth of forest mandini, more than anywhere else, a playful aesthetic is at work, made possible paradoxically by a widespread consensus on the fact that British takeover of forests was a blow to all Dangis. Thus, while goth of forest mandini vary widely in their themes and concerns, and there are few attempts to present any one goth as more

---

[1] Kishan Vaghmare, 7.3.1990, Ahwa.

correct than any of the others — all these versions coexist, sardonic, sceptical, or angry narratives of loss.

But these very different goth do share some broad themes, those of trickery, illiteracy, domination and ignorance. Many goth ascribe the mandini to the overwhelming power of the British lashkar, and to the chiefs being coerced into leases. Memories are still evidently strong of the Bhil corps that was deployed with such devastating effect against Silput in the early nineteenth century, and of the forces used against other rebels in the early twentieth century. Some goth, in fact, specifically associate the leases of Dangi forests with Silput's military defeat, and the dominance that the British gained after that. Others focus on deception:

> The gora saheb and *sahebin* [white man and woman] came one night to the house of the Bhil raja. The saheb said, 'it is night, and your jungle is not safe for me, and the sahebin is unwell. Give me space to sleep for the night'. The raja said, 'How much space do you require?' The saheb said, 'I want only enough space to spread a tiger skin'. The raja said, 'You may have it'. But at night, when the raja was asleep, the saheb cut the skin into thin strips, and used it to cover all of Dangs. In the morning, after the raja had woken, the saheb said, 'Raja saheb, you had told me to take as much space as I could spread a tiger skin on. Now the entire Dangs belongs to me.'[2]

This goth draws upon older traditions in the devdevina goth, where the motif of a skin being cut into strips and used to encompass a region crops up occasionally.

Other goth focus on how the mandini was made possible by Dangi ignorance of British technologies. Many characterize the rajas as illiterate — more broadly, ignorant. Some narrators describe the saheb as having sought shelter from the raja for a night, and then having gone and measured the trees and the forests while the chief was sleeping.[3] Here, the act of measuring carries with it intimations of sovereignty. Its power lies in the information it gives of the exact area, and other details that, as prominent aspects of colonial forestry, have come to be imbued with power. For the British to have measured the forests was for them to establish control over it.

Enhanced vision, and the power of writing and naming are also invoked in this way — to contrast British technology and Dangi

2 Ibid.
3 Gangaram Mahadu, 26.4.1990, Nilsakia.

ignorance. Some accounts explicitly stress how written documents were used to cheat the illiterate rajas: the rajas were called to Dhulia, their *sahi-anguthas* (thumb-mark as signature) were taken on a blank piece of paper. The saheb then wrote on the paper an agreement taking the forests away from the chiefs.[4] And according to another goth:

> Even before coming to Dangs, the saheb had seen the forests with a *durbhin* [telescope]. He said to himself, 'these are forests of gold. I must get them for myself'. He went to the raja and asked for one year's permission to move in the forests. He went with the rajas for shikar, and saw the jungle more closely. While moving in the jungle, he asked for the names of trees, which he wrote down immediately in his book. With the names in his book, he did not need the rajas any longer, for he knew everything about the forests himself.[5]

It is the power of writing and the accretion of knowledge which enables the saheb to overturn the relation of supplication with which he first came to Dangs. In one instance, initial hostility to me from a vadil in Kirli village drew on these memories of the past. When I went to meet him, along with several others from the village, he initially refused to tell any goth. When pressed by some of the younger Dangis with me, he exploded at them: 'This was how the saheb came, asking "what is the name of that tree, what is the name of that dungar", writing them down, and then they took away the forests. But even they did not ask questions like his, about our vadils. What will you do if tomorrow he comes and takes away the *raj* [specifically, pensions]? Do you know what he will do with the goth?'

In some goth, colonial knowledge was literally inscribed onto Dangs, and created the Dangi ignorance that led to the mandini. Thus, the absence of roads is one of the markers of moglai in oral traditions, for it is often described as a time when there were only footpaths. And the mandini of the forests, with the subordination to colonial power that it implies, is described often as being centred around the colonial construction of roads. Similarly, the construction of forest rest-houses, which took place on a large scale in early-twentieth-century Dangs and facilitated forest officials' tours, are sometimes mentioned as a part of the mandini.

4 Linga Partam, 17.3.1990, Ghavria.
5 Surya Kosu, 31.3.1990, Chikar.

THE TRANSFORMATIONS OF WILDNESS

In the last two chapters, I have suggested how older forms of wildness were extirpated in the plains of Khandesh, and how a particular British notion of civilization was not only imposed there, but came to be dominant in relation to the wildness of the dang. This construction of an opposition between the wild and the civilized, and the accompanying subordination of the wild, was to transform Dangi notions of what was involved in being wild. Here, I would like to explore these transformations by focusing on the British leases of the early 1840s.

These leases, it seems to me, are a particularly suggestive parallel to goth of mandini. The figures associated with the mandini — Udesinh raja of Ghadvi, Hasusinh raja of Amala, Ankus raja of Deher and Aundya raja of Vasurna amongst others — are those who negotiated with the British for these leases. And certainly, more than any other event, the leases enabled British access to and control over the forests. The leases represented a moment when the growing subordination of the forest polity was made vividly manifest, a poignant moment in the transition from the world of shared sovereignty and multiple alliances to one of exclusive sovereignty and singular allegiances. Taking my cues from goth, I would like to suggest here that, with the leases, the wildness of being Dangi was refigured as ignorance.

As a point of contrast, consider first the precolonial and paracolonial trade in timber and forest products, where wildness was associated more with political power. Timber trade was already extensive in Dangs by the early nineteenth century. Timber was principally used for indigenous shipbuilding activities along the Surat coast.[6] In 1825, Silput raja of Ghadvi had an income of about Rs 5000 annually from the tax of Rs 2½ that was levied on each cart of timber that left Dangs. This amount was shared at some nakas with the Mulher deshmukh, and at some with Baroda. Murharrao claimed in 1843 to have received 4 annas on every cartload

---

6 John Vaupell, 'Continuation of desultory notes and observations on various places in Guzerat and Western India', *Transactions of the Bombay Geographical Society*, vol. 7, May 1844–December 1846, p. 100; R.A. Wadia, *The Bombay dockyard and the Wadia master builders*, Bombay, 1957, pp. 22–4; Nathan Crow to Committee for Investigating the Timber Resources of the Western Side of India, 31.5.1806, *BA.PD.–42.Vol 631/1164.Comp 669.*

of timber — a fee which yielded between Rs 100 and Rs 500 for each tract in which he had rights.[7]

The 1830s possibly saw an intensification of timber trade. Merchants sought to work Dangs not just through sporadic fellings, but by cornering tracts through lease agreements with the chiefs. Maybe the chiefs' receptivity to these lease agreements had to do in part with the near-extinction of raids by 1830: the intensification of the timber trade could have compensated for the loss of resources previously secured through raiding. The first such lease was signed with the Ghadvi chiefs in 1836. That one, for six years, undertook to pay the chiefs Rs 1833 annually. In 1841, partially because of resistance from chiefs, it was superseded by another one which was to run for three years. So great was the demand that an agreement was also signed that year for another lease which was to commence in 1844 after the existing one expired.[8]

Timber trade was the most major axis along which Dangis participated in the regional economy. The payments that the merchants made to the chiefs were, like giras or spoils from raids, very widely distributed amongst bhauband, and thus reached many ordinary Dangis, especially Bhils. Besides, while merchants brought their own labourers, Dangis too regularly worked as labourers for merchants, and were paid for this. The merchants often tried to strengthen their authority in the region by extending loans to the chiefs and thus becoming more central in the local economy. In 1841, the trader who secured a lease of the Ghadvi forests which was due to commence in 1844 did so by undertaking to pay off a portion of the chiefs' debts.[9]

In addition, timber trade was part of the construction of alliances and patterns of authority in the region. The power of the merchants owed much to their close association with Gaekwadi officials. One of them was described as the ijaradar of Dangs. After his leases commenced, he paid annually the Gaekwadi bhet and bakra (goat) to the chiefs, presumably the dues given when the Gaekwadi flag in Ghadvi was renewed. The merchants also drew sometimes on British presence to buttress their authority. The 1836 lease was drafted by the Khandesh Collector, specifying that he would look

[7] British officials however considered this estimate excessive. See H.W. Reeves to Secy., GoB, 1.7.1843, *IOL.F.4.2074.* See also 'Tabular List of Chiefs', Rigby to Robertson, 30.10.1825, *BRO.RR.DN 144.FN 719.*

[8] See *BA.PD.1847.Vol 21/1902. Comp 9731.*

[9] Text of agreement with Nathubhai Rahimbhai and Udechand Tarachand, 23.5.1841, *BA.PD.1845.Vol 16/1648.Comp 444.* Lease to Nathubhai Rahimbhai and Syed Ali Ashkar, *BA.PD.1847.Vol 21/1902.Comp 9731.*

into any of the merchants' complaints. The 1841 agreement stipulated that a clerk of the deshmukh — identified by the chiefs with
the British — would be stationed in Dangs, and he would report
any infractions of the lease by the chiefs to the British.[10]

Because of the growing strength of the British and (in the 1820s
and 1830s) the Gaekwads, the merchants were possibly becoming
dominant over Dangi chiefs during this period. Nevertheless, the
political power of the Bhil chiefs, with its connotations of wildness,
was still significant. The traders worked through idioms that acknowledged the chiefs' authority: the 1836 agreements stipulated
that the charges of maintaining 'for purposes of state, cushions,
pillows, floor cloth and other articles, as well as Lamp and Light, with
oil for the same' was to be borne by the merchants. Nor was this
acknowledgement a mere formality. The bhauband were powerful
enough to repudiate agreements: the 1836 lease broke down in 1839
because of resistance from them. When the leases were renegotiated
in 1841, the power of the bhauband was again acknowledged in the
shares they received.[11]

Nor did the merchants' style of operations involve restrictions
on bhauband or ordinary Dangis. Though they invested money in
making Dangi routes passable for large timber, they did not work
the forests themselves, preferring instead to levy duties of around
Rs 3 per cart that left Dangs. In addition, local bhauband continued
to collect small amounts as dues from timber-cutters. These dues,
known as khuti, represented an acknowledgement by merchants of
the sovereignty and power of the chiefs of each small dang that
the timber passed through.[12] And ordinary Dangis continued to use
the forests as they had before.

LEASES AND ALLIANCES

In all these respects, the British leases were quite different. By the
1840s, colonial officials of the nearby British districts — Surat to

[10] Udesinh to Blanc, 24.8.1838, *BRO.RR.DN 144.FN 719*. Boyce to Reeves,
19.2.1844, *BA.PD.1845.Vol 16/1648.Comp 444*; Udesinh Jararsinh and others
to Syed Ali Ashkar, 23.5.1841, *BA.PD.1847.Vol 21/1902.Comp 973*. Elliot and
Simson to Secy., GoB., 11.12.1842 *IOL.F.4.2074*; Mr Boyce's memorandum,
n.d., 1842, also Morriss to Reeves, 22.5.1843, *IOL.F.4.2074*.
[11] Text of lease of Nathubhai and Syed Ali Ashkar, *BA.PD.1847.Vol 21/1902.
Comp 9731*; *DCR.DN 2.FN 4Uc*.
[12] G. Inveriarity to Secy., GoB, 1.10.1847, *BA.PD.1847.Vol 21/1902. Comp
9731*.

the northwest and Khandesh to the southeast — desired direct leases of the forests. Such leases seemed important because they would enable direct access to forests. During the 1830s, the British had been content to obtain Dangi timber through the merchants. But as the demand for it increased, there was a growing sentiment that direct leases would trim costs by cutting out the merchants' commissions, and allow the control over felling operations needed to produce the large timber that the British required for shipbuilding. Combined with this was the fear that if the merchants continued their 'indiscriminate' removal of timber, there would be little left for 'extraction' in future years.[13]

The British Timber Agent at Surat, W. Boyce set out in January 1842 for Dangs to secure leases. At Kalibel, on the borders of Dangs, he was met by Khursal raja, one of the Ghadvi bhauband, who 'appeared quite delighted and without hesitation signed a document transferring his share of the Dang to the British govt'. Accompanied by Khursal, Boyce proceeded towards Ghadvi, where he met the principal chief, Udesinh raja. Udesinh and other bhauband initially tried to hold out for Rs 6000 annually, but finally leased the forests to Boyce for Rs 2300. On another trip to Dangs in May, Boyce entered into lease agreements with the chiefs of Vasurna and Pimpri. Boyce and other officials justified the colonial action in overriding the already existing leases of merchants for the same forests by arguing that Dangis, because of their 'low degraded habits', had always been cheated by the merchants. As protectors of such a 'wild and untutored' people, the British had an obligation to set aside the merchants' leases, which were 'unworthy of consideration'.[14]

But the colonial leases did not last. Problems began in September, when Udesinh raja attacked and drove away the men who had been stationed by Boyce at a naka. Then, in November, when money was sent to the Vasurna chief Aundya (Anandrao) raja as part of the lease payment, he 'not only refused to take it but has also sent back my letter unopened'. And in February, Aundya raja's karbhari prevented timber-cutters sent in by Boyce 'from cutting timber and

13 See Wadia, *The Bombay dockyard*, pp. 216–28; Elliot and Simson to Secy., GoB, 6.8.1841, *BA.PD.1840–2.Vol 63/1164. Comp 641*; and the proceedings in *IOL.F.4.2074*.

14 Mr Boyce's memorandum, n.d., 1842; R. Oliver to Anderson, 23.3.1842, Boyce to Arbuthnot and Elliot, 28.5.1842; Reeves to Willoughby, 20.9.1843, all in *IOL.F.4.2074*; Morriss to Bell, 28.5.1844, *BRO.DDR.DN 1.FN 4*.

says if anybody steals their cloths and things, then he will not be answerable, therefore they may look out for themselves'. In subsequent months, the leases completely broke down.[15]

However, British officials were by that time quite set on leasing the forest, and decided to try again. Morriss, the Bhil Agent for Khandesh, went in May 1843 to Songadh, where he met Boyce. Both proceeded together into Dangs. At Bardipada, along the northern frontiers of Dangs, the chiefs had assembled to meet him. The joint persuasion of Boyce and Morriss was successful, and the chiefs of Amala, Vasurna, Pimpri, Deher or Dherbhavti, Ghadvi, Avchar and Chinchli agreed to enter into leases. Morriss then brought the chiefs to Mulher, where they met the Khandesh Collector, Reeves, and formally signed the agreements.[16] This time round, there were to be no repudiations, and the leases were to last.

The initial agreements, their repudiation within three to six months, and new leases within a year betoken a significant transformation in Dangi understandings. Through the initial agreements, it could be argued, the chiefs sought alliances with the British, as they had with the merchants before them. These alliances were intended to affirm the political power and wildness of Bhil raj. However, this reading of the leases could not be maintained, and the leases broke down. By the time the new set of leases had been negotiated, the chiefs still did seek alliances with the British, but more apprehensively — the leases no longer seemed to affirm the wildness of Bhil raj but rather to show it up as a form of ignorance.

For the British, the leases were of significance not so much as alliance but as contracts which gave them direct control over forests. For Dangis, in contrast, direct British control did not seem to mean much. The merchants' leases had not hindered Dangi use of forests; and there was little reason to believe that British control over forests would be different. What made the chiefs accept the leases was their importance as an alliance. (As commercial transactions, the colonial leases were not even particularly attractive. The British offered only slightly more than the Rs 1833 that the merchants were already paying, and the merchants would possibly have been willing to top that offer.) After all, the British were far

15 Boyce to Arbuthnot, 19.1.1843, *BA.PD.1846.Vol 16/1781.Comp 222*; see also proceedings in *IOL.F.4.2074.*

16 Reeves to Willoughby, 1.7.1843, and Morriss to Reeves, 22.5.1843, *IOL.F.4.2074.*

more powerful than either the merchants or the Gaekwadi officials that most merchants could claim ties with. The morning after the lease had been signed, Udesinh came to Boyce and said he wished to 'show his sense' of satisfaction with the leases 'in a becoming manner'. He gave Boyce a deed for Rs 50, to be paid to the British as long as the lease continued. Boyce described this gesture as an act of goodwill.[17] The word 'goodwill' is suggestive, and Udesinh's gesture will merit closer attention. Till then, the leases could have been read as an occasion characterized by balanced reciprocity where the chiefs gave the forests and received money in return. But alliances, like gifts, are not about balanced reciprocity — they are about the creation of surplus. It is the surplus beyond the final discharge of reciprocal obligations that creates alliances. By gifting back a portion of the money, Udesinh situated the leases as an alliance.

It was because leases were alliances that the British distribution of gifts was especially charged: as an acknowledgement of authority by the sarkar, it could affect hierarchies. When Khursal raja first met Boyce, though he accepted liquor from Boyce and even signed a lease, he refused to accept any presents, 'stating that it would displease Oodeysing; however in his [Udesinh's] presence he would willingly receive anything which I might offer . . . '. To have accepted presents directly from the British sarkar would have been to convert the leases into an alliance, and to implicitly claim a degree of power which might have offended Udesinh. Indeed, Udesinh and his bhauband tried to direct Boyce's distribution of the markers. As Boyce was leaving after securing the leases, they 'presented me with a list of several Rajas and others who were shareholders and requested that the British would send a trifling present such as a turban to each as it would conciliate them and prevent jealousy'. Udesinh also tried to ensure that his alliance with the British involved more exclusive markers than those distributed to other bhauband. When Boyce was leaving, 'as a parting request, Oodeysing begged that a chair might be sent to him'. The significance of the chair lay, quite obviously, not in its material value but in the fact that it would be a special gift from Boyce, almost literally a seat of authority.[18]

[17] Mr Boyce's memorandum, n.d., 1842, *IOL.F.4.2074*. The rest of the section is based on this memorandum, unless otherwise specified.
[18] Udesinh to Boyce, Appendix 1, Boyce to Arbuthnot, 19.1.1843, *IOL.F. 4.2074*.

WILDNESS AND IGNORANCE

But the chiefs found it difficult to sustain their readings of the leases primarily as alliances that affirmed Bhil raj and its wildness. British officials were too set on treating the leases as granting them a control over forests which excluded even Dangi chiefs. At the request of the chiefs, the leases had permitted Dangis to retain the ability to cut timber for their own use. But colonial officials interpreted these provisions very restrictively, and tried to prevent Dangis from felling timber or using the forests. This radical departure from the merchants' style of functioning was more than the chiefs had bargained for. Aundya raja of Vasurna complained: 'the Bheels in Dangs . . . subsist by cutting and selling wood. They have no other means of support than this trade. No interruption was ever experienced by us during the Moghul and the Peishwa's government, nor under the British government till now'. He pleaded: 'the Sarkar must not take this [the forests] away from us.'[19] Besides, by excluding Dangis from use of trees, the British implicitly made a claim to political sovereignty, and denied Bhil raj. And all this for a payment that the merchants would have willingly topped.

But challenging the leases was difficult, because wildness itself was taking on new meanings. These new meanings emerge in the four starkly varying accounts that Aundya raja provided of why he did not wish to continue with the leases. In his initial petition to the Khandesh *mamlatdar* (revenue official), he claimed that '[s]ome Parsee [a community whose members in the region ran liquor shops and engaged in timber trade] has come and obtained a lease of the Rambaj district under false pretences'. Since then, the Parsi had prevented the cutting of wood, 'in consequence of which we are starving'. He pleaded with the mamlatdar to quickly make some arrangement so that timber could be felled again.[20]

Then there was the account that Aundya's karbhari later gave to the mamlatdar. A 'Mussalman' sipai, he said, came to Aundya raja and said 'that a Saheb has come from Surat and wishes to see the Raja, therefore you must come quickly, if not he will seize and take you by force'. The sipai gave the raja a letter in Gujarati, 'with

---

[19] Mr Boyce's memorandum, n.d., 1842; Boyce to Arbuthnot and Elliot. 28.5.1842; Aundya to Boyce, 8.1.1843; Petition from Aundya raja, 15.3.1843, all in *IOL.F.4.2074.*

[20] Aundya to Mamlatdar, Baglan, n.d., *IOL.F.4.2074.*

a seal and English signature'. Since the raja did not have anybody who could read Gujarati, he took the letter and went to Karzai, the spot where the saheb was supposed to be. But:

there was no Gentleman there, a Parsee and a person in black dress and a dozen or so Mussalman sepoys were there, without any badges. The Raja asked where the saheb was. The Parsee said he is gone but give me a lease of your territory. The Raja replied I will not do so, the chief is another, and I must ask my co-sharers and afterwards give you an answer.[21]

The Parsi then 'wrote what he pleased' on a piece of paper, and asked the raja to sign it. Anandrao replied that he had no *karkun* (clerk), no seal, and would not sign it. Afterwards, the karbhari said, the Parsi sent presents to the raja, which he did not accept. Despite this, the Parsi was living at Rambaj village in Vasurna, had established nakas, and prevented the cutting of bamboo and timber.[22]

Yet another account was given in November, in a reply by Aundya to a letter from Boyce saying that he would visit Dangs soon to make the lease payment:

I have no power to grant you a lease as I told you at Karjaee and now again. I state that if government insist upon the treaty I cannot restrain my co-sharers from breaking it and I shall receive the blame — to prevent this the Government must consider that they have not received a lease from me and must remove all the chowkies.[23]

Later, in another letter to Boyce, Aundya changed tack somewhat. He said he was sent for, and when he reached Karzai

some Saheb was there whom I did not know, but he detained me and asked me for a lease of my territory and offered me 850 Rupees . . . taking me by the hand [he] took me from one place to another and threatened to take me to Surat. Seeing he was determined to use compulsion I said if you will force me I must submit, what was obtained from me in writing I did not understand and whilst the writing was in progress I told him he had the power of forcing me that I did not agree of my own free will.[24]

To colonial officials, with their emphasis on the 'what really happened', these starkly varying, contradictory accounts seemed, quite simply, a tangle of 'false allegations'. But if Aundya resorted

21 Mamlatdar, Baglan, to Pringle, 7.11.1842, *IOL.F.4.2074.*
22 *IOL.F.4.2074.*
23 Aundya to Boyce, n.d. (after 12 November 1842), *IOL.F.4.2074.*
24 *IOL.F.4.2074.*

to these contradictory accounts, this was because of the ways in which wildness had been refigured in the preceding decades. Because of the power of the British, direct repudiations of the sort that Silput had resorted to, with their defiant affirmation of the wildness of Bhil raj, were no longer possible. Indeed, Aundya was very careful to avoid these. Repeatedly, he ended his protests with avowals of loyalty. 'Whatever the sarkar decides, I will do.'[25] This reluctance to resort to open defiance may also have been why Aundya cast Boyce as an unknown saheb or a fair-complexioned Parsi of the sort who could easily be mistaken for a saheb: to deny leases to such figures was obviously a less hostile act than denying them to the sarkar. Now, wildness was marginality; it had to acknowledge subordination to the newly constituted civilized.

It was because of this marginality of wildness that Aundya focused so obsessively on questioning the written agreements. Recall: the lessors were not the right ones, being unknown sahebs or Parsis. The lessee was not the right one either: Aundya claimed repeatedly that he did not have the authority to sign leases, that he was not the chief, that he needed the permission of his bhau-band, and that he could not make the bhauband stick to the agreements. The occasion at which the agreement had been secured was not right: there were insinuations of deception and impropriety in a Parsi having been at Karzai instead of a saheb, in the sipais being without badges, in Aundya being without his seal or karkun, and in the coercion that the unknown saheb resorted to. Finally, even the written document itself is not quite right: the Parsi wrote 'what he pleased', and Aundya did not understand what the unknown saheb had written.[26]

If the chiefs focused so single-mindedly on the written agreements, this was because writing had come for them to represent the growing inadequacy of their wildness; it had become the event which refigured their wildness as ignorance. Increasingly by the late nineteenth and early twentieth century, the chiefs and the Dangis were to represent themselves as 'ignorant people'.[27] With the connotations of social and political power which claims to wildness had formerly enacted becoming difficult to maintain,

[25] Aundya to Mamlatdar, Baglan, n.d. (Oct.–7 Nov. 1842?), *IOL.F.4.2074.*
[26] Anandrao to Boyce, 8.1.1843, *IOL.F.4.2074.*
[27] Petition from Aundya raja, 15.3.1843, *IOL.F.4.2074*; Petition from rajas to Coll., Kh., 26.6.1892, *BRO.DDR.DN 4.FN 24*; Petition from rajas to Coll., Kh., n.d., *BRO.DDR.DN 4.FN 26.*

wildness was now associated with being ignorant of the workings of social and political power. Maybe even the starkly varying accounts that Aundya provided were part of the construction of ignorance: he could claim to unclear about what happened, after all, precisely because of his claim to be ignorant.

It is not surprising that the writing of the dominant should have become the occasion which transmuted wildness into ignorance. As I have argued at length elsewhere, while written agreements had been used in relations with the Gaekwads and the deshmukh, their tenuous dominance meant that the meanings of the documents could be challenged by the chiefs. But the British, because of their power, were able to give effect to the written agreements they engineered around giras, raids and forests. They not only used writing extensively in subordinating forest polities, but did so with deliberate spectacular intent. After Silput and the other chiefs had been captured and taken to Khandesh following the 1830 expedition, the Bhil corps commandant Outram 'went through the form of making a list of them and their villages in front of them and informing them that they are now known and can be easily apprehended'.[28] Already, the written agreements that the timber merchants entered into in the 1830s and 1840s seemed a bit more fearsome and prone to create ignorance, for the merchants were backed not only by Gaekwadi officials but by the British, who emphasized an exclusive control of writing as a source of their power. With the British directly entering into leases in the early 1840s, the written agreement now took on for the Dangis a relatively independent existence.[29]

Claims to having been bamboozled by the technology of writing were the rhetorical deployment of a major cultural fear, an expression of their sense of inadequacy when it came to handling the plains technology. Inscrutable, dominant, capable of taking away rights, writing could no longer be challenged by Dangi wildness; rather, it betokened the transformation of wildness into ignorance. In more muted ways, other Dangi goth also reflect on this transformation of wildness into ignorance, on the subordination of wildness by technologies that marginalized it. This is why the telescopes, the rest-houses, the roads and measuring tape loom so large in Dangi goth: all of them created ignorance.

---

28 Outram to Boyd, 24.5.1830, *BRO.DDR.DN 1.FN 3.*
29 See my 'Writing, orality and power'.

DOMINATION AND IGNORANCE

This context of ignorance, and the persistent fear of deception and coercion, suggests interesting perspectives on the consent of the chiefs to the fresh set of leases in 1843. This time, the leases allowed for greater Dangi use of forests. This would have, from the point of view of ordinary Dangis, left the necessary leeway to continue with old modes of subsistence.[30] Also, there was an upward revision of payments. Though not much in actual terms (save in the case of Aundya, whose allowance was doubled),[31] the hike would have satisfied the principal chiefs, and possibly helped them incorporate dissenting bhauband more effectively into the network of alliances around the British. Now, evidently, there were fewer attendant discomforts to viewing the leases as alliances with the British.

But it would be mistaken to see the 1843 leases as something that the chiefs entered into because it satisfied their rational interests. Even more importantly, British domination seemed overwhelming, and made the leases almost inescapable. While the deshmukh had assisted the chiefs in opposing the leases the first time, he now supported the British, possibly because he realized that this was the safest way to ensure that his rights in the region were preserved.[32] Also, the first time round, the leases were secured by Boyce, an unknown figure based in a British district with whose officials the chiefs had few dealings. Now they were asked for by the Khandesh officials whom the Dangi chiefs were both familiar with and afraid of: Morriss, in fact, had led a Bhil corps punitive expedition into Dangs in 1839. Aundya had already been apprehensive about denying leases to the unknown saheb; how much more difficult, then, to deny leases to Morriss! Indeed, there are several signs that the chiefs entered into the alliances apprehensively, maybe fearful of the consequences of their novel ignorance. The chiefs who attended had to be 'persuaded' for nearly two days before they assented to the leases. And many smaller chiefs preferred to stay away from the meeting rather than deny leases outright to the British. Even amongst those who granted leases, many concealed from colonial officials, where possible, the existence of villages and territory controlled by them.[33]

30 Boyce to Coll., Surat, n.d., *DFR.DN 3.FN 4Uc.*

31 Political Letter of 15.6.1844, no 42, *IOL.F.4.2074.*

32 By shifting allegiances, he got his timber haks commuted to an annual payment of Rs 700. Reeves to Willoughby, 1.7.1843, *IOL.F.4.2074.*

33 Campbell to Ashburner, 11.3.1873, *BA.PD.1873.Vol 87.Comp 2039*; 'List of concealed villages', *DFR.DN 3.FN 2Uc.*

And maybe the chiefs still hoped (not an entirely implausible hope in the 1840s) that British domination was temporary, and that the leases could be challenged later. Murharrao Deshmukh's heir, Laxmanrao, astutely remarked on this in the 1870s: 'if they [the chiefs] were freed for a day from the Political charge under which Government have kept connection with them they will not fail to say that their ancestors used to tell them that the Dang forests were never leased to the British.'[34] In this sense, the longevity of the leases the second time round was itself a deception, made possible above all by what followed after the leases — the growth of British domination and the creation of an inner frontier.

Undermining Fixity

All this is very well, but there remains one question. Clearly, deception did not inhere in the leases, which provided neither for long-term permanence nor for the exclusion of Dangis from the forests. Rather, deception and dispossession were the result of the slow consolidation of the inner frontier, of ways in which the leases were interpreted in later decades. So why do goth now, and most Dangis by the early twentieth century, condense the process of dispossession and deception into one marker — the leases?

Maybe because of the power of writing. While Morriss and Boyce may have explained some of the meanings of the leases, they did not explain all its meanings. They could not have. There was in colonial ideology the perception that meanings, once inscribed in writing, were stable, fixed, and inviolable. This rhetoric of fixity was what allowed Morriss and Boyce to even think that they were explaining all the implications of the meanings of the leases to the chiefs. Yet, as we know only too well, the rhetoric of fixity is constantly undermined by a politics of reading: written documents had to be constantly interpreted and reinterpreted. And, as Chapter 14 shows, colonial officials in the late nineteenth century did precisely this: they repeatedly restricted Dangi access to the forests by reading new meanings and implications into the leases.

Yet Dangis could not participate in this process of interpretation. Formerly, this did not matter, for they could challenge interpretations of written documents by invoking their political power and

[34] Laxman Murharrao to Governor of Bombay, n.d., *BA.PD.1874. Vol 108.Comp 897.*

wildness. Now this was not possible, and their powerlessness relative to colonial officials meant that they could not persuade the British with their interpretations of the leases. Now, for them, these agreements were protean and threatening, a fount of meaning over which they had no control, which threatened them, which created and sustained their ignorance and subordination.

The almost exclusive focus on the leases, then, can be read as a riposte to the colonial rhetoric of fixity, to the British claim that the rationale for all their actions always already resided in the original leases. If it is from the original moment of the leases that colonial and postcolonial power derives legitimacy, then it is that original moment which has to be challenged, questioned and dislodged. By claiming to have been deceived and coerced into the leases, Dangis deny the legitimacy of the mandini and state control of forests; they invoke instead the moglai of chhut or freedom to move. Indeed through much of the nineteenth and twentieth centuries, Dangis have tried to challenge the mandini by producing moglai and enacting chhut as everyday practice.

(4)

13

The Violence of Environmentalism

Soon after the leases, the management of Dangs was taken over by the Forest Department. As is well known, the Department emerged by the late nineteenth century as one of the most powerful institutions in colonial India, controlling over a quarter of the land in British India, managing these lands under separate forest laws, and maintaining its own separate police force and administrative cadre.[1] The Department's practices can be fruitfully understood as attempts at the refiguration of wild spaces seen as outside and before civilization. What is especially interesting about thinking of Forest Department practices in this way is that it allows an attention to geographical specificity, to the close relationship between managing wild spaces and wild peoples and, through all of this, to the violence of colonial environmentalism.

The western opposition between the wild and the civilized was itself inflected with new uncertainties in the colonial context. In some ways it seemed clear who and what were wild — forests, deserts, mountains, forest communities, pastoralists, and all mobile groups — and who and what were civilized — areas of settled agriculture and urban growth, and the upper and middle castes. But in a profound and pervasive sense, no colonized place or people could be civilized. Colonial rule drew implicitly and explicitly on the idea that the colonized, whether as people or space, were always carriers of a particular wildness that had to be acted on. After all British colonialism had from around the late eighteenth century increasingly legitimated itself as an imperialism of improvement,

---

[1] The literature on colonial forestry in India is by now immense. But see especially Ramachandra Guha's path-breaking article, which virtually created the whole field of study, 'Forestry in British and post-British India: An historical analysis', *Economic and Political Weekly*, vol. 18, nos 44–5, 1983.

as one that would bring the barbarian and the savage into the circle of the civilized.[2]

But could the civilizing mission mean the erasure of the wildness of the colonized? Maybe in Australia and the Americas, where European settlers not only took over the land, but converted it, in Crosby's evocative phrase, into neo-Europes, or places whose floral and faunal configurations came to resemble those of Europe.[3] Here, wildness was literally extirpated by the civilized: by European settlers and European biota. Where, as in Africa and Asia, indigenous biota and indigenous peoples continued to be important, matters were different. Here, colonialism was founded on the impossibility of the civilizing mission, on what Partha Chatterjee has evocatively called 'the rule of difference' — the idea that the colonized were fundamentally different from the colonizers.[4] If the difference between the colonizers and the colonized was erased, so was the justification for colonial presence. The civilizing mission thus never could be about erasing wildness: it always had to be about subordinating the wild, construing the colonized as wild, and sustaining that construction.

Celebrations of Wildness

In this context, the difference between the plains and forests or the communities that lived in them was not, for the British, one between the civilized and the wild: it was rather about different forms of wildness. As is well known, by the late nineteenth century, the British saw almost all communities in India as either castes or tribes. The Bhils and other forest communities were amongst the communities that were often referred to as the 'wild tribes' of India, so much so that the adjective wild was almost a superfluity — the tribes were by definition wild. The distinction between castes and tribes can be very helpfully understood as a colonial attempt to

2 Richard Drayton, 'Empire as "Development": The new imperialisms of the enlightenment, 1780–1815 and 1880–1914', unpublished paper.

3 Alfred Crosby, *Ecological imperialism: The biological expansion of Europe, 900–1900*, Cambridge, 1986. Crosby's work has been rightly criticized for being ecologically deterministic, and for not recognizing the significant ecological transformations that took place outside the neo-Europes. See, for example, David Arnold, 'The Indian Ocean as a contact zone, 1500–1950', *South Asia*, vol. 14, no. 2, 1991, pp. 1–21, and also his *The problem of nature: Environment, culture and European expansion*, Oxford, 1996.

4 Partha Chatterjee, *The nation and its fragments*, Princeton, 1993.

differentiate the wildness of the colonized through two interlinked tropes: those of anachronism and gender. The tribes were wild because they were 'primitive', anachronistic in the sense that they were from a time before civilization, a time that had been left behind by more evolved societies.[5] Of course, it was not as though the castes were in the same time as western or European societies — it was only that they were in a more advanced time than the tribes and in this sense less wild than tribes. Here, then, different societies could be mapped onto different locations on a continuum between the wild and the civilized.

It is less evident that the ascription of wildness was also gendered. As has been pointed out, feminizing the colonized was crucial to colonialism both as a metaphor and as a constitutive dynamic.[6] I do not so much wish to dissent from this understanding as to suggest that colonial domination could also be on the basis of the ascription to the colonized of particular forms of masculinity. That is to say, the colonized were not always only feminized; there also existed British constructions of colonized masculinities which enabled and sustained imperial domination.

For British officials, broadly speaking, tribe was to caste as male to female. The castes of the plains represented, in colonial imagination, the potential site of a wild disorder, distinctively feminine. The nineteenth-century British historian Grant Duff said of the Marathas that 'perfidy and want of principle are the strongest features in their character, and their successes have perhaps been less owing to their activity and courage than to their artifice and treachery'.[7] Marathas and other castes were often described as lying, treacherous, and effeminate groups.[8]

In contrast to this, the tribes, and especially the Bhils, were viewed as masculine. This masculinity was emphasized in the whole slew of qualities — nobility, honesty, loyalty, and rugged independence

[5] This point has been made most famously by Johannes Fabian in his *Time and the other*. For a fuller discussion of anachronism in relation to castes and tribes, see my 'Shades of wildness'. Fuller references to the sources employed in this chapter's discussion of tribes and castes are also provided in 'Shades of wildness'.

[6] The literature on this point is by now immense. But see especially Anne McClintock, *Imperial leather: Race, gender and sexuality in the colonial context*, New York, 1995.

[7] Quoted in Andre Wink, *Land and sovereignty in India*, Cambridge, 1986, p. 5.

[8] The obvious exceptions to this were the masculine 'martial races' and 'sturdy farmers'. On martial races, see Lionel Caplan, *Warrior gentlemen: 'Gurkhas' in the western imagination*, Providence, 1995.

amongst them — that they were presumed to possess. If anything, their problem was that their masculinity was unbridled. It was amongst other things this surplus of masculinity which in colonial imagination made communities like Bhils resort to raids on the castes of the plains. (Possibly because officials saw Bhils as so decidedly masculine, they also did not sexualize and eroticize the Bhil woman the way plains women were in colonial imagination.)

The two wildnesses — the female wildness of castes, and the male wildness of tribes — required very different civilizing missions. The wild tribes were often portrayed in terms akin to those used in nostalgic colonial descriptions of British public school boys. This is significant, for the honourable public school boy represented the adolescence of the Victorian gentleman, and the colonial official was above all a gentleman. Unlike the English public school boy, however, the Bhil or tribal man did not ever quite grow up. His distance from English gentlemen was basically because of his primitiveness. It was manifest in his inability to hold his liquor, his proclivity to quarrel and carry on feuds, his impulsiveness, and his thriftlessness and aversion to work.[9] As a result, he never became fit for self-rule — he was the perpetual subject, and one happy to be subject.

Controlling boisterous boys required masculinity. It was because of the effeminacy of plains castes that the Bhils had been restive and resorted to raids in precolonial times. British gazetteers often claimed that precolonial relations between Bhils and the surrounding Maratha plains states had been those of unremitting hostility. Left to themselves, upper caste native officials, whether in princely states or British territory, were prone to be cruel to the Bhils, to deceive them, or to resort to treachery.[10]

In contrast, the British were masculine. In British accounts, it was the demonstration of colonial masculinity which persuaded the Bhils to halt raids. Even in later decades, the Bhil Agents, the British officials responsible for looking after the forest communities, conformed closely to British conceptions of what was involved in being particularly masculine — they had to be capable of hard riding, very good at sports and hunting, and so on. And the implications

9 For a rehearsal of these common perceptions about Bhils, see E. Barnes, 'The Bhils of western India', *Journal of Arts and Ideas*, vol. LV, no. 2829, 1907, p. 325.

10 For fairly typical examples, see *NAI.FD.21.11.1846.FC 66–88*; *NAI.FD.1 8.4.1845.FC 54–75*.

of the Englishman's mastery of the wild tribes stretched outwards into the plains — their ability to master the Bhils demonstrated their fitness to master the plains.

It was in the context of the masculinity of Bhils and British mastery of them that colonial celebrations of Bhil wildness have to be placed. Because they were like public school boys, Bhils were believed to recognize British gentlemanliness. They had 'reverence' and 'affection' for the British',[11] they had 'unbounded confidence in European Gentlemen, whose character they think they understand'.[12] Perennial boys, and likeable ones at that, the Bhils and the wild tribes made ideal subjects. And the affection of such subjects affirmed imperial masculinity and nobility. It was, so to speak, a man-to-man recognition . . . or should one say a boy-to-man recognition? The nobility of the Bhils provided British officials a means of thinking about themselves, of locating the essence of imperial masculinity. It was a way of thinking fondly about the courage, truthfulness, honesty and rugged simplicity that was the essence of being British back home, and even more so in the colonies.

Their mastery of the Bhils made these officials quite like kings. Describing the Bhil-dominated region of Panchmahals in eastern Gujarat, the civil servant Maconochie reminiscenced: 'such was the domain in which Raja Propert [the prefix, meaning king, was often applied to W.H. Propert, a mid-nineteenth-century Collector of the district] hunted his tigers, spanked his wild children with paternal hand and ruled with untrammelled authority.'[13] The British officer-king had no bhauband, only children-subjects. In Kipling's 'The tomb of his ancestors', the main protagonist John Chinn, a Bhil Agent of Satpura range (a post held by his father and grandfather before him) who is treated as a demigod by 'his own people' the Bhils, declares: 'The Bhils are my children.'[14]

The overlaps between these colonial understandings of wild tribes and of forests are striking (as possibly are those between castes and agricultural 'wastes', though I shall not explore these).[15]

[11] See *BA.RD.1848.Vol 96.Comp 514*.

[12] *BA.PD.1858.Vol 95.Comp 734*.

[13] Evan Maconochie, *Life in the Indian Civil Service*, London, 1926, p. 36. On paternal rule over the Bhils, see also David Hardiman, 'Power in the forest: The Dangs, 1820–1940', *Subaltern studies*, vol. VIII, Delhi, 1994.

[14] Rudyard Kipling, 'The tomb of his ancestors', in *The day's work*, London, 1988 (1898), pp. 99, 105.

[15] On the colonial discourse around 'wastes', see Vinay Gidwani's insightful

Just as the Bhils were before civilization, the forests were in colonial understanding before cultivation (and therefore civilization). Of course, forests and more broadly jungles were sites of danger and disorder in colonial thought. Yet these apprehensions usually centred around the interrupted forests of the plains. In both the plains of Awadh in northern India, and in the Mysore region in southern India, colonial officials were most worried by the forests around plains forts, and tried to clear these. In other words, when the jungles were infested by the castes, less trustworthy and sometimes effeminate, they came to be imbued with danger and disorder. They then came to embody the otherness of the colonized, and the threat that the colonized represented to the colonizer. This was the sense in which the Indian subcontinent as a whole was often seen as a jungle, the site of a wildness that threatened colonial order.

But the large forests in the hills, especially those inhabited by the wild tribes, were regarded slightly differently. True, here too, malaria killed, and the weather was hardly very prepossessing from the point of view of the British. Yet these forests were the abode of the wild tribes, where they had their 'wild inhospitable mountain homes'[16] and that itself already made the forests more attractive. The nobility, simplicity and sense of honour of the wild tribes refigured these forests and made them a more masculine and friendly place — repeatedly, officials remarked on how while their provisions had been stolen from camp in the plains, in the forests there was no such worry.

Because the forests were a space of masculine wildness, the ideal forester was ascribed qualities similar to those expected of the Bhil Agent: he had to be a man capable of riding long distances on horseback, camping in rough conditions, handling the wild tribes, and a handy man with a rifle. Indeed, shikhar was a much-emphasized part of being a British forest officer. Even after the Indian Civil Service lost its associations with a rugged physical masculinity, colonial forestry continued to carry these associations.[17]

And the implications of mastering the forests stretched outwards into the plains. As we know, shikhar was important not only to

---

' "Waste" and the permanent settlement in Bengal', *Economic and Political Weekly*, 25 January 1992.

16 *BA.PD.1858.Vol 95.Comp 734*. On British celebration of forests, see also J.M. MacKenzie, *The empire of nature: Hunting, conservation and British imperialism*, Manchester, 1988, pp. 191f.

17 See, for example, the remarks in *DCR.DN 3.FN 4Uc*.

foresters but to colonial officials more broadly. By mastering the forests, as with mastering the Bhils, colonial officials demonstrated to themselves their suitability for mastery over the more effeminate plains. In this sense, the forests were a space of colonial masculine communion, a space which recharged officials to deal again with the effeminate plains.[18]

Colonial celebrations of wild tribes and forests are best understood as a civilized dalliance with wildness — the dalliance that often goes by the name of primitivism. Here, as always, primitivism was premised on domination and mastery — it was the fact that the tribes and forests had already been mastered that made their celebration possible. And again, as is often the case, primitivism was profoundly masculine: it was the affirmation of imperial masculinity as reflected in the wildness of tribes and forests.

Taming and Excluding

Celebrations of wildness existed however in uneasy and complementary conjunction with another discourse: that on the need to tame wildness. The 'civilizing mission', central to colonialism in general, was carried out especially enthusiastically by British officials when amongst the wild tribes. Not only were these their children but, equally importantly, since they were always children, the civilizing mission would never threaten to erase the difference between them and the colonizers. Here, therefore, the ways in which the civilizing mission was about subordination could remain obscured.

Under the steadying influence of a British officer, it was envisioned that tribes would abandon their wild and wandering ways, take to settled agriculture, and become steady, yeoman cultivators. One of the tasks of the Khandesh Bhil Agency was to extend loans to tribes in order to make them take up settled agriculture.[19] This emphasis on settling wild tribes has already been well explored: everywhere that the British consolidated control, they tried to

---

[18] On imperial hunting, see MacKenzie, *The empire of nature*; see also Rangarajan, *Fencing the forest*, ch. 4. On the use of hunting to draw a distinction between the British and the effeminate castes, see Mrinalini Sinha, *Colonial masculinity: The 'manly Englishman' and the 'effeminate Bengali' in the late nineteenth century*, Manchester, 1995, pp. 41–2.

[19] For colonial practices in Khandesh, see Stewart Gordon, 'Bhils and the idea of a criminal tribe in nineteenth century India', in his *Marathas, marauders and state formation*, Delhi, 1994.

impose fixity of residence on pastoralists, forest communities, and other mobile groups. Involved in these efforts was a distinctive ideology which emphasized economic efficiency, and which was dismissive of mobile groups because of the assumption that they did not use resources efficiently.[20] Civilizing the wild tribes, then, was about bringing them closer to British ideas of efficient and rational use of resources.

In many ways, the working of the Forest Department paralleled this civilizing mission in intention and scope: just as colonial officials civilized the tribes, so did the Department civilize the forests. As has been pointed out, colonial forestry was in many ways 'an industrial science . . . informed by a conception of the "rational" use of natural resources intrinsic to industrial capitalism'. As part of the articulation of a Cartesian scientificity, plantations were set out in straight lines, an almost geometrical order was imposed on forests, and they were converted into industrial resources that had to be rationally utilized.[21]

Whether it was the tribes or forests that were being civilized, there were some common themes in the strategies adopted. For one, to civilize them, both tribes and forests had to be protected from the outside. The wild tribes had to be protected against the liquor merchants of the plains and other plains figures. Simple upright folk like the wild tribes were lamentably prone to being deceived by devious plains merchants and traders, as well as by plains powers like the Gaekwads or the Rajput states.[22] Besides, contact with the effeminate castes of the plains had a corrupting influence on the wild tribes. In the Bhil corps, formerly 'the Bhil, when he was questioned, always spoke the truth . . . But, unfortunately, he had learned to lie with the advent of Brahman native officers who had taught him the drill'.[23] Similarly, the forests too had to be protected from the outside — from plains timber traders and the large numbers of peasants who regularly visited the forests

20 See especially Neeladri Bhattacharya, 'Pastoralists in a colonial world', Jacques Pouchpedass, 'British attitudes towards shifting cultivation in colonial south India', both in Arnold and Guha (eds), *Nature, culture, imperialism*.

21 Ramachandra Guha, 'Scientific forestry and social change', *Economic and Political Weekly*, vol. 20, Special Number, November 1985. p. 1949. For another fascinating account of the imposition of Cartesian scientificity on forests, see Peter Sahlins, *Forest rites*, Cambridge, Mass., 1994.

22 See, for example, *BA.PD.1864.Vol 28.Comp 394*; Reeves to Willoughby, 20.9.1843, Morriss to Reeves, 22.5.1843, *IOL.F.4.2074*; see also *BRO.DDR.DN 1.FN 4*.

23 Barnes, 'The Bhils', p. 339.

and took away timber. Their activities were now viewed as the crime of pilferage and theft, one more serious than similar criminal activities by forest communities. Amongst the first tasks of the Forest Department was the setting up of posts to guard against incursions into Dangi forests from merchants or plains peasants from Gaekwadi territories.[24] There was the possibility of the corruption of forests too: if they were misused by tribes or castes, they could degenerate into wastelands.

Second, civilizing the tribes and forests involved protecting them from themselves. There was their high-spirited boisterousness — boys will be boys — which might lead to plundering and other troubles if not kept in check by an understanding but firm British official.[25] The forests too had to be protected from themselves; their wildness could not be allowed to consume them. A whole range of silvicultural techniques existed for this purpose. They had to be cleared of undergrowth, so that combustible material which could trigger off fires did not build up. Trees had to be trimmed so that they grew properly; plantations had to be created.

Third, and most relevant here, civilizing the tribes and forests involved excluding each from the other. In the perceptions of colonial officials and foresters, the coming together of the forests and the wild tribes was what spoilt both of them. The Bhils and other wild tribes were made indolent by their ability to depend on the forests to give them an easy life. Access to forests and timber led to sloppy cultivation. Forests too were damaged: tribes wrecked forests, and prevented them from being used rationally. One Conservator of Forests expostulated: 'the people [of Dangs] . . . have no idea that the teak tree has a much higher value to the general public and for the good of the country at large, than to be destroyed for their private purposes.'[26] For the good of both, forests and tribes had to be kept apart from each other.

This emphasis on excluding the wild tribes from the forests was the basic thrust of desiccationist practice right from the early days of its influence in India. An ideology deeply influenced by edenic visions of the garden, desiccationism was basically characterized by its aggressive assertion of a connection between the depletion

[24] Annual Report, 1844–5, BA.PD.1846.Vol 16/1781.Comp 1368; BA.RD. 1851.Vol 120.Comp 1247.

[25] Lt Hutchinson to Agent to the Governor General, Indore, 12.5.1856, NAI.FD.Pol.1856.Nos 31–45.

[26] Shuttleworth to Comm., CD, 24.3.1893, BA.RD.1893.Vol 133.Comp 948.

of tree cover and phenomena like droughts or soil erosion. Many East India Company botanists and surgeons were passionate desiccationists, and the setting up of Forest Departments in the British Presidencies of Madras and Bombay in the 1840s was the result of their desiccationist arguments that ecological doom would follow if trees were not preserved.[27] Yet it would be a mistake to treat desiccationist environmentalism as innocent of colonial domination. The point is not so much that imperialism was green as that green or environmentalist discourses were imperialist. The violent and often brutal domination and exclusion of colonized peoples practised by the Forest Department was part of environmentalist idealism rather than separate from it.

In 1849, Dr Gibson, the founder of the Bombay Presidency Forest Department and one of the key figures in the desiccationist movement in India, visited Dangs and issued a memo to the chiefs directing them how to do cultivation without damaging 'valuable timber'. Cultivators were to refrain from agriculture in areas 'thickly covered with [young or mature] teak Tiwas or "Sissoo" timber'.[28] Around 1855, a more comprehensive set of rules was promulgated. Khandad in teak forests was prohibited. If unavoidable, then the cultivator was instructed to either put a heap of stones or remove the grass around the teak trees so that they would not be affected by fires. The selling of headloads of teak, *sisu* and khair was also prohibited. The manufacture of kath, an astringent extract popularly eaten with betel leaves, and made from khair trees, continued to be banned.[29] These rules provided, till 1901, the framework within which the Dangs was managed.

As this suggests, desiccationist taxonomies graded Dangi social practices by the extent of 'damage' they caused to 'valuable timber' such as teak. By such criteria, most Dangi modes of subsistence were harmful. Cultivation, and khandad in particular, was especially reprehensible. It involved firing the forests, lopping trees, and clearing wooded patches — all of which were seen as either killing trees or at least preventing the production of long straight boles of timber because of the knots and twists they caused.[30] The regular

[27] Richard Grove, *Green Imperialism: Colonial expansion, tropical edens, and the origins of environmentalism, 1600–1860*, Cambridge, 1994.

[28] Memo from Dr A. Gibson, 16.5.1849, *BA.PD.1852.Vol 41.Comp 851*.

[29] Rules for the forests of Dangs, *BA.PD.1856.Vol 48.Comp 1104*.

[30] Shuttleworth to Chief Secy., GoB, 27.8.1877, *BA.RD.1877.Vol 69.Comp 1566*.

migration to new spots for cultivation was also seen as inimical to the production of large timber, since new houses had to be built and new land cleared for cultivation at the freshly chosen site.[31] Hunting and mahua collection, similarly, were considered objectionable because they involved firing.[32] All these Dangi activities, then, had to be excluded from forests.

The problem, in the eyes of later colonial officials, was that Gibson's prohibitions did not achieve this task efficiently enough. Disparaging remarks already commenced in the 1860s about the 'loose system' of managing the Dangs.[33] Gibson's techniques had treated entire forests uniformly, imposing the same restrictions over the whole area. These rules, though good on paper, and in principle very far-reaching in the exclusion of Dangis that they sought, proved difficult to implement. Now forest officials were concerned with developing systems that, even if less far-reaching in principle, were nevertheless more effective in excluding Dangis and securing the production of large timber.[34]

Maybe nothing is more representative of this new system than demarcations. By the late nineteenth century, demarcations had almost become a rite of passage which had to precede the establishment of scientific forestry.[35] In Dangs, the Inspector General of Forests for India, Dietrich Brandis, had already in 1870 recommended a quick demarcation. A survey for the purpose was undertaken, and a Commission submitted in 1879 a report on how the demarcation should be carried out. In 1891, a Forest Demarcation Officer was appointed, and the demarcation was carried out. It was implemented in 1901.

The importance of demarcations derived from their role as the technology of exclusion in the new intensive systems of forest management that were becoming dominant by the 1870s. These systems proposed setting apart smaller tracts of forests than formerly by picking out the especially dense parts. Here, popular rights

[31] Propert to Comm., CD, 26.3.1878. *BA.RD.1878.Vol 58.Comp 127*; Morriss to Mansfield, 9.12.1853, *BA.RD.1854.Vol 63.Comp 182.*

[32] Shuttleworth to Chief Secy.; GoB, 19.6.1888, *BA.RD.1889.Vol 164.Comp 948*; *FRBP, 1884–5*, p. 23.

[33] RC to Secy., GoB, 1.7.1864, *BA.PD.1864.Vol 15.Comp 906.*

[34] See, for example, 'Remarks of Mr Muller', 27.4.1867, *BRO.DDR.DN 3.FN 12*; Brandis to Chief Secy., GoB, 13.6.1870, *BRO.DDR.DN 3.FN 18*; and Shuttleworth to Chief Secy., *BA.RD.1879.Vol 90.Comp 947.*

[35] This shift is explored very persuasively in Guha's 'Scientific forestry and social change'.

were to be severely restricted: cultivation, felling or the removal of timber by local communities, hunting or firing were to be banned. As compensation for the extinction of rights in these 'reserved forests', there were the 'protected forests', the less dense areas to which local communities were shifted from reserves, and 'given' what officials claimed was adequate land for their needs.

But demarcation was not only a technical task which involved identifying as reserves the densest forests or those with the most valuable timber. Equally, it was about the conversion of wild spaces into wild places — into areas with specific ecological and social configurations of wildness. Local details were overwhelmingly important. When the Demarcation Officer set aside around 219 square miles or approximately a third of the Dangs as reserved forests (much less than the two-thirds which had been recommended by an earlier Commission), he justified what he considered his moderation on the grounds that cultivation had increased enormously since the Commission's report, and that since 'the sole object of demarcation is the curtailment of privileges at present enjoyed' in the reserved areas, enough land should therefore be left aside as protected forests to meet 'all popular needs'.[36] Similar considerations influenced the imposition of restrictions. He permitted Dangis to retain their 'privilege' of hunting and collecting mahua flowers in the reserved forest, as also, very unusually, that of lopping any tree, including teak, in the protected areas.[37] These concessions were because he was trying to engineer a demarcation which would not be derailed by popular hostility. Thus, the demarcation converted Dangs from an abstract wild space into a wild place with a particular history, one which needed a specific kind of treatment.

It has sometimes been implied that desiccationism was not involved in converting forests into economic resources, and that the Department in concentrating by the turn of the century on meeting imperial needs, abandoned desiccationist environmentalism.[38] But this is not the case. Desiccationism was also about

36 Gibbs to Loch, 8.7.1890, *BA.RD.1890.Vol 93.Comp 947.*

37 The redefinition of popular rights as 'privileges' was often characteristic of scientific forestry. See Guha, 'Forestry and social protest', pp. 68f.

38 This argument is implicit in Richard Grove's *Green imperialism.* I had also implied something similar in an earlier paper, 'From desiccationism to scientific forestry: The Dangs, 1840s–1920s', in Richard Grove, Vinita Damodaran and S. Sangwan (eds), *Nature and the orient: Environmental history of south and southeast Asia,* Delhi, 1998. This paper was completed in 1992; my views have changed much since then.

civilizing the forests, converting them into economic resources that could be efficiently utilized. The demarcation, and later scientific forestry more broadly, were deeply influenced by desiccationist environmentalism. In the 1880s and 1890s, Khandesh officials were reluctant to sanction the demarcation, fearing that it would anger Dangis. But there was a shrill and rising crescendo of protests from forest officials, who argued that Dangs was a natural forest area, that ecological disaster would follow if the demarcation was not done immediately, and that water in Dangs was already scarce because of deforestation.[39] If the demarcation was finally sanctioned in 1901, it had to do most of all with this persistent invocation of desiccationist themes. That is to say, desiccationist environmentalism led to a more forceful and emphatic exclusion of Dangis than might have been the case otherwise.

After the demarcation, the exclusion of Dangis from forests was carried out very effectively. As Chapter 15 argues in detail, Dangi cultivation in what had been deemed reserved forests was entirely halted, and styles of cultivation in the protected forests were forcibly modified so that they would do less 'damage' to valuable timber. Similarly, the fires that Dangis deployed during cultivation, hunting, or mahua-collection were excluded. Though nineteenth-century officials had repeatedly complained that fires hindered 'the chief aim of the forest officer' — the production of 'large straight and sound' timber, their control over the region was too limited to permit any sustained attempts to halt fires.[40] With the acquisition of these powers in 1901–2, there were no further stumbling blocks to the introduction of 'fire conservancy', felt to be '50 years behind the times' in the Dangs.[41] Preparatory measures began with fire-tracing, a process involving the clearing of trees and vegetation from 100-feet wide strips around the reserves, so that fires from the protected areas could not spread into the reserves. After some trial attempts, a comprehensive fire protection scheme prepared by the Divisional Forest Officer, E.M. Hodgson was implemented with remarkable results. In its first year, only around 22 per cent of the forests were traversed by fires. During

39 F. Gleadow to Coll., Kh., 6.6.1887, *DCR.DN 1.FN 19B.*
40 Surat Forest Administration Report, 1890–1, *DFR.DN 2.FN 17*; Surat Forest Administration Report, 1889–90, *DFR.DN 2.FN 18.* For one attempt at fire control, see Surat Forest Administration Report, 1890–1, ibid.
41 Surat Forest Administration Report, 1904–5, *DFR.DN 3.FN 38.*

the next decade, the area traversed by fires was to quite consistently stay below five per cent.[42]

TOWARDS DICHOTOMOUS FORESTS

The civilizing mission of colonial forestry — the exclusion of Dangis, and the 'rational' and 'efficient' use of Dangi timber — reconstituted and transformed the forests in several ways. Earlier, the annual fires had helped a fresh crop of sweet grass to spring up every year in the forests. In the absence of fires, the grass in the reserves, as well as the protected areas that were no longer traversed by fires, became coarser and less suitable for grazing by cattle. It is likely that this was offset to some degree by the fact that more grass was available in the summer months, when fodder was often in acute short supply.[43] Also, paradoxically, since fires had played a major role in the germination of teak seeds, their cessation possibly led to a rapid drop in the reproduction of teak. This would explain the barrage of complaints by Surat forest officials from the 1910s onwards regarding the way in which teak tended to reproduce poorly in 'natural' conditions — that is to say, in the absence of fires by the Dangis.

Another kind of reconstitution of forests was the denudation caused by the mid-twentieth century owing to the extraction of large amounts of timber as part of the rational use of forests. Though we do not know the actual volume of timber felled, it is indicated by the rising revenue from timber sales. In 1901–2, the revenue of the Surat division, which consisted principally of Dangs, stood at around Rs 28,109. By 1910–11, it had climbed to Rs 108,633, and by 1920–1 to Rs 224,171. By the time of Indian independence in 1948–9, the revenue from Dangs stood at Rs 1,520,489.[44] Quite evidently, despite the official Department commitment to reproduction, the necessity for higher revenue had, as was usually the case, taken precedence in the way the forests were actually worked. Such

42 Surat Forest Administration Report, 1901–2, *DFR.DN 2.FN 19*; Hodgson to Coll., Surat, 22.12.1906, *BA.RD.1907.Vol 126.Comp 632*; Surat Forest Administration Report, 1907–8, *DFR.DN 1.FN 2*; Dangs Annual Administration Report, 1906–7, *BA.ED.Vol 63.Comp 7390*. See *FRBP*, 1907–20 for the areas burnt annually.

43 From E.M. Hodgson, 25.12.1906, *DFR.DN 1.FN 2Uc*.

44 These figures are taken from the annually published *Forest Reports of the Bombay Presidency*. While there were sharp annual fluctuations in the revenue secured, the figures serve as a broad indicator of the increase in Forest Department exploitation.

denudation directly affected fauna too. Game had already been scarce in the late nineteenth century as a result of Dangi practices and departmental exploitation; the Department's working of the forests now led to the extinction of species like the flying squirrel, as also virtual disappearance of the large number of antelopes and wild boar that the Dangis had subsisted on.

The reconstitution of forests led in Dangs, as possibly in many other areas of British India, to a slow and partial shift away from mosaic forests to what almost might be called dichotomous forests. This was because the protected forests — the zone to which Dangi cultivation and modes of subsistence were to be largely confined — were reconstituted in ways very different from the reserved forests, the zone the Department had tried to arrogate to itself. Within the reserves, all 'unsound' or crooked trees were gradually felled. Only valuable species, especially teak, were allowed to survive: 'the unmarketable species must be felled wherever they are interfering with or threatening valuable growth.' Nurseries (note the word, with its civilized and civilizing connotations of gardening) were set up on a large scale to supply seedlings of valuable timber trees, especially of teak, for filling 'blanks' left by old fellings or cultivation.[45]

The densest tracts of present-day Dangs, the Mahal and Bardipada forests are believed to be, from the regularity of their growth, the result of departmental plantations between seventy and eighty years back.[46] In most reserved forests, because teak had been systematically replanted while other species had not, it may have become more predominant relative to other species than formerly, even if overall forest cover was less because of denudation.

In contrast to the strategy in reserves, the Department tried to reduce the density of tree growth and remove valuable species in protected forests. As part of an effort to regenerate forests in reserves, little or no felling was done in them for ten years or more after 1901.[47] Till 1916 at least, the sizeable revenue secured by the Department was generated entirely from the fellings conducted in the protected forests, and these continued to provide a major chunk

[45] See, for some reports, *DWP*, pp. 13f; *FRBP*, 1912–13, pp. 35ff; *FRBP*, 1913–14, p. 36; *FRBP*, 1916–17, pp. 32ff; *FRBP*, 1916–17, pp. 32ff; *FRBP*, 1919–20, p. 12.
[46] I am grateful to Sejal Vohra for pointing this out, and for sharing with me the insights from her work on Dangi ecosystems.
[47] 'Report on the future administration of the Dangs', *BA.RD.1902.Vol 107. Comp 949.Part II.*

of the Department's revenue in the ensuing decades. The Department's focus in protected forests was on cornering 'the revenue from sound timber of marketable size before it is ruined by lopping'.[48] So while lopped or 'unsound' timber was being removed from the reserves and 'sound' timber grown, precisely the opposite policy was being followed in the protected areas.

Other measures too fed into this dichotomization of the two areas. Dangis had been excluded from the reserves, and had to depend entirely on the protected areas for loppings and their more general timber requirements. Fires were permitted in the protected areas, but not in the reserves. Finally, the Department undertook few reproduction operations or seedling plantations in the protected areas. All this meant that the protected forests were denuded much faster than the reserves.

At the turn of the century, the difference between protected and reserved forests had not been much. The latter were often more dense, but only slightly so. Several dense patches were not taken into the reserved forests for a variety of reasons — because of the fear of resistance by local villagers, because they were isolated patches, because of proximity to a village, or because there was not too much valuable timber in them. Later forest officers claimed that 'the original Forest Settlement Officers . . . searched for the hilliest tracts and studiously avoided interfering with any cultivation found . . . certain areas eminently suitable for reserves were excluded in the year 1890 owing to the existence at the time of a small area of cultivation therein'.[49] By the mid-twentieth century, this was no longer the case. Few large trees remained in the protected areas, while the reserves increasingly consisted of them; the former were denuded at a rapid pace, the latter more slowly, leading to their being relatively more dense; in the former, teak was present but heavily lopped and not regenerating very well because of the decline of fires; in the latter, teak was becoming the predominant species. The mosaic forests were slowly being transformed into dichotomous ones. One might say, then, that a double dichotomization of western India occurred. In the plains, with the dominance of settled cultivation, interrupted forests disappeared: now the dichotomy was between the forestless plains and forested hills. Within the forested areas themselves, mosaic growth was

48 *DWP*, pp. 7f, 12.
49 Hodgson to PA, 31.3.1910, *BA.RD.1911.Vol 120.Comp 636.*

increasingly transformed into dichotomized tracts of reserved and protected forests.

The Anxieties of Mastery

Whether the wildness of forests and tribes was celebrated or assimilated into a civilizing mission, there was a consistent emphasis on mastery. It was precisely the anxieties accompanying this emphasis on mastery which formed another important theme in colonial relationships with wildness. In British understandings, with a wild people like the Bhils, mastery was never complete, not even after they had been protected and transformed. They could be instigated by mischief-makers, and they had this habit of breaking into revolt at the drop of a pin. In some senses, true, British officials felt that there was something exasperatingly endearing about the impossibility of mastery over the wild tribes. This was because, as Chinn remarks to his colonel: 'There isn't an ounce of real vice in them.'[50] Their proclivity to rebel was not because they were devious or deceitful; it was because they were natural and irrepressible. This irrepressible wildness was what made both forests and forest communities attractive: the desire for mastery was authorized and legitimated by its very impossibility. To seek mastery over the wild tribes was a challenge, and the element of danger which accompanied it was a clean one, suitable to honourable Englishmen.

Nevertheless, revolts dangerously foregrounded the limits of mastery, and of colonial stereotypes about wild tribes. To conceive of genuine rather than misplaced hostility from the masculine wild tribes undermined British notions of themselves, their masculinity, their gentlemanliness and their civilizing mission far too drastically; it threatened to show up the awfulness and raw domination of colonialism. To conceive of Bhil hostility as no different from plains hostility was to allow that Bhil wildness too might be like that of the feminine castes, that there was no site anywhere in the colonies for the affirmation of imperial masculinity — a deeply troubling thought. Revolts had to be suppressed brutally, and then either forgotten or else recast as boisterousness. This may be why, despite the fact that the Bhils possibly revolted more often than any other

---

[50] Kipling, 'The tomb of his ancestors', in *The day's work*, London, 1988 (1898), p. 120.

community in India, colonial officials clung desperately, almost touchingly, to the idea that Bhils were especially loyal subjects, more so than any others.

As with tribes, though the forests could be transformed, their wildness could never be entirely erased. Again, it was the very persistence of wildness which made forests occupy such a special place in colonial discourse, which made them objects fit for mastery. Shikhar always carried with it more than a element of danger, especially in regions like the Dangs where tigers and panthers abounded, and where at least one British forest officer, Dalzell, was attacked by a tiger during the nineteenth century.

But the coming together of the wildness of the tribes and the forests, during rebellions or even the pursuit of everyday modes of subsistence, made both the tribes and the forests dangerously wild. In this sense, the dichotomization of the forests, and the exclusion of forest communities, was an emphatic act of mastery spurred also by colonial apprehensions about the threatening wildness of the colonized.

Colonial officials could never be sure that they had mastered this wildness. Dangis could never after all be entirely excluded from the forests. In innumerable ways, they invaded the forests, and were involved with it. Because of these threats to mastery, colonial officials could never view forestry as a completed project; rather, as Ramachandra Guha has pointed out, the techniques of forestry such as demarcation developed through an engagement with the resistance that local communities put up.[51] It is to these irruptions of what colonial officials saw as wildness that the rest of the book will turn.

(14)

51 Guha, 'Scientific forestry and social change', *Economic and Political Weekly*, vol. 20, Special number, November 1985.

14

Demarcation and Domination

Goth of the mandini are often about the demarcation of 1901–2. The specific measures often ascribed to it — the creation of reserved forests where Dangis were not permitted to cultivate or the setting up of cairns to denote reserves — are those which accompanied it. The officials associated with it — Hokson Saheb (E.M. Hodgson) and Nilkantrao Diwan (N.M. Deshmukh) — are those involved in implementing the demarcation. Indeed, maybe mandini itself, meaning as it does dividing or apportioning, emerged as an important concept after the demarcation.

> The gora saheb came to the raja and said, 'Rajasaheb, give me permission to cut wood from your forests'. The raja asked, 'What will you do with the wood?' The saheb said, 'I shall sell it at Surat and get money, and give you a pension from that money'. The raja said, 'Do not cut too much wood. Cut only the *ubha sukha lakda* [standing dead timber]. Do not cut the green timber. I do not want damage to my forests. Set up nakas and protect my timber from being stolen'.[1]

It is of course tempting to read the goth as a statement of an ecological concern quite close to what environmentalists are now concerned with. That would also unfortunately be misleading, for it is more an inversion of the symbols of colonial domination. The naka, that ubiquitous emblem of the sarkar, is set up at the raja's instructions. The restrictions that the raja imposes on the British are precisely those which colonial officials were to insist that the Dangis observe; this goth mocks colonial and postcolonial forest restrictions by associating the restrictions with Bhil raj, and making the Forest Department and the saheb the victims of restrictions.

But such inversions are not only playful; they are also bitter. Sometimes, the demarcation is associated with the lashkar.

---

[1] Surya Kosu, 31.3.1990, Chikar.

When the sarkar came, they put up cairns in the reserved areas first. The rajas said,'let them put up cairns, it will not change matters'. But the sarkar had the lashkar, and the cairns stayed despite the opposition of the rajas. After this, they put up cairns for the protected areas.[2]

Evidently, many goth question the legitimacy of the demarcation:

Hokson saheb came to house of the raja. He said, 'Rajasaheb, ram ram'. The rajasaheb said, 'what do you want?' Hokson saheb said, 'Rajasaheb, we have a jodi. But I am a shikari, and I often roam in the jungle. I am afraid that I might by mistake come into your house, and you might become angry and kill me. So give me a portion of the forests, and I shall stay within it, and will not be afraid of coming into your house by mistake'. So cairns were put up, and a portion became the banbhag [reserved forest]. But Hokson saheb did not stay within these bounds; he expanded his territory till all the forests had been taken over.[3]

In another goth:

Only three jungles were initially given to the saheb: those of Kot, Barda ni Khadi and Bhuria Sadada ni Vangan. But they did not stay to these, they took over other forests too.[4]

The specifying of the three areas is significant, since these are the densest surviving tracts in Dangs. In acknowledging the legitimacy of departmental control over them, its authority over the rest of Dangs is implicitly questioned.[5]

In describing gora raj — associated with mandini — several narrators characterized it with one phrase: *khavana pivana changla, pan kayda kadak* (eating and drinking were good, but the laws were strict). Another characterization of it was as a *markhub raj* (a *raj* of much beating and violence). For most of my fieldwork, I ignored such remarks, treating them as a sort of prefatory routinized memory, a harbinger of the specifics to follow. It took an inordinate amount of time to realize that these routinized statements were the pithiest accounts possible of gora raj.

2 Jiva Kharsu, 20.3.1990, Ghadvi.
3 Rahirao Bhagirao, 29.4.1990, Deher.
4 Surya Kosu, 31.3.1990, Chikar.
5 The connection between resistance today and such goth is explored systematically by Shiney Varghese in 'Women, development and resistance: A case study of Dangs, India', *Development in Practice*, vol. 3, no. 1, 1993.

CULTURES OF DOMINATION

Maybe goth of mandini and gora raj can provide cues for exploring
an unsaid of the previous chapter — what the violence of environmentalism and its culture of domination meant to Dangis, and how
this violence and culture was shaped through an engagement with
Dangis. Khavana pivana changla: here, gora raj is being thought of
in terms of the break that the present involves from it. While
mandini extends to the present, gora raj obviously does not. And
the differences from the present are clear. During gora raj land was
more productive compared to the present. Since cultivators could,
till two or three decades back, shift around from field to field, plots
recovered their fertility, and the nagli could be reaped with less
effort and seed. There were low prices — either eight, twelve or
sixteen champas (a measure of volume) of nagli was available for
a rupee. Whatever the figure, the contrast with the present is
dramatic. The price of turbans, shelas, or dhotur form part of this
contrastive complex — they are low enough to evoke both anger
at the present, and laughter.

But this is not so much nostalgia for gora raj as a critique of the
present: simultaneously, recall, there is the all-important qualifica-
tion 'pan kayda kadak', or even simply in the description of British
rule as markhub raj. These are references to draconian restrictions
and the punitive powers of colonial officials. Two officials figure
above all in these goth: the DFO saheb, and the Diwan Saheb. Dangs
forests were managed throughout the period by the Divisional Forest
Officer (DFO) of Surat district (the post that Hodgson held).

What is striking about Diwans and DFOs, both in records and
goth, is their enormous power. In the mid-1850s, a Diwan was
appointed (over the fierce opposition of the chiefs, who feared the
greater British control this would result in)[6] to look after Dangs,
and this post was continued till the mid-twentieth century, shortly
after Indian independence. In the nineteenth century, the Diwan
was based in Khandesh and toured Dangs for two or three months
annually; after the demarcation, he was based in the new British
capital in Dangs, Ahwa. He investigated any 'crimes' or complaints
against rajas by Bhils or Koknis, and settled minor disputes. The
major 'crimes' or disputes were referred to the Khandesh Collector
for settlement.

6 Inveriarty to Secy., GoB, 15.6.1847, *BA.PD.1847.Vol 21/1902.Comp 973*;
Coll., Kh., to Secy., GoB. 24.7.1855, *BA.PD.1855.Vol 36.Comp 1242*.

The first Diwan, Kadar Ali, extorted money from the rajas and others as fines and forced Trimbak raja of Pimpri to buy through him a shela for the bloated sum of Rs 400. In another case, the Diwan arbitrarily kept Trimbak's father-in-law, Jewa, bound and confined for four days because he would not hand over a chillum or pipe to which the Diwan took a fancy. When Jewa was asked later why he had not complained to the Collector about the Diwan, he said that he was in 'greater awe [of the Diwan] than the Saheb'. Trimbak too was terrified of the Diwan. When Kadar Ali threatened him with terrible consequences if he complained to the saheb, Trimbak began to cry.[7]

The point about stories such as these is not whether they were true or false; rather, the very fact that they were widely retailed was part of the way in which the colonial culture of domination over the forests was sustained. Nor was there fear only of these high officials. At a more local level, there were the forest guards — the village-level officials who were supposed to actually ensure that Dangis did not use forests save in the ways that the Department prescribed. The power of guards was all too evident to Dangis — they could demand forced labour, impose restrictions on forest use, stop cultivation on any site on the grounds that rules were being violated, or even in some cases order the evacuation of villages. They used their position to make heavy demands from villagers: 'a forest *pattevala's* [peon's] food does not cost him an anna in the month, everything he requires being taken from the people without payment . . . if a Forest Sepoy comes to [a] . . . village, he always gets his rice or other food for nothing.'[8]

Quite apart from officials' demands, there were heavy levies for Forest Department works. Many goth of gora raj dwell especially on *bigar*, whether paid or unpaid, which was systematically demanded by the British from Dangis, and which ceased only with the end of colonial rule. In 1874, the Assistant Conservator of Forests, Captain MacRae, kept an unspecified number of Dangis continually at work for nearly forty days without any payment, making them carry their own food when accompanying him on tours. Even more pervasive problems were those created by routine Forest Department demands (which increased after the 1901 demarcation) for bigar to carry baggage, post, to clear fire lines, to work in sawmills and so on. If

---

7 Mansfield to Secy., GoB, 8.5.1857, and attached case records, in *BA.PD. 1857.Vol 82.Comp 584.*
8 Nice to MacRae, 25.4.1874, *BA.RD.1875.Vol 48.Comp 1279.*

refused bigar, villagers said, forest officials 'threaten they will beat us and order us to leave the village'.[9]

> The engine *malik* [sawmill (engine) owner] would come and call out to us for bigar. If nobody was at home, he would drop the money into the pot kept outside. When we came back, we would see the money. [T]hen we would prepare sida pani for eight days and go. There was no question of not going; we would be beaten if we did not. It was a markhub raj. If the malik did not like the work, he would take out his belt and beat us, 'Saala . . . have you come here to work or smoke bidis'. I was not beaten, but some of my companions were.[10]

Still another dimension of the kadak kayda of gora raj was the fire restrictions. As remarked earlier, from the 1910s, fires swept less than five per cent of Dangs every year. In few other areas of India had comparable results been obtained: it was almost normal for 10 to 20 per cent of the forest area to be annually traversed by fires. The restrictions that Hodgson imposed were no different from those elsewhere in India. But he had almost unique magisterial powers, and he exercised them. Thus, a Bhil who in 1904–5 had been sentenced to 15 days' rigorous imprisonment for firing a forest was sentenced a year later to four months' imprisonment for the same offence. Terms of four months to a year's imprisonment for even accidentally setting a patch of forest on fire were not uncommon. As Hodgson argued, '[l]ight sentences . . . only make the villagers think that the authorities are not really in earnest'.[11] These savage sentences were considered legitimate, surely, because of the prior ascription of savagery and wildness to forest communities.[12]

---

[9] Ibid.; deposition of Lanu Kusba, Chikatia 6.5.1874, *BA.RD.1875.Vol 48. Comp 1279.* Chhotubhai naik, untitled MSS autobiography (Gujarati, photocopy in my possession). Such demands were common to forest tracts almost all over India. See Guha, 'Forestry and social protest in Kumaon, c. 1893–1921', in Ranajit Guha (ed.), *Subaltern studies* IV, Delhi, 1985, pp. 73–7.

[10] Govinda Vanju, 8.6.1990, Kodmal.

[11] Hodgson to Coll., Surat, 22.12.1906, *BA.RD.1907.Vol 126.Comp 632.*

[12] The magisterial powers that Hodgson exercised were the consequence of Dangs being technically outside British India, though under colonial administration. Elsewhere in British India, cases were tried by Revenue Department officials, who, in the opinion of foresters, did not pass sentences that were stringent enough. A national forest conference in 1910 took special note of Hodgson's success, and argued for similar powers to forest officials elsewhere in India. The proposal was rejected on the grounds that officials should not in principle be given magisterial powers to try cases in which they were concerned, even if this 'general principle was not applicable to such a wild and primitive country as Dangs'. *BA.RD.1910.Vol 105.Comp 660.*

Goth too dwell on the draconian kayda.

> We could not even carry anything that might be used to make fire into the forests. And if there was a fire, the guard would come to the village and ask, 'who started it?' If nobody said anything, he would beat people in the village till they confessed. Or he would just take away somebody who he thought was likely to have started the fire.[13]

Similarly:

> If there was a fire, everybody in the village had to turn out and go to extinguish it. We did not wait for the guard to come and tell us. The patil would gather everybody and go out to the forest. If there was somebody in the village who had not gone when the guard reached, the guard would pull him out and beat him with his lathi. Even the patil was beaten if he did not go: I have seen the Ghadvi patil being beaten by the guard because there was a fire.[14]

According to goth, nine persons were burnt to death in a forest fire, including seven villagers who had been mobilized to go and put it out. These stories, circulating and recirculating, created part of the fear of the sarkar.

BHIL RAJ AND THE DEMARCATION

What had necessitated this culture of domination? Maybe it was a colonial attempt to engage with the constant exceeding of colonial restrictions by the everyday enactment of moglai, which I explore in Chapters 4 and 5. Moglai, in a sense, was about a culture of resistance, one that undermined the workings of colonial power in various subterranean and overt ways. The trope drawn on most often for articulating hostility to gora raj and mandini was one which we encountered in goth of moglai — Bhil raj. An official remarked: 'one of the most curious points I noticed in Dangs was that in no case are the wild inhabitants, although used to timber cutting, willing to fell trees for the Forest Department. This I cannot understand.'[15] Except when compelled to do so as *bigaris*, Dangis refused to do paid or unpaid labour for the Department. Even

[13] Khandu Ravji, 9.6.1990, Vakaria.
[14] Jiva Kharsu, 17.4.1990, Ghadvi.
[15] KPAAR, 1876–7, *BA.PD.1877.Vol 106.Comp 1383*; see also Gibb to Loch, 8.7.1890, *BA.RD.1890.Vol 93.Comp 948*.

during the severe famine of 1899–1901, contractors had to import over 500 of the 600 labourers working on the site in Dangs.[16]

Officials reported that Bhils did not work for the Department because they considered themselves rajas.[17] This is true, but being a raja did not rule out wage labour. Many Bhils, including poorer members of the bhauband, did wage labour for prosperous Koknis.[18] If despite this both Bhils and Koknis refused to work for the Department, this may have been for other reasons: the activities of the Department seemed to directly threaten and question Bhil raj by claiming control over forests, and to refuse to work for it was to refuse to recognize it as sarkar, to assert the prevalence of Bhil raj.

The trope of Bhil raj was even more in evidence after 1874, when, following the appointment of an Indian as the DFO, senior white officials stripped the post of its magisterial powers as the Khandesh Collector's deputy. For the rest of the nineteenth century, despite district officials' efforts to restore these powers after a white man was appointed, the DFO was to be without magisterial powers. This transformed Dangi attitudes to the Department: now it was no longer part of the feared Khandesh sarkar which had organized the military expeditions and leases, and departmental domination no longer seemed so terrifying. The Indian's successor complained that 'the people will not listen to them [Forest Department employees] and tell them their raj is over . . . the effect on the forest is only too apparent . . . Thousands of young teak have been cut down or stripped of their branches.'[19] Some years later, when the demarcation was proposed, the chiefs protested:

we do not wish to let the Dang jungle [be] demarcated, for thereby we shall lose our rights and we and our poor rayat shall always be under the control of the Forest Deptt and the Deptt will always oppress us. Altho' [sic] the demarcation has not yet been finally settled the Forest people oppress our rayat and they have become sarkar.[20]

This was what the Department had been before 1874, and never again, evidently, did the Dangis want the Department to become the sarkar.

16 Hodgson to Political Agent, Khandesh, 17.7.1901, *DFR.DN 1.FN 8.*
17 KPAAR, 1876–7, *BA.PD.1877.Vol 106.Comp 1383.*
18 *KDG*, p. 601.
19 MacRae to CF, 1.3.1874, Extract from monthly diary of Dy. CF, April 1875, *BA.RD.1875.Vol 48.Comp 1279.* Administration Report, Gujarat Circle, 1874–5, *DFR.DN 1.FN 10.*
20 Petition, n.d., *BRO.DDR.DN 5.FN 25.*

Maybe as an assertion of Bhil raj, forest guards, the feared symbol of the sarkar, were in some cases seized, stripped naked and beaten. Almost in purposive protest against the demarcation, Dangis abandoned fertile lands in the valleys to take up cultivation in the proposed reserves. The Amala raja, like many other chiefs, even threatened to fine cultivators Rs 5 each if they left the reserves as the Forest Department had ordered. This defiance made sense as a strategy of livelihood too: forest official who toured the area was told by many Dangis 'that it was advisable in their interest to cultivate the "closed" forest — now while no obstacles were placed in the way & to leave the open blocks until such time as the Gov. might prevent cultivation in the demarcated area'.[21]

The alternatives that the chiefs proposed to the demarcation were premised on Bhil raj, and on Dangi understandings of rightful use of land. Realizing that the leases were inescapable, the chiefs had tried from the 1850s to limit these to as few species of trees as possible, thus leaving their authority over most forests intact. In 1852, they had already petitioned the Khandesh Collector against the prohibition on the manufacture of kath from the khair tree, claiming that the British had leased only teak, *tiwas* and sisu. At the time, the Collector reiterated the British reading of the leases — that all trees were covered by them. This explanation, he remarked satisfiedly, made the rajas fall silent.[22]

Silence did not however indicate assent. The chiefs consistently tried to interpret the leases in ways that restricted British use of the forests. Lacking access to the written word, their evaluation of the leases was based not on the documents but on colonial practice. Till 1852, the British felled principally teak, tiwas and *sisu*, and it was only these that the chiefs were willing to concede a right to. Involved in the Dangi understanding was a species-specific understanding of the leases, and they tried to limit the British to as few species as possible. Maybe species-specific restrictions also seemed preferable to the chiefs and many ordinary Dangis, for these still allowed them to move freely in the forests. In contrast, region-specific restrictions such as those proposed in the demarcation excluded them from entire tracts of forests. Also, these denied Bhil raj over the entire tracts that became reserves. During the struggle

21 Fry to Comm., CD, 1.12.1898, *BA.RD.1899.Vol 119.Comp 947*; note by Wallinger, 22.4.1894, *BRO.DDR.DN 4.FN 24*; see also *DFR.DN 1.FN 15*; DFAR, Surat Circle, 1898–9, *DFR.DN 2.FN 19*.
22 Annual Report, 1850, *BA.PD.1852.Vol 42.Comp 1415*.

over demarcation, the chiefs again tried to reiterate a species-specific understanding of the leases, this time claiming that the British had rented only teak, tiwas, sisu, and khair.[23]

Sensing however, that region-specific demarcations were inevitable, the bhauband also tried to govern the form these would take. Already in 1881, when the demarcation had been first suggested to them, they had insisted that they would allow only a fourth of the land to be reserved, and that they would select these areas — a proposal which the Department evidently found unacceptable. The only tracts the rajas were willing to countenance as reserves, it turned out later, were the 'unarable rocky uplands'.[24] Surely, these were the vanarkilla or makadkilla — the lands that conformed in Dangi usage to 'useless' patches.

The rajas also challenged the written documents that British officials claimed authorized the demarcation. Since 1881, the British had been trying to get the chiefs to sign an agreement assenting to the demarcation; after refusing to do so for several years, the chiefs finally signed the agreement in 1889. The agreement specified that once the demarcation was completed, 'no one would be allowed to enter [the forests] without permission of the forest officer'.[25] The rajas were suspicious and unwilling to sign the document. It was secured finally because of what the Khandesh Collector called the 'influence', 'patience and tact' of the Dangs Diwan, Kutubuddin.

Three years later, the rajas claimed that the agreement had been obtained unfairly, and demanded that it be set aside. The Collector had 'brought forward a certain paper in the Durbar and obtained the signatures of our Dewans to that document'. The rajas 'did not know what the document contained or that it was intended . ... to coerce us and our . . . cultivators to forsake our lands and villages'. The Collector, they said, had taken advantage of the fact that they were 'poor, illiterate and jungly people'.[26] These motifs are by now familiar: they are part of the seguing of wildness into ignorance, quite similar to that which Aundya raja had sensed in the 1840s. By claiming to have not understood it, the chiefs were attempting to delegitimize the agreement, and deny its fiction of being a

23 Petition, n.d., 1894, *BRO.DDR.DN 5.FN 25*.
24 DFAR, Gujarat Circle, 1881–2, *DFR.DN 1.FN 16*; Cumine to Comm.,CD, 9.7.1895, *BA.RD.1895.Vol 314.Comp 948*.
25 Agreement to Demarcation, *BA.RD.1889.Vol 164.Comp 948*.
26 Petition from rajas, 26.6.1892, *BRO.DDR.DN 4.FN 24*. See also the petition in *BRO.DDR.DN 5.FN 25*.

contract between equal and independent parties: the Diwan's 'tact' and other sundry qualities, for example, must have appeared quite coercive to the chiefs.

But the juggernaut of scientific forestry was, despite the occasional stumble, unstoppable. Late in 1901, on the grounds that the chiefs had violated the 1889 agreement by permitting lopping and clearing, the Bombay Government authorized the demarcation. E.M. Hodgson was appointed the Special DFO of Dangs and given the magisterial powers that Assistant Political Agents had wielded before 1874.[27]

AN END TO BHIL RAJ?

All of this raises one perplexing question. When Hodgson started driving Dangis out of the reserved forests, he did not meet with much resistance, and nor did cultivators return to the forests in subsequent years.[28] Why was this so, especially when in earlier decades Dangis had resorted to myriad forms of everyday resistance, both open and hidden, to fight the demarcation. Partly because the years from 1899 to 1901 had been a time of a devastating drought: several thousands died, others migrated out, and the population of Dangs fell to half its former level. And there was sufficient land for such a reduced population.

But surely this is not all. The refusal to fight back this time may also have been related to the consolidation once again, with even more scope, of colonial domination. Now the DFO had magisterial powers, the Diwan stayed round the years in Dangs, and the Surat Collector visited regularly. Besides, colonial power had only recently been made evident afresh to Dangis: in 1901, an expedition was sent into Dangs to capture some Amala bhauband, and it succeeded with an ease that might have surprised even the British. This was followed by the imposition of the demarcation, which after all represented a very extensive negation of Bhil raj. Maybe many Dangis felt that Bhil raj was over, and that it could not be invoked so easily as an everyday alternative to the British sarkar, which had become more powerful and fearsome than formerly. Of course, this feeling was not shared by everybody. Many narrators associate the end of Bhil raj with Indian independence, and others claim that it still continues now.

27 GR.RD.8495, 6 December 1901, in *BA.RD.1902.Vol 107.Comp 949, Part II.*
28 DFAR, Surat Circle, 1901–2, *DFR.DN 2.FN 19.*

Still, the early-twentieth-century apprehension that Bhil raj was over throws light on a striking phenomenon. As we saw earlier, Dangis in the nineteenth century were reluctant to work for the Forest Department. Yet, from the early twentieth century, when the departmental need for labour increased manifold, there is the complete disappearance of complaints about such refusals, without so much as a swan-song explanation. By 1910, nearly all the workers at forest sites were Dangis.[29] How should we explain such a transformation? One thing is clear: resentment of the sarkar continued unabated. The anthropologist Khanapurkar reported that the Dangis did not like outsiders, and considered it 'dishonourable to serve foreigners'.[30]

> If an outsider orders them to perform a thing, they will do it, thinking that he is an officer. But a request from an outsider is always spurned. They have a peculiar way of expressing themselves when taken to task by officers. Their reply is 'Ami anadi loka, bimjat nahi' [We are simpletons ('ignorant people', more accurately), we cannot grasp anything.][31]

If despite this Dangis suddenly commenced working for the Department, this may have been because of a perception that Bhil raj was now over. Now, there was greater fear of the Department, and it was much more an act of defiance to refuse to work for it. The Department now seemed so powerful that even paid labour for it seemed an unavoidable exaction. In the 1940s, an official reported: 'Dangi villagers consider any Government work as 'veth' [bigar] even though they are paid for the same. The Dangi calls it "veth" because he considers that being a Government work he is bound to do the same.'[32]

With this end of Bhil raj, maybe everyday Dangi resistance became even more subterranean than it had been. There is an early-twentieth-century song about a forest guard's visit to a village.

> The patil has gone to the bungalow, the bungalow,
> Comes the sarkari sipai, sipai
> The sipai does *tirimiri, tirimiri,*
> He demands a fowl immediately, immediately
> Our karbhari is not at home, not at home,

[29] Hodgson to PA, Surat, 31.3.1910, *BA.RD.1911.Vol 120.Comp 636.*
[30] Khanapurkar, 'The aborigines of south Gujarat', vol. II, p. 913
[31] Khanapurkar, 'The aborigines of south Gujarat', vol. I, pp. 74f.
[32] Chief Forest Officer to Coll., Dangs, 8.6.1949, *DCR.DN 8.FN 14.*

He has gone to the Ahwa office, office
Comes the saheb sipai, sipai
He demands sida immediately, immediately
My *patilin* [patil's wife] is not at home, not at home[33]

(15)

---

33 The bungalow is a reference to the government office, during the period amongst the few brick structures in Dangs. Tirimiri refers to showing off: here, it is possibly a reference to the sipai throwing his weight about. 'Saheb sipai' is the description of a senior forest official, as opposed to the ordinary sipai. The last line describes the patil claiming that his wife is not at home and that he cannot therefore supply food. Khanapurkar, 'The aborigines of south Gujarat', vol. II, p. 953. I have translated the song afresh from the Dangi text he provides.

15

Redefinitions of Mobility

Mandini is also about the end of chhut or mobility. It marked the end of hunting, gathering, mahua-collection, khandad and dahi, all of which are identified almost exclusively with moglai. In the nineteenth and early twentieth century, Dangi lifestyles and modes of subsistence were transformed as a result of the demarcation and the colonial reconstitution of the forests. Take cultivation. Like his nineteenth-century predecessors, Hodgson believed that 90 per cent of the 'injury' to 'valuable' timber was because of the lopping, firing, clearing and migration involved in cultivation. Unlike them, he had the power to do something about it, and he initiated a range of measures.

One of the first steps he took was to completely ban khandad, the form of cultivation which involved firing the entire field. Those who practised khandad were pushed to take up dahi, the form of cultivation which involved firing only seedbeds. Hodgson claimed that it was necessary to ban khandad since '[s]teep slopes treated in this way become denuded of soil, and so unfit for either forestry or cultivation; elevated plateaus, which are very numerous, produce a dense growth of reeds and grass, tree growth only very slowly establishing itself '.[1] He deliberately took undulating, sloping areas into reserves so that no land would be left for khandad.[2] The Dangs Diwan was instructed to discourage hand cultivation and permit only plough cultivation. By 1904, it was reported that khandad was 'rapidly dying a natural [sic] death'.[3] By 1909, it was claimed to have been completely stopped, and 'no one in the Dangs, except a few idle and destructive Bhils desire to revert to this destructive method'.[4]

---

[1] Report on the Future Administration of the Dangs Forests, *BA.RD.1902.Vol 107.Comp 949, Part II.*

[2] Hodgson to Coll., Surat, 31.3.1910, *BA.RD.1911.Vol 198.Comp 944.*

[3] Hodgson to Deshmukh, 5.5.1906, *BRO.DDR.DN 5.FN 29*; Annual Report for 16 months ending July 1904, *BA.ED.1904.Vol 62.Comp 739.*

[4] Hodgson to CF, 27.7.1909, *DFR.DN7.Case 3 of 1909–10.*

Colonial officials also tried to modify dahi. Formerly, it had involved cultivation with ploughs and transplantings seeds which had earlier been grown on a seedbed fired with lopping from trees. Possibly because the Department had burnt its fingers badly when trying to halt similar practices in nearby Thana in the 1870s, it proceeded cautiously. Hodgson did not ban dahi outright. Instead, the preparation of seed beds which used a lot of timber was banned; cultivators were now to use cowdung, grass and small branches for seedbeds. Furthermore, the felling of any trees was banned, as was lopping and cultivation on slopes, the cutting of footsteps into tree stems, and the lopping of bamboos and saplings anywhere.[5]

Colonial restrictions did not easily succeed. The 'people are more obstinate about this matter than any other . . . [they] do just as much damage as they think will be suffered to pass, in order to save themselves trouble.'[6] Bhil resistance posed the greatest problem: '10 Koknis together probably do less damage than one Bhil.'[7] In the more remote hills, 'where Bhils consider the chances of being caught not worth worrying about', lopping went on virtually unchecked.[8]

Still, Dangi methods of cultivation were pushed by the culture of domination towards a decreased use of fire and loppings. If the entire cowdung in the area around the village had not been collected for *gawari dahi*, the forest guard could stop the villagers from preparing seed beds with other material till this was done. Stiff fines were imposed on those who lopped the upper third of trees, practised cultivation using methods disallowed by the Department, or caused fires. By 1913, it was reported that protected forests were treated 'better' by the Dangis than previously.[9]

SETTLING DANGIS

Along with this shift in dahi to fewer loppings and fewer fires, Hodgson's measures engineered a decline in the agricultural mobility

5 Dangs Administration Report, 1906–7, *BA.ED.Vol 63.Comp 739*. See also the Surat Forest Administration Report, 1908–9, *DFR.DN 6.FN 17*, Dangs Diwan to DFO, 30.3.1907, *DFR.DN 7.Case 48 of 1907–8*; Surat Forest Administration Report, 1907–8, *DFR.DN 1.FN 2*. Dangs Standing Orders, *BRO.DDR.DN 6.FN 36/1*.

6 Surat Forest Administration Report, 1913–14, *DFR.DN 3.FN 41*.

7 *FRBP*, 1910–11, p. 5.

8 Surat Forest Administration Report, 1914–15, *DFR.DN 3.FN 42*.

9 Surat Forest Administration Report, 1904–5, *DFR.DN 3.FN 38*; Surat Forest Administration Report, 1912–13, *DFR.DN 3.FN 40*, Surat Forest Administration Report, 1908–9, *DFR.DN 6.FN 17*.

which had been characteristic of both khandad and dahi. Mobility was sharply circumscribed, first, by the ban on all residence or cultivation in the reserves. The area designated as reserves was 217 square miles at the time of the demarcation. By 1911 it had been increased to nearly 331 square miles, primarily on the grounds that much land in the protected areas lay uncultivated and could easily be added to the reserves without hurting Dangis.[10] Residents of over three hundred villages in the reserves were forcibly evacuated and made to settle down in other villages in the protected forests. Individual agriculturists did resist this massive displacement, attempting surreptitious cultivation in the reserves till around 1911.[11] But the consequences of being found out were too heavy — loppings were confiscated or removed outside the reserves, making cultivation that year difficult or impossible — for such resistance to be worth it against a powerful sarkar. In effect, the ban on cultivation in reserves meant that Dangis were confined in their agricultural mobility to only half the Dangs.

Mobility was further circumscribed by the second measure that Hodgson initiated: that of prohibiting migration even in protected forests without prior permission. The patil was held accountable for reporting new cultivators to the government, and for not permitting cultivators to settle in a village without prior official permission. Many Dangis, especially Koknis, soon began seeking permission from the Department before they moved to a fresh village. Bhils continued to try and move without seeking permission, maybe because they felt that such mobility was connected to Bhil raj.[12]

Only some kinds of migration were permitted. Hodgson prepared a list of three classes of villages, in which 'list A included the best villages as regards land, water and situation, B included villages which though requiring a population were not so urgently needed as A, while list C comprised those village[s] in which the land being poor or water scarce, a population was not desirable'. Only migration to villages on lists A and B was permitted. These had usually already been cleared of 'valuable' timber; were on sites suitable to settled cultivation; and were often so situated as to provide pools for the supply of bigar for departmental works such as fire protection.[13]

---

[10] Hodgson to PA, 31.3.1910, *BA.RD.1911.Vol 120.Comp 636.*
[11] Surat Forest Administration Report, 1911–12, *DFR.DN 3.FN 39.*
[12] Hodgson to Coll., Surat, 31.3.1910, *BA.RD.1911.Vol 120.Comp 636.* Coll., Dangs to Secy., GoB, 28.1.1949, *DCR.DN 3.FN 2Uc.*
[13] Hodgson to Coll., Surat, 31.3.1910, *BA.RD.1911.Vol 120.Comp 636;*

The settlement pattern of the 315 villages that survive today indicates that Hodgson succeeded: all the villages that survive are those enumerated in lists A and B, and virtually none of those in list C survive.[14] This is one sense in which chhut indeed ended with the mandini or the demarcation. Dangis had to not only stay out of the reserves but had to primarily confine themselves to the village assigned to them. Now both Koknis and Bhils took to a style of cultivation which combined fixity of residence in one village with the shifting of fields. After one patch of land had been exhausted, they would abandon it for a few years, and take up cultivation on another patch in the same village.[15]

Two intertwined developments also put an end to non-agricultural forms of livelihood, and to the seasonal mobility they were associated with. First, as Chapter 18 explores in further detail, there was a new ambivalence towards wildness, which led to a reduction in Dangi enthusiasm for hunting, fishing, and mahua-collection. Second, colonial restrictions and ecological changes made these modes of subsistence more difficult. Hunting now had to be carried out without fires; besides, the Department's working of forests disturbed the ecology of the area, and animals were increasingly scarce by the mid-twentieth century. Hunting was virtually extinguished as a major activity.

Similarly, under the vigorously implemented new excise laws designed to generate more revenue for colonial coffers, the distillation of mahua liquor was made a crime. Dangis now perforce had to buy liquor for cash from British-authorized liquor dealers. Even the possession of mahua before mid-March or after the end of May was made an offence, an indicator of the intention to brew liquor.[16] Because of these developments, the use of mahua flowers either for distilling liquor or for food declined dramatically. In the long run, mahua trees became fewer. Mahua trees had been planted normally by Dangis near any new village site that they migrated to. Now, with little migration, such seeding of the forests had ground to a halt. (Goth now ascribe the decline to a mistake by

Hodgson to Coll., Surat, 22.12.1906, *BA.RD.1907.Vol 126.Comp 632*. See also 'Dangs fire protection scheme', *BA.RD.1910.Vol 105.Comp 660*. Madho Bhivsan, 25.4.1990, Nadagkhadi.

[14] For a broadly indicative list of the villages in Dangs today, see *DDG*, pp. 155–7.

[15] Khandu Ravji, 9.6.1990, Vakaria.

[16] *BRO.DDR.DN 6.FN 36/1*.

colonial foresters, who were instructed to cut down all trees of another species, but felled all mahua and toddy trees instead by mistake. This story even has a touch of archival authenticity: it is retailed in the Dangs administration report for 1944–6. Still, we cannot be sure that colonial officials were not simply having their legs pulled by straightfaced Dangis: an almost identical tale of a departmental mistake exists in Madhya Pradesh, several hundred kilometres away.) By the 1940s, the role of fishing, hunting, gathering, or mahua-collection in livelihood was much too reduced to justify staying by riverbanks for the summer months.

Maybe one crucial indicator of the decline of seasonal mobility is the transformation of Dangi residences that began in the 1950s. Till then, most houses in the Dangs (save those of very prosperous Koknis who had settled in one village) had been round, supported by one big upright pole in the middle, a bamboo matting in a circle all around, and a sloping roof of teak leaves. Such houses, which served as abodes even for important rajas like those of Pimpri or Vasurna, allowed for quick dismantling and quick construction; they could be abandoned too without many qualms. From the 1950s, however, these houses were replaced by more permanent structures — rectangular houses with two large upright poles and four smaller ones. Such replacement took place at an especially rapid pace in the 1970s, when a sudden (and brief) spurt of prosperity because of intensified timber removal operations by the Department provided many Dangis with the resources to build these houses.

The Return of Seasonal Mobility

The impact of the ban on cultivation in nearly half of Dangs was softened initially by the drop in population that had taken place around the turn of the century. The late 1890s was a terrible decade for the Dangs, when a combination of disease and the famine of 1899–1901 reduced its population from 32,920 in 1891 to 18,633 in 1901.[17] By the 1930s, however, population was comparable with that in the 1890s. Techniques such as leaving lands in the same village fallow for some years could scarcely succeed in the face of these mounting population pressures. Fallows could not be maintained for as long as before, and the same plot usually came back

[17] Government of Gujarat, *Dangs District Gazetteer*, Ahmedabad, 1971, p. 159.

into cultivation within four or five years. Thus, in addition to increasingly smaller landholdings, over-cultivation led to the erosion of the thin topsoil of Dangs in many areas, and a consequent decline in productivity.

Increasingly by the 1950s, the very Dangis who had refused to work for the Department had to search out wage labour with it. And that was only a taste of things to come. Now, in the 1990s, even the wage labour generated through agricultural or departmental needs is not adequate to meet the shortfall in subsistence for most Dangis. A fourth or more of the Dangi population is compelled to resort to seasonal migration to the plains for wage labour in sugarcane fields in order to make ends meet. So by the late twentieth century, seasonal migration has come back with a vengeance as a livelihood strategy.

But this is seasonal mobility with a difference. It is now not within and around but far beyond Dangs; it is no longer about subsistence but about wage labour; it is not part of a strategy to deal with mosaic forests but the consequence of the exclusion of Dangis from forests.[18] Most of all, seasonal mobility now for reaping sugarcane or other wage labour is part of a very different aesthetics, and of a very different way of imagining wildness. We saw that the various non-agricultural modes of subsistence affirmed in different ways the wildness and otherness of being Dangi. Also, some of them, such as hunting, fishing and mahua-collection were part of an aesthetics of pleasure.

Now, though some Dangis do occasionally dwell on the novelty of the world of the plains, their accounts of seasonal migration for wage labour on the sugarcane fields are overwhelmingly laced with metaphors of drudgery. In part, this is part of the continuing hostility to wage labour where it involves subordination to the government or plains figures. As the post-independence *Dangs District Gazetteer* complained, the 'Dangi is never eager to do hard manual labour for the sake of wages'. And sugarcane reaping is arduous work. The migrants work in gangs, the basic unit of which is a *koyta*, or a unit of two persons, a man and a woman. The head of the gang is assigned a specified amount of work daily, and payments are made on the basis of each ton of sugarcane that the workers cut, strip, bundle and load. An average day involves twelve to fifteen hours of backbreaking work with few breaks, in the midst

---

18 Breman, *Of peasants, migrants and paupers*, Delhi, 1985.

of sugarcane fields whose sharp leaves lacerate hands and bare feet. The payment too is far below the minimum wages.

Most of all, this mobility is no longer about the wildness of the Dangis in relation to the plains; rather, it is an enactment of their subordination to the plains. This is partially why, as Chapter 18 suggests, the growing irrelevance of non-agricultural modes of livelihood and the transformation of mobility has been associated with a reimagining of wildness itself.

Back to Vanarkillas

In thinking about these transformations, memories of moglai become ways of creating alternative and angry histories that engage with mandini and bring out its oppressive meanings, of emphasizing practices that exceed mandini. The older understanding of the Dangs, we saw, drew on three categories — those of vanarkilla panlot and sapati — to render the region intelligible as cultivable space. The demarcation rendered these meaningless. The vanarkilla became part of the reserved forest, as did large portions of the panlot. Most of the land that was left to the Dangis for cultivation was in the sapati and some portions of panlot.

Maybe this is why there was the slow disappearance till recently of the word vanarkilla or makadkilla. I learnt the term from Khandu Ravji, the jagirdar of Vakaria village in southeastern Dangs, who was born around 1899. Quite often, when I used the word in the early part of my fieldwork in conversations with others, they were not familiar with it. Even amongst older men, knowledge of it was partial. When identified, it was often described as a word of ancestors or vadil. Unlike sapati and panlot, useful categories even for thinking of cultivable space within the protected forest, the vanarkilla has none of the older relevance to daily life.

But it may be developing a new kind of relevance, one deeply involved in Dangi goth of mandini, and the way these invert statist narratives. In the course of a major agitation in the early 1990s for forest rights, Dangis questioned the Department's control of the reserved forests by insisting that their vadils had given it only the vanarkilla, and that it should go back and confine itself to these. It is difficult to say whether this new centrality of vanarkilla will last. For the present, however, the notion of the vanarkilla embodies within it an agenda for rolling back the state's control of forests.[19]

19 I am not sure about the extent to which my own fieldwork may have

That control is articulated through two words which had emerged already by 1902. The protected forests were referred to as the *kartuk*, and the reserved forests as the *banbhag* or *gairan*.[20] Kartuk literally meant 'freedom to do [cultivation]'. In contrast, gairan meant 'the area where cattle graze' and banbhag can be translated as 'the closed portion'. Gairans existed formerly, but the synonym for it, banbhag, brought out the new dimension of gairans: they were now irreversibly closed to cultivation, rather than being of shifting patterns of land use. The binary opposition which many Dangis set up between banbhag and kartuk brings out starkly the manner in which they thought of the region after the demarcation as dichotomous forests. Indeed, it is likely that the forest had, because of restrictions, become more dichotomous to them than the Department had actually managed to make it silviculturally.

Simultaneously, the extinction of mobility led to a transformation of the process of naming villages and sites. As we saw, nineteenth-century Dangi naming was both connotative — referring to the meaning of the name — and denotative — referring to the name only as a marker of a specific site. But after the extinction of mobility, the names of the new permanent villages acquired a fixed dimension, a meaning simply and primarily as the designation of the village. Because of this foregrounding of the denotative dimension of names, the connotative aspect soon withered away, and names lost their tendency to shift around physically, or change in different contexts. One striking case is Nanapada village, which we know to have been named after an important late-eighteenth- or early-nineteenth-century patil, known as Nana patil.[21] There are now no descendants of Nana patil in the village, nor is the genealogy of the name very widely known: it has acquired a fixity which has outlived collective memories of Nana patil. Naming was transformed in another way in the gairan or banbhag. Old village sites are of course recognized by the remains of old wells, or trees like the mango, usually planted in villages. But here both the connotative and denotative dimensions of names have been erased. Now,

---

contributed to the renewed centrality of the vanarkilla as a theme around which resistance is organized. It may be that my repeated questions about vanarkilla coincided in several villages with the beginnings of the agitation for forest rights.

[20] 'Proposal for . . . Dang forests', *BA.RD.1902.Vol 107.Comp 949, Part II*.

[21] Khanapurkar, 'The aborigines of south Gujarat', vol. I, p. 92. Budea Ganguda, 21.4.1991, Nanapada.

few village sites within the reserved forests are popularly remembered by the names on nineteenth-century maps, or indeed by any names at all.

These abandoned villages are crucial to Dangi goth of mandini and moglai. All of them are described by one word: the *junigavthad*, or old village sites. We do not know whether the word existed in the nineteenth century; in all likelihood, it did. But with the ban on mobility, it took on a politically combustible dimension. Dangis often claimed that they have a right to cultivate in the junigavthad, since their ancestors had lived in the villages.[22] In May 1990, persons from Dhulda and other villages moved into the reserves and occupied two junigavthad where they claimed their vadils had cultivated. The spots, they claimed, should be given back by the Department. Needless to say, their demands were not met; the Forest Department moved in with an armed force to drive the villagers out. The concept of the junigavthad carries within it, then, a loaded history, a history which seizes on and deploys simmering accounts of the manner in which the Dangis were driven out of the reserved forests nearly a century back.

(5)

22 For an analysis of the motifs involved in rebellions, see Shiney Varghese, 'Women, resistance and development', *Development in Practice*, vol. 3, no. 1, 1993.

16

The Fullness of Kingship

Related to the mandini of the forests is that of the raj or kingship, which led to *panch raja ani nau naik* (five rajas and nine naiks) being designated as the chiefs. In many goth, the descendants of these chiefs are now the rajas and naiks of Dangs:

> In moglai, there were only naiks, no rajas. All the naiks were called to Bhavani cha killa. There, the sahebs said, 'do you agree to have nine naiks and five rajas on the gadi'. They agreed, and these fourteen were put on the gadi. Bhil raj was given by the *devs*, but it was the British who gave the gadi.[1]

To goth such as these, there are startlingly close parallels possible. In thinking of the ways in which kingship was transformed in western India with the consolidation of colonial rule, it might be misleading to focus on the hollowing out of an originally full kingly power. As I have already suggested in Chapter 6, Dangi kingship during moglai was characterized by a profound lack, and by the absence of any singular gadis or loci of power. Taking these points further, I suggest here that the consolidation of colonial rule was associated with attempts to create singular gadis that were characterized by a relatively novel fullness of power.

The Emergence of a List

In 1830, as part of his attempt to locate those with whom he should enter into agreements to prevent future raids, Outram had identified five figures as the principal chiefs to whom all the rest were subordinate. By the time of the leases of 1843, seven independent chiefs had been identified. The process of finding new chiefs continued through the 1840s and 1850s. When the leases came up for renewal in the early 1860s, sixteen chiefs had been identified. And

---

[1] Indrasinh Keshavrao, 29.3.1990, Dhondunia.

by the late nineteenth century, a definitive list of fourteen chiefs had emerged.[2]

The list was accurate in the sense that it did include many of the powerful chiefs in Dangs. It could hardly have been otherwise, since it had been prepared to identify the chiefs whom the British could deal with, sign agreements, or hold responsible for 'offences'. Colonial officials were acutely aware that successful control depended to a great extent on identifying the powerful chiefs. All the same, it was arbitrary in the Dangi context of shared authority. Authority was too deeply shared for any set of figures to be designated as the only legitimate chiefs of the region. The list was the result of the exigencies and conjunctures of colonial knowledge and power. For instance, the chief of Kadmal, mentioned separately by Outram as one of the six principal mewas chiefs of Dangs, was absent from the list: he was treated as a feudatory of Dherbavti.

The list was even more arbitrary in its choice of the nine naiks who were treated as independent. All the nine were from the northeastern region of Dangs. It is highly unlikely that these nine were substantially more independent of the principal chiefs than those members of the bhauband elsewhere who were not accorded the status of independent naiks. But the northeastern tracts were well integrated into the plains economy of neighbouring Khandesh and these chiefs possessed extensive contact with colonial intermediaries such as the deshmukh, whose co-shared villages were principally here.[3] So, being more visible to colonial officials, they were included in the list. In another instance, the chiefs of Sivbara and Kirli had leased their forests to a Gaekwadi timber merchant. To set these leases aside, colonial officials had to secure separate agreements from the two naiks. Consequently, they were treated as independent chiefs, rather than feudatories of the Deher chiefs, as they would otherwise have been regarded.[4]

Within the list, colonial categories also initially floundered in the flux of the dangi distinctions between raja and naik. It was only

2 Outram to Boyd, 2.6.1830, *BRO.DDR.DN 1.FN 3*; Crawford and Reid to Court of Directors, 15.6.1844, *IOL.F.4.2074*; Fenner to Robertson, March 1860, *BRO.DDR.DN 2.FN 9*; *KDG*, 597, and the correspondence in *BA.PD.1890.Vol 122.Comp 1841*.

3 See Shuttleworth to Secy., GoB, 6.4.1871, *BA.PD.1871.Vol 18. Comp 552*; Shuttleworth to Secy., GoB, 19.1.1872, *BA.RD.1872.Vol 17.Comp 556*; Gibb to Loch, 8.7.1890, *BA.RD.1890.Vol 93.Comp 948*; Rigby to Briggs, 18.6.1822, *BRO.DDR.DN 1.FN 1*; *BRO.DDR.DN 6.FN 34*.

4 Fenner to Gibson, 15.9.1857, *BA.PD.1858. Vol 96.Comp 1123*.

by the late nineteenth century that colonial taxonomies firmed up. Four chiefs — those of Ghadvi, Amala, Vasurna, and Dherbhavti — were invariably described as rajas. A borderline case was that of the chief of Pimpri, who was described as a naik throughout the nineteenth and twentieth centuries. But because of his large territories comparable to the four rajas, he was sometimes clubbed together with them in discussions.[5] And the other nine were decidedly naiks.

<h2 style="text-align:center">CONSTITUTING FOURTEEN DANGS</h2>

That the list was in places arbitrary or misleading is by itself a minor point — after all, any list, by any group, would have been somewhat misleading given the complex relations of power in Dangs, and there could have been no accurate list of chiefs. The importance of the list was because of the late-nineteenth-century context in which it emerged, a context marked by the extirpation of raids, the leases, the expulsion of merchants, the exclusion of the Gaekwads and deshmukhs, and the general extension of British power. These developments reduced the ability of the chiefs to assert power, and established an overwhelming British domination. Precisely because the British were so powerful, actual patterns of power came to resemble those that the British invested in the list.

One way in which the list became real involved the constitution of fourteen exclusive dangs. Formerly, intimate ties and the exercise of authority by chiefs beyond their dang had been common, even constitutive of their power: it was rarely clear what were the boundaries of a dang or how many dangs there were, and there were many dangs within and across dangs. But this web of overlapping, contested authority could not be accommodated within colonial categories. The British operated with a notion of a chief's authority being limited to what they designated as his own dang; they did not recognize his exercise of authority beyond it. Consider the case of Ghadvi, the most influential of Dangi chiefs. British domination was accompanied by the decline of Ghadvi's ability to directly exercise authority over regions that had been defined by the British as being outside it. The dismantling of the Ghadvi chief's authority started in 1829, when the giras agreements bypassed Silput. This not only reduced his control over resources but

5 Briggs to Elphinstone, 19.11.1818, *PA.DCR.Vol 173*; *KDG*, p. 597.

demonstrated to other chiefs that the British were willing to support them against Silput. The dismantling of Ghadvi's influence was accelerated in 1830, when both Khem and Silput were captured and imprisoned following Outram's expedition. Outram received many complaints about the villages which Khem and Silput had taken away from the other chiefs in the past.[6] By the time Silput returned to Dangs in 1833, his power had been almost 'completely broken'.[7] Increasingly, the power of the Ghadvi chiefs was confined to Ghadvi itself. Similarly, the influence that other chiefs wielded outside what had been decided to be their dang was whittled down. Slowly, all of Dangs became part of one or the other of these fourteen recognized dangs; the unrecognized ones faded into being only feudatories of these fourteen.

ONE DANG, ONE RAJA

Simultaneously, within each of the fourteen officially recognized dangs, there was the consolidation of the authority of the chief recognized by colonial officials as the principal one. Formerly, we saw, kingship had been so deeply shared that there were several bhauband who were almost as powerful as the holder of the gadi. However, Khandesh officials desired sovereignty to be singular and exclusive, where a chief possessed comparatively unquestioned authority over the tract he held. Several colonial measures affirmed the authority of the recognized chiefs to the exclusion of other bhauband, and spurred the emergence of distinct gadis within each of the fourteen dangs.

In contrast to older Dangi practices where primogeniture had provided only a loose claim to succession which had to be backed up with alliances, the British insisted on primogeniture or succession by the eldest legitimate son of the ruling chief in all cases.[8] This was why they favoured Kerulsinh over Devisinh in the Ghadvi succession dispute, and Bapu over Shendia in the Vasurna dispute. With the introduction of primogeniture, the succession of the eldest male son could no longer be seriously challenged by rivals: he was too visibly backed by the much-feared military might of the British sarkar.

6 Outram to Boyd, 2.6.1830, *BRO.DDR.DN 1.FN 3*.
7 There was however no conscious colonial policy of reducing the power of the Ghadvi chief. See Graham to Blanc, 25.3.1839, ibid.
8 *SRBG 26*, p. 166; *KDG*, pp. 604–6.

Similarly, the cessation of raiding strengthened the domination of the recognized chiefs within each dang. Their authority could be sustained through the distribution of resources provided by the British. But unrecognized bhauband who wished to improve their position could no longer create new entitlements or resources through raids. Also, the recognized chiefs had not formerly possessed the sort of authority necessary to obtain an exclusive control over resources. Minor bhauband had enough followers to harass the principal ones if they did not receive what they considered a fair share. Even timber merchants had to pay dues not only to the principal chief, but also to the minor bhauband of areas where felling operations were conducted, or through which carts had to pass.[9] However, when the British entered into giras and lease agreements, they made the entire payment to the chiefs they recognized. These chiefs were supposed to distribute the money amongst their followers. The chiefs now gained greater control over the distribution of money and could quite effectively pay less to rival members of the bhauband.[10] Shendia kuver, one of the Vasurna bhauband, complained that out of the timber lease payment of Rs 700, Anandrao raja gave him only Rs 100, 'and my brothers and huckdars tease me for their dues, but what can I give out of Rs 100'.[11] Figures like Shendia could not even easily retaliate by attacking Aundya: that would again have invited reprisals from the British.

The support of the British also increased the ability of officially recognized chiefs to allocate other kinds of resources, most importantly villages, as jagir grants. Rescinding village grants had always been a complex process, requiring considerable power on the part of the chief who wished to claim them back. But British officials were keen to ensure that the recognized chiefs controlled as much land as possible directly (this, it was felt, would avoid interference by outside powers like the Gaekwads or the deshmukh). After 1853, they prohibited the chiefs from making village grants. For older grants, they also demanded written proof — something most grantees did not possess. In cases where the officially recognized chiefs wished to claim villages back, they now found it easy to appeal to the British for support and claim back a village. Furthermore, the

9 *DBD*, II, pp. 190f.
10 Morriss to Bell, 28.5.1844, *BRO.DDR.DN 1.FN 4.*
11 Statement of Shendia kuver, Case II, Annual Darbar Report, 1848, *BRO. DDR.DN 1.FN 2.*

British ban did not effectively stop the officially recognized chiefs from making new grants. British surveillance of the region was limited, and as long as both the chief and the grantee did not raise the issue with colonial officials, there was little way the latter could come to know of it.[12]

This kind of consolidation of authority of recognized chiefs, and the emergence of singular hierarchies occurred possibly in many large and small plains kingdoms too. The support of the British was deployed by the rajas of Jaipur to strengthen their authority over nobles.[13] Similarly, by the late nineteenth century, the recognized Gaekwadi family had gained superiority over most rivals for power in and around Baroda. In this sense, relative to bhauband and other similarly powerful rivals within each kingdom, the gadi held by the principal chiefs came to have a certain fullness of authority.

THE CENTRALITY OF BRITISH AFFIRMATION

The power of the principal chiefs was derived from colonial affirmation, and developments in the twentieth century made this all the more clear. After the 1901 demarcation, the new revenue system prohibited the chiefs and bhauband from directly collecting the annual tax assessment or halpatti, and the nau kayda or nine levies, from the villages. Instead, these were commuted into cash payments, collected by colonial staff and distributed to the chiefs at the annual darbar.[14] These measures affected both the principal chiefs and the bhauband, though it might have hit the latter more. Given the latter's more limited resources, the nau kayda had been one of the sources of generating resources for subsistence, and indeed one of the most important ways in which they had demonstrated their authority in the villages.

In the wake of the demarcation, colonial officials again prohibited the chiefs from giving jagirs, and this time they enforced the prohibition. This seriously curbed the latter's ability to create followers or demonstrate their authority. A list was now prepared which listed the bhauband of each principal chief and their shares.[15]

12 *BRO.DDR.DN 8.FN 34*; *BRO.DDR.DN 4.FN 2Uc*.

13 Robert W. Stern, *The cat and the lion: Jaipur state in the British Raj*, Leiden, 1988.

14 Report on the Future Administration of Dangs, *BA.RD.1902.Vol 107. Comp 949, Part II*.

15 *BRO.DDR.DN 8.FN 34*; See *DCR.DN 3.FN 4Uc*.

The principal rajas could no longer attempt to control the distribution of payments amongst the bhauband; they were now paid only their personal share of the giras and lease dues. Besides, on the grounds that the chiefs spent the money foolishly, it was decided that they should not be given even their entire personal allowance in hand. They were given a portion of it, and the rest was deposited in their name in post office personal savings accounts, to be accessed only with the consent of the administration. This was another blow to the ability of the chiefs to construct their power independently, for what seemed to be excessive expenditure was actually part of the attempt to maintain their authority by distributing their personal allowances.[16]

Effectively, then, the authority of the chiefs over the bhauband seemed increasingly derivative, created and sustained almost exclusively through affirmation by the British. Derivative power was not new in itself. To the extent that kingship had formerly been constructed through affirmation by bhauband, it had always been derivative, it had never been sufficient in itself. But the authority of the principal chiefs was now derivative in a new kind of way, for unlike former times, there was only one source which could affirm their authority — the British.

The power of the chiefs over bhauband was no less for being derived exclusively from the British. If anything, there was after the demarcation a hardening of those British attitudes which treated the fourteen officially recognized chiefs as the only ones, and saw the rest as feudatories over whom the chiefs had extensive rights. The British attempted to make the principal rajas behave in the manner befitting kings. For instance, they built a stone house twice for the Pimpri raja, and once for the Ghadvi chief. They also attempted to separate the principal chiefs from their 'hangers-on' (the bhauband) and to make the chiefs spend their money only on their immediate families. The authority of the fourteen chiefs was most explicitly acknowledged at the colonial darbar, which was filigreed by early-twentieth-century officials to include rituals that marked out the fourteen chiefs from others. While turbans and shawls were distributed to all those bhauband entitled to it, the lease and revenue payments were handed over only to the fourteen chiefs.[17] In these and several other ways, the

16 See, for example, Annual Report, 1906–7, *BA.ED.1908.Vol 63.Comp 739.*
17 *BA.RD.1911.Vol 120.Comp 113*; P.A., Surat, to Comm., ND, 12.10.1911, *BA.PD.1913.Vol 126.Comp 54*; Annual Report, 1917–18, *BA.JD.1919.Comp*

fourteen chiefs were set apart from their bhauband through their power being derivative rather than despite it.

The emergence of fourteen distinct gadis did not however put an end to the sharing of authority and lifestyles with the bhauband. The rajas lived in the British-provided stone houses for one or two years, and liked these. But not enough: when some misfortune like the death of a relative took place, they readily abandoned these houses and built beside them mud huts just like their bhauband's. The recognized chiefs of Amala and Pimpri continued to be surrounded, despite British efforts, by bhauband who they even protected against the arm of colonial law.[18] Similarly, in 1910, the Ghadvi chief spent unauthorized money on the marriage of his brother, pretending that it was his own.[19] This sharing of authority continues down to the present: now too, the allowances that both the recognized chiefs and the bhauband receive are very widely distributed.

The enactment of authority as shared was part of the ways in which moglai always exceeded mandini. It is striking that though goth about the sharing of authority are narrated as part of moglai, they are often set in the same period or years as goth about the mandini, or about the creation of fourteen distinct gadis. British affirmation could not cover the lack which the sharing of authority addressed. The gadi, we saw, was in many ways constituted by markers of authority, with all their contingency and alienability. Though British recognition emerged as the most important marker, there were several others which could not be claimed exclusively by the recognized chiefs. Meanings were not inherent in markers but had to be read into them by bhauband and other important Dangis. To sustain their preferred readings, the recognized chiefs had to redistribute their resources and share their authority with bhauband.

Furthermore, even if the bhauband could no longer seize the gadi or militarily challenge the principal chief, they were still very

---

412; *DCR.DN 3.FN 4Uc*; and Indrasinh Keshavrao, 4.3.1991, Ahwa; Annual Report, 1912–13, *BA.ED.1914.Comp 739*; see also Hardiman, 'The fight for the forest', my 'Ritual and authority in western India', and *Dangs District Gazetteer*, p. 132.

18 Marjoribanks to Coll., Surat, 3.7.1911, *BA.RD.1911.Vol 120.Comp 636*.

19 Annual Report, 1909–10, *BA.RD.1911.Vol 22.Comp 1595*.

powerful in Dangs. They held villages on their own, collected revenue from these, and commanded the allegiance of at least some section of bhauband. So powerful were the bhauband that the fourteen gadis were still not widely accepted or regarded as the only ones. There was still a multiplicity of markers of authority, and these could be invoked by the bhauband to effectively deny their subordination to the British-recognized chiefs, or even to claim (as the Ghadvi chief Devisinh did in the 1860s) that they held the gadi. The meanings of kingship could not thus be subsumed within mandini: they always exceeded it, and were situated to a significant degree in moglai, and its sharing of authority.

This exceeding was so forceful that even the British were compelled to face up to it. Because of the power of the bhauband, the British were keen to ensure that they did not have too many causes for complaint: 'should it happen that the Rajahs, from motives of a private nature, withhold shares of the annual stipend from relatives or subordinates who may deem themselves entitled to a participation, we may look for attempts at evasion, destruction of Government property, and other means of annoyance.'[20] The British, therefore, responded with alacrity to complaints from bhauband about not having received a fair share.

This exceeding of mandini by moglai is also evident in the ways in which goth of mandini rarely involve women. With the centrality it accorded to male primogeniture and singular gadis, mandini was a historical time inhabited largely by men. Of course ranis as well as ordinary women remained important through the nineteenth and early twentieth centuries. But as figures whose authority was not provided for in the mandini and had no legitimacy within the goth about them, even when from the same chronological period, are part of moglai.

THE POLITICS OF KHARI RAJ

The exceeding of mandini by moglai is also enacted in the motif of *khari raj* or true kingship. Dispossessed bhauband frequently claim that the mandini was wrongly done, or that a wrong chief was recognized amongst the panch raja ani nau naik, as the officially recognized five rajas and nine naiks are often described.

Our ancestors were formerly the rajas of Linga [Amala.] When the mandini was held, our vadil could not go, since he was young. His chakardar went, and claimed to be the Amala chief, and he got the entire raj transferred to his name. We thus became one of the bhauband and lost the gadi.[21]

Such claims, postulating the accidental absence of the rightful chief at the mandini are made in virtually every dang by dissenting bhauband. Furthermore, claims to khari raj are made not only within each dang but also over Dangs as a whole. The Amala bhauband often insist that they, not Ghadvi, have the khari raj of Dangs. But the Ghadvi chief reached the site of the mandini first, and when the saheb asked who was the principal raja, the Ghadvi chief declared himself so. Nor is it only powerful bhauband who are concerned with khari raj. More ordinary Dangis, both Koknis and Bhils, often speculate about who has the khari raj of various dangs, and the questions I asked during fieldwork were also often treated as spurred by this concern with establishing khari raj.

The conception of khari raj bears unmistakable traces of long imbrication in colonial categories, and is founded on beliefs that have accompanied the creation of singular hierarchies. It takes as given and natural the existence of fourteen gadis, and proceeds on the assumption that each dang has a single gadi and font of authority. Colonial ancestries are even more evident in the question of which bhauband possesses the khari raj over Dangs as a whole — now, unlike formerly, a single gadi is imagined for the entire region. Also, through all the extravagant emphasis on the role of the British in setting up chiefs in Dangs, goth of the mandini almost never question the right of the British to decide on who the chiefs should be. Even accounts by dispossessed bhauband only charge the British with having been misled or having made a mistake, never with having actively dislodged them. Maybe this is because acknowledgement by the British has been an important source of legitimacy for so long that it is difficult to conceive of the very existence of gadis without the British. And, of course, the centrality accorded to the British is not misplaced: it was they, after all, who made possible singular gadis.

But while Dangi evocations of the gadi have a decidedly colonial ancestry, the notion of khari raj also questions the British conferral of authority. Its basic insistence is that British investitures of

---

[21] Chandu Bhausinh, 30.4.1990, Anjankund.

authority during the mandini are khari only if the figures so recognized held the gadi during moglai too. And since there were no clearly defined gadis in moglai, to insist on this is to effectively undercut all claims to a singular gadi. Challenges articulated in this manner, by questioning the rightfulness of colonial affirmation, must have developed in the nineteenth and early twentieth centuries, the period which saw the making real of the list and the marginalizing of many bhauband even as the power of the fourteen recognized chiefs seemed increasingly derived only from colonial support.

The fact that the authority of the principal chiefs is derived exclusively from British recognition has also refigured the ways disputes are cast. As already seen, the loss of gadi as a result of struggles amongst the bhauband was not uncommon in precolonial or early colonial Dangs. But British intervention through the mandini provided a new means to reflect on and think about these struggles. Now, cases of dispossession which had occurred under very different circumstances, which preceded colonial rule or had nothing to do with it, are recast and accounted for by invoking the mandini. In this way, the mandini has emerged as a paradigmatic way of thinking about the loss or acquisition of gadis. Ironically, then, despite its concern to arrive at a singular resolution of who truly holds the gadi, the notion of khari raj has actually spawned and sustained multiple claims to the gadi; despite its colonial ancestries, it traverses and exceeds mandini to situate itself in moglai.

(6)

17

Disputes and Transformations

In the nineteenth-century confrontation between the bhauband associated with Devisinh and Udesinh, colonial intervention was decisive at several points. It was principally because of British support that Udesinh and especially his son Kerulsinh succeeded to the gadi. In 1849, colonial officials summoned Devisinh to Pimpalner following complaints from Kerulsinh, and it was they who seized him at Pimpalner after his attack on Kerulsinh and Dadaji. In the 1850s, Daulat was imprisoned by them on the basis of complaints from Kerulsinh. And after Devisinh and Daulat killed Kerulsinh, it was Khandesh officials who sent in the expedition that captured Devisinh, hanged Daulat, and restored the gadi to Kerulsinh's descendants. Nor was this exceptional. The centrality of colonial power in the construction of Dangi authority meant that the British were often involved in disputes, and that both disputes and markers of kingship were transformed in fundamental ways.

All bhauband making claims to political power necessarily had to engage with the British after the mid-nineteenth century. Such engagement could take the form of direct and armed confrontation. This was what Devisinh resorted to after he escaped to Dangs in 1859 from the lunatic asylum in Bombay to which he had been confined, and launched his most sustained effort to reclaim the gadi from Kerulsinh. British support to Kerulsinh led him to attack them. In September or early October 1860, when the Dangs Diwan, Shaikh Ibrahim, visited Dangs, Kerulsinh complained to him against Devisinh. Shaikh Ibrahim sent four men to summon Devisinh. Devisinh detained three of them and sent the fourth back with the message that the Diwan should come to him if he wished to hold discussions.

Thus did the defiance of colonial authority begin — with the refusal of the powerful Diwan's summons and its inversion by summoning the Diwan instead. Devisinh resorted to such inversions

with several colonial officials. To attend is usually an act of subordination; to remain stationary and receive a person is an assertion
of superiority. Later, he carried his hostility even further, and tried
to kill the Diwan (the latter escaped).[1] The Forest Department
formed another target. In May 1861, Devisinh and Daulat, accompanied by around fifty armed followers, forced the Assistant Conservator of Forests to give a written undertaking that they would
be paid Rs 250 instead of the Rs 40 to which Department officials
thought they were entitled.[2] When that undertaking was not hon-
oured by officials at Surat to whom Devisinh's followers took it,
the two brothers stopped departmental operations in Dangs from
around July, causing the Department to lose Rs 50,000 in 1861. If
sarkari cartmen came, Devisinh said, he would 'rob them all', and
if sarkari peons came, 'I will have them bound and kept here'.[3]

Such hostility to the Department and the Khandesh sarkar, fitting
in as it did with widespread popular resentment, could easily find
extensive support. After he killed Kerulsinh in November 1861,
defiance of the Department was widespread, going far beyond the
bhauband. And by early 1862, 'dignified already with the name of
a bund [insurrection]', it showed signs of spreading beyond Dangs.
It was rumoured that 'the Raj of the Sahib log had passed away
and that the Brahmans ruled over the land now',[4] an especially
suggestive rumour since Brahmans had been crucial figures in
Maratha rule under the Peshwas, and just five years ago, some
Brahmans had played an important role in the 1857 uprising.

Understandably, colonial officials were keen to put Devisinh's
rebellion down quickly. Failing in efforts to get other Dangi rajas
to capture him, the Khandesh Political Agent, Ashburner, eventually
led an expedition into Dangs against Devisinh in early 1862. His
task was not easy. He complained that Devisinh was 'wary, like a
tiger in the cold weather, easily disturbed and not remaining long
in one place'. And though the recognized rajas were allied against
Devisinh, he enjoyed considerable support from other bhauband,

1 Mamlatdar to Coll., Kh., n.d., *BRO.DDR. DN 3. FN 13*; Sheikh Ibrahim to
Grant, 12.10.1860, ibid.
2 2nd Asst. CF to Grant, 25.5.1861, ibid.
3 2nd Asst. CF to Grant, 3.6.1861, *BRO.DDR.DN 2.FN 10*. Forest Jamadar
to 1st Asst. CF, 17.7.1861, ibid.; Forest Havildar to 1st Asst. CF, 4.11.1861,
Ibid. Mehta, Kurzai to 2nd Asst. CF, 4.11.1861, ibid. 1st Asst. CF to PA, Kh.,
11.1.1862, ibid.
4 Ashburner to Secy., GoB, 29.12.1869, *BRO.DDR.DN 3.FN 13*.

and his spy system reported from every village to him on the movements of the police.[5]

But the odds were stacked against him. In February, pursued closely by colonial forces, abandoned by all his followers except one, he surrendered. His brothers Daulat and Rupdev, who had also been involved in the confrontation with the sarkar, were captured shortly afterwards. All three were put on trial for the killing of Kerulsinh. Daulat was found guilty and condemned to be hanged, Rupdev was sentenced to several years in prison. As for Devisinh, it was decided that he was insane, and he was committed again to the lunatic asylum at Colaba in Bombay.[6]

Nothing was more poignantly indicative of the distance between Dangi and British conceptions of authority than the relegation of Devisinh's claim to the gadi and confrontation to the marginalia of colonial lunacy. Devisinh certainly was enraged at Kerulsinh, at Kerulsinh's bhauband, and at the British: he felt that his claim to the gadi had been unjustly set aside. Maybe it was this rage that uncomprehending colonial officials had begun regarding as insanity by 1853, during his first imprisonment. An official reported that year that he appeared 'sane' but had 'expressed strong resentment at his detention from home for an indefinite period'.[7] In 1854, after he had a 'paroxysm of fury' and attacked some guards, he was declared insane and confined to an asylum. When his term was over, his bhauband refused to stand security for him, since they felt that he was bent on retaliation against Kerulsinh, who had by that time added insult to injury by 'seducing' Devisinh's wife. So he was confined to a lunatic asylum till his escape in late 1859.

After he killed Kerulsinh, during the trial in 1862, the Khandesh surgeon testified that Devisinh's incoherence, the 'insane look' in his eyes, and other signs made it clear that he was of 'unsound mind'. Aware that insanity had an exculpatory role to play in English judicial discourse, and that it would allow Devisinh to escape 'punishment', Ashburner marshalled the evidence of several Bhil and Kokni cultivators to argue that Devisinh had not been insane either before or after his escape from asylum, and sentenced Devisinh to death. But the imperial discourse on madness had

[5] Ashburner to Secy., GoB, 4.1.1862, *BRO.DDR.DN 3.FN 13*; Trial of Devisinh, 1862, *BRO.DDR.DN 2.FN 10*.

[6] See the correspondence in *BRO.DDR.DN 2.FN 10*. Mansfield to Secy., GoB, 22.1.1862, *BRO.DDR.DN 3.FN 13*.

[7] Dy. Coll., Kh., to PA, Kh., 8.1.1853, *BRO.DDR.DN 2.FN 10*.

developed too far to be appropriated this way: the Bombay government overturned his verdict, and ordered that Devisinh be confined to the Colaba asylum. Some years later, he died there.[8]

Deploying British Power

In extending his dispute with Kerulsinh to rebel against the sarkar, Devisinh was exceptional. Usually, Dangi chiefs shied away from direct or armed confrontations with the British after the 1840s, realizing that the latter were too powerful for them to win. Even Devisinh had tried to avoid open defiance for as long as possible. When Ashburner summoned him in 1862, Devisinh did not refuse to attend. He only claimed that he was too busy with agricultural operations to come immediately. And in later months, when Devisinh reflected on his defiance, he viewed it as an act so final that it left no option other than suicide: 'I'll kill the Saheb first, and then myself.'[9]

Because authority was now so dependent on the British, the bhauband brought their complaints against each other to colonial officials: 'every little squabble which in former days used to be settled among themselves . . . is now referred by them for adjudication by the Collector as their common umpire.'[10] Going to the sarkar was a way of deploying it in disputes, an attempt to make the British an ally against rivals. Without the British as an ally, claims to kingship were anyway increasingly impossible to sustain. During the dispute between Aundya raja and Shendia kuver in the late 1840s, both orchestrated charges against each other to the Khandesh Political Agent. Kerulsinh and his allies repeatedly got cultivators and others with grievances against Devisinh or Daulat to complain to the British. These accusations led to the imprisonment of Devisinh in 1849, and of Daulat in 1853.[11] Nor was it necessary to even complain to the sarkar. The threat of doing so was adequate. In 1849, Kerulsinh demanded the seal of Ghadvi, which was in Devisinh's possession. Devisinh returned it primarily in the hope that Kerulsinh would not take his complaints about that and other matters to the British.[12]

8 Trial of Devisinh, *BRO.DDR.DN 2.FN 10*.

9 Forest Havildar to Forster, 4.11.1861, *BRO.DDR.DN 3.FN 13*; Ashburner to Secy., GoB, 2.1.1862, *BRO.DDR.DN 2.FN 10*.

10 Elphinstone to Secy., GoB, 26.4.1852, *BA.PD.1852.Vol 42.Comp 1415*; note by Comm., SD, 4.4.1888, *BA.PD.1888.Vol 115.Comp 1683*.

11 *BRO.DDR.DN 2.FN 10*.

12 Trial of Devisinh, *BA.PD.1850.Vol 38/2404.Comp 830*.

After Kerulsinh's death, his bhauband deployed British authority in their attempt to avenge themselves on Daulat for the dishonourable way Kerulsinh was killed, with his body left in the forests. The Khandesh Superintendent of Police, Bell, brought Daulat to Chankhal village in Dangs to be hanged. The choice of Chankhal as a site was a symbol of the dominance of Kerulsinh's bhauband, for this was the village where Kerulsinh had stayed.[13] Kerulsinh's bhauband demanded that Daulat's body should be thrown to dogs and vultures, as he had done with Kerulsinh. When Bell refused to permit this, and offered an option between burial and cremation, the bhauband settled for the former — another insult, for it was less honourable than burning.

Overcoming the dishonour of his death became one of the major concerns of Daulat's descendants. His son, Chipat, repeatedly clashed with the ruling descendants of Kerulsinh because, it was claimed, of his rage over it. Chipat felt that the participation of their ancestors in Daulat's killing through complaining to the sarkar made them responsible for it. He demanded compensation, and finally, because of his constant attacks, secured it. The Ghadvi chief, Nathu raja gave him two villages, Chankhal and Hindla, in jagir. By obtaining the jagirs, especially that of Chankhal, the shame of the event was being erased. In later decades, Chipat and his descendants would not allow villagers to cut or lop the *asan* tree from which Daulat had been hanged, describing it as their ancestor's tree. Once, at least, when the original tree fell, another was planted in its stead.[14]

In the decades that followed, Kerulsinh's sons, Fatehsinh and Nathu, were to again deploy colonial machinery against their opponents, and complaints engineered by them led to both Chipat

---

13 Bell to Ag. SP, June 1862, Ashburner to Secy., GoB, 29.12.1861, *BRO.DDR.DN 2.FN 10*; Sheikh Ibrahim to Grant, 12.10.1860, *BRO.DDR.DN 3.FN 13*.

14 Statements of Vanvasia Devisinh, Somansinh Umbarsinh, Kanirao Rupdev, and others, July–August 1919, *BRO.DDR.DN 6.FN 34*. If the investiture of the spot with this positive symbolism has not continued to the present, this is possibly because of the extinction of Chipat's lineage in the early twentieth century, enabling Kerulsinh's descendants to claim back the village (APA to Diwan, 23.8.1919, *BRO.DDR.DN 6.FN 34*.) But after resuming control of the villages, Kerulsinh's lineage did not attempt to consciously desacralize the spot, possibly because they wanted to avoid clashes with other lineages associated with Daulat. Slowly, however, by the 1950s, the importance of the site appears to have declined.

and Tikam being imprisoned for varying terms.[15] Descendants of Devisinh's lineage too deployed British power against Udesinh's descendants. In 1898, when the reigning Ghadvi chief and Udesinh's descendant Umbarsinh Devrao was convicted for allegedly killing his wife,[16] he claimed that he had been framed: 'Raja Vanwasia [Devisinh's son] being on inimical terms with me in connection with the gadi got up false witnesses by means of threats &c.'[17]

<h2 style="text-align:center">THE EMERGENCE OF LINEAGES</h2>

The centrality of the British to the construction of kingship may also explain a curious convergence. The mandini is associated with Udesinh raja in Ghadvi, with Ankus raja in Deher, Aundya raja in Vasurna, and Trimbak naik in Pimpri. These, according to records, are precisely the figures who signed the 1843 leases. This striking overlap, however, is only partially because of the factual accuracy of goth. It is more because they are the founding ancestors of the kind of lineage that conformed to colonial officials' understandings, one that traced descent through primogeniture and was a basis for social organization.

Formerly, while the language of kinship suffused alliances and ties amongst bhauband, disputes over the gadi rarely took place amongst sharply defined lineages; rather, bhauband could ally in a range of ways. This changed with the colonial emphasis from the mid-nineteenth century on male primogeniture, and the British shoring up of the fourteen chiefs they recognized. The figures who were chiefs around the time that colonial rule was consolidated — like Trimbak, Udesinh, Aundya and Ankus — thus effectively established novel kinds of lineages, where descent was directly correlated to power.

Associated with this was a transformation of disputes. Previously, as I have already suggested, disputes involved not just kin groups but the bhauband more broadly. With the British imposition of primogeniture and the emergence of a kingship more exclusively derived from colonial support, other chiefs were no longer as significant in constructing authority. In this context,

---

15 See *BA.PD.1882.Vol 50.Comp 1452*, *BA.PD.1881.Vol 73.Comp 1518*, *BA.PD.1879.Vol 94.Comp 1404*, and *BRO.DDR.DN 4.FN 23*.

16 Trial of Umbarsinh Devrao, *BA.PD.1898.Vol 75.Comp 798*.

17 Petition of Umbarsinh, 24.3.1898; Finding of Political Agent's Court, Khandesh, *BA.PD.1898.Vol 75.Comp 798*.

disputes increasingly came to be seen as between lineages rather
than between different groups of allies. In the later stages of the
dispute between Devisinh's descendants and Kerulsinh's descendants, thus, alliances with other chiefs faded into relative insig-
nificance. Ironically, then, it was because of the consolidation of
colonial power that disputes were transformed into something that
could be seen as very close to that anthropological staple about
'traditional' societies — feuds.

New Markers of Kingship

Even after the consolidation of colonial power, many markers of
authority continued to carry broadly the same meanings as before.
The markers discussed in Chapter 7, with all their contingency and
alienability, were important not only before but also during colonial
rule. It was not so much that these were marginalized as that now
those conferred by British officials came to be especially valued.
Thus, the question of how chiefs were treated by the British and
what they received at the colonial darbars — a turban or the more
valued shawl (usually only given to the five rajas), an expensive
turban or a cheaper one — became subtle indicators of the degree
of authority a chief possessed, more important indicators than
similar markers given by other chiefs.

But a most profound transformation was indicated by the emergence of a new marker of authority — the sikka-daftar. We do not
know exactly when the sikka-daftar became important as a marker
of authority, for it is not mentioned in records. But in goth now, it
looms large. According to many descendants of Silput, for example,
Udesinh went to the houses of Daulat and Devisinh after killing
Rajhans and took away their sikka-daftar. This loss of sikka-daftar
is seen now both as the loss of proof of having held the gadi, and
as one way in which Udesinh seized the gadi.

Because of this crucial role, both sikkas and daftars are very
important in Dangs today. Some families, such as the descendants
in Jakhana village of Shendia kuver, or the former ruling lineage
of Vasurna, preserve sikkas as proof of raj. These are usually metal
armbands issued by the Khandesh collectorate in the late nineteenth
century to the sipais of the principal bhauband. More commonly,
neither ruling lineages nor dispossessed ones possess sikkas, and
both are sometimes uncomfortable about this. Bhauband often
claim that their ancestors lost their sikkas because of the practice

of keeping precious objects hidden in the hollow of bamboo culms in the forest, the destruction caused in fires, or — once again that motif — the ignorance of ancestors who were jangli and did not appreciate their value.

While sikkas are important, daftars are far more so. Descendants in Uga village of the former ruling Deher lineage preserve carefully some daftars which they believe to be proof of their raj (these are handwritten early-twentieth-century notes by a British forest officer on how the forests should be worked). On the whole, however, unlike sikkas, daftars are not expected to be found in a village. Extended forms of writing in a largely non-literate society, they are explicitly associated with the sarkar. And the sarkar's daftars, it is believed, can prove or disprove claims to khari raj. The descendants of Devisinh and Daulat, dispossessed since the mid-nineteenth century, have even in recent years undertaken searches in government offices in Ahwa, Dhulia and Sakri in order to locate such documents, hoping that these will persuade the government of the admissibility of their claims to the allowances which are granted to former gadi holders.

It seems likely that the emergence of the sikka-daftar as a conjoined marker of authority was part of the process explored earlier — the accordance of enormous power to writing because of the role that it played in the consolidation of colonial authority. The sikka, as I have suggested in Chapter 7, had already been important in Dangi politics by the nineteenth century. But its power derived not so much from its association with writing as from it being constructed, like some kinds of arrows, as an inalienable possession of major chiefs. By contrast, the power of the sikka-daftar, lay in its written form. With the consolidation of British power, the power of colonial writing (maybe best represented by the daftar) came to epitomize British dominance and Dangi ignorance. This was why the legitimacy of the sikka was now greatest when it was conjoined with the daftar. The sikka-daftar indexed the colonial domination of Dangs, for it made explicit the point that the daftar was now necessary to affirm and sustain the authority already displayed in the sikka.

In the perceptions of Devisinh's descendants and many other Dangis, the writing of the daftar directly determined the actions of the sarkar. How should we treat this centrality? At one level, it is a sensitive barometer of the extent to which the writing of the sarkar has shaped Dangi reality for well over a century now. The written genealogies prepared by colonial officials provided the guiding principles in settling questions of succession to the gadi. After the 1900s, claims to jagirs or shares of lease allowances were granted or denied in keeping with what the daftars or records indicated.[18] The trace created by the colonial written word stretched out from the past to determine the present.

At another level, the centrality was indicative of the fetishization of the daftar. In seeing the inscriptions in the daftar as almost entirely determining the sarkar's actions, the rhetoric of fixity — the claim that colonial actions were determined by records, or by the 'rule of law' — and iconic centrality accorded to the daftar in colonial discourse was taken at face value by many Dangis. This was in part because of the radical unknowability of the daftar, caused by the limited Dangi access both to the daftar and to the means of interpreting it. As a result, the colonial politics of interpretation, which fundamentally modified the rhetoric of fixity, remained invisible (like it was to most British officials for different reasons). Combined with the enormous power that records did possess in determining social change within the Dangs, this seemingly ineradicable fixity of the daftar led to its fetishization.

Paradoxically, a second and equally important cause of fetishization was the surplus of meaning of the daftar. It was, as we saw, invoked often by the colonial state to legitimate coercive agendas that, in Dangi perception, had no precisely delineated genealogy within it. Radically unknowable, the epitome of state writing, it was thus the source from which coercive agendas inexplicably sprang. It had a frighteningly protean quality to it. Reconsider, for instance, the case of the 1843 lease agreements, which provided in their text for the leasing of the entire Dangs forests.[19] The specifics were possibly soon forgotten by the rajas. Their understanding of the lease was organized around customary usage, and since the British initially cut only teak, tiwas and sisu, they believed that only these had been leased.[20] But the British, too powerful to be defied openly, insisted on their interpretation and kept increasing restrictions, always with reference to the leases. In a non-literate and subordinated Dangs, where the only producers and purveyors

[18] See, for instance, the proceedings of various disputes in *BRO.DDR.DN 6.FN 34.*

[19] For the text of the leases, see Government of Gujarat, *The Dangs District Gazetteer*, Ahmedabad, 1971, pp. 138–41.

[20] Annual Report, 1850, *BA.PD.1852.Vol 42.Comp 1415.*

of meaning from daftars were colonial officials, the daftar must have been a frightening reminder of the sarkar's domination.

The invocation of the fetishized daftar was in evidence in 1924, when Sakharam Gana deshmukh of Mahalpada village claimed a share of Rs 500 from the lease amount paid to the Amala raja. The 'Conservator Governor', he said, had visited Mahalpada around forty years back and told his grandfather Kalu deshmukh to accept a subsidy of Rs 500. The Conservator 'noted this amount of Hapta [regular payment] on the map'. But Kalu deshmukh had not been willing to lease the forests, and the saheb had told him that arrangements for him would be made later, when five European officials came. Some years later, the officials arrived, noted the boundaries of his jagir, 'but the money remained noted on the map'.[21] There is good reason to think that Sakharam invented this story. Be that as it may, the point is that in searching for potent and persuasive images that could strengthen his claim, he settled on those of the saheb writing on the map, and for the inordinate wait for the five Europeans who would implement that writing. Colonial maps, after all, were an essential part of daftars, and had been highly visible during the demarcation.

REMEMBERING DISPUTES

It is from the vantage point of these transformations that goth emphasize the centrality of the colonial sarkar and its actions. There is the account by Devisinh's descendants of Daulat's hanging and dishonourable death.

> After Kerulsinh's killing, his family complained to Dhulia Sakri. Then the sarkar said, 'enquire whether Devisinh raja did kill Kerulsinh?' The enquiry was held, and they found Kerulsinh's plated tooth. The sarkar was now sure that Devisinh raja had killed Kerulsinh. Then it came to catch him. Devisinh raja heard of this and he went in to Dhulia Sakri and gave himself in. In the meantime, the saheb in Dangs caught Daulat raja and decided to hang him. The saheb at Dhulia Sakri wrote a letter to the saheb in Dangs, saying, 'Devisinh raja has come to Dhulia, so do not hang Daulat raja'. At that time, the sarkar's mail used to come from Dhulia Sakri by bigar. By the time the letter reached Dangs,

---

21 Statement by Sakharam Gana, and Case 7 (1924), *BRO.DDR.DN 6.FN 34.* A version of the story is still narrated by Sakharam's descendants at Mahalpada, and either Sakharam or his descendants have written out their account. A copy of this document is in my possession.

the saheb had already hanged Daulat raja from an asan tree in Chankhal. When the saheb read the letter, tears came to his eyes. He wrote to the Dhulia Sakri saheb, saying, 'Daulat raja has already been hanged'. The Dhulia Sakri saheb wrote back, saying 'by what authority did you hang Daulat raja?' The Dhulia Sakri saheb then called the Chankhal saheb back, and there, he was hanged for having hanged Daulat raja.[22]

This recasting by his descendants of Daulat's death as grotesque error is part of the effort to minimize the shame and obloquy of his being hanged by the sarkar. By walking in and surrendering, Devisinh creates a situation where retaliation against Daulat is unnecessary. If the revocation of the order did not have effect, this was only because of a delay in communication. So enormous is the British transgression in hanging Daulat that the Chankhal saheb is hanged as retaliation. The goth is also a claim to raj and legitimacy: Devisinh's surrender is an act of expiation which makes up for the transgression of norms which was committed when Kerulsinh was killed.

Other goth dwell on details of how the gadi was held by Devisinh's descendants:

When Kerulsinh's men came to burn Devisinh raja's *mahal* [palace], Jivli rani [Devisinh's elder wife] took her son Rahirao and ran away. She went to the naik of Palasvihir, who was then staying at Ghogli village. She gave Rahirao to Govinda Naik, Nanju Naik and Shevu naik, saying, 'take care of him, else he will be killed'. Rahirao was then given by the naiks to the Vasurna raja. The naiks said, 'this is the son of the raja of the entire Dangs. If anything happens to him, then the sarkar will harass us'. So Jararsinh raja of Vasurna kept Rahirao at Deodosi [a village near Vasurna.] Two sipais were kept near him all the time to guard him.

Then Jivli Rani went away to the Baduda [Baroda] sarkar [after Devisinh was confined at Dhulia.] Devisinh's younger wife, Sharju Rani, she went to the Dhulia Sakri sarkar. At the time, the Diwan was an Arab, Ibram Diwan. She told the sarkar, 'give me the powers of the raja, or restore the raja'. She was put with Devisinh raja. She started speaking to the raja, and she got the kayda [laws] and other things in her raj.

Then she was pregnant. So the Diwan and the rani went to Bhavani cha killa for the delivery. The child was born at the killa. The Diwan said, 'call her *killin*' [of the fort]. Then Sharju rani came home. Then she felt, 'I should leave no kayda with the

[22] Raisinh Gondusar, 2.4.1990, Jamulvihir.

sarkar. I should take all the kayda myself. So she went to the Dhulia sarkar again [and met Devisinh.]

She was pregnant again. When she had finished nine months and nine days of her pregnancy, the Diwan gave the entire kayda of the raj to her. She was to go back through the forests to Dangs. The Diwan said, 'if it is a girl, call her Vanwasin [resident of the forests] and if it is a boy, call him Vanwasia. The child was born in the forests, when she was returning with her sipai from Bhavani killa to Ghadvi. She named him Vanwasia. Then they came to Ghadvi raj, and Sharju rani asked, 'Where is Rahirao?' So he was brought and the gadi was divided. Rs 400 was given to Rahirao, Rs 400 to Vanwasia, Rs 150 to Daulat's son, that is, Chipat, and Rs 40 to Rupdev's family. The *nishankar* [person who carries the raja's flag] and the *nagarachi* [the raja's drummer] were also given Rs 5 each. Thus was Rs 1000 divided amongst the family.[23]

Leave aside the parallels to this goth in the records (the Diwan at the time indeed was Ibrahim; and Devisinh's wife, Sharju, briefly stayed with him in prison and was reported to be pregnant in 1853).[24] More striking, really, is the depiction of Devisinh's sons Vanwasia and Rahirao — both figures important till the early twentieth century — as continuing to hold the gadi. (And, ironically, in another reflection of the pivotal role of the sarkar in Dangi historical imagination now, the Diwan, the very person to whom Devisinh was so hostile, is assigned a major role in this continuation.)

The loss of the gadi itself remains an unclear moment. Devisinh's descendants obviously feel that it was lost, but the question of when or how is never really pinned down, nor is it considered necessary to answer these questions. Again, this fuzziness may not be because of forgetfulness but because the gadi had not become irrevocably singular in the nineteenth century. With the British emphasis on primogeniture, of course, the officially recognized lineages slowly came to possess a singular gadi. Only, it was such a contested and partial process that there is still no moment definitively associated by dispossessed lineages with the loss of gadi.

CAVEATS

Having stressed the centrality of the sarkar in the narration of goth, some qualifications remain. For through all the stories told by

23 Ibid.
24 Mansfield to Morriss, 31.3.1853, *BRO.DDR.DN 2.FN 10*; *BA.PD.1855.Vol 37.Comp 930.*

members of Devisinh's lineage, there is an intriguing silence. The confrontation between Devisinh and the sarkar is, as one might say of a more literate culture, written out: only that with Kerulsinh is remembered. Instead of challenging the sarkar, Devisinh walks into Dhulia and surrenders to it, and that not because he had rebelled against it, but because he had killed Kerulsinh. This surrender is not even a defeat: by turning himself in, Devisinh so gained the favour of the sarkar that the saheb revoked Daulat's hanging. Indeed, goth emphasize how Devisinh was confined not in a jail but in a house, and how he was accorded the respect due to a chief rather than being treated as an ordinary convict.[25] Nor is it only Devisinh's lineage which has forgotten his clash with the sarkar. Even Udesinh's lineage, which might seem to have every reason to remember the confrontation as a means to discredit Devisinh's lineage, has forgotten about the matter.

This total erasure from memory of Devisinh's clash with the sarkar is suggestive of the profound marginality of the sarkar in Dangi imaginations even as they appropriated it most actively in their politics. The dhum between Devisinh and Kerulsinh and their bhauband is basically recalled as clashes over the gadi, and the confrontation with the sarkar, while crucial in terms of its consequences, was secondary to and a result of the confrontation over the gadi. As such, these are goth primarily of moglai and only secondarily of the mandini; in this profound sense, moglai again traverses the mandini and displaces it.

(7)

---

[25] Records mention that in 1850 a house was built for Devisinh at Dhulia at the cost of Rs 80. See *BA.PD.1850.Vol 38/2404.Comp 593.*

18

Reimagining Wildness

After these mandinis, being jangli could obviously not have meant the same things as before. The word jangli itself, formerly affirmed and celebrated, is now almost universally rejected by Dangis as a description of themselves, with many younger Dangis viewing it as an upper caste, plains societies' characterization of them. Older Dangis too share this hostility, though they sometimes recall a time when their vadils called themselves jangli.

By the late nineteenth century, there was a sense of deep malaise amongst many forest communities. One official remarked in 1875 that though Bhil sepoys offered their respects to the image of a local goddess, they 'say it is of little use doing so, as the power of the goddess has failed since British influence became supreme. . . . Most Bhils think the strong English Gods too much for the weak deities of their country, hence their desire to adopt Brahminism. . . '.[1] Being jangli was evidently no longer enough. That sense of malaise fuelled a series of religious movements amongst the forest communities of India from the mid-nineteenth century. These movements involved, to varying degrees, appropriation of upper caste norms around eating, drinking and personal hygiene, hostility to colonial power and upper castes, and in some cases millenarian confrontations with the British.[2]

In Dangs and surrounding regions, the most influential of these was the Devi movement of 1922. The movement spread over a large stretch inhabited by the forest communities of western India — from Palghar and Dahanu in the south to Mandvi and beyond in the north, from Mulher and Kalvan in the east to Navsari and Valsad in the west. A new goddess, Salabai, supposed to have

---

[1] T.H. Hendley, 'An account of the Maiwar Bhils', *Journal of the Royal Asiatic Society of Bombay*, no. 4, 1875, p. 349.

[2] For a pan-Indian survey of these movements, see Stephen Fuchs, *Rebellious prophets*, Bombay, 1965 and his *Godmen on the warpath: A study of messianic movements in India*, New Delhi, 1992.

emerged from the mountains to the east, was carried from village to village. She spoke through mediums, usually ordinary people with no previous history of spirit possession who were suddenly seized by Salabai. They pronounced her commands

> Stop drinking liquor and toddy,
> Stop eating meat and fish,
> Live a clean and simple life,
> Men should take a bath twice daily.
> Women should take a bath thrice a day,
> Have nothing to do with Parsis.

At the height of the movement, for about a year, 'everywhere, *adivasis* [forest communities] were gathering together in large numbers to listen to the commands of the Devi. It was believed that those who failed to obey her would suffer misfortune at the least and perhaps become mad or die'.[3] Several thousands followed these commands for a year or more, and the more faithful were to stick by her injunctions for the rest of their lives.

Such movements can evidently not be treated as a form of Sanskritization — the adoption by lower castes of higher caste values in an attempt to increase their status. As several scholars have shown — Hardiman's path-breaking oral history of the Devi movement in particular — Sanskritization as a concept glosses over the contestation of upper caste power by lower castes. Hardiman points out that the Devi movement was not simply about adopting upper caste norms; it was also characterized by hostility to the upper castes involved in exploiting forest communities, especially Parsis. By appropriating the values of the Brahmans and Vaniyas who were dominant in the plains, followers effectively challenged upper caste plains figures.[4]

Maybe we can take Hardiman's point further by thinking of Dangi actions as a process of keeping a distance from a wildness that was no longer associated with power, but with marginality, ignorance and subordination. The centrality of forest spirits and village deities in the Dangi ritual order was attacked. 'Their [Devi devotees] mission was to drive away the *bhuts* [ghosts or demons] from the villages, and also to drive out the belief in bhuts.'[5] Animal sacrifice was rejected, and the offering of coconuts emphasized

---

3 Hardiman, *The coming of the Devi*, Delhi, 1987, pp. 1, 4.
4 Ibid., pp. 158ff.
5 Ibid., p. 38.

instead. In other words, an effort was made to mute the wilder dimensions of Dangi ritual power.

Also, the Devi's injunctions attacked Dangi livelihood practices organized around pleasure and wildness. A new ambivalence towards metaphors of pleasure was most marked in the case of mahua-collection. Quite apart from British restrictions, Salabai had specifically commanded that no liquor was to be drunk. For that year and the next, according to goth, mahua flowers rotted under the trees, with nobody picking them. More broadly, Salabai challenged the centrality of liquor in Dangi culture. Before the movement

In marked contrast to Brahmanical, Jain and Islamic beliefs, adivasis accorded great honour to spirituous drinks. They believed that their deities were extremely fond of daru and toddy and that they could be appeased by such offerings. It was common to pour a libation before starting to drink. Alcohol was considered a 'food of the gods' and drunkenness incurred during the act of worship was seen as a form of intoxication by the divine spirit . . . In the words of a local proverb, 'God gave the Brahmins ghi [clarified butter, used extensively in upper caste religious rituals] and the Bhils liquor' . . . the spirit-mediums who divined the causes of diseases and other misfortunes while in a state of trance often enhanced their state of possession with the help of alcohol. It was normal to pay these mediums for their services with chickens, goats and liquor, which they consumed.[6]

The new bhagats associated with the Devi movement departed from these practices. They not only refused to accept offerings of liquor, but considered these highly impure. Even after the heyday of the movement, many Dangis (though more Koknis than Bhils) withdrew from the collection and consumption of mahua flowers. Other modes of subsistence subsumed under metaphors of pleasure, such as hunting or fishing also effectively came under attack, since both meat- and fish-eating were prohibited by the movement. Similarly, gathering, which we saw connoted a female wildness, was deeply problematic. Salabai's mediums, it is significant, stuck most of all to the consumption of cultivated grains, millets and pulses. It seems possible that they actively avoided gathered food where possible and called for women to abstain from gathering, though there is no consistent picture in this regard. All these attacks were indicative of the crisis of old notions, for the very modes of livelihood that had been affirmed as constituting a jangli identity now connoted inferiority.

6 Ibid., pp. 99f.

THE WILDNESS OF WOMEN

Distance from wildness had specific connotations for women, as is already indicated by the rejection of gathering. The mandini is often associated with a ban on killing dakans.

> The saheb called all the rajas to the Bhavani cha killa. He said, 'Rajasaheb, till now you have caught and killed the dakans. In my raj, this will not be permitted. You may catch dakans, but you must take the Diwan's permission before beating them. And you must not kill them. If you kill them, I will send you and the bhagats who find them to *kalapani* [prison, across the seas].[7]

The ban on killing dakans was possibly an important reason for the sense of deep malaise amongst forest communities in the late nineteenth century. In the initial years of British rule, Dangis had assumed that the British too would punish dakans — one of the things that kings were supposed to do, both in the plains and the forests. In 1844, a suspected dakan, 'seated in a basket, her eyes crammed with a paste of Chillies and bound with leaves', was brought by villagers to British officials at Khandesh in order that she be punished.[8] They were soon disabused of any such hopes. The British banned witch-killings in Dangs and surrounding regions around 1847.

The ban, accompanied as it was by tough measures, was quite effective, and witch-killings soon declined. What gave teeth to the ban were the dissensions that already existed within adivasi society. The ban increased the resources of supporters of women accused of witchcraft: they could now complain to the British and ensure retribution against those who swung or attacked witches. In fact, this was how colonial officials came to know of most witch-killings. Also, the role of bhagats and chiefs in swingings declined because they were singled out for punishment by the British when involved. By 1901, it was reported that 'so many Bhils have suffered for their share in these [witch] murders, that, as a rule, the holy man now keeps to himself his knowledge of the witch's name'.[9]

The practical everyday business of controlling witches, however, was not much affected by the ban on swinging. Less violent methods

---

[7] Manglia Rayji, 30.4.1990, Garmal.

[8] Coll., Kh., to Secy., GoB, 11.6.1844, *BRO.DDR.DN 1.FN 4*. I draw this account from my 'Women, witchcraft and gratuitous violence', and provide footnotes only where I quote.

[9] *Gazetteer of the Bombay Presidency*, vol. IX, part I, p. 293; Khanapurkar, 'The aborigines of south Gujarat', vol. I, p. 63.

of dealing with witches, always possibly predominant, continued with the encouragement of colonial officials: the Diwan often sent for the witch to reprimand her, allowed 'minor bullying', and local constables authorized beatings.[10]

Still, most Dangis responded to the ban with hostility and resistance. The trial of witch-killers was considered particularly unjust. In 1873, it was reported that the prohibition on witch-killings was 'almost the only thing they have now to complain of '.[11] In a lunge at wit, another official remarked:

Several Chiefs whom I asked about the witchcraft situation, much as one asks about the crops elsewhere, said it was shocking; we really should appoint a Government Bhagat with authority to handle it. One chief whom I asked, 'What would you do if allowed a free hand?' said 'I will kill two women in each of my villages for you if I may'. Another said he wished to beat five or six dakins severely; he would find them alright if permitted.[12]

And the ban produced a sense of profound unease. Swingings had a sense of rightness to them: they were part of the ways in which dangerous female wildness was to be controlled. To be prohibited by law from swinging in general (as opposed to being unable to swing a specific woman because of dissensions) seemed profoundly wrong and crippling, and the ban rendered impossible one crucial way of performing Dangi masculinity. Furthermore, since swingings had been part of the enactment of kingship, the ban also implicitly undermined the performance of Bhil kingship.

Not surprisingly, many Dangis felt 'that since the Dakuns had received our [British] sympathy, they had become quite outrageous.'[13] Others remarked that dakans had increased since the British had established their rule. These claims cannot of course be taken at face value: they were at least partially rhetorical, designed to persuade colonial officials to revoke the ban. And the data is too scanty for us to speculate whether an increase really took place. Still, an increase in dakans would fit very well into the general pattern which anthropologists and historians have found of witchcraft accusations increasing in times of social stress, such as the late nineteenth and early twentieth centuries certainly were.

10 T.B. Creagh Coon, 'Witchcraft in the Dangs', *Man in India*, vol. 25, 1945. Khandu Ravji, 2.5.1990, Vakaria.
11 Administration Report, 1872–3, *BA.PD.1873.Vol 87.Comp 1551*.
12 Creagh-Coon, 'Witchcraft', pp. 187f.
13 Fenner to Robertson, March 1860, *BRO.DDR.DN2.FN9*.

In addition to the general stress, there may have been very specific reasons for a perceived increase in dakans. The perception of women as dakans had to do with the relatively greater power that women wielded in Dangs, and the fact that this power was not considered legitimate. Now, with the subordination of forest polities and communities, and with the growing distancing from wildness, the power that women wielded appeared in all likelihood even more unacceptable and problematic. This could have spurred the perceived increase in the number of dakans. That is to say, witchcraft accusations increased because female wildness had become even less acceptable. Also, the British ban appeared to rob Dangis of the principal means that they had formerly used to control this wildness.

Fundamentally, then, the Devi movement was an effort to control female wildness in the face of the colonial ban and the declining role of bhagats and chiefs. As Shiney Varghese and I were told in 1994, all the women in the village also had to assemble and undergo a simple test (which varied from village to village) to establish that they were not dakans. Those who were dakans were then exorcized. Hardiman was told of a similar incident:

After that we went to a place where a stream flows. There the gaulas [mediums] told all of the women to give up witchcraft. A small stick was placed on the head of each woman and it was announced that she had given up the evil crafts. Tea was then prepared. The women, both Bhils and Kunbis (i.e. Konkanas) had been asked to bring three or four rotis or pieces of coconut. They then took a vow that they would not use evil crafts against others.[14]

The nature of the test is revealing: it made up for the loss of the special vision of the bhagat through a comprehensiveness that would sieve out the practitioners of gratuitous violence.

No Longer Bhil

There are very distinctively Kokni goth of the mandini:

At Sattarsingi, there was the Rao Saheb. He had a gun, cartridges and other things. The Rao gave an order that there is going to be a mandini at Bhavani cha killa. So the Bhils and naiks went to Sattarsingi. But the chiefs were afraid. They stayed at the bottom [Bhavani killa is on the top of a hill] and the patils climbed to the

14 Hardiman, *The coming of the Devi*, Delhi, 1987, p. 39.

top of the killa. The Rao Saheb was there. The patils removed their pagdis, touched his feet, and said, 'Ram, ram'. Then Rao Saheb said, '*Hoi, tuj raja has?*' [are you the rajas?] They said, 'No, like your *patavala*, we are *sirbandi* patils of the rajas'. The Rao asked, 'where are the rajas?' The patils said, 'they are at the bottom'. Then the Rao said, 'call them up'. So they went and called the rajas up. There, those who were rajas were noted as rajas, those who were naiks were noted as naiks, and the khutibandi patils were noted down too.[15]

This goth accords to Koknis and their khutibandi patils a constitutive role right at the beginning of the present, the mandini, and is in the older tradition of Kokni participation in Bhil raj. But many goth emphasize how the mandini was because Koknis refused to participate in Bhil raj, and sought to undermine it.

The rajas did much dhum in Bhil raj. For quite some time the patils did nothing about the matter. Then they heard that the saheb had come to Poona. So they went to Poona and told the saheb, 'the Dang rajas do a lot of dhum, please come and stop them'. So the saheb came, and he took away all the rajas who were doing dhum to kalapani. After that, the dhum of the rajas reduced.[16]

Bhils too realize and emphasize how the relationship with Koknis changed since the colonial mandini: after that, it is commonplace to remark, Koknis have become more influential and arrogant.

Khandesh officials had by the 1840s begun taking action against Bhils involved in 'excesses' against Koknis. What officials called excesses were, of course, nothing other than the practice of ikki khavana which accompanied the collection of the nau kayda. By 1888, the Political Agent mentioned that cases were often brought up to him where the bhauband had killed the cow of a Kokni or Varli without taking his leave, or had taken cattle without paying for it. In many of these cases, the Bhils were made to pay compensation.[17]

All this did not lead to a halting of ikki khavana; the 1890s saw an increase in it, partially because of a succession of bad years that left the Bhils with few resources.[18] This decade saw the dominance of many figures synonymous in goth with the looting of Koknis: Mahipu kuver, Rajhans kuver, and Ikia kuver amongst others. In the famine of 1899–1901, it was reported that

15 Lasu Jiva, 29.5.1990, Kotba.
16 Balu Kalu, 29.5.1990, Dhavalidod.
17 Note by Loch, 18.4.1888, *BA.PD.1888.Vol 115.Comp 1683*; KPAAR, 1889–90, *BA.PD.1890.Vol 122.Comp 205*.
18 *BA.PD.1899.Vol 75.Comp 797*.

Most of the grain grown eventually found its way to the buniyahs and the Bhils. The cultivating castes, therefore, khunbis, Warlis, etc are in a poor way and reported to be leaving the Dangs, especially the Upper Dangs, in large numbers owing to the oppression of the Bhils. The latter are said to be in as good a condition as they usually are, which is explained by the fact that they depend on berries and roots to a great extent, while at the same time they manage to extort quantities of grain from the unfortunate cultivating classes.[19]

Nevertheless, there was a significant transformation of the attitudes of Koknis. The volume of reports about 'loot' received by the British indicates that their sources of information were not only feuding Bhil chiefs deploying Kokni complaints against each other, but also independent complaints by Koknis against the bhauband. There was growing knowledge amongst Koknis by the late nineteenth century that they could draw on British support. Already, in 1868, a patil told an official that he would be willing to revive a disused well, bring more land under cultivation and even grow sugarcane, if only he could be sure that there would be no 'oppression' by Bhils or Gaekwadi officials.[20] Such agricultural transformations were what officials were most interested in. Increasingly, colonial officials focused on the patils, treating them as the agents for change. As one official said, a 'more civilized system of revenue and police administration' would be 'most distinctly opposed by the majority especially of the Bhils who hate any change but I do believe a portion of the Kunbi population would hail any reform which would be to their ultimate benefit with delight'.[21]

But Bhil chiefs remained powerful in the nineteenth century, and Kokni participation in Bhil kingship was far more substantive than these challenges to it. It was only after the 1902 demarcation, with the further reduction of the power of the chiefs, that Kokni participation in Bhil kingship declined, and an opposition between Kokni and Bhil values began to be emphasized. Now a new revenue system was introduced since Hodgson found several aspects of the old system unpalatable. The irregular instalments in which the halpatti or land revenue was collected was replaced by annual collections at a fixed time. The collection itself was taken over by the Forest Department, which then distributed the amount amongst the rajas at the annual

19 DFO to Coll., Surat, 15.2.1901, *DFR.DN 1.FN 8.*
20 Remarks by Mr Muller, 27.4.1868, *BRO.DDR.DN 3.FN 12.*
21 Hexton to Loch, 13.4.1889, *BA.RD.1889.Vol 164.Comp 948.*

darbar. The nau kayda were done away with. As compensation to the rajas, the halpatti was increased to Rs 6 per plough for cultivation with plough and Rs 2–8–0 for cultivation by hand. It was also decided that ikki khavana, described now as the '[p]romiscuous begging by the Rajas or their impecunious idle relatives for install-ments of revenue in advance of the time fixed for the payment thereof in full should be sternly put down'.[22]

The new revenue system and the presence of the British led to a significant decrease in ikki khavana. The demarcation had been followed by the capture of several Bhil bhauband who were in-dulging in 'dacoities', as the British described the more extensive cases of ikki khavana by the Bhil kuvers. Many dacoities were reported from the Dangs in the late 1890s and finally, around 1902, a 300-strong colonial force went in and captured Ikia kuver, the bhauband most involved in exactions from Koknis. Again in 1911, Rajhans kuver, another member of the bhauband involved in similar dhum was captured by a British force.[23] It was at least clear that the bhauband could not get beyond the reach of colonial authorities as easily as before. Now even more everyday ikki-khavana, till very recently quite legitimate, declined sharply, for it could easily lead to Kokni complaints to the British.[24]

The power of Kokni patils relative to Bhil chiefs also increased after the demarcation. While Bhil chiefs participated little in colo-nial administration, 'civilized' Koknis had a substantive role to play. The fire protection scheme instituted a separate darbar for Kokni patils, where they were paid for their role in protecting the reserves, and providing bigar to the Department. Again, in the promotion of cultivation in class A villages, or paying revenue, the patils were the node at which colonial administration intersected with Dangi society.

Because of colonial protection for Koknis, there was substantial 'improvement' in Kokni cultivation, with the construction of wells, and the introduction of new techniques.[25] During the early twen-tieth century, these measures led to a widening cleavage between Kokni and Bhil interests. Hodgson, for instance, reported that he

[22] Report on the Future Administration of the Dangs, *BA.RD.1902.Vol 107.Comp 949, Part II.*

[23] Marjoribanks to PA, 3.7.1911, *BA.PD.1911.Vol 191.Comp 1621.*

[24] For such complaints, see *DCR.DN 1.FN 20.*

[25] *BA.ED.1905.Vol 59.Comp 739*; *BA.ED.1909.Vol 54.Comp 739*; Annual Report, 1914–15, *DCR.DN 3. FN 4Uc.*

was receiving a good deal of support in his fire-protection schemes from 'intelligent villagers', 'except Bhils'.[26] The higher degree of support for the scheme from the Koknis was not surprising. They required grass for their cattle, and loppings for their cultivation much more than the Bhils did. Abstention from firing did possibly increase the amount of loppings and grass available, even if these were of lower quality than formerly, and Koknis strengthened their economic power even further. A mid-twentieth-century song dwells on the new-found prosperity of the Koknis:

> . . . the Kunbi [Kokni] finds his purse heavy . . .
> In former times *bhaji-bhakar* was difficult to get
> Now the Koknis and Kolis think of *tup* and sugar.[27]

Accompanying this was a profound transformation. Somewhere in the early twentieth century, goth indicate, Koknis became increasingly reluctant to call themselves Bhil. That shared political identity, which had formerly constituted a constantly affirmed alternative universal, was now marginalized. Now, for Koknis at least, the word Bhil connoted a wildness and inferiority that they were no longer willing to be associated with.

Again, of course, it was not as though Bhil domination over Koknis ended. Though officials managed to halt the collection by bhauband of halpatti directly from villages, Bhils continued to collect the nau kayda, one of the most visible symbols of Bhil raj, from villages till well after independence. Other Bhil demands too continued on a muted scale: even if Koknis could complain to the British, they ran the risk of assaults from Bhils later, who viewed these payments as their rightful dues.[28]

Similarly, the more powerful Koknis, such as the patils or village headmen, continued to play significant roles in Bhil kingship right down till Indian independence in the 1940s. Because of their new proximity to the colonial state, that role even increased. The khuti patils who helped the rajas manage their villages were even more powerful now, and the literacy of some Koknis became an additional asset for the chiefs in dealing with the British. As for ordinary Koknis, despite protestations, many of them were and are willing to concede the legitimacy of the nau kayda and ikki khavana.

26 Hodgson to Coll., Surat, 22.12.1906, *BA.RD.1907.Vol 126.Comp 632.*
27 Khanapurkar, 'The aborigines of south Gujarat', vol. II, song 59. Bhaji-bhakar is a reference to vegetables-and-bread, tup to clarified butter.
28 See *DCR.DN 1.FN 20*, for several instances of Koknis being beaten by Bhils when they tried to evade these dues.

Many of them were also still part of the groups that went for ikki khavana.[29]

THE INESCAPABILITY OF WILDNESS

As this suggests, the process of keeping a distance from wildness should not be confused with its rejection. After all, wildness was not only something that Dangis affirmed of their own volition; it was also seen as something involuntary, something so much part of being Dangi that even those who wished to could not really take distance from it. Consider the ambivalences in the rejection of female wildness. Even after the Devi movement had subsided, women, unlike men, never did return in quite the same degree to drinking. By the mid-twentieth century, drinking had become a primarily male activity. Similarly with gathering, from which women increasingly withdrew. As a mode of subsistence, it was by the mid-twentieth century relatively marginal, though (unlike the other modes of subsistence) the forests could still support a significant degree of gathering. Now only some leaves, fruits or mushrooms were gathered; it was no longer considered desirable to gather the tubers that had been a central part of Dangi diets formerly.

The distance from female wildness should not, however, be confused with any greater social or political subordination of women. Women continued to play a crucial role in various modes of subsistence. In some ways women came to play an even more crucial role in subsistence strategies with the cessation of mobility: the agricultural tasks that they performed became more important than ever. Women also continued to exercise within Dangi society their relatively substantive power to choose or divorce their spouses, or to secure subsistence independently. Even after land titles were formalized in the names of male cultivators in the 1960s and 1970s, women retained considerable control over the cash generated from wage labour.

And while the Devi movement attacked women as dakans, it alongwith other movements also represented the creation by women of a distinctive devotional and ritual space for themselves, a space of the sort that had not existed. Women were major actors in all these movements. Though not numerous amongst the mediums

29 30.3.1990, Nadagkhadi.

that carried Salabai's message, they were a significant presence amongst her followers. In the Gula Maharaj movement in neighbouring Khandesh, they accounted for the bulk of the followers, often trekking for miles in groups to attend meetings. Furthermore, it was women devotees above all who sustained these movements when the backlashes against them developed. After most male followers had given up following the Devi's injunctions by late 1923, women were most involved in campaigning against drinking, and the consumption of meat and fish. Through these activities, they not only distanced themselves from wildness; they also transformed the movements into sites for the enactment of a distinctive power.[30] In this important sense, the wildness associated with being a dakan was no longer the only way that women could think about their power.

It is not even clear that Dangis thought that there was a significant decline in the prevalence of dakans after the movement. While the number of women killed as dakans declined, this may have had to do as much with tighter colonial control — the number had been declining ever since the British banned it. Certainly, after the movements too, many women were thought to be (and some claimed to be) dakans. The persistence of the image of the dakan had to do with the continuing power of women, and the simultaneous illegitimacy of that power.

Quite apart from this sort of inescapable wildness of women, other forms of wildness continued to be affirmed too. Most Bhils followed Salabai's injunctions very briefly, usually only for the time that the mediums in their village were possessed, and then they went back emphatically to drinking, meat-eating and other activities that Salabai had prohibited. The bulk of Koknis too quickly reverted to older lifestyles which involved drinking, hunting and fishing. Within a few years of Salabai's movement, those Bhils and Koknis who continued to follow her were besieged. Other Dangis, both Kokni and Bhil, refused to give their daughters in marriage to these families, and refused to marry women from families devoted to Salabai. As Hardiman notes, they sometimes also polluted devotees' food with liquor or meat, and forcibly made them abandon their vows.

Even the religious movements remained caught up in wildness. Dangi mediums of Salabai were in fact considered particularly

30 Lasu Jiva, 29.5.1990, Kotba.

powerful in surrounding areas because of 'the belief that the forests and hills of the Dangs harboured spirits of unusual power, so that the local mediums had out of necessity to be more skilled in their craft than those of the plains'.[31] Salabai, the Devi that abjured wildness, was after all herself from the forests and mountains, and thus was in many ways wild.

In these ways, though many Dangis felt a novel and passionate need to keep a distance from wildness, their identities continued to be shot through in all kinds of inescapable ways with wildness. There was not so much a wholesale repudiation of wildness as an increase in the deep ambivalence towards it. It may have been because of this deep and profound doubt that many of them were to return repeatedly to other movements which abjured drinking and the eating of meat.

The complexities of the process that was taking place are indicated by the infusion of the old motif, Bhil raj, with new meanings. We do not know whether Salabai's devotees invoked Bhil raj, though it is likely that they did. Certainly, they emphasized the unity of the three major Dangi jatis: "'All are one. Bhil, Kunbi [Kokni] and Varli — all should behave as one!" Everyone, including the Bhil chiefs, took this oath and resolved to reform their lives together.'[32] The other major nineteenth- and early-twentieth-century religious movements elsewhere amongst the forest communities of western India, such as the Govindgiri movement in Panchmahals in 1914 or the Gula Maharaj movement in Khandesh, explicitly called for Bhil raj.

What did these calls for the restoration of Bhil raj mean? Maybe they evoked, above all, a refigured notion of wildness. This wildness was not about Bhil domination over Koknis or other such communities — after all, the latter were those most deeply involved in the movements. Nor was it a celebration of modes of livelihood associated with pleasure. Rather, involved here was an evocation of wildness to oppose upper caste values. In this changed context, to affirm Bhil raj was to adopt a novel subaltern position, and to simultaneously question this subalternity by invoking and enacting moglai, with all its attendant wildness.

(8)

31 Hardiman, *The coming of the Devi*, Delhi, 1987, p. 44.
32 Ibid., p. 40.

19

Insurgent Adivasis

In goth, dhum or rebellion against the sarkar is treated as almost natural, as not requiring any explanation. But this kind of attitude itself is a recent development, the result of the reimagining of forest communities that took place from the late nineteenth century. This newly imagined community involved, most of all, the affirmation of a subaltern and insurgent identity in relation to the state and plains groups.

The reimagining of forest communities was in evidence during three rebellions between 1907 and 1914. In early September 1907, the patil of Ahwa (the village in Amala raj which served as the British capital in Dangs) died. Some days later, on 7 September, Nilu kuver, a son of the Amala raja, came and took 'forcible possession of two bullocks from the son' of the patil, a reversion to an older custom of taking away a Kokni patil's grain and cattle if he died without adult male heirs.[1] The patil's son complained to the Diwan, who sent a constable to look into the matter. Nilu kuver, along with other bhauband, was found at the liquor shop at Ahwa. There, two constables and the bhauband had 'high words' which ended in blows. Receiving reports of this, the Diwan went there with some of his staff. Nilu and the others were allegedly 'beaten by the sipais with the butts of their guns, and . . . the Divan himself belaboured Nilu'.

Temporary peace restored, the Diwan went back to the *kacheri* (office). But many more Bhils, 'who seem to have been sent for', arrived a little while later

and a good company of them, with bows and arrows and a gun or two, sat by the liquor shop and caroused freely, the Parsi liquor shopkeeper, Dhanbai, perforce supplying their wants and quite diplomatically keeping them there instead of letting them go to the kacheri

---

[1] H.L. Painter, Collector, Surat to Secy., Political Dept, GoB, 23.9.1907, *NAI Foreign Department.Intl-B.Proceedings, March, 1908*. The account of the rebellion, including quotes, which follows is drawn from this letter.

as they were very angry with the Dewan who they considered ought to have done justice (*nishabi insaf*) instead of *zulum* [oppression] and talked of beating him. Dhanbai however sent to the kacheri half a mile distant and warned the Dewan to be on his guard.

Some time later, the Diwan was told by a patil that the Pimpri naik and the Ghadvi raja had also been sent to by the Bhils for reinforcements. A rebellion appeared to be building up. Apprehensive, and feeling that his men were inadequate in numbers and arms, he and most other government officials, along with their families, made a stealthy departure during the night.

The next morning, the Bhils, who had remained near the liquor shop at night, went to the kacheri. Finding it empty, they started smashing things. Officials later discovered that the damage done had been considerable:

Trees in the compound had been hacked down, the ground was littered with torn up files, and books and the debris of broken lamps, the lock up door was smashed in, tables, chairs and desks had been mutilated and worst of all, many of the surgical and medical instruments and medicine bottles in the dispensary lay about hopelessly shattered.

The Bhils also attacked and looted the houses of several Koknis who stayed nearby. Soon after this, the Amala raja came on the scene, saw the damage in Ahwa, and 'expressed his great regret to Dhanbai, and sent all his Bhils home'.

That, in a sense, was the end of the revolt. Colonial reinforcements marched into Dangs some days later. When the detachment from Surat camped in Vansda, just outside Dangs, the officer in command reported seeing 'Bhils armed with bows and arrows on the other side of the river [Ambika] . . . our passage was likely to be disputed'. The next morning, however, when the detachment crossed the Ambika and entered Dangs, it met with no resistance. That night, the detachment camped at Pimpri, and its naik warned officials that they might face resistance near Ahwa. Again, they met with none. They reached Ahwa, to find the place deserted and the Bhils 'conspicuous by their absence'. The Surat Collector, Painter, set about restoring order by reinstating government officials in Ahwa.

The re-establishment of colonial order was not however as effective as officials would have liked. In 1911, Sonji Kakdia, a Bhil of Kadmal village, in the extreme north of Dangs, wanted some wood to rebuild his hut. Under the new forest restrictions, permission had to be taken from the Department before timber, especially teak, was felled for such purposes.[2] But when Sonji told his chief, the Kadmal raja Sukria kuver, that he wanted timber for his house, Sukria 'suggested to him that he should take teak and said that since he [Sukria] was the "Master of the Kadmal Forests" there was no need to ask the permission of the Sarkar'. Sonji went ahead and cut the timber he required. When the guard came to know of this and descended on the village to arrest Sonji, Sukria told Sonji 'that it was not worth being taken before the Court for such a trifle and urged him to set fire to all the forests and if anybody came to interfere with him, he should shoot them'. Sukria had for some time past been inciting Bhils to burn the forests. He had also threatened to kill a round guard if he set foot in the village again. Now Sonji threatened the guard, who beat a hasty retreat. Then, armed with his bow and arrows, Sonji went around the forests, setting them afire, 'intimidating the [forest] subordinates and Kokani villagers from interfering and extinguishing the fires'. He also sent word to the Koknis of nearby Kasarbari village that he was going to burn their village.

Meanwhile, on receiving reports of the incendiarism, a party of three armed policemen was sent by the local authorities. They reached Kadmal at night, and awoke Sonji by mistake while trying to ascertain whether he was at home. A clash ensued, with Sonji shooting his arrows at the police. Finally, finding himself with only two arrows left, Sonji rushed out and shot the Havildar, Ibrahim, through the body with an arrow, killing him. But Sonji was also shot in the leg by one of the policemen. He fell down and was captured immediately.

Officials, thinking his hostility to be 'an isolated case of defiance' initially believed that there would be no further trouble. Their hopes were soon belied. Many Bhils had already been in an offensive mood when Sonji was arrested. They had been armed in readiness against his arrest and had gathered together when Sonji called out for help as he fell wounded. But the appearance of the DFO, Marjoribanks, with reinforcements possibly made them shy away from a confrontation. Marjoribanks, however, left soon. Around two days later, the Ranger who had been sent to estimate the area burnt by Sonji returned with reports that he had been followed and closely watched by the Kadmal and Subir Bhils and kuvers, and

---

[2] This account is drawn from: Report by F. Anderson, PA, Surat, 3.8.1911, G.E. Marjoribanks to Anderson, forwarded 16.5.1911, *BA.RD.1911.Vol 120.Comp 1113*, and the proceedings in *BA.PD.1911.Vol 121.Comp 1443*.

that the local round guard and beat guard had fled after their lives had been threatened. The Ranger too 'had been frightened into granting an unusually large number of permits for free wood'. By 22 April, seven days after Sonji's arrest, the confrontation had escalated. Marjoribanks complained that the Bhils were 'setting the forest rules at defiance and [were] likely to subject officials to violence'; that a liquor shop had been looted; and that a Kokni patil had been threatened.

Marjoribanks left the next morning for Kadmal to enquire into the outbreak. But he had hardly got as far as Mahal when he was informed that fires had started in Pipaldahad, in the extreme east of Dangs. These fires, spreading in several directions, were accompanied by intimidation of the forest guards. The rebellion was spreading. Marjoribanks retreated to Surat to call for assistance. Around thirty armed police from Surat, in addition to a force of thirty from the Khandesh Bhil Corps, proceeded into Dangs. Details from this point onwards are frustratingly scanty. We know only that the Surat Collector by 22 May felt that the rebellion had been more or less suppressed.

Three years later, in 1914, yet another rebellion commenced. 'The Bhils were excited about the war in Europe and imagining the government to be in sore straits considered it a good opportunity to throw off its authority.'[3] It began with an outbreak of fires being reported from Ghadvi. Police were rushed there. They returned complaining that the 'Ghadvi chief himself, his bhauband and Bhils and Koknis totalling more than 100 were burning fire; the Bhils and chiefs were armed with bows, arrows and guns . . . they [the guards] were informed that anybody extinguishing fires would be killed'. A day or two later, the Pimpri raja too commenced firing the forests. The Dangs Diwan rushed to the areas from where these had been reported. Reports he received indicated that 'all the Dang chiefs and naiks had planned secretly to harm the forests'. He immediately sent messages to the Deher, Vasurna and Amala rajas, who reassured him in their replies that they would not join the uprising. Two days later, however, the Amala raja came to Ahwa with about twenty armed men. Another fifty men from Amala occupied Surkhai hill just outside Ahwa, which they commenced

---

3 This account is drawn from: Annual Report, 1914–15, *BA.ED.1916.Comp 739*; Diwan to PA, Surat, 7.12.1914, and Range Forest Officer to Diwan, 2.12.1914, 'Details of recoveries proposed', 17.3.1915, 'Fire cases in the Dangs', n.d., note by Diwan, 12.12.1914, all in *DCR.DN 1.FN 20*.

burning. Representatives sent into Ahwa by the raja demanded that his money, which was in the custody of the Diwan, should be handed over immediately. The Diwan reported that they were handled with 'tact' and sent back. In the evening, the Amala chief went back home after seeing the armed police around. Nevertheless, people began to flee Ahwa as rumours spread that the Pimpri and Ghadvi chiefs were heading towards the village with their men.

And the firings continued. The chiefs of Kirli, Sivbara, Piplaidevi and Vadiavan also joined in. It was reported that 'bands of several hundred of Bhils and others met in many localities and began systematically burning the forests and in many cases interfering with road construction and other works'. There were 'hundreds of different attempts to set fire by torches. . . . These places could be seen nearly all over Dangs'. Around 6 December, the Assistant Political Agent arrived, along with a force of around 110 men. We do not have any information of what happened after that, but the rebellion appears to have been put down without much difficulty. Within a week, the Pimpri naik was on trial for having fired the forests, and he was sentenced to six months rigorous imprisonment.

Becoming Insurgent

To British officials, the rebellions were simply part of the boisterousness of public school boys. The 1907 uprising was described as 'not a rebellion but a mere drunken escapade'.[4] Of the 1911 revolt, officials remarked: 'there was nothing to account for it except only that among the Kadmal Bhils there are some notorious firebrands who had been quiet longer than their patience could hold out and therefore these disturbances occurred merely as the result of pent up hotheadedness'.[5] The 1914 rebellion was described as 'mainly due to wild rumours about the war — a regular case of naughty boys making a disturbance in the school-room when they believed the school-master's attention was momentarily diverted'.[6]

But involved here was a profoundly novel phenomenon: the imagining of insurgent communities. It is easy to forget how radically new such an imagining was. Yet, in 1861, Devisinh did not think of himself as rebelling against the British, and his acts are

[4] H.L. Painter, Coll., Surat to Secy., Political Dept, GoB, 23.9.1907, *NAI Foreign Department.Intl-B.Proceedings, March, 1908.*
[5] Letter from PA, Surat, 3.8.1911, *BA.RD.1911.Vol 120.Comp 1113.*
[6] Annual Report, 1914–15, *BA.ED.1916.Comp 739.*

not even remembered that way in goth. For that matter, virtually no Dangis in the nineteenth century who confronted the state in the nineteenth century thought of themselves as rebels, or are cast now as rebels. But in 1907, 1911, and 1914, the Bhils did think of themselves as rising against the sarkar. What had changed so dramatically in this short span of less than fifty years that impelled Dangis to make this conceptual leap? Why did they think so differently from their grandparents or even parents?

To ask these questions is to problematize rebelliousness and subalternity. These have sometimes been treated as innate to South Asian forest communities; more broadly, subaltern identities have been often ascribed a kind of pre-existing factity.[7] Yet subaltern identities are historically constituted, and the nature of resistance that communities put up changes with their understandings of themselves. Insurgency is just one form of resistance, it is not an always-present option: both the idea of insurgency and the community of insurgents have to be constructed and, as times change, constructed anew.

The constitution of Dangis as a subaltern community commenced in the nineteenth century and was broadly completed by the early twentieth. There was no dearth, as we have seen, of clashes or confrontations in the eighteenth and nineteenth centuries. But to call these instances of insurgency would be to mistake their character. In the attacks of Silput raja and others on the deshmukh or the Gaekwad, in their raids on villages, or in their defiance of the British, it was not insurgency that was being contemplated or undertaken. These acts were located at the juncture of two opposed but complementary polities, with only a notional subordination of forest polities; in them, power was being negotiated, even if this took place in contexts where the forest chiefs were aware of the balance being skewed against them.

In later decades, the power of the sarkar could be invoked, as in the dispute between Devisinh and Kerulsinh. But the sarkar was still an external force. In this, it was to be appropriated as an ally, with its power often made manifest in the development of feuds and disputes. Thus, the shared fear of the sarkar did not necessarily translate into a shared hostility. The attitudes of the Bhil bhauband to the sarkar depended much more on the alliances that were

---

7 Some essays in the first four volumes of *Subaltern studies* occasionally incline towards such a treatment of forest communities and more broadly of subaltern communities.

constructed with it by different lineages: the sarkar was still a potentially complementary force from the plains.

All this started changing after the forest demarcation. Older forms of alliance-building with the sarkar by appealing to it in internal disputes were less feasible. With its now-extensive judicial and official machinery, the sarkar constituted itself in a resolutely panopticist manner. Not only could it no longer be easily appropriated along the grooves of existing disputes, but it often acted unilaterally, without being appealed to by anybody. More clearly than ever before, it had become by the early twentieth century a destabilizing, unmanageable force, invasive in the extreme, a force from the outside, the symbol above all of the desh and Gujarat, but located almost inescapably within Dangs. For Dangis, the clearest indicator of this must have been that the much-disliked Forest Department had become the sarkar. The very existence of this sarkar symbolized Dangi subordination, and to that extent the end of Bhil raj.

Now, a shared hostility to the sarkar was possible, and was articulated in the notion of Bhil raj. Formerly, the invocation of Bhil raj had represented the assertion of an extant and locally dominant identity, an assertion of wildness. With the completion of the inner frontier, Bhil raj was increasingly something of the past. Now it evoked loss, juxtaposed past against present, and represented a charged call that a newly defined subaltern insurgent community could respond to. Because the sarkar was now seen as having extinguished Bhil raj, insurgency against it in the name of Bhil raj became possible, plausible, and even desirable.

Bhil raj was invoked in many ways. There was drinking — part of popular rebellions almost everywhere, and usually treated as a carnivalesque element of rebellions. In Dangs, however, it was also more, for it evoked Bhil raj and wildness. Two rebellions involved attacks on liquor shops. As Hardiman has demonstrated, colonial support had made Parsi liquor merchants powerful amongst the forest communities of nineteenth- and early-twentieth-century western India. Colonial officials pushed through abkari laws that prohibited the home distillation of liquor; the chiefs too no longer had the authority to challenge Parsis. From the point of view of officials, Parsi liquor merchants helped them control a lightly administered region. One merchant reminiscenced that his brother and he had 'rendered services to the Government at the time of rioting by getting some of the culprits arrested. We also used to help officials in the detection and arrest of criminals, and we were in the good graces of all Government officials, as we were useful to them during their touring and camping'.[8]

The power of Parsis was also derived from the cultivation and money lending they engaged in, principally lending grain to Dangis at exorbitant rates of interest, sometimes over a hundred per cent. The cultivation itself was very oppressive, with Dangis having to work on shopkeepers' fields to pay off the loans that they had incurred. And during the rebellions, the Bhils gave vent to their hostility to the Parsi merchants. In some cases, they demanded the reduction of liquor prices, which were pegged about as high as they could go without leading to illicit distilling. In 1911, the Bhils attacked a liquor shop at Mokhanamal village and forced the dealer to supply them liquor at half the price, telling him that 'the Bhils were now sole authority in the Dangs' (a translation of "Bhil raj"?)[9]

Second, the re-establishment of Bhil raj involved attacking the Forest Department, and flouting its restrictions. Thus, during the rebellions of 1911 and 1914, the forest guards and other officials were repeatedly intimidated. Especially striking is the incendiarism involved in both rebellions. In the nineteenth century, as we saw, firing had been part of the way in which subsistence was secured. It was then put down by the Department. Its resurgence in the rebellions heralds a transposition of the valencies of the act: from a means of securing subsistence, it had become one way of resisting and defying the colonial state. The notorious obsession of officials with preventing fires imbued such incendiarism with even greater import.[10]

8 Manaji Tamboli to Diwan, 28.1.1948, *DCR.DN 4.FN 20*; Hardiman, *The coming of the Devi.*

9 Marjoribanks to Anderson, n.d., forwarded 16.5.1911, *BA.RD.1911.Vol 120.Comp 1113*; Hodgson to PA, Surat, 31.7.1907, Case 49, *DFR.DN 7.FN 1*; Diwan to APA, 26.3.1922, *BRO.DDR.DN 6.FN 34 Part IV*; Joju Joshya, 30.4.1990, Borkhet.

10 Ramachandra Guha has argued that there was a specificity to the targets chosen by the residents of Kumaun in their incendiarism: it was always the *chir* forests propagated by the Department that were burnt and virtually never the broad-leaved forests that were locally useful ('Forestry and social protest in British Kumaun, 1893–1921', in Ranajit Guha [ed.], *Subaltern studies: Writings on South Asian history and society*, vol. IV, Delhi, 1985. pp. 89f.) It is difficult to make this kind of distinction for the Dangs, since the silvicultural strategies of the Department had not led to the creation of forests which had no relation to local needs. Teak, though important to the Forest Department for commerce and the profits it yielded, was also important to the Dangis for their subsistence needs.

The attack on the Department was just part of the story; more broadly the sarkar as a whole was a target during the rebellions. Bhil understandings of the sarkar are instanced in the destruction they wrought in the Diwan's office during the 1907 revolt. The lockup which they broke open and destroyed had acquired a special significance since the turn of the century, when the imposition of forest conservancy had led to the repeated imprisonment of Dangis, especially Bhils. In destroying it, the punitive power of the sarkar was being negated. Similarly, tearing up files was a symbolically charged act. Files epitomized daftars and the written word, and it was to a large extent from forms of writing that the sarkar derived its enormous power. In choosing the dispensary as a target, they were again attacking a particularly despised symbol of the sarkar. Vaccinators had been around in Dangs since the nineteenth century, and while the scale of their operations was not very extensive, knowledge of their existence, and fear of them, was. Officials complained often about hostility to vaccinators. One powerful Kokni khuti patil and jagirdar, Khandu Ravji, successfully defied the British and drove away the vaccinators who came to his village till the 1930s.[11]

Third, Koknis, and especially powerful patils amongst them who were asserting their independence, were often amongst the prime targets of the Bhils. In 1907, the resistance of the Ahwa patil to Bhil demands sparked off the revolt, and Koknis' houses were amongst those looted when many Bhils retaliated against the Diwan by going on a rampage in Ahwa. Again, in 1911, the Koknis of Kasarbari and the patil of Subir were amongst those who were threatened by Sonji and other Bhils. In attacking Koknis in this manner, the old traditions of Bhil raj, when such exactions enjoyed borderline legitimacy, were being reasserted.

Predictably, the rebellions were viewed at best ambivalently by Koknis. Of the fifty-five persons tried for incendiarism in 1914, only four were Koknis.[12] At least some Koknis were actively hostile to the revolts. As Marjoribanks remarked in 1911, all 'decent villagers' (a prim synonym for Koknis in the local patois of scientific forestry) were 'thoroughly disgusted at having the forest burnt and no grazing for their cattle in the hot weather'.[13] In 1914, again, the

[11] *KDG*, p. 604; Khandu Ravji, Vakaria, 30.5.1990.
[12] 'Fire cases in the Dangs', *DCR.DN 1.FN 20*.
[13] Marjoribanks to Coll., 2.6.1911, *BA.RD.1911.Vol 120.Comp 1113*.

patils and village karbharis were reported to have given 'loyal help in quelling the disturbance'.[14]

But within a few decades, Koknis also came to participate in this insurgent identity. Affected almost as much as the Bhils by the forest restrictions, the participation of the Koknis in insurgency had always been a possibility. It was precluded in the initial decades of the twentieth century, however, by a perception amongst many Koknis that British presence also gave them protection from the Bhil chiefs, and by their distancing from Bhil raj. By the mid-twentieth century, faced with growing population pressures and less of a threat from Bhil domination, forest restrictions began to seem especially harsh even to most Koknis. In 1931, the population had reached 33,495 persons. By 1941, it stood at 40,236, and by 1951, it had risen to 47,282.[15] In a rebellion in 1949, quite soon after the feared British sarkar had been replaced by a nationalist one, Koknis were to participate in large numbers, and they have been active in later rebellions too.[16]

BECOMING ADIVASI

Insurgency against the sarkar, or at least of resistance to it and the adoption of a subaltern position relative to it, has now become pervasive amongst forest communities throughout South Asia. Forest communities have from the late nineteenth century been engaged in more rebellions and insurgencies against the state than probably any other section of Indian society. In post-independence India too, some of the most famous insurgencies have often had substantial following amongst them — the Naxalbari movement, the Telengana movement, and the Naxalite movement in contemporary Andhra Pradesh, to name some. In the long run, then, the nineteenth-century colonial consolidation of the inner frontier had profound consequences: it led to a relatively new identity that involved subalternity, insurgency and resistance.

In many parts of the subcontinent, this oppositional and often insurgent identity is articulated in the word adivasi. The word, which has a chequered history, drew implicitly on the colonial ideology that distinguished between caste and tribe; that identified

---

[14] Annual Report, 1914–15, *BA.ED.1916.Comp 739*.

[15] *Dangs District Gazetteer*, p. 159.

[16] For an account of the rebellion, see *DCR.DN 2.FN 36*. These rebellions have also included women. See Varghese, 'Women, resistance and development'.

the 'caste system' with plains communities and saw tribes as isolated, primitive, less Hinduized and autochthonous communities
that usually lived in the forests.[17] Literally meaning 'inhabitant from
the earliest times' or autochthons, the word was meant as a non-
derogatory alternative the perceived racist connotations of older
words like kaliparaj. It originated in the Chhotanagpur region of
Bihar in the 1930s, and was popularized on a national level by the
Gandhian A.V. Thakkar, who worked amongst the 'tribes' of western
India.[18] The prefix adi was very popular at the time, and was used
a lot by nationalists to describe oppressed communities — adi-
Dravida, adi-Hindu, and so on.

While less derogatory terms were used, the colonial trope of
anachronism and the accompanying view of these communities as
primitive were taken over and became deeply entrenched in the
perceptions of dominant Indian groups.[19] The tribes were the
younger brothers of the more advanced plains nationalists, to be
helped out of their primitiveness. This kind of reform of the forest
communities was a central theme of Gandhian and nationalist
thought and social work. It may not be accidental that Gandhian
ashrams, the paradigmatic physical space of nationalist reform and
spiritual regeneration, are far more numerous today in adivasi
areas of western India than in plains regions.[20]

Nevertheless, the proto-nationalist and nationalist evocation of
primitiveness was very differently gendered from its colonial ancestor. In his insightful article, Ghosh has explored the theme of
primitivism in Bengali modernity, focusing specifically on how Kol
societies were imagined by the Bengali middle class. Pointing out
that Bengali nationalism internalized the colonial characterization
of Indians as effete, he suggests that the ascription of masculinity
to Kol society was part of an attempt to recover masculinity for the
middle class. Second, he suggests that the sexual objectification of
Kol women was especially significant since it occurred at a time

[17] For a survey and critique of these distinctions, see Stuart Corbridge, 'The
ideology of tribal economy and society: Politics in Jharkhand, 1950–80', *Modern
Asian Studies*, no. 22, 1, 1988; Crispin Bates, 'Race, caste and tribe in central
India: The early origins of Indian anthropometry', in Peter Robb (ed.), *The
concept of race in South Asia*, Delhi, 1995.

[18] Hardiman, *The coming of the Devi*, Delhi, 1987, p. 13.

[19] Premanand Patel, *Navsari prantni kaliparaj*, Baroda, 1901, pp. 1–10.

[20] On Gandhian ashrams in the adivasi areas of south Gujarat, see Ghanshyam Shah and H.R. Chaturvedi, *Gandhian approach to rural development:
The Valod experiment*, New Delhi, 1983.

when nationalist discourse was constructing the Bengali woman in a language that erased her sexuality, and cast her basically as an embodiment of motherhood and sacrifice.[21]

These two attitudes — adivasi society as highly male, and adivasi women as highly sexual and erotic figures — were in all likelihood common to late-nineteenth and early-twentieth-century Indian middle-class attitudes towards tribes. The emphasis on the sexuality of adivasi women continues today.[22] But the ascription in middle-class discourse of masculinity to adivasi society was a more short-lived and tenuous affair. Late Indian nationalism often denied masculinity to adivasi societies, or at least marginalized adivasi masculinity as something quite different from what the Indian nation required. The nationalist movement was, as scholars have demonstrated, a claim for the masculinity of the Indian people, and especially of the Indian middle class. What made the Indian middle class especially masculine, in this representation, was its claim to control of the project of modernization. Modernity, rather than a splotchy palette of truthfulness, loyalty, bravery, and primitiveness, came to be the central defining parameter of masculinity.

In a sense, all the protagonists in the famous 1940s' debate — where important figures like Ghurye, Elwin and Thakkar discussed the policies to be adopted towards tribals in independent India — accepted this equation of modernity and masculinity. Persons like Elwin felt that adivasis needed to be protected. However, this protection was sought for a fragile adivasi culture which could not survive the onslaught of modernity. And those like Ghurye (who accused Elwin of wanting to preserve adivasis as though they were in a zoo) argued for the assimilation of adivasis into the Indian mainstream. If they were marginalized in the process and incapable of coping with masculine modernity, those like Ghurye seemed to argue, then so be it.[23]

---

21 Kaushik Ghosh, 'Primitivism in Bengali modernity: The imagining of tribal society in 19th century Bengali nationalist culture', unpublished manuscript, 1994.

22 Maya Unnithan points to this sexualization of adivasi women in her 'Constructing difference: Social categories and Girahya women, kinship and resources in South Rajasthan', PhD, University of Cambridge, 1991; see also her 'Gender and tribal identity in western India', *Economic and Political Weekly*, 27 April 1991, vol. 26, no. 17.

23 Verrier Elwin, *A philosophy for NEFA*, Shillong, 1964, and G.S. Ghurye, *The aborigines 'so-called' and their future*, Poona, 1943; and its revised edition, *The scheduled tribes*, Bombay, 1963.

Indeed, Indian nationalists were very suspicious of words like adivasi. To concede to these communities an autochthonous status which could not be claimed by dominant plains groups seemed to accord to them a power prior to the nation state. Predictably, the postcolonial Indian government, while it did not actively reject the word, was careful to specify that these communities were 'tribes' not because they were autochthons but because they were deemed so through a government list — they were the Scheduled Tribes.[24] Others such as the aggressively assimilationist sociologist Ghurye were more vitriolic, describing it as 'question-begging and pregnant with mischief'.[25] More recently, right wing Hindu organizations have been actively hostile to it. To accept its implications, after all, would be to undermine their own claims to an autochthonous status in India. They have systematically tried to promote other words such as *vanyajati*, literally forest castes or communities.

These nationalist fears were quite astute: the trope of autochthonicity itself continues to be very powerful and persuasive to dominant groups in ways that have sometimes disrupted nationalist projects. When, recently, the World Bank review mission had to decide whether funding for the Indian government's controversial multimillion Sardar Sarovar dam project should be continued, one of the criteria it employed was whether the several hundreds of thousands of Bhils and other forest communities which the project would render homeless were 'indigenous peoples'. If they were, it was felt, then the Bank could not, by its criteria, continue funding the dam. Using a range of indices, and relying on the evidence of several social scientists, the review mission finally decided that the Bhils and others were indigenous peoples. On this and other grounds, the Bank withdrew from the project.[26]

The way forest communities used the words being attributed to them was of course quite different. It is significant that of the various words for them which flourished in the early twentieth century, only one — adivasi — found any substantial degree of favour with them. The history, necessarily subcontinental in scope, of why and how this happened remains to be written. Till then, it

[24] For a survey of some of these developments, see Crispin Bates, 'Congress and the tribals', in M. Shepperdson and C. Simmons, *The Indian National Congress and the political economy of India, 1885–1985*, Aldershot, 1988.

[25] Ghurye, Foreword, *The scheduled tribes*, Bombay, 1963, p. ix.

[26] See Bradford Morse and Thomas Berger, *Sardar Sarovar: The report of the independent review*, Pune, 1992, ch. 5.

may be worth speculating about. One striking feature of almost all the other words used for them was a reference to the forests: *vanwasi, vanyajati, girijan* or *raniparaj* all meant, in different ways, 'residents of the forests'. That reference was one which many members of early-twentieth-century forest communities would have felt ambivalent about, engaged as they were in assuming a distance from wildness. Adivasi, in contrast, was a free-floating signifier in relation to the forests, not necessarily involving identity with all of it. In addition, its connotation of autochthonous power must have been important. Not only did such autochthonicity create power within dominant plains values, but it made possible a claim to wildness that did not imply inferiority.

But maybe we can read the word adivasi more metaphorically, as connoting not simply autochthonicity but a distinctive way of being outside the narratives of the Indian nation state. It seems to me that in Dangs the word adivasi traverses the mandini and situates itself in the excess represented by moglai. Being adivasi is about shared experiences of the loss of the forests, the alienation of land, repeated displacements since independence in the name of 'development projects', and much more.[27] Central to the whole notion of being adivasi, then, has been a perception of subalternity, of a novel marginality created by the mandini, with its dichotomy between wildness and civilization, and its emphasis on subordinating wildness. In opposition to this mandini, the word adivasi evokes those histories associated with moglai, or with times when subordination to plains societies was not so marked. Maybe, then, the power of the word adivasi does not have to do simply with some lexical meaning — original inhabitants — but with being outside domination by surrounding plains societies? Like Bhil raj earlier, now the word adivasi, should one say, both points to subalternity and refuses to accept that subalternity?

(20)

---

[27] For movements that draw on adivasi identities, see Bates, 'Lost innocents and the loss of innocence: Interpreting *adivasi* movements in South Asia' in R.H. Barnes, A. Gray and B. Kingsbury, *Indigenous peoples of Asia*, American Association for Asian Studies, Michigan, 1995; Baviskar, *In the belly of the river*, Delhi, 1995; R.B. Lal, 'Socio-religious movements among the tribals of south Gujarat', and I.P. Desai, 'The tribal autonomy movement in south Gujarat', both in K.S. Singh (ed.), *Tribal movements in India*, New Delhi, 1983.

20

Epic Resistance

I have tried to elaborate on how the Dangi epochs of mandini and moglai enable us to go beyond what Guha has so appropriately called 'the arbitrary singularity, the so-called principal contradiction, that between the colonizer and the colonized'.[1] Goth of mandini tell of the interventions of the British, but from perspectives that extensively displace the statist discourses of British power, and focus instead on Dangi encounters with and refiguring of that power. Goth of moglai carry this process further: they traverse mandini and create a multiplicity of local and regional narratives that have little do with the concerns of statist power.

Consider now what this kind of understanding can mean for the ways we think of resistance and rebellion. Radical historians and social theorists have focused on many aspects of these: the visions of the rebels, the moral economies within which they operated, the carnivalesque dimensions of rebellion, the forms of everyday resistance, and the hidden and public transcripts involved in resistance and rebellion. Chapter 19 implicitly draws on much of this work in exploring Dangi rebellions: it explores insurgency, Dangi visions of Bhil raj, and the creation of subaltern identities such as adivasi. It is clear that I do not wish to deny the continuing importance and value of such work. But precisely because this work is about rebellion and resistance there is a pervasive tendency to focus on the 'so-called principal contradiction' between the subaltern and dominant. Taking my cues from goth, I instead pursue here a supplementary strategy: of foregrounding the ways in which resistance and rebellion were directed not only at opposition and inversion but were also about exceeding the dominant through local and regional narratives, through invoking moglai, and sometimes through enacting what might be called epic resistance.[2]

---

[1] Ranajit Guha, 'The small voice of history', p. 6.
[2] I thank Shahid Amin for suggesting ways to explore 'epic resistance'.

LIQUOR AND POWER

One of the more detailed stories I learnt about the Ahwa dhum, as the professional historian's 1907 rebellion is known, was from Kewar Naik of Gondalvihir, the great-grandson of the Amala chief involved in the revolt, Ratansinh raja.

Nilu Kuver and Navlu Kuver came to Ahwa to ask for the Dashera *paiha* [Money, a reference to the lease instalments paid at the time of Dashera]. They sat at the shop of the Parsin, Dhanbai, drinking. Then Nilkantrao Diwan's peon came by to take the *phuldaru* [the first pressing or take of liquor]. They asked him, 'where are you taking this'? He said, 'I am taking it for *dada*' [a term of respect which can also mean father]. They said, 'is he your *bahas* [father] that you call him dada? Give some to us'. But he refused to. So they slapped him twice.

The peon went and told Nilkantrao Diwan, 'Nilu and Navlu beat me'. So the Diwan came to Dhanbai's shop with ten policemen. There was a young man with them, Haipat. His son is still there at Borkhal. Haipat saw them coming, jumped over the compound wall, and ran away. He went and told Kamansinh Kuver that they have come and killed Nilu and Navlu. So all the bhauband got ready. Kamansinh said to Ratansinh, 'come, bahas'. [Ratansinh was at the time the raja of Amala, and Kamansinh was his son who later succeeded him]. Ratansinh said, 'let us not go today, we shall go tomorrow. If they have been killed, then we shall take blood for blood'.

But Kamansinh did not listen, and he went to Ahwa with many men. They went to Dhanbai's shop. Dhanbai said, 'why have you come'. He said, 'I have come to beat Nilkantrao diwan'. Dhanbai said, 'do not go today, go tomorrow. I shall give you Rs 100 worth of liquor'. She opened a keg and gave daru to everyone. Quietly, she sent a messenger from the backdoor to the Diwan, with the message, 'you and the karkun must go away because they are coming to get you'. Nilkantrao Diwan and the others then ran away to Songadh. From Songadh he sent a letter to the saheb at Surat, saying, 'there is dhum at Ahwa'.

The saheb got the letter at Surat and picked up his durbhin and he looked through it and he saw that there was really dhum in Dangs. So he took his lashkar [army] and came to Billimora. From Billimora he came to Vaghai, and from Vaghai he came to Ghogli. From Ghogli he looked at Ahwa again with his durbhin and saw that there was nobody at Ahwa. He came to Ahwa. The saheb was there at the Forest [Department] rest-house, and Ratansinh came there. The saheb told Ratansinh, your people did a lot of dhum at Ahwa. The bhauband were also caught and brought to the forest rest-house. The saheb took away the money from Ratansinh Raja because of the dhum, two sacks of it every year for four years.[3]

Goth of the Ahwa dhum are often appropriated into the complex of local and regional narratives around Dhanbai, one of the most powerful of early-twentieth-century liquor merchants. The Surat Collector had remarked after the 1907 rebellion on her power and role in 'keeping the Bhils comparatively quiet. It may be noted that Dhanbai has been in the Dangs for many years and has great influence with the Bhils. She employs them on her lands, supplies them with drink, acts as general provider and confidential agent, and if necessary, lends them money'.[4]

In goth now, Dhanbai is central to the beginning of sarkar, and of liquor.

> Formerly, there was no sarkar. There was only Dhanbai. She had her factory at Ahwa, where there is the PWD [Public Works Department] office now. She would make daru [liquor] there. Daru would come from Surat and she would mix it. Then she would send it all over Dangs, to Galkund, Bardipada, Singana, everywhere. She had her shop at Borkhet.[5]

> Earlier there was no sarkar in Dangs. The sipai would come to Dangs once a year at Dashera to look at the major cases. Dhanbai was at that time the only sarkar.[6]

> Dhanbai? She was a rani. She was the sarkar. She distributed the lease payments. She told the rajas to go to Bhavani cha killa and do the mandini.[7]

If Dhanbai's shop existed in Ahwa before the 1901 demarcation, she would certainly have preceded the sarkar there, and of course been crucial to the colonial management of Dangs. The concatenation of signs associated with her is a powerful one: the mandini is the founding event of the present, the sarkar is enormously powerful, and the lease amounts provided the chiefs' main income.

And though Dhanbai's power is crucially constituted by her association with the sarkar, it is also part of other narratives that have little or nothing to do with state power.

[3] Kewar naik, 21.5.1990, Gondalvihir.
[4] Painter to Secy., GoB, 12.9.1907, *NAI.Foreign Department.Intl-B.Proceedings, March, 1908.*
[5] Nathu Dhavji, 25.4.1990, Ghavria.
[6] Ramu Kharsu, 23.4.1990, Pipalghodi.
[7] Nanu Jivlia, 29.5.1990, Nadagkhadi.

She was very fat, and very fair. She was so fat that she needed three bamboos for making her *ghungro*.[8] She had a sewing machine and she would make clothes on it. Nobody had seen a sewing machine before, and so people would gather to have a look at it. That was how sewing machines came to the *dang*.[9]

Dhanbai's power is nowhere so clear as in accounts of how she conducted herself. She addressed the Amala chief by his name alone, as 'Ratan' or, worse, 'Ratnio' (rather than the more respectful 'Ratansinh raja' or 'Rajasaheb') and was often abusive:

> She gave respect to no one, neither the rajas nor the sarkar. When the rajas came, she would ask them, *kai muha*. She made them keep the bows and arrows outside, and only then would she allow them to drink.[10]

· The description of Dhanbai calling the rajas 'kai muha' is always amusing to listeners. My efforts to get a translation of the word proved baffling initially. The problem resides in the polysemous nature of the term. When I used to ask immediately after the goth for the meaning of the phrase, I was told that the term was one of abuse, and did not mean anything in particular. It meant, I slowly began to think, something like an idiot. Yet I soon discovered another everyday use of the word. Muha is sometimes used by many Dangis as an affectionate invective to call their male children. Used for the rajas, kai ['what', here a salutation] muha infantalized them, and therefore became an abusive term. This was why the ostensibly affectionate epithet evoked such laughter, for it was to dismiss their power as inconsequential.[11] Again, there is the significance of the chiefs leaving bows and arrows outside when they went into her shop. Until as recently as the 1960s, Bhils rarely moved anywhere without the bows and arrows. They were not only used for hunting or for protection in the forests; they also symbolized Bhil power. In making even rajas leave these outside, her authority over them was being rendered highly visible.

Because of this independent power, Dhanbai is often regarded as having been a mediator between the rajas and the British.

---

8 A ghungro is a bamboo basket worn over the head during the rains for protecting oneself. Normally, one bamboo or vas is adequate for making a ghungro for a person.

， 9 Dasari Chandrasinh, 26.4.1990, Pipliamal.

10 Pavji Ravji, 1.5.1990, Lahanchariya.

11 Khandu Ravji, 2.5.1990, Vakaria.

When the lashkar came after the dhum, she sent it back because she said she did not want violence.[12]

In various goth, she was the one who warned the rajas that the British were returning with reinforcements, who suggested how the wrath of the British could be deflected, or who arranged for the reconciliatory meeting of the rajas with the British. Certainly, she was close to the rajas even according to records: in 1907, the chiefs had asked Dhanbai to 'go to Surat and intercede with me [the Surat Collector] on behalf of the offenders'.[13]

Such ambivalence towards liquor merchants or *kalals* occurs repeatedly in goth. Of course, they were extremely exploitative of Dangis.[14] Goth about Dhanbai too dwell on her exploitativeness, how she would make people work in her fields for little or no payment, and how her assistants would beat Dangis. But despite this, loans from the liquor shopkeepers made survival easier in the monsoons or bad seasons. Besides, they lived in the same villages, in conditions not very different (relative to the British) from those of most Dangis. As one official ruminated about the kalals in Dangs: 'their life must be a hard one . . . It is true that they act as saukars and also deal in grain, but the country people are so utterly poor and wild that anything like a steady trade must be out of question.'[15] Another official remarked on how 'Parsis and Mohameddans who have lived one or two generations in the vicinity of these people retrograde [sic] almost to the level of the Bheels themselves, believing in the supernatural power of witchcraft and Dakuns [witches].'[16] Such beliefs were again an indicator of the proximity of the Parsis to the Dangis: however powerful they were, they could not place themselves beyond the reach of Dangi ritual power. In contrast, the distance of the sahebs from this ritual power was epitomized in their ban on witch-killings — read by Dangis not only as the abdication of the responsibilities of kingship but also as an indicator that the sahebs themselves were not vulnerable to Dangi witchcraft.

In Dhanbai's case, there may have been a greater ambivalence still because, as a woman, her oppressiveness took on a different

[12] Dasari Chandrasinh, 26.4.1990, Pipliamal.
[13] Painter to Secy., GoB, 23.9.1907, *NAI.Foreign Department, March, 1908.*
[14] Diwan to Ag. PA, 4.10.1887, *DCR.DN 1.FN 19B.* See also Elphinstone to Secy., GoB, 14.5.1852, *BA.PD.1852.Vol 42.Comp 1415* and KPAAR, 1876–7, *BA.PD.1877.Vol 106.Comp 1383.*
[15] KPAAR, 1876–7, *BA.PD.1877.Vol 106.Comp 1383.*
[16] Fenner to Mansfield, 30.8.1858, *BA.PD.1858.Vol 95.Comp 734.*

quality. Reconsider her calling the rajas 'kai muha', or Ratansinh raja as 'Ratnio'. From a male kalal, such remarks may have crossed the boundaries of acceptability, for the attack on Bhil raj involved in such remarks would have been very threatening. But because women, despite their power, were too marginal to threaten any specific raja in the way that another man could, the threat of Dhanbai's remarks was defused, and there was even a touch of the ludicrous and improbable to them. That is to say, the very marginality of Dhanbai as a woman may have made for some of her power and influence with Bhil chiefs, and for the fact that she is remembered now more than any other kalal.[17]

The way in which many goth cast Dhanbai's death epitomizes the ambiguity of her power.

> She used to abuse the women who came to work on the field, because they did not work properly. Then one of the women, who knows who, put a *danch* [curse or spell] on her. Her tongue became swollen and she was taken to the dispensary for treatment, but she died nonetheless.[18]

According to other goth, it was a retaliation in which the colonial state participated.

> Dhanbai was hit by *dukh* [sorrow/ill-fortune often associated with witchcraft] and her tongue became large and she forgot her children's names. She had not listened to anybody, not even the sarkar. So when the sarkar came to know that the woman who does not listen to anybody is sick, they took her away to the dispensary on the pretext of medical treatment, and there they cut her tongue off. That was how she died.[19]

It was her manner of conducting herself, and the power inherent in this manner, which was also the cause of her downfall. The retaliation against her came through one of the few types of power strong enough to hold out: witchcraft, almost the sole survivor (and that a besieged one) amongst the practices which had marked out the fearsomeness of forest communities. And maybe the retaliation was directed at her tongue because it was a major element in the articulation of her power: she was abusive. And of course it is scarcely surprising that the sarkar should be suspected in killing her — it was hostile to her power and her proximity to Dangis.

---

17 I thank Shahid Amin for a discussion which clarified this point.
18 Dasari Chandrasinh, 26.4.1990, Pipliamal.
19 Khandu Ravji, 1.5.1990, Vakaria.

Confronting the Sarkar

There are also local and regional narratives of the dhum, some of which dwell on details of pursuit and confrontation which colonial officials would not even have been aware of. Thus, for instance, the accounts of how the Amala chiefs evaded capture.

> After the dhum the lashkar came, one company from Khandesh, and one from Surat. They came to Ahwa and asked '*Chuha kothe aha*' [Where have the rats gone?] But the Borkhal people had already run away, and the sarkar could not catch them. So the saheb said, 'we shall go at midnight to catch them'. At night they reached Payarghodi, and asked Diwa patil 'where is Borkhal village', where do the rajas live now?' The patil said, 'they live in Borkhal village, but right now they have run away. What will you do, going there now?' In the meantime, he had already sent someone to tell the kuvers at Borkhal 'the lashkar has arrived, run away fast'. When the lashkar came to Borkhal after spending some more time talking to the patil, there was nobody there.[20]

Other goth dwell on how the chiefs made their peace with the British.

> After the dhum, the police came into Dangs. Dhanbai warned the Borkhal [Amala] chiefs, 'the saheb is coming. Go away and hide'. So when the British came to Ahwa, there was nobody there. Then they went to Borkhal, but everybody had run away into the forests. So the sahebs came back to Ahwa. Then the Borkhal rajas came to Dhanbai, and said, 'what do we do now?' Dhanbai said, 'go and give them a *bhet* [gift] of *komda* [fowl] and say 'Ram Ram Saheb'. So they went. The British said, 'Raja Saheb, your people have done a lot of dhum in Ahwa. But now that you have come on your own with a komda, I don't want to take up the issue. You may go'. The saheb let Ratansinh Raja and his bhauband go back. He did not do anything to them.[21]

The giving of a komda is a gesture laden with acerbic humour, for it draws on a vivid detail from the everyday business of satisfying the demands of forest guards with fowls. Conciliating the saheb is thus not that very different from keeping on the right side of the comparatively lowly forest guard.

[20] Jiva Kharsu, 26.4.1990, Ghadvi. During the 1914 rebellion, interestingly, a march was undertaken to Borkhal to capture the Amala bhauband. The party found nobody in the village. Diwan to APA., 12.12.1914, *DCR.DN 1.FN 20*; see also Secy., GoB to Secy., GoI, 24.12.1914, *NAI.Foreign Department.Intl-B.January 15.Nos 74–5.*

[21] Sayaji Pandu, Nadagkhadi, 11.6.1990.

But through all these various versions, goth are very clear that
the dhum was about overturning the sarkar and restoring Bhil raj.

> First there was nobody at Ahwa, only two *saukars*, one *telia*
> [oil-presser] and two Bhils. Then Dhanbai's bungalow came, and
> she was the sarkar. The sipais came once a year only. Or Kutubud
> diwan would come, he was the first sarkari Diwan. Then there
> was Nilkantrao Diwan, he was from Chalisgaon in Maharashtra.
> He came to Ahwa, saw it, and said, 'this is a nice place'. So the
> sarkar came to Ahwa. But the rajas said, we will not let the sarkar
> stay here, and they went to Ahwa and did dhum.[22]

In a similar vein, there is the goth of Bapu Naik of Gundia village,
who caught Suryawanshi Diwan (around in the 1920s) by his neck
and demanded that Bhils be given the raj.[23]

The concern with dislodging the British and reinstituting Bhil
raj is also clear in the stress on attacks on the *thambla*, or the pole
from which the British flag or nishan flew.

> The rajas went to Dhanbai. They told her, 'we do not want the
> sarkar here'. She said, 'don't do dhum, the sarkar will kill you'.
> She gave them sida pani and said, 'don't go today, go tomorrow.
> I will give you daru today'. The next morning the rajas went to
> the kacheri and saw that the sarkar had run away. They did dhum
> for one day at Ahwa. Chimnia kuver, Rajhans kuver, Mahipu
> kuver, Ikia kuver, Dasru kuver, Kamansinh raja, they were all
> there for the dhum. They shot at the thambla from which the
> sarkar's flag was flying and hit it several times, but they could not
> break it. The thambla is still there, near the hospital. You can see
> the marks left by their arrows.[24]

For many Dangis, this is (and almost certainly was) the most
important incident in the 1907 dhum, though the British possibly
never even learnt of it. The failure to bring the thambla down that
day often explains the return of the sarkar.

> When Nilubhau went to Ahwa, the sarkar ran away. But their
> nishan remained flying. Then the British looked from Surat, and
> saw that their flag was still flying. So they said, 'we can go still
> back' and they returned. Had the thambla been broken, the sarkar
> would not have come back.[25]

[22] Khandu Ravji, 2.5.1990, Vakaria. Kutubud diwan is Kutubuddin, who
was the Diwan of the Dangs in the 1880s. Nilkantrao is N.M. Deshmukh, the
Diwan from the time of the demarcation till the 1907 uprising.

[23] Nanju Raut, 8.6.1990, Payarghodi.

[24] Pavji Ravji, 1.5.1990, Lahanchariya, and Khandu Ravji, 2.5.1990, Vakaria.

[25] Ramju patil, 6.6.1990, Pandva.

The flag was already a key marker of authority by the early nineteenth century.[26] By attempting to bring it down, the Bhils were making clear the nature of their protest: it was not about specific grievances like the restrictions on lopping, felling, or hunting but rather about the rejection of colonial rule.

In the interrogation and undercutting of the authority of the sarkar, ridicule is another element that figures repeatedly.

> Dhanbai told Nilkantrao Diwan about the plan to attack him. He decided to run away. But he was so nervous that while tying the reins of his horse, he tied them to the hind of the animal instead of the head. The police were in such a hurry that they tied the saddles to their own stomachs instead of the horses. The *amaldar* [a revenue official] and others had made some *khichdi*, but they did not even wait to eat it before running away. They ran away leaving it untouched.[27]

Notice the motifs. The Diwan is so nervous that he cannot put the bit properly, the amaldar does not even wait to eat. And the police, the persons who usually terrorize Dangis, tie themselves up instead of their saddles. This is delegitimizing caricature at its chortling best; it is the portrayal, gleeful, of a sarkar on the run. Earlier too, there was the same element of mirth directed at the sarkar: as Nilu and Navlu insinuated, is the peon a bastard son of the Diwan that he should refer to the latter as dada?

SONJI'S DHUM

A similar kind of engagement with, and displacement of, the sarkar pervades goth of the 1911 revolt.

> Sonji Bhil went and cut some *sagoti* [teak timber] for building a house. Muckun beat guard came to know of it, and he said, 'I shall go to Sonji and catch him'. Sonji heard of this and he said, 'I shall go and meet the guard first'. So he went from Kadmal to Subir to meet the guard. Muckun guard came to know of Sonji's coming and he ran away. Sonji reached the house of Muckun guard, but did not find him there. So he shot some arrows into the house, extracted them out again, and went off. From Subir he went to

26 *BA.PD.1874.Vol 109.Comp 619.*
27 Khandu Ravji, 2.5.1990, Vakaria. The eating of khichdi is often used as a means to mark out officials or non-Dangis. Khichdi is a dish of rice and lentil, not part of the regular Dangi diet. Dangis often offer it to visiting officers or outsiders, since they presume that the local millet, nagli, will not be liked.

Garbari, and from Garbari he went to Singana, burning forests on the way.

The Parsi at Singana came to know that he was coming and he ran away. He left the liquor behind. Sonji took daru from the keg after breaking open the cock. He poured some daru out for Vadudev and then he took some himself. He swirled it round his mouth and then spat out. He did not drink, but he destroyed all the daru.

Then he left Singana and went to Jamniamal. There, the patil offered him some tobacco. Sonji told the patil, 'I have all I need, I do not need tobacco'.

Then he left Jamniamal and went to Monginamal. Firing the forests along the way, he finally came back to Kadmal. That night he stayed at home. The next day he went to Hadol, burning all the forests on the way. From Hadol, he went to Borumal, and came back again at night. The next day, again burning the forests, he went to Bhondmal, near Uga. From there he went round, and came back home at night.

The dhum started that night. From Khandesh and from Surat, the police came that night. The Khandesh police reached first, and started firing at Sonji, who was in his hut. Sonji shot back arrows at them.

At that time Sonji's wife ran out. They caught her in the dark, felt the bangles on her wrists, and said, this is a woman. She was taken to another house, and was told to stay there till the whole affair was over.

Finally, Sonji had only one arrow left in his quiver. Abrun Fauzdar from Khandesh was outside. He stood outside the hut with his arms outstretched, wearing a *saatcoat* [here, a kind of armour.] Sonji shot an arrow. This went through the saatcoat and killed Abrun on the spot. Abrun pulled the arrow out of his chest, and shot Sonji with his rifle, hitting him in the knee.

Sonji had a sword also. If he had not been hurt, he would have killed with the sword. Radhu patil of Deher was there. He began beating Sonji on the hands till Sonji finally dropped the sword. The police then caught Sonji, and they took him away. They took him to the hospital, and he was given good food there. Then his health improved.[28]

As with stories of the Ahwa dhum, goth about Sonji are imbued with an implacable hostility to the sarkar, and dwell on how colonial authority was defied, on parodying and scorning its power. As we have seen, Ibrahim havildar came, confident in his saatcoat, dismissive of the dangers of a mere bow-wielding Sonji.

---

[28] Sukria Kakad, 9.6.1990, Subir. See also *BA.PD.1911.Vol 121.Comp 1443.*

> Ibram Havildar roamed for 2–3 days, hunting for Sonji Bhil. He
> went asking, 'is Sonji here? is Sonji there? Where is Sonji?' He
> was carrying a pistol, and he kept making the sound of a pistol
> with it as he went along.[29]

The pistol was a weapon far above the bow and arrow. The sound
of the pistol was itself enough, in usual contexts, to frighten people
into surrender.

But how did Sonji react to the pistol and to the hunt for him?

> The patil told Sonji, 'they are coming to catch you. The sarkar will
> kill you if it catches you'. Sonji said, 'when are they coming?' The
> patil said, 'I don't know, they may come at any time'. Sonji said,
> 'let them come, I am ready'.[30]

Sonji, then, was not worried at the approach of Authority. He
would not be, of course. Sonji was no ordinary person:

> The Diwan told Ibram havildar, 'if you capture Sonji Bhil, I shall
> go back to Chalisgaon [the village the Diwan hailed from] and
> you can have my job'. So Ibram Havildar left from Ahwa. He went
> to Borkhet and from Borkhet he went to Lavchali. At Lavchali he
> crossed the river, and his horse stumbled. The Lavchali patil told
> him, 'your horse has stumbled. This does not bode well. You
> should go back'. Ibram laughed and said, 'what can Sonji Bhil do,
> he has bows and arrows and I have a rifle, and I am wearing my
> saatcoat'. And Ibram went ahead. But it was Sonji who killed
> Ibram, not Ibram who killed Sonji.[31]

This, then, is the paradox that gives the approach of Sonji its special
flavour, its potential to be developed. It was the approach of Authority, better armed, better equipped and confident of the outcome.
Yet it was Authority which was to lose out in the encounter, making
for event which many Dangis still savour with delight. This defeat
of Authority was driven home even after Sonji's capture.

> The Dangi Saheb came with the lashkar almost immediately after
> Ibram's death. They made hammocks to carry Ibram's body and
> Sonji to Ahwa. Ibram was carried ahead. But Sonji said, 'It is I
> who should be carried ahead'. The sarkar gave in and he was
> carried ahead.[32]

The insistence on being carried ahead of Ibram is, in a sense,

---

29 Jiva Kharsu, 25.4.1990, Ghadvi.
30 Ibid.
31 Chandarsinh Somalsinh, 1.6.1990, Kadmal.
32 Jiva Kharsu, 27.4.1990, Ghadvi.

political. It is to assert, once again, the priority of Bhil raj, and the correctness of Sonji's action in felling the teak tree.

It may seem, on first consideration, that what is involved in goth like these, in addition of course to rich local and regional detail, is the pervasive trope of subaltern resistance: inversion. To espy more than rich local detail and inversion in these goth may seem unnecessary. Yet, consider closely the divergences from the categories which professional historians use to think of resistance. The principal criteria used by historians for gauging the magnitude of rebellions would be the number of people involved, or the degree of popular resistance. By both these criteria, the 1914 rebellion would be the most important and the 1907 rebellion the least. Yet the 1914 rebellion, or the much more recent 1949 revolt, are not recalled much. When they are, it is usually as several separate and unconnected incidents of firing. Often, even the fact that these incidents took place around the same time is not recalled. Also, they remain known within a small region, usually the villages around that in which the persons involved in it lived. In contrast, goth of the much earlier Ahwa dhum and Sonji's dhum are known very widely and told very often. Why should this be so?

Perhaps because the latter involve what might be called epic resistance. I use the phrase here in two senses. First, to loosely connote acts that went beyond defiance to gestures that refigured the mandini dramatically, as for instance Sonji's killing of a sarkari havildar, or the attempt to fell the flag during the Ahwa dhum. In comparison, the firing of forests, the principal gesture of resistance in the 1914 and 1949 rebellions, while it also refigures the mandini, is quotidian. Second, and far more importantly, to indicate goth about subaltern resistance which draw, flamboyantly and exultantly, on the tropes of imaginary goth.

Consider for example the detail of these goth. Both here and elsewhere, the frugality of the records and the articulateness of the goth are significant. Detail, in the colonial discourse of counterinsurgency, was deployed only to the extent that it was necessary for maintaining the continuity of this discourse. One aspect of the resultant sparseness is that colonial records are frugal with their names, both of persons and places. Thus, the precise areas that Sonji fired are not mentioned: this is a matter only of silvicultural importance, certainly not directly related to the question of law and order which the records we examined were generated to serve. Again, it was only the broad fact of Sonji's eventual capture — and the killing of a government official in the process — which is mentioned. In the 1907 rebellion, there are only three named actors: Dhanbai, Nilu kuver and Ratansinh raja. The rest, including the Diwan, remain unnamed. In archival accounts of the 1911 rebellion, only Sonji Kakdia and Sukria kuver are named in the context of the rebellion itself.

Now, why are these goth so generous with detail? One explanation, reasonably conventional, could be that since the goth are concerned with an immediate past, naming is central to personhood in the goth. Whether Nilubhau or Sonji Bhil, the rebels existed as persons of flesh and blood, who had lived in nearby villages, or had been their ancestors, and whom their parents had often seen. The officials, whether it was Konjia sipai whom Nilu was rude to and fought with, or Ibrahim Havildar and Karim sipai whom Sonji confronted, or Sathiya Ranger whom the Vakaria zamindar defied,[33] were part of a web of control which these ancestors had to contend with.

Such an explanation would only be partial. The richness of detail should not be confused with that facticity or immediacy which western historiographical traditions admire as indicative of solidity. Rather, detail is here one of the ways in which the confrontation with the British is exceeded, in which the goth appropriate the event for local and regional narratives where the British are marginal. Detail is here also part of the conventions of story-telling such as in imaginary goth. Therefore, names are, within generative schemes governed by the scatter of plausibility, invoked without any necessary relation to that factual past which historians sedulously and serious-mindedly seek to excavate. While naming the spots that Sonji Bhil burnt, all narrators recited names of sites around and near Kadmal, but no two recitations, even by the same person, were identical. Yet the idea of hammering out a definitive single list would be somewhat laughable. Dangi goth are concerned here not with factually reproducing the past but with evoking Bhil dhum, a task which can almost as legitimately be carried out by conjuring names out of thin air as by naming any actual persons or places.

Consider another point: the convergence between narratives of

---

[33] Khandu Ravji, 1.5.1990, Vakaria.

Sonji and those imaginary goth of heroes capable of superhuman feats. In some accounts, Sonji is depicted as possessing tremendous strength, so that even four policemen could not hold him down.[34] And there is Sonji's appetite: as the patil of Pandva village said, he could eat one bullock a day. Rajhans kuver has a similar complex of goth developing around him. We met Rajhans in Chapters 6 and 8, when his rani, Jegi, rode and subordinated Ghobria patil. Rajhans too was a very interesting person. One of the most prominent Amala bhauband, he was, according to some goth, involved in the Ahwa dhum, and in many other confrontations with the British. In 1911, a British expedition was sent in to capture him and other bhauband.[35] He was, according to persons who saw him before he died around four decades ago, a very large man. According to some goth, he ate one bullock a day. He also had the power of fooling people. Once, when he was surrounded on all sides by the lashkar, he dressed himself in a hat like a saheb. Then he passed through the ranks of the army, with all soldiers saluting him because they thought he was a saheb, and he escaped.

Another theme, again with parallels to imaginary goth, concerns the ultimate fate of Sonji.

> Sonji was caught and taken to Dhulia. The sarkar said, if you had brought him without injury, we could have used a strong and brave man like him in the lashkar. They took him to the hospital, where they kept him till he got well. Then they opened a shop for him at Dhulia. He would sit there and eat.[36]

Thus, caught finally, Sonji escapes retribution because he has given the good fight. We noticed a similar reprieve for Devisinh in a previous chapter. Rajhans kuver too, in some goth, is taken to Dhulia and kept there.

Why should it be significant that stories of Sonji or the Ahwa dhum are shot through with the tropes of imaginary goth? Recall, imaginary goth are outside concern with being khari or true. Because of this, accounts of dhum can be spectacular refigurings of statist discourses rather than only inversions; they create a multiplicity of local and regional narratives about mandini, moglai and dhum. The connection with mandini is of course evident: it is in response to it that all the dhum takes place. In addition, it could

---

[34] Navsu sipai, 23.3.1990, Diwantembrun.
[35] Marjoribanks to PA, 3.7.1911, *BA.PD.1911.Vol 191.Comp 1621.*
[36] Ramju patil, 6.6.1990, Pandva.

be argued, the goth are invocations of moglai, made spectacular and dramatic because they draw on the tropes of imaginary goth. The parallels between goth of dhum, and of the major chiefs during moglai is striking. Janak raja, you will recall from Chapter 3, is ascribed a gargantuan appetite in many goth. In Ghadvi, there are similar stories about the prowess of Silput and Khem; in many villages, there are such goth about vadils who were great hunters.

POPULAR RESISTANCE?

Finally, there is the intriguing absence of other actors from the goth of Sonji Bhil. Sukria kuver, the arch villian in colonial accounts, is almost entirely missing from goth. While the liquor shop at Mo-khanamal was looted by Bhils after Sonji's arrest, goth across virtual-ly all of Dangs are unanimous in ascribing the act to him. Nor do the goth speak of other Bhils firing the forests during the revolt, as was clearly the case. The same with the Ahwa dhum: there are no goth of all the popular resistance that took place — no accounts of the firing of forests, threats to forest guards, or attacks on offices. But when asked specifically whether their vadils had at the time burnt the forest, narrators are quite likely to answer in the affirmative.[37] There is, in other words, a curious disjunction. On the one hand, the dhum is entirely ascribed to Sonji or the Ahwa bhauband; on the other, there are local or even familial memories that acknowledge the role of other men and women in the dhum.

This, it may seem, is a case of epic resistance slowly overshadow-ing more mundane acts of resistance, of the disappearance and marginalization of popular resistance in Dangi memories. But let us treat this commonsensical interpretation with caution. The devalu-ing of the 1914 and 1949 rebellions is precisely because of the everyday resistance that Dangis put up now and in the past. The narration of the past as moglai — often in the same chronological period as mandini, but outside it — is about the production of everyday resistance. And as forest officials never tire of complaining, Dangis often set fire to forests for no reason other than to harass the Department. Such sporadic incendiarism is the backdrop against which firing during rebellions is looked at; and it is one which makes the act seem less striking. Dangi goth, in other words, proceed by assuming the existence of popular hostility and resistance to the sarkar; they do not tie themselves up in knots to demonstrate it.

37 For example, Gajesinh Monsu, 26.4.1990, Kadmal.

Thus, though ordinary actors in revolts have been forgotten, the notion of an extensive popular resistance runs strongly in goth, and is intertwined with celebrations of epic resistance. In Jamulvihir, quite early on in my fieldwork, Raisinh Gondusar pointed at the shoes that I was wearing and told me with much glee that his vadils would shoot at shoeprints if they saw them in Dangs. As I moved across more villages, this story was to be repeated over and again. In those days, they said, only the sahebs and people from outside Dangs wore shoes, and so the Bhils shot at shoeprints. The vadils did not want *seekhel bhanel lok* (educated persons) in Dangs.

It is significant that the appurtenances of the desh are symbolized in footwear. The rejection of either colonial authority or the authority of the plains cannot in Dangi memory take the form of explicit hostility to persons from the desh, except when in open rebellion. Colonial authority is invested with too much authority and power for such a challenge to be lightly conceived. Attacks on the person were prone to provoke retaliation. Footprints however are unproblematic: they are tangible markers of the presence of the desh, but at the same time too peripheral for attacks on them to provoke retaliation. As I was told once, 'how could you shoot at the sahebs themselves — *dhak lage ni'* [would one not be scared?]

We have, obviously, no way of knowing whether this is really a powerful vestigial memory of times when shoes and outsiders were rare, when Dangis actually did shoot at footprints. I would certainly like to think so. Be that as it may, consider the wider implications of both the act, and its remembering. In shooting at shoeprints, Dangis were rejecting the plains domination associated with mandini (should we think of shoeprints as analogous to the script produced by writing?) and affirming the wildness of their footprints. And in remarking on it now, there is often a harkening back to that rejection. That is to say, the insistent remembering of shooting at shoeprints is a way to think about the injustices of the Forest Department and the sarkar, about the subordination of Dangis to plains traders and government officials. Like the images of the vanarkilla, of the dang and the desh, the junigavthad, Sonji's dhum, or the Ahwa dhum, the image of shooting arrows at shoeprints is a political one, forged and reforged by Dangis at the intersections of their pasts and presents. This is why all these images are so important. Passionate, murky with meaning, they carry not just histories of exploitation and resistance, but also intimations of potential languages and visions to overturn this state of affairs — intimations, in other words, of hope.

Afterword:
Loss, Hope, and Hybridity

Reclaiming Bhil raj, shooting at footprints, fighting for junigav-thad or old villages, insisting that the Department be confined only to the vanarkilla or fortress of monkeys — running through all these is a thread too prominent to be missed: that of loss. These evocations of loss have not only created Dangi subalternity; they also make possible a politics of hope, for they involve visions that challenge subalternity.

This might seen a deeply problematic thing to say. As post-colonial historians, we have learnt to be suspicious of narratives of loss. And rightly so. In their colonial, nationalist or liberal forms, narratives of loss are about a transition from homogeneity to dif-ferentiation, from the originary fullness of autonomy to a degraded condition of subalternity. These narratives suffer from a pervasive nostalgia, a yearning for unity with the homogeneous past, a desire for the closure of difference, and any politics associated with them would be profoundly conservative and restorative. For example, the politics of the invention of tradition is above all about nostalgia, about claiming unity and continuity with a time before history and difference. It is not surprising that the invention of tradition is most resorted to by dominant social groups, or powerful groups making a claim to dominance.

But what sense would it make to characterize goth of moglai as the invention of tradition, or as nostalgic invocations of a prelap-sarian past? Moglai is never tradition or anything akin to it. And moglai and mandini are not even two distinct and chronologically sequential epochs. Rather, to return to a point already made in Chapter 2, involved in vadilcha goth is a counter-aesthetic of mod-ernity. Unlike the invention of tradition, this counter-aesthetic does not seek to deny or freeze modernity and history. Rather, it engages with the modern and the historical and foregrounds the relations of domination involved in them. Goth of mandini are precisely about that foregrounding. They tell stories of modernity from a very distinctive perspective, that of those groups such as adivasis whose identities have been created by modernity, but who have also been made marginal by that very modernity. This marginality becomes especially evocative in the context of evocations of moglai, which tell not of the precolonial or traditional but the extra-colonial, of times outside (not always before) marginality. What is constructed as moglai is not innocent of relations of power, nor is it about any originary fullness. It is marked by profound fissures and tensions — around loci of kingship and masculinity, around female wildness, around the dangers lurking in the pleasures of livelihood, and around the oppression of Koknis by Bhils, to name but a few.

That is to say, goth of mandini and moglai, like many other subaltern narratives, are hybrid, and they exceed the modern and historical. And it is precisely this hybridity which makes possible a politics of hope. For involved in these goth are ways of envisioning social relations which are radically outside dominant narratives — think for example of the junigavthad, the vanarkilla, and the arrows shot at footprints, and Sonji Bhil. Memories that are seized hold of as they flash 'up at a moment of danger',[1] involved in them, at least potentially, is a politics organized around wildness, one that questions the narratives of the postcolonial nation state.

Of course, this politics is agonizingly worrisome. It is replete with relations of exploitation or domination: it can carry connotations of accentuated masculinity, of hierarchical violence, of an original and exclusionary autochthonous relationship with the land, even of ethnic purity. Nevertheless, these connotations are also under siege. Besides, surely, it would be mistaken to search for a subaltern identity not marked by these troubling ambivalences. Such identities do not exist, and cannot provide any site for our politics. A politics of hope would lie in recognizing that subaltern identities are contested terrains, the meanings of which are open to redetermination in all kinds of ways. A politics of hope would lie in constantly challenging and undermining the relations of domination involved in them, in retaining and sharpening that subaltern and radical edge which questions Indian narratives of the nation, and of citizenship. And it is here, maybe, that some tasks

---

[1] I quote here from Walter Benjamin, 'Theses on the philosophy of history', *Illuminations*, London, 1973, p. 247.

of the radical historian lie: in learning from the hybridity and surplus of subaltern bricolage, in working together on programmatic montages of resistance against the dominant — in dreaming, with trepidation and hope, of different pasts and futures.

Bibliography

A. Recordings

Fieldwork interviews were recorded on 62 tapes, covering over 75 hours of recording time. Recordings have been supplemented by field-notes and transcripts of interviews which could not be recorded.

B. Archives Consulted

India Office Library: Boards Collection.
Maharashtra State Archives, Mumbai: Revenue Department Proceedings; Political Department Proceedings; Secret and Political Department Proceedings; Education Department Proceedings; Judicial Department Proceedings.
Maharashtra State Archives, Pune: Deccan Commissioner's Records.
Gujarat State Archives, Vadodara: Huzur Political Office Proceedings; Residency Records; Dangs District Records.
Dangs Collectorate Records, Ahwa, Dangs district.
Dangs Forest (North Range) Records, Ahwa, Dangs district.
Walker of Bowland Papers, University of Edinburgh Library, MS 13861
National Archives, New Delhi, India.

C. Government Publications

Anon., *A Concise Manual of Sylviculture for the Use of Forestry Students in India*, Calcutta, 1906.
Bomanji, K.R. (ed.), *The Dangs Boundary Dispute*, Bombay, 1903.
British Parliamentary Papers, Colonies and East India, vol. 19, Session 1871.
Central Provinces Ethnographic Survey, *Draft Articles on Forest Tribes*, Allahabad: Pioneer Press, 3rd series, 1911.
D'Arcy, W.E., *Preparation of Forest Working Plans in India*, 4th edition, Calcutta, 1910.
Government of Baroda, *Selections from the Records of the Baroda Government, no. X, vol. I, Dang Case*, Baroda, 1891.

Government of Bombay, *Dangs Working Plan,* Bombay, 1926.
—— *Forest Reports of the Bombay Presidency,* Bombay 1847–1945.
—— *Gazetteer of the Bombay Presidency, vol. VI, Rewa Kantha, Narukot and Surat States,* Bombay, 1880.
—— *Gazetteer of the Bombay Presidency, vol. VII, Baroda,* Bombay, 1883.
—— *Gazetteer of the Bombay Presidency, vol. XII, Khandesh,* Bombay, 1880.
—— *Gazetteer of the Bombay Presidency, vol. XVI, Nasik,* Bombay, 1883.
—— *Gazetteer of the Bombay Presidency, vol. IX, part I, Gujarat Population: Hindus,* Bombay, 1901.
—— *North Dangs Working Plan,* Bombay, 1913.
—— *Selections from the Records of the Bombay Government* (henceforth SRBG) New Series, no. 6, *Report on the Experimental Revenue Settlement of Kowonee Taluka of Nasik Sub-Collectorate,* Bombay, 1853.
—— *South Dangs Working Plan,* Bombay, 1916.
—— *SRBG 216 (new series), Papers Relating to the Revision Survey Settlement of 102 Dangi Villages of Akola Taluka of Ahmednagar Collectorate,* Bombay, 1888.
—— *SRBG 23 (new series), Miscellaneous Information Connected with the Petty States in the Rewa Kantha in Gujarat,* Bombay, 1856.
—— *SRBG 26 (new series), Rough Notes Containing Historical, Statistical and Other Information,* Bombay, 1856.
—— *SRBG 366 (new series), Survey Settlement of the Talukdari Villages of Jhalod, the Petha Mahal of the Dahod Mahal of the Panchmahals Collectorate,* Bombay, 1898.
Government of Gujarat, *Dangs District Gazetteer,* Ahmedabad, 1971.
Government of India, *Report of Bombay Forest Commission,* Calcutta, 1887, vol. I.
—— *The Imperial Gazetteer of India: The Indian Empire, Economic,* vol. 3, Oxford, 1907.

D. OTHER WORKS CONSULTED

Alatas, Syed Hussain, *The Myth of the Lazy Native: A Study of the Image of the Malays, Filipinos and Javanese from the 16th to the 20th Century and its Function in the Ideology of Colonial Capitalism,* London: Cass, 1977.
Alavi, Seema, *The Sepoys and the Company: Tradition and Transition in Northern India,* Delhi: Oxford University Press, 1996.
Amery, C.F., 'On the Relation Between District and Forest Officers', *Indian Forester,* vol. I, 1875, pp. 294–7.
Amin, Shahid, *Event, Metaphor, Memory,* Delhi: Oxford University Press, 1995.

Amin, Shahid and Dipesh Chakrabarty (eds), *Subaltern Studies IX: Writings on South Asian History and Society*, Delhi: Oxford University Press, 1996.

Anderson, Benedict, *Imagined Communities: Reflections on the Origins and Spread of Nationalism*, London: Verso, 2nd revised edition, 1991.

Ankersmit, Frank and Hans Kellner (eds), *A New Philosophy of History*, Chicago: University of Chicago Press, 1995.

Anon., 'Forest Administration and Revenue Making', *Indian Forester*, vol. 31, no. 5, 1905, pp. 243–8.

—— *Notes on the Criminal Classes in the Bombay Presidency*, Bombay, 1908.

—— 'Rab in Thana', *Indian Forester*, vol. 12, 1886, pp. 186–90.

Arnold, David, 'The Indian Ocean as a Contact Zone, 1500–1950', *South Asia*, vol. 14, no. 2, 1991.

—— *The Problem of Nature: Environment, Culture and European Expansion*, Oxford: Blackwell, 1996.

Arnold, David and David Hardiman, *Subaltern Studies VIII: Essays in Honour of Ranajit Guha*, Delhi: Oxford University Press, 1994.

Arnold, David and Ramachandra Guha (eds), *Nature, Culture, Imperialism: Essays on the Environmental History of South Asia*, Delhi: Oxford University Press, 1994.

Asad, Talal, 'Afterword: From the History of Colonial Anthropology to the Anthropology of Western Hegemony', in George Stocking (ed.), *Colonial Situations: Essays on the Contextualization of Ethnographic Knowledge*, Madison: University of Wisconsin Press, 1991.

Bann, Stephen, *Romanticism and the Rise of History*, New York: Maxwell Macmillan, 1995.

—— *The Inventions of History: Essays on the Representation of the Past*, Manchester: Manchester University Press, 1990.

Barnes, E., 'The Bhils of Western India', *Journal of Arts and Ideas*, vol. LV, no. 2829, 1907.

Barthes, Roland, *Mythologies*, trans. Annete Lavers, New York: Noonday Press, 1972.

—— 'Change in the Object: Mythology Today', in his *Image Music Text*, trans. Stephen Heath, London: Fontana, 1977.

Bartra, Roger, *Wild Men in the Looking Glass: The Mythic Origins of European Otherness*, trans. Carl T. Berrisford, Ann Arbor: University of Michigan Press, 1994.

Bates, Crispin, 'Congress and the Tribals', in M. Shepperdson and C. Simmons, *The Indian National Congress and the Political Economy of India, 1885–1985*, Aldershot: Avebury, 1988.

—— 'Lost Innocents and the Loss of Innocence: Interpreting *adivasi* Movements in South Asia', in R.H. Barnes, A. Gray and B. Kingsbury,

Indigenous Peoples of Asia, Michigan: American Association for Asian Studies, 1995.

Bates, Crispin, 'Race, Caste and Tribe in Central India: The Early Origins of Indian Anthropometry', in Peter Robb (ed.), *The Concept of Race in South Asia*, Delhi: Oxford University Press, 1995.

Baviskar, Amita, *In the Belly of the River: Tribal Conflicts over Development in the Narmada Valley*, Delhi: Oxford University Press, 1995.

Bayly, C.A., *Rulers, Townsmen and Bazaars: North Indian Society in the Age of British Expansion, 1770–1870*, Cambridge: Cambridge University Press, 1983, also Delhi: Oxford University Press, 1993.

—— *Indian Society and the Making of the British Empire*, Cambridge: Cambridge University Press, 1988.

Benjamin, Walter, 'Theses on the Philosophy of History', in his *Illuminations*, London: Fontana, 1973.

Bennet, Jane and William Chaloupka (eds), *In the Nature of Things: Language, Politics and the Environment*, Minneapolis: University of Minnesota Press, 1993.

Bennington, Geoff, 'Demanding History', in Derek Attridge, Geoff Bennington and Robert Young (eds), *Post-structuralism and the Question of History*, Cambridge: Cambridge University Press, 1987.

Berkhofer Jr., Robert F., *The White Man's Indian: The History of an Idea from Columbus to the Present*, New York: Knopf, 1978.

Bernheimer, Richard, *Wild Men in the Middle Ages*, Cambridge, Mass.: Harvard University Press, 1952.

Bhabha, Homi K., 'Are you a Man or a Mouse', in Maurice Berger, Brian Wallis and Simon Watson, *Constructing Masculinity*, New York: Routledge, 1995.

Bhattacharya, Neeladri, 'Pastoralists in a Colonial World', in Arnold and Guha (eds), *Nature, Culture, Imperialism*.

Billington, Ray Allen, *Land of Savagery, Land of Promise: The European Image of the American Frontier in the Nineteenth Century*, New York: Norton, 1981.

Borofsky, Robert, *Making History: Pukapukan and Anthropological Constructions of Knowledge*, Cambridge: Cambridge University Press, 1987.

Breman, Jan, *Of Peasants, Migrants and Paupers: Rural Labour Circulation and Capitalist Production in West India*, Delhi: Oxford University Press, 1985.

—— *Beyond Patronage and Exploitation: Changing Agrarian Relations in South Gujarat*, Delhi: Oxford University Press, 1993.

Briggs, John, *Memoirs of General John Briggs of the Madras Army*, London: Chatto and Windus, 1885.

Butler, Judith, *Gender Trouble: Feminism and the Subversion of Identity*, London: Routledge, 1990.

Callicot, J. Baird and Roger T. Ames (eds), *Nature in Asian Traditions of Thought: Essays in Environmental Philosophy*, Albany: State University of New York Press, 1989.

Caplan, Lionel, *Warrior Gentlemen: 'Gurkhas' in the Western Imagination*, Providence: Berghahn Books, 1995.

Carruthers, Mary, *The Book of Memory: A Study of Memory in Medieval Culture*, Cambridge: Cambridge University Press, 1990.

Carter, Paul, *The Road to Botany Bay: An Exploration of Landscape and History*, New York: Alfred A. Knopf, 1987.

Chakrabarty, Dipesh, 'History as Critique and Critique(s) of History', *Economic and Political Weekly*, vol. 26, no. 37, 1991.

—— 'Postcoloniality and the Artifice of History: Who Speaks for the "Indian" Pasts', *Representations*, 37, Winter, 1992.

—— 'Marx After Marxism: History, Subalternity and Difference', in Saree Makdisi, Cesare Casarino and Rebecca E. Karl (eds), *Marxism Beyond Marxism*, New York: Routledge, 1996.

Chatterjee, Partha, *The Nation and its Fragments*, Delhi: Oxford University Press, 1993.

Chavda, V.K., *Gaekwads and the British: A Study of their Problems, 1875–1920*, New Delhi: University Publishers, 1966.

—— 'Dharavi Deer Preserve: A Note on Ecology, Royal Past-time, and Peasant Unrest, 1856–1940', *Proceedings of the Forty-fifth Session of the Indian History Congress, 1984*, New Delhi, 1985.

Chowdhry, Prem, *The Veiled Women: Shifting Gender Equations in Rural Haryana, 1880–1990*, Delhi: Oxford University Press, 1994.

Chowdhury-Sengupta, Indira, 'Mother India and Mother Victoria: Motherhood and Nationalism in Nineteenth Century Bengal', *South Asia Research*, vol. 12, no. 1, 1992.

Cixous, Helene and Catherine Clement, *The Newly Born Woman*, trans. Betsy Wing, Minneapolis: University of Minnesota Press, 1986.

Clanchy, M.T., *From Memory to Written Record: England, 1066–1307*, Oxford: Blackwell Publishers, 2nd edition, 1993.

Clastres, Pierre, *Society Against the State*, trans. Robert Hurley in collaboration with Abe Stein, New York: Zone Books, 1993.

Coetzee, J.M., 'Idleness in South Africa', in his *White Writing: On the Culture of Letters in South Africa*, New Haven: Yale University Press, 1988.

Cohen, David William, *The Combing of History*, Chicago: University of Chicago Press, 1994.

Cooper, Frederick, 'Colonizing Time: Work Rhythms and Labor Conflict in Colonial Mombasa', in Nicholas Dirks (ed.), *Colonialism and Culture*, Ann Arbor: University of Michigan Press, 1992.

Corbridge, Stuart, 'The Ideology of Tribal Economy and Society: Politics in Jharkhand, 1950–80', *Modern Asian Studies*, no. 22, 1, 1988.

Creagh Coon, T.B., 'Witchcraft in the Dangs', *Man in India*, vol. 25, 1945.

Croll, Elisabeth and David Parkin, 'Cultural Understandings of the Environment', in Elisabeth Croll and David Parkin (eds), *Bush Base, Forest Farm: Culture, Environment and Development*, London: Routledge, 1992.

Cronon, William, *Changes in the Land: Indians, Colonists and the Ecology of New England*, New York: Hill and Wang, 1983.

Crosby, Alfred, *Ecological Imperialism: The Biological Expansion of Europe, 900–1900*, Cambridge: Cambridge University Press, 1986.

Crosby, Christina, *The Ends of History: Victorians and the 'Woman Question'*, London: Routledge, 1991.

De Certeau, Michel, *The Practice of Everyday Life*, Berkeley: University of California Press, 1984.

Derrida, Jacques, *Of Grammatology*, trans. Gayatri Chakravorty Spivak, Baltimore: Johns Hopkins University Press, 1974.

Desai, I.P., 'The Tribal Autonomy Movement in South Gujarat', in K.S. Singh (ed.), *Tribal Movements in India*, New Delhi: Manohar, 1983.

Deshpande, Arvind M., *John Briggs in Maharashtra: A Study of District Administration under Early British Rule*, New Delhi: Manohar, 1987.

Dirks, Nicholas, *The Hollow Crown: Ethnohistory of an Indian Kingdom*, Cambridge: Cambridge University Press, 1987.

—— 'The Original Caste: Power, History and Hierarchy in South Asia', *Contributions to Indian Sociology*, 23 (1), 1989.

—— 'History as a Sign of the Modern', *Public Culture*, 2, no. 2, Spring, 1990.

Dove, Michael, ' "Jungle" in Nature and Culture', in Ramachandra Guha (ed.), *Social Ecology*, Delhi: Oxford University Press, 1994.

Drayton, Richard, n.d., 'Empire as "Development": The New Imperialisms of the Enlightenment, 1780–1815 and 1880–1914', unpublished paper.

Dudley, E. and M. Novak (eds), *The Wild Man Within: An Image in Western Thought from the Renaissance to Romanticism*, Pittsburgh: University of Pittsburgh Press, 1972.

Duerr, Hans Peter, *Dreamtime: Concerning the Boundary Between Wilderness and Civilisation*, trans. Felicitas Goodman, New York: B. Blackwell, 1987.

Dumont, Louis, *Homo Hierarchicus: The Caste System and its Implications*, Chicago: University of Chicago Press, 1980.

Elwin, Verrier, *A Philosophy for NEFA*, Shillong: P.C. Dutta on behalf of the Adviser to the Governor of Assam, 1964.

Embree, Ainslee, *Imagining India: Essays on Indian History*, Delhi: Oxford University Press, 1989.

Enthoven, R.E., *The Tribes and Castes of Bombay*, Bombay: Cosmo Publications, vol. 1, 1975 (1920).

Ermarth, Elizabeth Deeds, *Sequel to History: Postmodernism and the Crisis of Representational Time*, New Jersey: Princeton University Press, 1992.

Errington, Shelly, 'Some Comments on Style in the Meaning of the Past', *Journal of Asian Studies*, vol. 28, no. 2, 1979.

Fabian, Johannes, *Time and the Other: How Anthropology Makes its Object*, New York: Columbia University Press, 1983.

Falk, Nancy, 'Wilderness and Kingship in Ancient South Asia', *History of Religions*, vol. 13, 1973.

Feierman, Steven, 'Africa in History: The End of Universal Narratives', in Gyan Prakash (ed.), *After Colonialism: Imperial Histories and Postcolonial Displacements*, New Jersey: Princeton University Press, 1995.

Forsyth, James, *The Highlands of Central India: Notes on their Forests and Wild Tribes, Natural History and Sports*, first Indian reprint, New Delhi: Asian Publication Services, 1975 (1919).

Foucault, Michel, *The History of Sexuality: An Introduction*, vol. I, New York: Vintage Books, 1978.

Fuchs, Stephen, *Godmen on the Warpath: A Study of Messianic Movements in India*, New Delhi: Munshiram Manoharlal, 1992.

—— *Rebellious Prophets*, Bombay: Asia Publishing House, 1965.

Gadgil, Madhav and Ramachandra Guha, 'Towards an Ecological History of India', *Economic and Political Weekly*, Special Number, November 1985.

Gadgil, Madhav and V.D. Vartak, 'The Sacred Uses of Nature', in Ramachandra Guha (ed.), *Social Ecology*, Delhi: Oxford University Press, 1994.

Geertz, Clifford, *Negara: The Theatre State in Nineteenth Century Bali*, New Jersey: Princeton University Press, 1980.

Ghosh, Kaushik, n.d., 'Primitivism in Bengali Modernity: The Imagining of Tribal Society in 19th Century Bengali Nationalist Culture', unpublished manuscript.

Ghurye, G.S., *The Aborigines 'So-called' and their Future*, Poona: Gokhale Institute of Politics and Economics, 1943.

—— *The Scheduled Tribes*, Bombay: Popular Prakashan, 1963.

Gidwani, Vinay K., '"Waste" and the Permanent Settlement in Bengal', *Economic and Political Weekly*, 25 January 1992.

Gilroy, Paul, *The Black Atlantic: Modernity and Double Consciousness*, Cambridge, Mass.: Harvard University Press, 1993.

Glacken, Clarence, *Traces on the Rhodian Shore: Nature and Culture in Western Thought from Ancient Times to the End of the Eighteenth Century*, Berkeley: University of California Press, 1967.

Goldsmid, F.J., *James Outram: A Biography*, vol. I, London: Elder and Co., 1880.

Gordon, David C., *Self-determination and History in the Third World*, New Jersey: Princeton University Press, 1971.

Gordon, Stewart, 'Forts and Social Control in the Maratha State', *Modern Asian Studies*, vol. 13, no. 1, 1979.

—— *The Marathas, 1600–1818*, Cambridge: Cambridge University Press, 1993.

—— *Marathas, Marauders and State Formation in the Eighteenth Century*, Delhi: Oxford University Press, 1994.

Graham, D.C., 'A Historical Sketch of the Bheel Tribes Inhabiting the Province of Khandesh', in Government of Bombay, *SRBG 26*, 1856.

Grinker, Roy Richard, *Houses in the Rainforest: Ethnicity and Inequality among Farmers and Foragers in Central Africa*, Berkeley: University of California Press, 1994.

Grove, Richard, *Green Imperialism: Colonial Expansion, Tropical Edens, and the Origins of Environmentalism, 1600–1860*, Cambridge: Cambridge University Press, 1994, also Delhi: Oxford University Press, 1995.

Gudeman, Stephen, *Economics as Culture: Models and Metaphors of Livelihood*, London: Routledge and Kegan Paul, 1986.

Guha, Ramachandra, 'Forestry in British and Post-British India: An Historical Analysis', *Economic and Political Weekly*, vol. 18, nos 44–5, 1983.

—— 'Forestry and Social Protest in Kumaon, c. 1893–1921', in Ranajit Guha (ed.), *Subaltern Studies IV: Writings on South Asian History and Society*, Delhi: Oxford University Press, 1985.

—— 'Scientific Forestry and Social Change', *Economic and Political Weekly*, vol. 20, Special Number, November 1985.

—— *The Unquiet Woods: Ecological Change and Peasant Resistance in the Himalaya*, Delhi: Oxford University Press, 1989.

Guha, Ranajit, 'The Small Voice of History', in Dipesh Chakrabarty and Shahid Amin (eds), *Subaltern Studies IX: Writings on South Asian History and Society*, Delhi: Oxford University Press, 1996.

Guha, Sumit, 'Forest Polities and Agrarian Empires: The Khandesh Bhils, c. 1700–1850', *Indian Economic and Social History Review*, vol. 33, no. 2, 1996.

—— n.d., 'Lords of the Land Versus Kings of the Forest: Conflict and Collaboration in Peninsular India, c. 1500–1981', unpublished paper.

Haberman, David L., *Journey Through the Twelve Forests: An Encounter with Krishna*, New York: Oxford University Press, 1994.

Habermas, Jurgen, *The Philosophical Discourse of Modernity*, Cambridge: Polity Press, 1987.

Halbwachs, Maurice, *The Collective Memory*, trans. F.J. Ditter, Jr. and V.Y. Ditter, New York, 1980 (1950).

Hans, Raj Kumar, 'The Grasia Chiefs and the British Power in the Beginning of the Nineteenth Century Gujarat', *Proceedings of the Indian History Congress*, Waltair, 1979.

—— 'Agrarian Economy of Broach District During the First Half of the Nineteenth Century', Ph.D. thesis, Baroda: MS University, 1987.

Haraway, Donna, *Primate Visions: Gender, Race and Nature in the World of Modern Science*, London: Routledge, 1989.

—— *Simians, Cyborgs, and Women: The Reinvention of Nature*, New York: Routledge, 1991.

Hardiman, David, *The Coming of the Devi: Adivasi Assertion in Western India*, Delhi: Oxford University Press, 1987.

—— 'Power in the Forest: The Dangs, 1820s–1940s', in Arnold and Hardiman (eds), *Subaltern Studies VIII*, Delhi: Oxford University Press, 1994.

—— 'Small Dam Systems of the Sahyadris', in Arnold and Guha, *Nature, Culture, Imperialism*.

—— *Feeding the Baniya: Peasants and Usurers in Western India*, Delhi: Oxford University Press, 1997.

Harms, Robert, with Joseph Miller, David Newbury, and Michele Wagner (eds), *Paths Toward the Past: African Historical Essays in Honor of Jan Vansina*, Atlanta: African Studies Association Press, 1994.

Harrison, Robert Pogue, *Forests: The Shadow of Civilisation*, Chicago: University of Chicago Press, 1992.

Heber, Reginald, *Narrative of a Journey through the Upper Provinces of India, from Calcutta to Bombay, 1824–1825*, 3 vols, Philadelphia: Carcy, Lea and Carcy, 1829.

Heehs, Peter, 'Myth, History and Theory', *History and Theory*, vol. 33, no. 1, 1994.

Heesterman, J.C., *The Inner Conflict of Tradition*, Chicago: University of Chicago Press, 1985.

Hendley, T.H., 'An Account of the Maiwar Bhils', *Journal of the Royal Asiatic Society of Bengal*, no. 4, 1875.

Hill, Jonathan, 'Introduction: Myth and History', in Jonathan Hill (ed.), *Rethinking History and Myth: Indigenous South American Perspectives on the Past*, Chicago: University of Chicago Press, 1988.

Hutton, Patrick, *History as an Art of Memory*, Hanover: University Press of New England, 1993.

Inden, Ronald, *Imagining India*, London: Blackwell, 1991.

Ingold, Tim, 'Culture and the Perception of the Environment', in Elisabeth Croll and David Parkin (eds), *Bush Base, Forest Farm: Culture, Environment and Development*.

Jameson, Frederic, *The Political Unconscious: Narrative as a Socially Symbolic Act*, London: Routledge, 1989.

Kemp, Antony, *The Estrangement of the Past: A Study in the Origins of Modern Historical Consciousness*, Oxford: Oxford University Press, 1991.

Kern, Stephen, *The Culture of Time and Place, 1880–1918*, Cambridge, Mass.: Harvard University Press, 1983.

Khanapurkar, D.P., 'The Aborigines of South Gujarat', PhD University of Bombay, 2 vols, 1944.

Kipling, Rudyard, 'The Tomb of his Ancestors', in *The Day's Work*, London: Macmillan, 1988 (1898).

Koch, Ebba, 'Hunt and Landscape in Imperial Mughal Paintings', Paper presented at the McIntire Department of Art, University of Virginia, 18 April 1996.

Kolff, D.H.A., *Naukar, Rajput and Sepoy: The Ethnohistory of the Military Labour Market in Hindustan, 1450–1850*, Cambridge: Cambridge University Press, 1990.

Kuklick, Henrietta, *The Savage Within: The Social History of British Anthropology, 1885–1945*, Cambridge: Cambridge University Press, 1991.

Kuper, Adam, *The Invention of Primitive Society: Transformations of an Illusion*, London: Routledge, 1988.

—— 'Lineage Theory: A Critical Retrospect', *Annual Review of Anthropology*, vol. 11, 1982.

Lal, R.B., 'Socio-religious Movements among the Tribals of South Gujarat', in K.S. Singh (ed.), *Tribal Movements in India*, New Delhi: Manohar, 1983.

Landes, David, *Revolution in Time: Clocks and the Making of the Modern World*, Cambridge, Mass.: Harvard University Press, 1983.

Lefebvre, Henri, *The Production of Space*, trans. Donald Nicholson-Smith, Oxford: Blackwell, 1991.

Le Goff, Jacques, *History and Memory*, trans. Steven Rendall and Elizabeth Claman, New York: Columbia University Press, 1992 (1977).

Levi-Strauss, Claude, *The Elementary Structures of Kinship*, Boston: Beacon Press, 1969.

—— *The Savage Mind*, Chicago: University of Chicago Press, 1966.

Liebersohn, Harry, 'Discovering Indigenous Nobility: Tocqueville, Chamisso, and Romantic Travel Writing', *American Historical Review*, vol. 99, no. 3, June 1994.

Lowenthal, David, *The Past is a Foreign Country*, Cambridge: Cambridge University Press, 1985.

MacCormack, Carol and Marylin Strathern (eds), *Nature, Culture, and Gender*, Cambridge: Cambridge University Press, 1980.

MacKenzie, John M., *The Empire of Nature: Hunting, Conservation and British Imperialism*, Manchester: Manchester University Press, 1988.

Maconochie, Evan, *Life in the Indian Civil Service*, London: Chapman and Hall, 1926.

Malcolm, John, 'Essay on Bhills', *Transactions of the Royal Asiatic Society of Great Britain and Ireland*, vol. I, 1827.

Malkki, Lisa H., *Purity and Exile: Violence, Memory and National Cosmology among Hutu Refugees in Tanzania*, Chicago: University of Chicago Press, 1995.

McClintock, Anne, *Imperial Leather: Race, Gender and Sexuality in the Colonial Context*, New York: Routledge, 1995.

Menen, Aubrey, *The Space Within the Heart*, London: Hamish Hamilton, 1970.

—— *The Prevalence of Witches*, New Delhi: Penguin, 1989 (1947).

Merchant, Carolyn, *The Death of Nature: Women, Ecology and the Scientific Revolution*, San Francisco: Harper and Row, 1980.

Miller, Joseph (ed.), *The African Past Speaks: Essays in Oral Tradition and History*, Fokestone: Dawson, 1980.

Mink, L.O., 'Narrative Form as Cognitive Instrument', reprinted in L.O. Mink, Brian Fay, Eugene O. Golob and Richard T. Vann (eds), *Historical Understanding*, Ithaca: Cornell University Press, 1987.

Mitchell, Timothy, 'Everyday Metaphors of Power', *Theory and Society*, vol. 19, 1990.

Morphy, Howard and Frances Morphy, 'The "myths" of Ngalakan History: Ideology and Images of the Past in Northern Australia', *Man*, n.s., vol. 19, no. 3, 1984.

Morse, Bradford and Thomas Berger, *Sardar Sarovar: The Report of the Independent Review*, Pune: Mudra, 1992.

Mudimbe, V.Y., *The Invention of Africa: Gnosis, Philosophy and the Order of Knowledge*, Bloomington: Indiana University Press, 1988.

Nandy, Ashis, 'History's Forgotten Doubles', *History and Theory*, vol. 34, no. 2, 1995.

Nash, Roderick, *Wilderness and the American Mind*, New Haven: Yale University Press, 1967.

Nath, Y.V.S., *Bhils of Ratanmal: An Analysis of the Social Structure of a Western Indian Community*, Baroda: MS University of Baroda Press, 1960.

Nietzsche, Friedrich, 'On the Uses and Disadvantages of History for Life', in Friedrich Nietzsche, *Untimely Meditations*, trans. R.J. Hollingdale, Cambridge: Cambridge University Press, 1983.

Nigam, Sanjay, 'Disciplining and Policing the "Criminals by Birth"' (2 parts), *Indian Economic and Social History Review*, vol. 27, nos 2 and 3, 1990.

Oelschlaeger, Max, *The Idea of Wilderness: From Prehistory to the Age of Ecology*, New Haven: Yale University Press, 1991.

Oelschlaeger, Max (ed.), *The Wilderness Condition: Essays on Environment and Civilization*, Washington, DC: Island Press, 1992.

O'Hanlon, Rosalind, 'Recovering the Subject: Subaltern Studies and Histories of Resistance in Colonial South Asia', *Modern Asian Studies*, vol. 22, no. 1, 1988.

Ohnukhi-Tierney, Emiko, *Rice as Self: Japanese Identities Through Time*, New Jersey: Princeton University Press, 1993.

Osborne, Peter, *The Politics of Time: Modernity and Avant-garde*, London: Verso, 1995.

Pagden, Anthony, *European Encounters with the New World: From Renaissance to Romanticism*, New Haven: Yale University Press, 1993.

Pandey, Gyanendra, 'Modes of History Writing: New Hindu History of Ayodhya', *Economic and Political Weekly*, vol. 29, no. 25, 1994.

Patel, Premanand, *Navsari Prantni Kaliparaj*, Baroda: Government of Baroda Press, 1901.

Pateman, Carole, *The Sexual Contract*, Cambridge: Polity Press, 1988.

Peabody, Norbert, 'Kota Mahajagat, or the Great Universe of Kota: Sovereignty and Territory in 18th Century Rajasthan', *Contributions to Indian Sociology*, vol. 25, no. 1, 1991.

Peel, J.D.Y., 'Making History: The Past in the Ijesha Present', *Man*, n.s., vol. 19, no. 1, 1984.

Portelli, Alessandro, *The Death of Luigi Trastulli and Other Stories: Form and Meaning in Oral History*, Albany: State University of New York Press, 1991.

Pouchpedass, Jacques, 'British Attitudes Towards Shifting Cultivation in Colonial South India: A Case Study of South Canara District, 1800–1920', in Arnold and Guha (eds), *Nature, Culture, Imperialism*.

Prakash, Gyan, *Bonded Histories: Genealogies of Labour Servitude in Colonial India*, Cambridge: Cambridge University Press, 1990.

—— 'Subaltern Studies as Postcolonial Criticism', *American Historical Review*, vol. 99, December 1994.

—— (ed.), *After Colonialism: Imperial Histories and Postcolonial Displacements*, New Jersey: Princeton University Press, 1995.

Prasad, A.K., *The Bhils of Khandesh under the British East India Company*, New Delhi: Konark Publishers, 1991.

Pratap, Ajay, 'Paharia Ethnohistory and the Archaeology of the Rajmahal Hills: Archaeological Implications of an Historical Study of Shifting Cultivation', PhD, University of Cambridge, 1988.

Price, Richard, *First-Time: The Historical Vision of an Afro-American People*, Baltimore: Johns Hopkins University Press, 1983.

Rabitoy, Neil, 'Administrative Modernisation and the Bhats of British Gujarat, 1800–1820', *Indian Economic and Social History Review*, 11 (1), 1974.

Rangarajan, Mahesh, *Fencing the Forest: Conservation and Ecological*

Change in India's Central Provinces, 1860–1914, Delhi: Oxford University Press, 1996.

Rao, V.N., D. Shulman and S. Subrahmanyam, *Symbols of Substance: Court and State in Nayaka Period Tamilnadu*, Delhi: Oxford University Press, 1996.

Rappaport, Joanne, *The Politics of Memory: Native Historical Interpretation in the Colombian Andes*, Cambridge: Cambridge University Press, 1990.

Richards, J.F. and V.N. Rao, 'Banditry in Mughal India: Historical and Folk Perceptions', *Indian Economic and Social History Review*, vol. 18, no. 1, 1980.

Richards, J.F. and Michelle B. McAlpin, 'Cotton Cultivating and Land Clearing in the Bombay Deccan and Karnatak: 1818–1920', in Richard Tucker and J.F. Richards (eds), *Global Deforestation and the Nineteenth Century World Economy*, Durham: Duke University Press, 1983.

Richards, J.F., E.S. Haynes and R. Hagen, 'Changes in Land-Use in Bihar, Punjab, and Haryana, 1850–1970', *Modern Asian Studies*, vol. 9, 1985.

Rosaldo, Renato, 'Doing Oral History', *Social Analysis*, no. 4, September 1980.

—— *Ilongot Headhunting, 1883–1974: A Study in Society and History*, Stanford: Stanford University Press, 1980.

Roy, Sarat Chandra, 'The Black Bhils of Jaisamand Lake', *Journal of Bihar and Orissa Research Society*, vol. x, 2 parts, 1924.

Rubin, Gayle, 'The Traffic in Women: Notes on the "Political Economy" of Sex', in Rayna Reiter (ed.), *Towards an Anthropology of Women*, New York: Monthly Review Press, 1975.

Russell, R.V. and Hira Lal, *The Tribes and Castes of the Central Provinces of India*, vol. ii, London: Macmillan, 1916.

Sahlins, Marshall, *Stone Age Economics*, Chicago: University of Chicago Press, 1972.

—— *Historical Metaphors and Mythical Realities: Structure in the Early History of the Sandwich Islands Kingdom*, Ann Arbor: Association for Social Anthropology in Oceania Special Publication No. 1, 1981.

—— *Islands of History*, Chicago: University of Chicago Press, 1985.

Sahlins, Peter, *Forest Rites: The War of the Demoiselles in Nineteenth Century France*, Cambridge, Mass.: Harvard University Press, 1994.

Saletore, B.A., 'Relations Between the Girassias and the Marathas', *New Indian Antiquary*, Extra Series i, 1939.

—— 'The Bhils of Maharashtra', *New Indian Antiquary*, vol. i, 1938–9.

Schneider, David, *A Critique of the Study of Kinship*, Ann Arbor: University of Michigan Press, 1984.

Scott, James C., *Domination and the Arts of Resistance: Hidden Transcripts*, New Haven: Yale University Press, 1990.

Shah, Ghanshyam and H.R. Chaturvedi, *Gandhian Approach to Rural Development: The Valod Experiment*, New Delhi: Ajanta Publications, 1983.

Sharma, Ursula, 'Dowry in India: Its Consequences for Women', in R. Hirschon (ed.), *Women and Property, Women as Property*, London: Croom Helm, 1984.

Shiva, Vandana, *Staying Alive: Women, Ecology and Survival in India*, New Delhi: Kali for Women, 1988.

Shull, E.M., 'Worship of the Tiger-god and Religious Rituals Associated with Tigers among the Dangi Hill Tribes of the Dangs District, Gujarat State, Western India', *Eastern Anthropologist*, vol. 21, no. 2, May–August 1968.

Shulman, David, 'On South Indian Bandits and Kings', *Indian Economic and Social History Review*, vol. XVII, no. 3, 1980.

Simcox, A.H.A., *A Memoir of the Khandesh Bhil Corps, 1825–1891*, Bombay: Thacker and Co., 1912.

Singh, Chetan, 'Conformity and Conflict: Tribes and the Agrarian System of Mughal India', *Indian Economic and Social History Review*, vol. 25, no. 3, 1988.

—— 'Forests, Pastoralists and Agrarian Society in Mughal India', in Arnold and Guha (eds), *Nature, Culture, Imperialism*.

Singh, K.S. (ed.), *The Mahabharata in the Tribal and Folk Traditions of India*, Simla and New Delhi: Indian Institute of Advanced Study and Anthropological Survey of India, 1993.

—— *Rama-katha in Tribal and Folk Traditions of India: Proceedings of a Seminar*, Calcutta: Seagull Books, 1993.

Sinha, M., *Colonial Masculinity: The 'Manly Englishman' and the 'Effeminate Bengali' in the Late Nineteenth Century*, Manchester: Manchester University Press, 1995.

Sivaramakrishnan, K., 'Colonialism and Forestry in India: Imagining the Past in Present Politics', *Comparative Studies in Society and History*, vol. 37, January 1995.

Skaria, Ajay, 'Shades of Wildness: Tribe, Caste and Gender in Western India', *Journal of Asian Studies*, vol. 56, no. 3, August 1997.

—— 'Women, Witchcraft, and Gratuitous Violence in Colonial Western India', *Past and Present*, no. 155, May 1997.

—— 'A Forest Polity in Western India: The Dangs, 1800s–1920s', PhD, University of Cambridge, 1992.

—— 'Writing, Orality and Power in Western India', in Amin and Chakrabarty (eds), *Subaltern Studies* IX, 1995.

—— 'From Desiccationism to Scientific Forestry: The Dangs, 1840s–1920s', in Richard Grove, Vinita Damodaran and Satpal Sangwan (eds), *Nature and the Orient: Environmental History of South and Southeast Asia*, Delhi: Oxford University Press, 1998.

Skaria, Ajay, n.d., 'Ritual and Authority in Western India: The Dangs Darbar', unpublished paper.

Sontheimer, G.D., *Pastoral Deities in Western India*, trans. Anne Feldhaus, New York: Oxford University Press, 1989.

Spivak, Gayatri Chakravorty, 'Subaltern Studies: Deconstructing Historiography', in Ranajit Guha (ed.), *Subaltern Studies IV: Writings on South Asian History and Society*, Delhi: Oxford University Press, 1985.

—— 'Can the Subaltern Speak', in Cary Nelson and Lawrence Grossberg (ed.), *Marxism and the Interpretation of Culture*, Urbana: University of Illinois Press, 1988.

Stebbing, E.P., *The Forests of India*, vol. I, London, 1921.

Stern, Robert W., *The Cat and the Lion: Jaipur State in the British Raj*, Leiden: E.J. Brill, 1988.

Stocking, George, *Victorian Anthropology*, New York: Free Press, 1987.

—— (ed.), *Colonial Situations: Essays on the Contextualization of Ethnographic Knowledge*, Madison: University of Wisconsin Press, 1991.

Sturrock, John, *Structuralism and Since: From Levi-Strauss to Derrida*, Oxford: Oxford University Press, 1979.

Sundar, Nandini, 'The Dreaded Danteshwari: Annals of Alleged Sacrifice', *Indian Economic and Social History Review*, vol. 32, no. 3, 1995.

Taussig, Michael, *Shamanism, Colonialism, and the Wild Man: A Study in Terror and Healing*, Chicago: University of Chicago Press, 1986.

Tiffany, Sharon and Kathleen Adams, *The Wild Woman: An Inquiry into the Anthropology of an Idea*, Cambridge, Mass.: Schenkman, 1985.

Torgovnick, Marianna, *Gone Primitive: Savage Intellects, Modern Lives*, Chicago: University of Chicago Press, 1990.

Tucker, Richard P., 'Forest Management and Imperial Politics: Thana District, Bombay, 1823–1887', *Indian Economic and Social History Review*, vol. 16, no. 3, 1979.

Tyler, Stephen, 'On Being Out of Words', in George Marcus (ed.), *Rereading Cultural Anthropology*, Durham: Duke University Press, 1992.

Unnithan, Maya, 'Constructing Difference: Social Categories and Girahya Women, Kinship and Resources in South Rajasthan', PhD, University of Cambridge, 1991.

—— 'Gender and Tribal Identity in Western India', *Economic and Political Weekly*, vol. 26, no. 17, 27 April 1991.

—— 'The Politics of Marriage Payments in South Rajasthan', *South Asia Research*, vol. 12, no. 1, 1992.

Vann, Richard T., 'Louis Mink's Linguistic Turn', *History and Theory*, vol. 26, no. 1, 1987.

Vansina, Jan, *Oral Tradition as History*, London: James Currey, 2nd revised edition, 1985.

Varghese, Shiney, 'Women, Development and Resistance: A Case Study of Dangs, India', *Development in Practice*, vol. 3, no. 1, 1993.

Vattimo, Giani, *The End of Modernity: Nihilism and Hermeneutics in Post Modern Culture*, trans. Jord R. Snyder, Baltimore: Johns Hopkins University Press, 1988.

Vaupell, John, 'Continuation of Desultory Notes and Observations on Various Places in Guzerat and Western India', *Transactions of the Bombay Geographical Society*, vol. 7, May 1844–December 1846.

Wadia, R.A., *The Bombay Dockyard and the Wadia Master Builders*, Bombay: Ruttonjee Ardeshir Wadia, 1947.

Waghorne, Joanne P., *The Raja's Magic Clothes: Re-visioning Kingship and Divinity in England's India*, Pennsylvania: Pennsylvania State University Press, 1994.

Weiner, Annete, *Inalienable Possessions: The Paradox of Keeping while Giving*, Berkeley: University of California Press, 1992.

White, Hayden, *Metahistory: The Historical Imagination in Nineteenth Century Europe*, Baltimore: Johns Hopkins University Press, 1971.

—— *Tropics of Discourse: Essays in Cultural Criticism*, Baltimore: Johns Hopkins University Press, 1978.

Wilmsen, Edwin, *Land Filled with Flies: A Political Economy of the Kalahari*, Chicago: University of Chicago Press, 1989.

Wink, Andre, *Land and Sovereignty in India: Agrarian Society and Politics Under the Eighteenth Century Maratha Svarajya*, Cambridge: Cambridge University Press, 1986.

—— 'Maratha Revenue Farming', *Modern Asian Studies*, vol. 17, no. 4, 1983.

Yates, Frances, *The Arts of Memory*, London: Pimlico, 1991 (1966).

Young, Robert, *White Mythologies: Writing History and the West*, London: Routledge, 1990.

Zimmerman, Francis, *The Jungle and the Aroma of Meats: An Ecological Theme in Hindu Medicine*, Berkeley: University of California Press, 1987.

Zizek, Slavoj, *The Sublime Object of Ideology*, London: Verso, 1989.

—— *For They Know Not What They Do*, London: Verso, 1994.

Index